Contents

Preface

Apparel and accessories marketing is the fiercely competitive, continually changing field in which workers buy, stock, advertise, display, and sell clothing and accessories. It is part of the broader field of fashion merchandising, which includes the design and production of ready-to-wear, the distribution of merchandise, and the selling of fashion apparel and accessories to the consumer. The text material and activities in *Apparel and Accessories* can be used by students who are preparing for careers in apparel and accessories—in retail firms, wholesale operations, buying offices, and fashion publication centers. It can be used by beginning workers who are employed in any phase of fashion merchandising and by fashion merchandising employees who wish to improve their knowledge and skills. Teachers will find this manual useful as a basic text on apparel and accessories retailing, adaptable to a variety of curricula and student needs.

COMPETENCY-BASED INSTRUCTION

Apparel and Accessories is part of the *Career Competencies in Marketing (CCM) Series,* which is designed to provide competency-building text material and activities for a variety of marketing industries. Each book in the series focuses on a particular field.

Students who have chosen apparel and accessories retailing for their careers may use this manual alone or in conjunction with the *Occupational Manuals and Projects in Marketing (OMPM)* series.

The flexible design of the *CCM Series* makes it appropriate for individualized instruction or for small- or large-group instruction. The entire series can be coordinated with the competency-based competitive events sponsored by the Distributive Education Clubs of America (DECA) to prepare students for their chosen marketing careers. The *CCM Series* can also be used with the learning activity packages (LAPS) developed by the Interstate Distributive Education Curriculum Consortium (IDECC). The Crawford study was used as the basis from which the LAPs were developed. That study was also used as one of the sources from which the books in the *CCM Series* were developed.

Activity-oriented learning experiences are interspersed throughout each chapter of the manual. These experiences give the student an opportunity to develop and demonstrate the needed competencies.

EMPLOYMENT LEVELS

The competencies considered in this book have been verified by professionals in the apparel and accessories industry as being critical or important for entry-level and mid-management employees.

Typical jobs at the entry level include:

- Salesperson of clothing and related items (men's, women's, youth, and children's wear, shoes, jewelry, and accessories)
- Customer service clerk
- Marking clerk
- Comparison shopper
- Display assistant
- Unit control clerk
- Gift wrapper
- Cashier
- Stock person
- Receiving clerk

Jobs at the mid-management, specialist, or supervisory level include:

- Department or unit manager (and assistant)
- Buyer (and assistant)
- Professional salesperson
- Fashion coordinator
- Training manager
- Fashion copywriter
- Jobber
- Wholesale account executive
- Wholesale or manufacturer's sales representative

SCOPE OF THE BOOK

Each book in the *CCM Series* is organized into four units:

1. An introduction to and overview of the industry
2. Basic and social skills
3. Product or service technology
4. Marketing skills

Within these units, the books are divided into chapters. Industry dictated the content the chapters would cover.

The sequence of chapters in *Apparel and Accessories* was designed for flexibility. Each chapter is a separate entity, and teachers may adapt the text to an outline appropriate for their particular apparel and accessories, fashion merchandising, or marketing course of study and the needs of their students.

The opening chapter provides an overview of the fashion merchandising industry, including entry-level and advanced jobs in manufacturing, promotion, and retailing. It explores the career opportunities in fashion merchandising and provides information that is needed for career decisions.

Chapters 2 through 4 cover the foundation skills necessary for success in an apparel and accessories career. Chapter 2 discusses human relation skills and their applications in a fashion merchandising career setting. In Chapter 3, students apply communication techniques; and in Chapter 4, students are asked to demonstrate the

Apparel and Accessories

Marilyn Purol Mathisen
Weber State College
Ogden, Utah

Consulting Editor
Richard L. Lynch
Program Leader, Distributive Education
Virginia Polytechnic Institute
and State University
Blacksburg, Virginia

GREGG DIVISION McGRAW-HILL BOOK COMPANY

New York St. Louis Dallas San Francisco Auckland
Bogotá Düsseldorf Johannesburg London Madrid
Mexico Montreal New Delhi Panama Paris São Paulo
Singapore Sydney Tokyo Toronto

Library of Congress Cataloging in Publication Data

Mathisen, Marilyn Purol.
Apparel and accessories.

(Career competencies in marketing series)
1. Clothing trade. I. Title. II. Series.
TT497.M37 658.89'687 78-12321
ISBN 0-07-040905-6

6 7 8 9 0 WCWC 8 5 4

Set in Optima by Waldman Graphics, Inc.
Printed and bound by Webcrafters.

Senior Editor: Mary Alice McGarry
Editing Supervisor: Frances D. Bond
Production Supervisor: May E. Konopka
Design Supervisor: Tracy A. Glasner
Art Supervisor: George T. Resch
Designer: A Good Thing, Inc.
Cover Designer: Graphic Arts International
Illustrator: Burmar Technical Corporation
Unit-Opening Artist: Pat Cummings

mathematical skills required for apparel and accessories careers.

Chapters 5 through 10 provide a detailed knowledge base of apparel and accessories products. In Chapter 5, information about fibers, yarns, fabrics, and finishes is presented in an easy-to-understand way. Chapter 6 describes the sizes, styles, and fitting, coordinating, and selling techniques for women's apparel. Men's clothing, including styles, sizes, fit, alterations, and sales techniques, is discussed in Chapter 7. Students have the opportunity of working with infants' and children's wear in Chapter 8. Chapter 9 discusses shoe materials, construction, and style details. Students are involved in measuring customers for shoes, determining proper fit, and selling shoes and related products. Accessories, including gloves, handbags, hats, belts, umbrellas, and costume jewelry, are discussed in Chapter 10.

Chapters 11 through 16 discuss the marketing and management skills required for an apparel and accessories retailing career. In Chapter 11, students plan apparel and accessories purchases by completing a six-month merchandise plan and evaluating unit-control records. They work with stock plans, decide what merchandise to purchase, write orders, and price apparel and accessories items. Chapter 12 discusses unit-control and dollar inventory control records and the procedures for receiving, checking, and storing newly received merchandise. Advertising responsibilities of apparel and accessories salespeople and buyers are discussed in Chapter 13. In this chapter, students prepare advertising budgets and make decisions about the sizes of ads, when to advertise, and what to advertise. They also "proof" advertisements and evaluate advertising effectiveness. Chapter 14 involves students in planning, building, and replenishing interior clothing displays. The selling steps are explained in Chapter 15, and students have the opportunity to practice each step when they complete the learning experiences. The final chapter focuses on the special management skills required of an apparel and accessories retail manager, including recruiting and hiring workers, training and supervising employees, and controlling expenses.

SUPPORTING MATERIALS

The *Teacher's Manual and Key for Apparel and Accessories* contains general teaching suggestions; a bibliography; specific teaching suggestions for each chapter, with the competencies considered in the chapter identified; and an answer key to the learning experiences.

The *General Methodology Manual,* which explains the philosophy of the entire *Career Competencies in Marketing Series* and offers suggestions for using it in the classroom, has also been prepared for teachers and administrators.

ACKNOWLEDGMENTS

The author wishes to express her appreciation to the many apparel and accessories retailers and educational associates who provided her their help, suggestions, and cooperation in completing this text.

Special thanks are extended to the reviewers of this text, who made many helpful suggestions: Elinor F. Burgess, Supervisor of Distributive Education, Fairfax County Public Schools, Fairfax, Virginia; Joseph Frodsham, Divisional Merchandise Manager, ZCMI, Salt Lake City, Utah; Elizabeth DeChurch Strenkowski, Director, Retail Division, The Bradford School, Pittsburgh, Pennsylvania; Ruth Pack, Personnel Director, Auerbach Company, Salt Lake City, Utah; and Eugene L. Dorr, Associate Director for Educational Services, State Board of Directors for Community Colleges of Arizona, Phoenix, Arizona.

Marilyn Purol Mathisen

UNIT 1

Introduction to Apparel and Accessories

Welcome to the exciting and challenging world of apparel and accessories marketing! In this first unit, you will read about the many careers the apparel and accessories industry offers you, including careers in manufacturing, promotion, and retailing. You'll explore the pros and cons of working in the different careers and also the interest, aptitudes, and skills you will need to succeed.

The multibillion dollar apparel and accessories industry is continually looking for intelligent, energetic people. This chapter should help you evaluate your personality and goals and decide if you want to pursue a career in apparel and accessories marketing.

1 Overview of the Apparel and Accessory Industry

Clothing—we wear it for warmth, for modesty, and for protection. Just as important as any of these reasons, though, is the fact that we also wear clothes to look attractive.

The apparel and accessory industry, which supplies clothing needs, is one of the largest in the country. By providing jobs and paying taxes, this industry has contributed greatly to the success of the nation's economy. Millions of workers produce the raw materials used to make clothing and accessories, design and sew garments, and sell these goods in stores. By the mid-1980s, it is estimated that each American will spend $630 for clothing and shoes, a total of approximately $145 billion. About 7 percent of all the money Americans spend, or $1 out of every $14, goes to the purchase of apparel and accessories.[1]

AN INSIDE LOOK AT READY-TO-WEAR

Less than a century ago, most Americans wore clothing made at home. Today the majority of people wear **ready-to-wear,** apparel made in factories in standard sizes.

THE BEGINNING OF READY-TO-WEAR

"Store-bought" clothes were first introduced in the 1800s with men's ready-to-wear. In 1818, a company called Brooks Brothers made and sold inexpensive ready-to-wear trousers and shirts to sailors who needed clothing quickly and inexpensively while on shore. The production of ready-to-wear expanded with the invention of the sewing machine in 1846. By the late 1800s, women's ready-to-wear began to catch up with men's. For the past 20 years, 65 percent of spending for apparel has been for women's and children's clothing.[2]

READY-TO-WEAR TODAY

Although many people still make their own clothes and some accessories, most Americans purchase them in stores. Every garment and accessory sold in stores has passed through the stages of design, manufacturing, and distribution. Apparel and accessory manufacturers begin planning the merchandise they will offer for sale to stores 6 months to 1 year before the merchandise reaches consumers. (See Figure 1-1.)

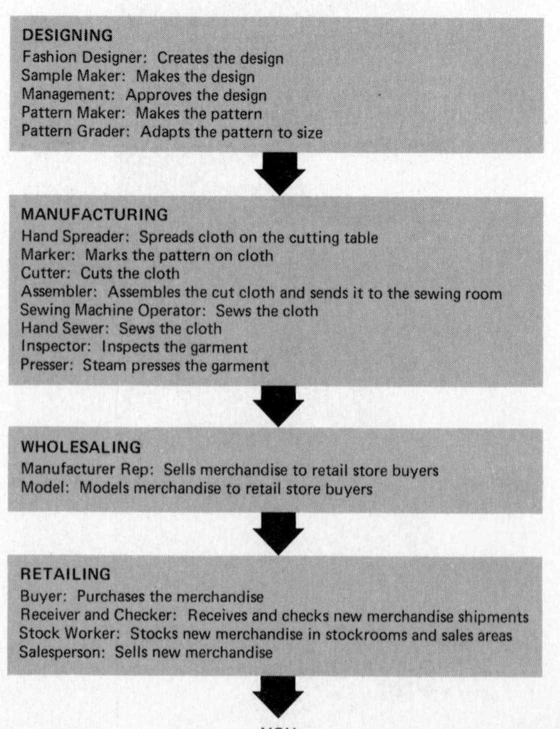

Fig. 1-1 Before you buy an item of merchandise, it has gone through these four stages.

Anthony Muto for Marita, New York. Photo: Daile Kaplan

Fig. 1-2 This fashion designer is discussing swatches of fabric samples with a client.

Designing Apparel and Accessories In fashion centers, such as New York, Dallas, and Los Angeles, **fashion designers** draw sketches of the new styles for clothing and accessories. (See Figure 1-2.) **Sample makers** prepare finished samples of the designers' styles. Using the designers' sketches, they cut and sew selected fabrics.

After a sample has been made, management of the company checks the profitability of making and selling that particular item. If the company feels it can make a profit, the item is sent to the pattern maker. The **pattern maker** constructs a master pattern from the designer's sketch using paper or fiberboard. This master pattern is used for cutting out the apparel or accessory item. The master pattern is then sent to a **pattern grader**, who measures the pieces that make up the master pattern and changes them to fit many size ranges.

Manufacturing Apparel and Accessories Many workers cut and sew apparel and accessories. **Hand spreaders**, or **machine spreaders**, lay out bolts of cloth into exact lengths on the cutting table. **Markers** arrange the pattern pieces on the cloth and trace the pattern. **Cutters** cut the pattern pieces from many layers of cloth. **Assemblers** bundle the cloth pieces and trims needed to make a complete garment and send them to the sewing room. (See Figure 1-3.)

Today, most apparel is sewn by machines. **Sewing machine operators** work on an assembly line, sewing one or two parts of the garment. Sections of better quality items are usually sewn by **hand sewers,** who do lapel basting and lining stitching.

Throughout the entire sewing process, **inspectors** and **checkers** examine the garments and mark defects. After the garments are sewn together, they are sent to **pressers.** These employees use steam pressing machines to flatten seams and shape parts of the finished garments.

Courtesy Kamehameha Garment Co., Ltd.

Fig. 1-3 By cutting through many layers of cloth, a cutter can turn out several pattern pieces at once.

Wholesaling Apparel and Accessories The newly made apparel and accessories are sold, or wholesaled, to retail stores. Apparel manufacturers have showrooms in fashion-center cities to display new fashions. **Retail store buyers** travel to the showrooms to examine the new clothing and accessories and to order those items they believe will attract customers. (See Figure 1-4.)

Manufacturing companies employ salespeople, also called **manufacturer representatives,** or reps. Many manufacturer reps call on buyers at their stores. Sometimes **models** display new fashions. Advertising, display, and public relations employees promote the sale of merchandise to retail stores and retail store customers.

Courtesy Anthony Muto, Marita. Photo: Daile Kaplan

Fig. 1-4 Buyers order the latest apparel and accessory items when they visit showrooms.

Behind the Price Tag of a $110 Summer Dress

Cotton and polyester dress: Wholesale price $59.75
Retail price $110.00

Manufacturer's Cost	
Fabric (2 11/16 yards at $1.60)	$4.30
Lining (1 3/4 yards at .75, plus interlining, 3/4 yards at .60)	1.54
Belt (Including covered snaps, elastic)	2.28
Labor, wages (Operator, finisher, presser)	21.03
Labor, fringe benefits (Health and welfare, Social Security, vacation, pension)	6.73
Overhead (Rent, insurance, utilities, salaries, costs of samples, trade discounts, etc.)	19.87
Total cost	$55.75
Taxes	2.00
Profit	2.00
Wholesale cost of dress	$59.75

Retailer's Cost	
$59.75 less discount for prompt payment	**$55.00**
Markdowns (Averaged over all dresses in stock)	**$11.00**
Shortages, pilferage, etc.	2.00
Alterations (Cost of maintaining department averaged out)	2.00
Salaries	
Sales staff	5.00
Merchandising and buying staff (Including expenses)	3.00
Clerical and stock room (Receiving, marking, deliveries, etc.; including expenses)	3.00
Advertising, display, sales promotion	4.00
Administrative (Executives, credit and accounting offices, including expenses)	8.00
Employe fringe benefits	2.00
Overhead (Rent, insurance, utilities, cleaning, security)	9.00
Miscellaneous	2.00
Total	$106.00
Taxes	2.00
Profit	2.00
Selling price	$110.00 (plus tax)

Fig. 1-5 This chart shows that apparel and accessory items may be among the consumer's best buys.

Retailing Apparel and Accessories After retail store buyers place their orders, the manufacturer prepares and assembles the merchandise to be shipped, usually by air or truck. At the store, the items are checked in, price-marked, and displayed on the sales floor. Advertising encourages customers to purchase new merchandise; and more salespeople may be hired to sell it.

THE PRICE OF APPAREL AND ACCESSORIES

A comparison of the costs of housing, food, transportation, and apparel has shown that, from 1967 to 1976, apparel prices rose at a smaller rate than that of the other items. And it is projected that the price of apparel will continue to increase at this smaller rate. One of the reasons for the lower increase rate is that competition in the American apparel industry is so strong that only companies that charge the lowest possible prices can survive.

The retail price of any apparel or accessory item includes the cost of producing it (manufacturer's cost) and the cost of selling it (wholesaler's and retailer's costs). The wholesale cost is paid by a retail store for merchandise. Thus, the retail cost, or the price consumers pay, includes the wholesale cost.

Figure 1-5 shows that a $110 dress brings the manufacturer 3 percent profit after taxes and the retailer 2 percent profit after taxes. This is a total of $4 profit. It's easy to see that apparel and accessory manufacturers and retailers are not making unfair profits. In fact, apparel and accessories may be one of America's best buys.

FASHION MERCHANDISING

Workers who plan to have the right fashion-oriented merchandise in the right place, in the right quantities, at the right prices, and at the right time are part of the exciting field called fashion merchandising. Designers, wholesalers, retail store buyers, store owners and managers, salespeople, and workers in advertising, display, and public relations are part of this fast-paced industry.

THE LANGUAGE OF FASHION

Fashion merchandising has developed its own vocabulary. Dr. Paul Nystrom, a leader in fashion merchandising, defined the words listed below. These definitions are very important because they are used in the daily work of fashion merchandising.

Fashion. The prevailing style accepted and used by a particular group of people at a particular time.

High Fashion. Fashions accepted by the elite among consumers, those who are first to accept fashion change. Usually, high fashions are produced and sold in small quantities at high prices.

Mass Fashion (or Volume Fashion). Styles widely accepted. These styles are manufactured and sold in large quantities at moderate to low prices.

Apparel. Everything that a person wears or carries to complete an outfit: undergarments, outerwear, jewelry, handbags, gloves, hats, shoes, and stockings. In the fashion industry "apparel" refers only to coats, suits, sportswear, and dresses. The industry uses different terms to describe other apparel items such as footwear, loungewear, sleepwear, casual wear, accessories, jewelry, and men's furnishings (shirts and ties), and so on.

Style. The characteristic or distinctive way a garment looks that makes it different from other garments. For example, dresses are one style of women's apparel, pants are another. Styles go in and out of fashion, but a specific style always remains a style. When people ask, "Is this in style?" they really mean, "Is this particular style in fashion?"

Design. A specific interpretation or variation of a style. For example, dresses are a distinct style in women's apparel. The shift, bouffant, and empire are three examples of different dress designs. In the fashion trade, a design is often referred to as a "style."

Fad. A short-lived fashion. Fads can come and go in a single season and usually affect a narrow group within a total population. The mood ring, popular in 1975-76, was a fad.

Classic. A style or design that remains "in fashion" over a long time. The cardigan sweater is an example of a classic.

FASHION PRINCIPLES

Some important principles of fashion remain the same year after year, season after season. Let's examine the following principles.

Change The look of clothing and accessories changes from season to season. For example, dresses may be one inch above the knee in spring. But in fall, dress lengths may be only one-half inch above the knee.

Change is one of the major principles of fashion. Usually change is gradual. For example, men's suit lapel widths may vary an inch or so from season to season. Because change is gradual, fashion merchandisers can study the fashions of the past and predict, with a fair accuracy, the fashions of the near future.

Fashions continue to change until they reach a point of excess. For example, the miniskirt continued to get shorter and shorter until, for modesty reasons, it could go no higher. A new fashion look begins when an extreme occurs.

Fashion Cycles Fashions are introduced, gain acceptance, become popular, decline, and pass out of fashion. Fashion moves in cycles of varying lengths. A fad has a very short cycle, whereas a classic has a long fashion cycle. (See Figure 1-6.)

Consumers Determine Fashion Fashions are not created by designers, manufacturers, or retailers. Rather, fashions are created by consumers. That is, people decide whether or not a style appeals to them. In fact, they choose the new styles.

All fashion merchandisers want to present merchandise that will appeal to consumers. Retail sales figures show if the right decision has been made. When consumers reject a style, no amount of advertising or sales promotion can change their minds. An example of this is the rejection of the midi, a long-skirted dress, in the late 1960s. The designers were wrong in their timing and choice of skirt length.

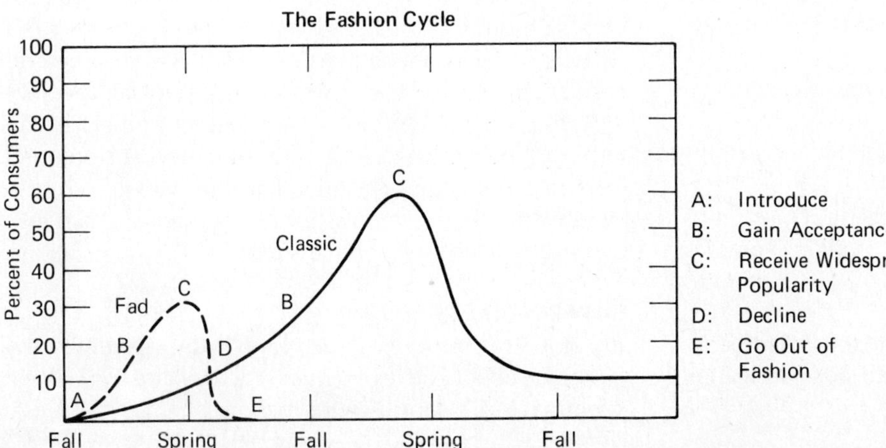

Fig. 1-6 Compare the short cycle of a fad with that of a classic.

Experience 1-1

Classics and Fads: Can You Tell the Difference?

Examine the following list of apparel items. In the space provided, write whether each item is a classic or a fad.

1. turtleneck sweater ______________
2. men's trench coat ______________
3. shirtwaist dress ______________
4. middy blouse ______________
5. kilt skirt ______________
6. A-line skirt ______________
7. bolero jacket ______________
8. polo shirt ______________
9. knickers ______________
10. Nehru jacket ______________

TYPES OF APPAREL AND ACCESSORY STORES

Department stores, specialty stores, self-service stores, and even supermarkets sell apparel and accessory items. Chain stores, mail-order houses, and direct-selling establishments are other sources of apparel and accessories. Let's examine each of these establishments.

DEPARTMENT STORES

Department stores, which originated in the United States between 1840 and 1880, offer a wide variety of merchandise. They are one-stop shopping stores in which almost everything people might want is brought together in one place and offered for sale.

Not every general merchandise store is a department store. The U.S. Department of Commerce defines a department store as a retail establishment that employs at least 25 or more people, has sales of apparel and soft goods combined amounting to 20 percent or more of total sales, and sells items in each of the following lines of merchandise:

Furniture, home furnishings, appliances, radios, and TV sets
General apparel for the family
Household linens and dry goods[3]

In department stores, merchandise is arranged in separate departments. Usually each department has a manager and one buyer, who purchases that department's merchandise. A typical department store may include any of the following apparel and accessory departments:

For Men. Suits, men's furnishings, preps' or students' clothing, shoes
For Children. Boys' clothing, girls' clothing, teen clothing, infants' clothing, shoes
For Women. Dresses, sportswear, lingerie, coats, hats, jewelry, hosiery, shoes, accessories, junior women's clothing

Department stores frequently have budget departments that feature less expensive apparel and accessories for children, men, and women.

Some well-known department stores are: Marshall Field (Chicago), May Company (Los Angeles), Macy's and Bloomingdale's (New York), J. L. Hudson (Detroit), John Wanamaker (Philadelphia), and Rich's (Atlanta).

SPECIALTY STORES

Specialty stores sell only one kind of merchandise, such as apparel, and items that go with that merchandise. For example, some specialty stores sell only uniforms. Others sell only clothing and accessories for a bride. Specialty stores sell merchandise that appeals to a very specific type of customer with specific needs. Their atmosphere, merchandise, displays, advertising, and salespeople are aimed at attracting that particular customer.

In 1975, men's, boys', and women's apparel specialty stores had a combined sales volume of $16,178,000—a total of 3 percent of all retail sales. Projected sales by 1985 are $30,692,000, a 90 percent increase in a 10-year period.[4]

Specialty stores can be large or small. It is not difficult to identify them. Remember that these stores specialize in selling one type of merchandise—apparel and accessories. Bonwit-Teller (New York) is an example of a specialty store.

SELF-SERVICE STORES

Like department stores, self-service stores usually have various departments and sell hard goods (appliances), cosmetics, apparel and accessories, and housewares. Unlike department stores, self-service stores do not provide salespeople. Customers select merchandise from shelves or racks and bring their purchases to a central cashier. Because these stores do not pay salespeople, they pass on some of their savings to customers in the form of lower prices. Most often, self-service stores sell low- to moderate-priced merchandise. Woolco (of the Woolworth chain) and K-Mart (of the Kresge chain) are two examples of self-service stores.

SUPERMARKETS

It's not uncommon to see pantyhose, aprons, baby clothes, socks, and even men's work shirts on sale at supermarkets. Many experts believe that in the future more and more apparel items will be sold at supermarkets. The basis for this reasoning is that at least one person within every family unit usually shops at a supermarket. This provides a ready market for apparel and accessories.

CHAIN STORES

Chain stores offer standardized merchandise and services to customers at 12 or more locations. They may be national, regional, or local. They may be department stores or self-service stores that offer apparel and accessories plus other types of merchandise. Or they may be specialty stores that sell only apparel and accessory merchandise. Sears, Roebuck and Company and J. C. Penney are two large department store chains that sell apparel and accessories. Thom McAn and Lerner Shops are chain specialty shops.

In chain store operations, the buying, merchandising, and distribution of merchandise are handled at a central office. For example, a chain store buyer, working at the central buying office, buys a particular type of merchandise for all the stores in the chain. This merchandise is then distributed to the retail outlets from a central or regional distribution center.

Chain stores often feature merchandise in low- to moderate-price ranges. They may provide customers with their own brand merchandise. Many chain stores encourage self-service.

MAIL-ORDER BUSINESSES

Before widespread use of the automobile, rural and small-town customers did most of their shopping from catalogs. Mail-order businesses still use catalogs to sell merchandise. Such companies as Sears, Roebuck and Company, Montgomery Ward, J. C. Penney, Alden's, and Spiegel print catalogs that let customers shop for apparel and accessories and other items at home. These catalogs feature popular priced, mass market merchandise, as well as some higher priced items.

Smaller mail-order businesses advertise in magazines and newspapers or mail brochures and catalogs to customers' homes. These brochures and catalogs usually show the merchandise and include a return coupon. (See Figure 1-7.)

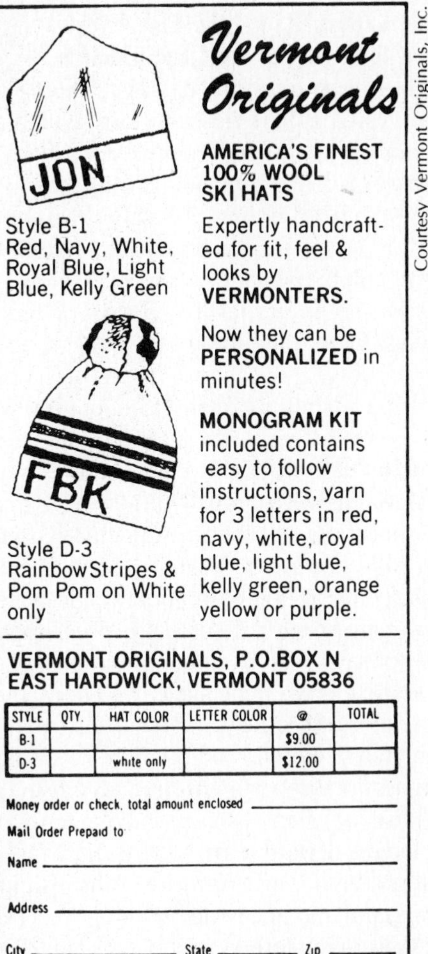

Fig. 1-7 Here's a typical ad for merchandise sold by a mail-order business.

DIRECT-SELLING ESTABLISHMENTS

Direct-selling establishments do not have stores. Rather, their salespeople sell door-to-door or arrange demonstration "parties." While in customer's homes, salespeople present the merchandise and take orders. The merchandise is delivered at a later date. Some direct-selling establishments are Avon cosmetics, Sarah Coventry jewelry, and Beeline Fashions.

Experience 1-2

Stores, Stores, Stores

On a separate sheet of paper, answer the following statements and questions.

1. Name a nearby department store that sells apparel and accessories. Is this store a chain store? How many stores are in this department store chain?
2. Name two local apparel and accessory specialty stores.
3. Name a local or nearby self-service store that sells apparel and accessories.
4. Visit a local supermarket. List the apparel and accessory items it sells.
5. In magazines or newspapers, locate two advertisements from mail-order houses for apparel and accessory items. Bring the ads to class and compare them with those of your classmates.

CAREER OPPORTUNITIES IN APPAREL AND ACCESSORIES

The field of apparel and accessories offers vast career opportunities. There are designer jobs, which require an ability to create and sketch new designs for fabrics, garments, and accessories. Manufacturing jobs extend from producing cloth to cutting and sewing a garment. Advertising or publishing careers are available to people who photograph, write, or sketch. Fashion promotion jobs involve preparing fashion shows or modeling the latest styles. Wholesale trade salesworkers or manufacturer reps show apparel and accessory merchandise samples or catalogs to retail store buyers. Wholesale trade salesworkers work for a wholesaler, a company, or an individual; they distribute hundreds of similar products. Manufacturer reps work for a particular manufacturer and only sell that manufacturer's products.

Rather than choose a position in one of those areas, you may decide to begin an apparel and accessory career in a retail store. In a retailing career, positions are available for salespersons, unit control clerks, stock persons, and cashiers. Higher-level positions include department managers, buyers, merchandise managers, and store managers. Retail stores employ people in their sales promotion departments to advertise or display merchandise or plan fashion shows. Employees also work in service departments, such as gift wrap, customer credit, and merchandise delivery. After gaining experience in apparel and accessory retailing, you may decide to open your own store.

This manual provides the information you need to begin or advance your career in an apparel and accessory store. The skills and aptitudes needed to work as a salesperson, manager, or buyer are presented. (See Table 1.) Unit 2 discusses the basic and social skills needed for an apparel and accessory retailing career. There are hints on how to get along with people and how to communicate. You will use your mathematics skills as retail apparel and accessory employees do every workday.

Unit 3 includes information about the many kinds of women's, men's, and infants' and children's apparel and accessories sold. Unit 4 discusses how apparel and accessories are purchased, received at the store, advertised, displayed, and sold. Also in this unit, you will learn how to manage yourself and others.

THE APPAREL AND ACCESSORY SALESPERSON

Salespersons work with many different kinds of merchandise and customers. They rearrange merchandise out on the sales floor, present the merchandise to customers, and answer their questions. They also ring up purchases on the cash register, handle money, and make change. Depending on the size of the store, salespersons may order merchandise and make merchandise displays, as well as receive, check, and ticket new merchandise. They may also take inventory and help keep their work area neat.

Successful salespeople enjoy working with the mer-

TABLE 1

PROFILE OF OCCUPATIONS IN FASHION MERCHANDISING

Entry Jobs

OCCUPATION	WHAT WORKERS DO
Stock Clerk	Receive and store incoming merchandise; keep merchandise properly arranged; participate in stock control
Merchandise Clerk	Record information on merchandise ordered, received, and sold; prepare special stock and sales reports
Office "Follow-up"	Follow up on buyers' orders for delivery and shipping dates; place special orders and reorders
Salesperson	Service customers; transact sales; help with stockkeeping
"Flying" Squad	Receive temporary selling and other assignments where needed
Merchandise Trainee	Receive periodic assignments in different merchandise departments to learn the various aspects of merchandising
Assistant to Fashion Coordinator	Help coordinator in producing fashion shows; research fashion; collect and cut fabric swatches
Executive Trainee	Receive temporary assignments in various departments of all the major divisions
Advertising Assistant	Follow through on ads; keep advertising sample books; assist where needed
Assistant to Copywriter	Assist in writing copy
Display Assistant	Collect merchandise from departments; help execute window and storewide displays
Photo Stylist	Accessorize and fix merchandise that is being photographed
Sales Assistant Showroom Sales Assistant	Assist salesperson when he or she shows merchandise to buyer, and render services to customers
Comparison Shopper	Shop competing stores; compare prices, observe active selling items; report findings to buyers
Merchandise Distributor	Collect information about individual store needs and allocate merchandise that has been bought
Shopper	Shop retail stores and textile firms; observe and report new and/or active selling items

PROFILE OF OCCUPATIONS IN FASHION MERCHANDISING (CONTINUED)

Advanced Career Opportunities

OCCUPATION	WHAT WORKERS DO
Head of Stock	Maintain stock from receipt to sale of merchandise
Assistant Buyer	Aid the buyer in most of his or her duties and take charge in absence of the buyer
Associate Buyer	Perform the buying function with its accompanying activities for a classification of merchandise rather than for an entire department
Branch Store Department Manager	Assist in handling the merchandising activities performed in the branch store; supervise sales personnel and store operations
Buyer	Anticipate wants; select merchandise; determine sources of supply and time of purchase; budget quantities; price merchandise; buy goods at a price which permits a profit; participate in selling; plan sales promotion activities
Divisional Merchandise Manager	Coordinate the activities of a group of related departments; advise and supervise the buyers; interpret and execute policies of management
General Merchandise Manager	Coordinate and supervise all the buying and selling activities of the entire organization; interpret and execute policies of management; advise and supervise divisional merchandise managers and buyers
Sales Manager	Hire, train, and supervise the activities of sales personnel, and participate in sales promotion activities
Fashion Coordinator	Research, analyze, and advise on fashion trends; produce fashion shows; prepare and distribute fashion information to company personnel
Comparison Office Manager	Supervise the activities of the shoppers who check the competing stores and participate in sales promotion by checking responses to the advertising of competing stores
Copywriter	Create the text, headlines, and slogans of ads
Advertising Manager	Direct a company's advertising program by setting policies concerning type of advertising, amount of advertising budget, and supervise the preparation of promotional material
Display Manager	Plan and direct the execution of window and interior displays

PROFILE OF OCCUPATIONS IN FASHION MERCHANDISING (CONTINUED)

OCCUPATION	WHAT WORKERS DO
Section Manager Service Manager	Maintain satisfactory standards of customer service throughout an assigned part of store; supervise sales personnel; handle emergencies arising in selling areas
Floor Superintendent	Supervise a group of section managers within a selling area
Sales Representative	Locate industrial customers; make products known to them; provide product information and services; take orders; follow up on customers

(Source: Career Exploration in the Fashion Industry: A Suggested Program Guide, Fashion Industry Series, No. 1, ERIC Reports ED 102 407 (New York.) Fashion Institute of Technology, 1973).

chandise they sell. They get excited about new fashions and convey that excitement to customers. They know about the merchandise they sell—its construction, style details, and care. To help their customers choose attractive clothing accessories, these salespeople have an eye for color, line, and design.

Successful salespeople are pleasant and like people. They make customers feel welcome and comfortable in the store. And they are able to remain calm when unpleasant situations occur with customers or coworkers.

Although full-time apparel and accessory salespeople may work a 40-hour, 5-day work week, they don't work regular 8 to 5 hours. Downtown stores are often open from 10 a.m. to 6 p.m. on Tuesday, Wednesday, and Saturday and from 10 a.m. to 9 p.m. on Monday, Thursday, and Friday. Suburban stores are usually open Monday through Friday from 10 a.m. to 9 p.m. and Saturday 10 a.m. to 6 p.m. Depending on the area, stores may be open on Sunday. During the weeks before Christmas, the busiest time of the retailing year, most stores are open from 10 a.m. to 9 p.m. Saturday through Sunday.

The working conditions in most apparel and accessory stores are very good. To attract customers, most stores are nicely decorated, well lighted and clean, and temperature-controlled. Some stores provide cafeterias for employees and/or customers.

Salespeople spend the majority of their day standing and walking. They need strong legs and feet and, occasionally, a strong back to lift merchandise. Good grooming is important for apparel and accessory salespeople. Usually salespeople are encouraged to wear clothing similar to that sold by the store. The clothing worn should allow the salespeople to bend over, lift, and stand comfortably for long periods.

Apparel and accessory employers prefer to hire high school graduates for sales jobs. They look for people who have had training in business mathematics, merchandising, and retail selling. Many employers prefer to hire people who have taken distributive education classes because these employees have a wide background in merchandising, physical distribution, advertising, display, sales, management, human relations, business communications, mathematics, and product and service technology. Employers are looking for new employees who have a neat appearance and are able to communicate clearly.

Beginning apparel and accessory salespeople earn a minimum wage. After a short time, they may earn a commission, or percentage of their sales, plus salary. Many stores offer their salespeople an employee discount, which allows them to buy merchandise below regular prices. Health and life insurance, retirement plans, credit union savings, and profit sharing are other fringe benefits.

Successful salespeople may be promoted to department managers or assistant buyers in 1 to 2 years. Usually salespeople with college training are promoted faster than those without it. The employment outlook for salespeople is expected to increase about as fast as the average for all occupations through the mid-1980s. People well trained in fashion and selling should be able to find good positions.

THE APPAREL AND ACCESSORY BUYER

Buyers go on buying trips to purchase merchandise for their stores. Successful buyers are familiar with the manufacturers that make the merchandise they need. They know about changes in products and the development of new ones. To learn about merchandise, buyers attend fashion shows and visit manufacturer showrooms. Buyers also regularly read trade journals, such as *Women's Wear Daily,* and fashion magazines, such as *Gentlemen's Quarterly*. On buying trips, they evaluate the merchandise offered by vendors.

Buyers have busy schedules. During a day, they may work with salespeople, manufacturer reps, store executives, and customers. They spend time in their offices, on the telephone, and on the sales floor. A buyer's job is fast-paced and full of constant pressure. Buyers may be away from home an average of one week a month, and they often work more than 40 hours a week.

Buyers use their mathematical skills in analyzing sales records, preparing merchandise buying plans, and computing the amount of money available for buying trips. They also need to be good at planning and decision making. A thorough knowledge of the merchandise they buy, leadership ability, and good communication skills are essential too.

Most buyers begin their careers as assistant buyers. Promising salespeople may be promoted to buying jobs or become assistant buyers. Stores usually prefer college or junior college graduates. These employees often have a liberal arts, business, retailing, distributive education, or fashion merchandising background. After training in the various operations of a store, assistant buyers are promoted to buying positions.

Assistant buyers usually earn between $8,500 and $14,000 a year. Some buyers earn $15,000 to $25,000 a year. Salaries for buyers at very large stores or chain stores are in the $30,000 to $50,000 range. Often, buyers are paid a bonus in addition to their regular salaries if they reach their store's sales objectives for the year.

The employment outlook for buyers is expected to grow faster than the average for all occupations through the mid-1980s. Competition for these jobs is keen. Apparel and accessory stores choose well-qualified people who enjoy the competitiveness of retailing and work best in a demanding, fast-paced job. Although there are buying positions in all parts of the country, most are in major metropolitan areas where there are many retail stores.[5]

THE APPAREL AND ACCESSORY MANAGER

Depending on the size and type of store, promotions to department manager, operations manager, merchandise manager, assistant manager, or store manager are available. Merchandise managers plan and coordinate buying and selling for the store, divide the store's buying budget among buyers, and assign buyers to purchase certain merchandise.

Although management jobs vary, all management positions require the ability to plan and organize, select and direct employees, and control particular business activities. A manager has increased responsibilities, works long hours, and makes important decisions. Managers may also be required to move, as are, for instance, chain store managers.

The National Retail Merchants Association reports that top executives in retailing management are younger and earn more than top executives in other fields. Persistence, ability, and hard work advance people into apparel and accessory management positions. For the right person, this job offers a satisfying career.

OWNING YOUR OWN STORE

There are many opportunities to open your own apparel and accessory store. Before opening your own store, though, you should be familiar with how a store operates, how merchandise is purchased, inventoried, and sold, as well as the ins and outs of the apparel and accessory industry. Working as a salesperson, department manager, or buyer is almost a necessity before starting a store of your own. Many new businesses fail due to lack of retailing experience.

You should realize that opening a store is risky because competition is intense. At this time, there are over 129,000 apparel and accessory specialty stores. Over half are small, with less than 20 employees.[6]

YOUR FUTURE IN APPAREL AND ACCESSORY RETAILING

Apparel and accessory retailing involves working in a fast-paced, dynamic environment. It's fun and exciting, but it's also hard work. Good mathematical skills, good communication skills, and the ability to get along with others are necessary. To be successful, you need to know the basic facts about your merchandise—their fabrics, style names, size ranges, and care. Familiarity with buying, receiving, advertising, display, and selling techniques is also important. As you advance on the career ladder, you also need to acquire management skills.

Here are a few suggestions to prepare yourself for a successful career in apparel and accessory retailing:

- If you are in high school and do not plan to attend college, start investigating the apparel and accessory stores in your area. Find out from managers which stores will have openings now or when you finish school. Ask about the kind of jobs in which you would start. Your first job may be as stock clerk, unit control clerk, cashier, or salesperson. The pay may not be as much as in beginning jobs in other fields, but the opportunities to advance will be greater.
- If you are in high school and plan to go to college, try to get a summer job in an apparel and accessory store. This will let you see if you like the work.
- In high school and college, take some basic courses in retailing, selling, and business. Try to get as much on-the-job experience as possible while still in school. If you enroll in the D. E. program at your school, you can "earn and learn" through on-the-job cooperative education and classroom training.
- If you are graduating from a junior college or four-year college, be sure to see the representatives of retail companies who visit your college placement office. Write to stores that do not visit your college that you would like to know more about, and ask for an employment interview. Campus recruiters hire college students for management training programs. These are excellent programs if you want to become a buyer or manager.

Your work will be challenging, fun, and interesting in an apparel and accessory retailing career. This is one field where you can test your knowledge almost daily and where you can tell almost immediately if you have made the right choice. Good luck with your career decision and welcome to the fascinating world of apparel and accessory retailing.

Experience 1-3

Is It Right for You?

Only you can tell if you will be happy in an apparel and accessory retailing career. Carefully examine your own personality and the requirements of the job. The following questions may help you decide if this career really interests you. Check them "yes" or "no" in the space provided. A "yes" answer to most of them may indicate that you would probably enjoy a career in the fascinating world of retailing.

	No	Yes
1. Do you like to do your own shopping?		
2. Do you like to browse through stores?		
3. Are you interested in what's "in fashion"?		
4. Do you notice what others are wearing?		
5. Do you like to read fashion magazines?		
6. Do you remember the prices of apparel you buy?		
7. Do you compare prices?		
8. Do you enjoy meeting people?		

	No	Yes
9. Do you like being around a lot of people?		
10. Do you try to figure out people?		
11. Is it easy for you to talk with strangers?		
12. Do you like change?		
13. Do you like your days to be very busy?		
14. Are you energetic?		
15. Do you like to compete with others?		
16. Do you enjoy making decisions?		
17. Would you take a risk for a big gain?		

NOTES

1. *Family Economics Review,* Consumer and Food Economics Insitute, U.S. Department of Agriculture, Winter 1977. Projection based on author's estimates.
2. Carl Priestland, *Focus, Economic Profile of the Apparel Industry* (Arlington: The American Apparel Manufacturers Association, 1976), p. 49.
3. G. Henry Richert et al., *Retailing Principles and Practices,* 6th ed. (New York: McGraw-Hill Book Company, 1974), p. 44.
4. *U.S. Industrial Outlook,* 1976, p. 176.
5. *Occupational Outlook Handbook,* U.S. Department of Labor, 1976-77, p. 129.
6. U.S. Department of Commerce, *County Business Patterns,* 1973, p. 29.
   U.S. Bureau of the Census, *1972 Census of Retail Trade,* RC72-A-52, July 1975.

UNIT 2

Basic and Social Skills

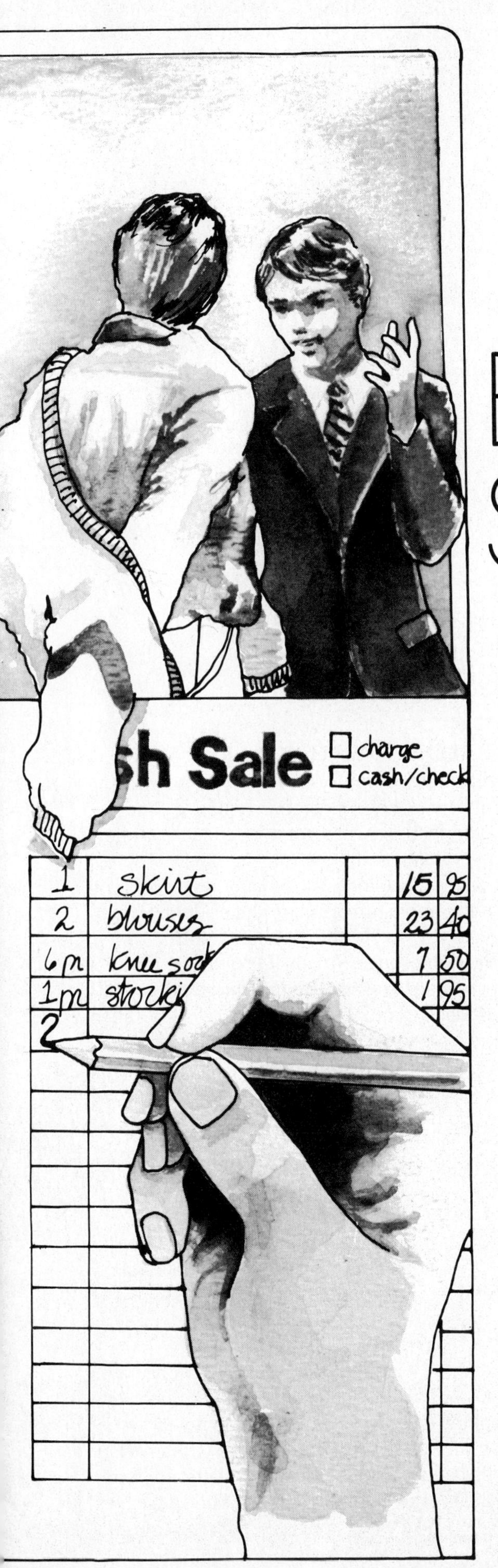

To succeed at any apparel and accessories career in marketing, you need certain "foundation" skills. For example, you need to know how to get along with people—customers, coworkers, supervisors, and suppliers. These skills are presented in Chapter 2. You also must know how to communicate with others—by speaking, listening, reading, and writing. These skills are discussed in Chapter 3. The mathematics skills you will use in your apparel and accessories marketing career are covered in Chapter 4.

If you master these "foundation" skills, you can build a good career on them—a career that will give you financial and personal rewards.

2 Human Relations

In an apparel and accessory store, it is important for you to cooperate and work effectively with coworkers, supervisors, and customers. You may not like some of your coworkers or customers, and some of them may not like you. But to do your job effectively, you have to learn how to get along with others. You must learn the art of human relations.

WHO ARE WE?

Each of us has personal characteristics that make us different from others. We are set apart by differences in personal appearance, and we are different because of personality traits. Each of us has a unique intelligence level and ability to learn. We are also set apart by our past experiences.

What has happened to us in the past may cause us to react, feel, or think in a way that is different from other people. For example, suppose when you were small you had a brother or sister who liked to scare you when it was dark. Although you are much older now and realize the dark shouldn't scare you, you still try to get out of working nights at the store. You don't like walking to your car or waiting for the bus after the sun goes down. This past experience affects the way you act. If your coworkers don't know why you try to get out of working nights, they may feel as though you are taking advantage of them.

To get along with others, we first need to look at ourselves and see who we are. What appearance characteristics, personality traits, intelligence level, experiences, attitudes, and opinions are combined to make each of us an individual? When we begin to understand ourselves, we can see our strengths and failings more clearly. We can become more objective, see ourselves the way others see us, and begin to understand why people react to us the way they do. With this information, we can set goals to become the persons we want to be.

GETTING ALONG WITH OTHERS

Apparel and accessory employers hire workers who can learn their jobs quickly, become productive, and get along with other people. They want individuals who are honest, dependable, and enthusiastic. They look for workers who will make the store a better place because they work there. In other words, employers look for employees who have good human relations skills.

Human relations concerns your behavior and how it affects other people. To see why human relations skills are important, let's examine a small apparel shop called Charlie's. There are four employees, and each employee demonstrates, or fails to demonstrate, certain personality traits, such as tolerance, understanding, interest in others, flexibility, and honesty. Their personality traits affect the way they get along with each other and with customers. (See Figure 2-1.)

TOLERANCE AND UNDERSTANDING

Rita is the most productive salesperson at Charlie's. She sells more than anyone else, works faster, seldom makes a mistake, and is punctual. When Rita is assigned a certain job, she can be depended upon to accomplish the task.

The other employees think Rita is a perfectionist and overachiever, and no one wants to work with her. Rita cannot accept the fact that other people do not catch on as quickly as she does. When Rita works with another employee, she cannot tolerate the smallest error or work slowdown. She is critical of others, but when she makes an occasional mistake, she is unable to accept criticism herself.

Fig. 2-1 Because Rita, Henry, Roger, and Joni (left to right) have unique personal characteristics, they relate to others differently.

Perhaps Rita's biggest weakness is that she doesn't realize good human relations is an important part of her job. She lacks tolerance—she doesn't realize that everyone does not think, act, or respond to situations as she does. And she doesn't take another person's viewpoint.

Tolerance and understanding are two important requirements for getting along with others. By developing these qualities, you can accept someone else's weaknesses without losing self-control, and you can accept another's accomplishments without jealousy.

INTEREST IN OTHERS

Henry is known for the interest he shows in others. He makes everybody feel special. Henry listens to others and gives each person his total attention. Henry's technique is to listen with his ears and watch with his eyes.

Henry says, "People always give verbal and nonverbal clues about how they feel or what's on their minds. The clues may say 'I'm not feeling well' or 'I have a problem I want to talk about.' It's not difficult to read these clues. It's just that many people are so involved with themselves that they don't hear someone else."

It's no secret Henry goes out of his way to be friendly. He always has a smile for everyone, and he remembers what someone has told him. Then Henry cares enough to ask about it in the future. For example, when another employee mentions she has to prepare an inventory report for the supervisor, Henry remembers to ask how it turned out.

ENTHUSIASM

Another of Henry's strong points is his enthusiasm; this generates more enthusiasm among his coworkers. He seems to make even the most boring job fun. Henry is a good influence on **morale**, a term that describes how employees feel about their jobs, their coworkers, and their employers. Workers with high morale are productive; they want to do a good job and enjoy coming to work.

Henry also generates enthusiasm in customers. He is enthusiastic about the merchandise he sells, creates a desire for customers to buy, and gives the feeling that he finds real enjoyment in his work.

INITIATIVE AND CREATIVITY

Henry's positive attitude is seen in his work. He's always eager to demonstrate his initiative and creativity—both good qualities. However, when Henry first started to work at the store, he didn't know how to take the initiative or show creativity in the right way. For example, the first day on the job, Henry rearranged the shirts. Although Henry was more familiar with this new system because of his work at another store, the other employees were not. The new arrangement caused confusion and angered other employees who lost sales because they couldn't find the proper sizes.

Henry's initiative shows that he is sincerely interested in doing a good job. Managers look for employees like Henry—self-starters who can begin a job without being told what to do. As a new employee, you should find out all you can about your job and the place you work before putting your ideas into action. Once you learn the store's operation, you can make suggestions for improvement. These suggestions are usually appreciated, and your initiative and creativity may be rewarded with a promotion.

FLEXIBILITY

At an apparel and accessory store, unplanned tasks occur all the time. For example, a customer may want to purchase the suit you just put on the window mannequin. Flexibility will help you adjust to unplanned events and to get along with your coworkers, supervisors, and customers.

Roger has a hot temper. When things go his way, he is responsible and productive. But when he must do something unplanned, he loses his temper. The other employees wish Roger were more flexibile and could accept changes without losing his self-control. His temper makes his coworkers uncomfortable.

PATIENCE AND TRUTHFULNESS

Roger's lack of patience affects the way he handles customers. When customers "get on his nerves," he sometimes misrepresents facts about the store or merchandise in order to make the sale quickly and leave the customer. For example, Roger misrepresented a raincoat as being washable when it could only be dry-cleaned. The store lost profit and credibility with the customer. The store replaced the damaged raincoat, but it also lost a valued customer.

Salespeople have to work with many different customers. Some customers are very quick in their decisions, others are slow and seem to take forever. As a salesperson, you must learn patience and courtesy when helping all customers. It's easy for salespeople to tell customers what they want to hear in order to make sales. But many future sales are lost when customers lose trust in a store, product, or salesperson. Management holds salespeople responsible to know the facts and honestly communicate them to customers.

SELF-CONTROL

Like his coworkers, Roger handles customer returns and complaints. When handling a complaint or return, Roger tries to listen courteously. When the customer's request for return or replacement is reasonable, and within store policy, Roger can correct the situation and keep a happy customer. But when customers are unreasonable, Roger becomes unreasonable too. Occasionally, when difficult customers throw insults at him, Roger insults the customers in return. When customers yell, he yells. Unfortunately, Roger has not learned that losing his temper does more damage than good. Store employees seldom win arguments with customers; they only lose sales.

When customers become difficult, remember the following important points:

- Get the customer off the sales floor and to the manager's office or another part of the store where other customers will not be disturbed.
- Appeal to the customer's sense of fairness and explain the store policies and reasons for those policies.
- Don't be frightened by the customer.

ASSERTIVENESS

Joni is the youngest salesperson at Charlie's. Although she just graduated with honors from high school, she doesn't have much self-confidence. Other salespeople do tell her that she has a talent for selling. Her coworkers like her because she shares work responsibilities, works her share of nights and Saturdays, and doesn't take long lunch periods.

Perhaps because of her lack of confidence, Joni is sometimes less assertive than she should be. For example, even though she has the authority to approve checks up to $50, Joni asks her coworkers to okay customer checks. During busy periods, this becomes a problem, because someone has to stop what he or she was doing and help Joni. The other employees wish Joni were confident enough to assert her own authority. They would like to discuss the problem with her, but they don't want to hurt her feelings.

Your first job in a store can be frightening because of the new things to learn and new responsibilities. It's important for all store employees to know their responsibilities. No one wants to work with someone who needs a second opinion before acting.

PROPER DRESS

The way you dress influences the way others think about you and react to what you say and do. Clothing and personal appearance create an impression on customers and business associates. A proper appearance establishes a good public image for the store. An employee who does not fit the store's image looks out of place.

Some stores have guidelines on what employees are to wear. The guidelines in Figure 2-2 are an example of dress standards at one apparel and accessory store. Stores without formal dress standards expect their employees to be clean and well groomed. Be sure to check with the personnel department about dress standards before you start a new job, as standards vary from store to store.

HONESTY

Most employers ask job applicants for character references. These references are asked if the applicant is honest, dependable, and a good worker. Some apparel and accessory stores ask employees to take a polygraph or lie detector test before they are hired. (See Figure 2-3.) The test can include such questions as "Have you ever stolen money?" or "Have you ever shoplifted?" The purpose of this test is not find how bad employees were in the past, but to see if they tell the truth.

Sometimes new employees are offended that their honesty is being questioned. But, after they work at the store for a while, they see the many opportunities for a

NAME ______________________________ DATE ______________

IN CASE YOU'RE IN DOUBT AS TO "WHAT SHALL I WEAR TO WORK TODAY?" HERE ARE SOME GUIDELINES:

FOR WOMEN	
Three-piece pantsuits, with proper accessories	Yes
Two-piece pantsuits in matching lightweight fabrics	Yes
Long skirts in fabrics for street wear, with proper accessories	Yes
Evening skirts, patio skirts, leisure skirts	No
"Slinky" fabrics in long-length skirts	No
Culottes, shorts, halter tops	No
The layered look (the layered look is a covered-up look rather than the bare look and includes a jacket or jacket-type sweater)	Yes
Slacks and sweaters or blouses	No
House slippers, athletic shoes on the selling floor	No
Knee socks to complete an appropriate costume	Yes
Hose	Yes
Stretch lace or see-through blouses with a jacket	Yes
Head scarves or head bands	No

FOR MEN	
Jacket and ties on the selling floor	Yes
Shirt tails tucked in	Yes
Polished shoes worn with socks	Yes
Fringed, slit jeans	No
T-shirts, tank tops	No
Jeans and knit shirts in certain nonselling areas	Yes

IN ALL AREAS	
Hair neat and clean, personal cleanliness	Yes
Hair length for men—no longer than the top edge of the back collar	Yes
Sideburns and mustaches, neatly trimmed	Yes
Closely clipped, short beards	Yes
If a uniform is furnished, the style should not be altered or any extras added.	
Gum chewing is not in good taste.	

(*Source:* Auerbach's, Inc.)

Fig. 2-2 Here are some typical guidelines to grooming for apparel and accessory salespeople.

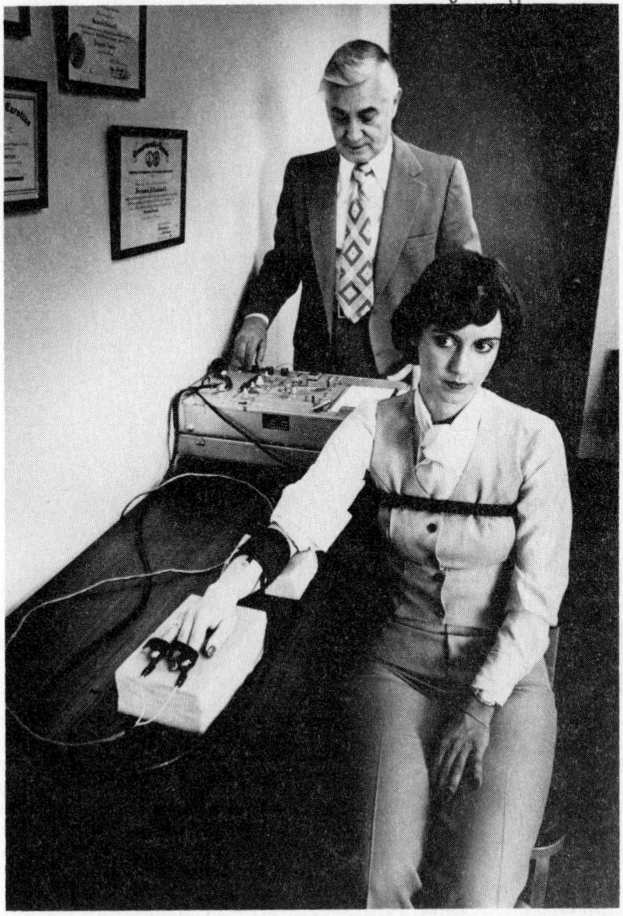

Bruce Roberts, 1977, for Photo Researchers, Inc.

Fig. 2-3 Why are some potential apparel and accessory employees required to take a lie detector test?

dishonest person to cheat or steal from the store. For example, employees who fail to punch their time cards when they go to lunch cheat the store of valuable selling time. Employees may be tempted to steal money from the cash register. Also, allowing friends to use your employee discount is a form of stealing.

Usually employees caught stealing or cheating are dismissed. This bad mark on their records may keep them from getting good jobs in the future.

Experience 2-1

These Words Mean Something Special

To get along with coworkers, supervisors, and customers, apparel and accessory salespeople need to have various desirable personal characteristics. Some of these characteristics are listed below. Following each word, write a definition of what that characteristic means to you. Then write an example of a situation demonstrating the use of each trait.

1. proper dress

   Definition: ______________________________

   ____

   Example: ______________________________

   ____

   ____

2. tolerance

   Definition: ______________________________

   ____

   Example: ______________________________

   ____

3. creativity

Definition: ______________________________

____

Example: ______________________________

____

4. dependability

Definition: ______________________________

____

Example: ______________________________

____

5. enthusiasm

Definition: ______________________________

____

Example: ______________________________

____

6. flexibility

Definition: ______________________________

____

Example: ______________________________

____

7. honesty

Definition: ______________________________

____

Example: ______________________________

____

8. initiative

Definition: ______________________________

____

Example: ______________________________

____

9. interest in others

Definition: ______________________________

____

Example: ______________________________

____

10. assertiveness

Definition: ______________________________

____

Example: ______________________________

____

11. self-control

Definition: ______________________________

____

Example: ______________________________

____

12. patience

Definition: ______________________________

____

Example: ______________________________

____

13. tact

Definition: ______________________________

____

Example: ______________________________

Experience 2-2

Taking Advantage

You work with three other part-time employees in the accessories department of a medium-sized department store. Your department manager prepares a work schedule that occasionally either you or the other part-time salespersons cannot meet. When this happens, you trade shifts with each other.

For the past three weeks, Chris, one of the other part-time employees, has asked you to work all his nights, and you agreed to the schedule change.

You are scheduled to work next Friday. But you have planned to attend a concert that night and ask Chris to work your shift. Chris says, "Me? I have a date Friday night. Why don't you ask Marty or Les to work for you?"

On a separate sheet of paper, answer the following about the situation described.

1. Identify the real problem in this human relations situation.
2. What are some important facts to be considered when evaluating this problem?
3. List several possible solutions to this problem.
4. Evaluate the results of each solution.
5. Which solution do you recommend and why?
6. How could this situation have been avoided by using better human relations skills?

Experience 2-3

Promise Anything to Make the Sale?

Tanya and Carol work in women's ready-to-wear. Both women receive a salary plus commission for their sales. This month there is a sales contest. The winner receives a three-day trip to San Diego. So far, Carol is leading the department in sales.

The other day, while Tanya was at lunch, Carol sold a jersey knit suit to a regular customer, Mrs. Clinton. Mrs. Clinton purchased the dress on sale for her daughter's birthday. Today, Carol's day off, Mrs. Clinton is returning the dress. She wants a cash refund.

The store's policy against refunds is clearly posted above the cash register. Tanya tries to explain the store policy to Mrs. Clinton, but the customer becomes firmer in her demands. Finally, Mrs. Clinton says, "The young lady that sold me this dress said I could return it and get my money back. That's the only reason I bought the dress. I told her I wasn't sure about the size, but she assured me returns would be no problem. I want my money back!"

1. Identify the real problem in this human relations situation.
2. What are some important facts to be considered when evaluating this problem?
3. List several possible solutions to this problem.
4. Evaluate the results of each solution.
5. Which solution do you recommend and why?
6. How do you think this situation will change Tanya's feeling toward Carol? Will the situation upset their working relationship?

Experience 2-4

What Do You Do When They Make a Scene?

Demonstrate how to handle two difficult customers who are trying to make a return. Assume your store does not allow customers to return merchandise for reasons such as (1) negligence and improper handling due to the customer's own abuse, (2) the merchandise has been worn, and (3) the merchandise was not purchased from your store, even though it is the same brand that your store sells.

Have two classmates play the parts of the following customers:

Customer 1 is returning a jacket received as a gift. The customer says it was purchased from your store. You carry that brand of clothing but not that particular style. Therefore, the jacket was purchased at another store.

Customer 2 is returning a pair of cotton denim pants. This customer wants a refund because after the pants were washed and dried, they shrank. (These pants have a merchandise tag that states the pants will shrink when washed in hot water or dried in a dryer.)

Note to "Customers" The items you are returning are expensive. You want the store to take back the merchandise and return your money or give you another item. If the salesperson fails to cooperate, get angrier and angrier. Try to cause a scene, so you can get your way.

After the role playing with the two classmates, describe how you felt about the situation. What human relations skills did you use? What skills did you not use that would have helped you handle both situations? On a separate sheet of paper, answer these questions and describe your feelings.

Experience 2-5

Is It Really Stealing?

You and Katie work in the Lingerie Department of a small store and have become good friends. The other day, Katie came to work wearing a new dress and a pair of textured hose.

During the day, Katie snagged her hose and developed a run in them. Katie said, "Will you watch the cash register while I slip in the dressing room and change my hose? I'll only be a minute."

Katie took a pair of hose from stock and went into the back. Later, you asked Katie if she paid for the merchandise. Katie answered, "Hey, that's a fringe benefit that comes with the job. They cost only $1.95."

You've thought about what Katie did. Your department manager, Mrs. Clegs, would be furious if she knew about Katie's behavior. Store management stresses that every employee has a responsibility to stop theft, and innocent employees who cover up for others are fired.

On a separate sheet of paper, analyze this situation. Identify the real problem and the factors that contribute to the problem. Prepare several alternatives that could solve the problem and analyze the results or consequences of each solution. Based on your evaluation, make a recommendation of how this problem should be handled. Then identify how you feel about the situation. Discuss such things as: Do you feel differently toward Katie? Will this situation affect your job performance? Do you feel good about the way that you handled the situation?

HUMAN RELATIONS RESPONSIBILITIES OF MANAGERS

Human relations is interdependence and cooperation among supervisors, coworkers, and customers. One of the most important jobs of apparel and accessory managers is to see that employees work together effectively. As an assistant department manager, merchandise manager, or store manager, you must organize your work and delegate it to the people who work for you. By training and encouraging your employees and monitoring their progress, you should achieve results. These results will be greater and more beneficial than if you did all the work yourself. If you find the productivity of your employees is disrupted because they do not work well together, you need to concentrate on improving the human relations skills of your staff.

THE MANAGER'S ROLE

Managers are responsible for the work and actions of the persons they supervise. They help new employees adjust to their jobs and see that they are acquainted with their fellow workers. Effective managers set good examples for their employees. In setting a good example, you become a role-model for your employees. For example, if you have a positive attitude toward work, enjoy doing a good job, and try to get along with others, so will your employees. If you display good work habits and ethical character, your staff will model their work behavior after yours. Your positive behavior may help your employees to change their actions and characteristics in a positive way.

Suppose, for example, that you worked for a person who was often late or who dressed sloppily. If this supervisor ever commented on your punctuality or dress, how would you react? You would probably think to yourself, "Why should I listen? I don't want to change my personality or behavior to become more like my supervisor!"

Managers must accept responsibility for influencing the attitudes of employees who work for them. Would you try to work hard and excel at your job if your manager did just enough to get by? Poor employee morale can often be caused by a manager who just doesn't care. Good employee morale can result from a manager who sets an example of personal work habits and character that people can admire and imitate.

Experience 2-6

What's the Problem?

Lily's Dress Salon recently added three new departments: sportswear, accessories, and shoes. To fill one of the new positions, Lily promoted her nephew, David, from receiving and stock clerk to manager of the Shoe Department. Although he has never worked on the sales floor before, David is responsible for training and supervising four salespeople.

Since David has become manager, he takes an hour for lunch rather than the usual half hour. When new shipments of shoes arrive, he gets his workers to put away the stock. He also asks the employees to prepare his merchandise and sales reports for his aunt. David spends lots of time on the phone with his friends. Many of his friends also drop in the store just to chat with him.

In the 3 months that David has been department manager, the store has hired nine salespersons for his department. The average time the employees stay at the store before quitting is 4½ weeks. The sales for the department have decreased by 35 percent.

On a separate sheet of paper, answer the following:

1. Identify the real problem.
2. What are the important facts to consider when solving this problem?
3. What are possible solutions to this problem?
4. Evaluate the results of each one of your possible solutions.
5. What is the best solution? Give reasons to support your choice.

USING HUMAN RELATIONS TO MOTIVATE OTHER PEOPLE

Because managers are responsible for the work of others, they spend much of their time motivating people to do a job and to do it well. **Motivation** is the reason that makes each of us act the way we do. Motivated workers have a goal in mind they want to achieve. Their motivations, or reasons why they want to accomplish a goal, influence their behavior. Apparel and accessory managers use many incentives to motivate their employees. Some of these incentives are:

Praise. When employees do a good job, their manager praises them. For example, a manager may say, "I saw last week's sales report, and you lead all the other salespersons in merchandise sales. I want you to know that I appreciate the work you've done. It reflects your ability and concern for our store and customers."

Public Recognition. With public recognition, the manager tells coworkers and other people who know the employee what a good job has been done. The store manager may sponsor an awards banquet and present outstanding workers with a plaque or trophy. (See Figure 2-4.)

Competition. Apparel stores sponsor sales contests to increase employee productivity. Prizes are usually money, trips, or merchandise. Many apparel stores publish weekly sales reports that list the sales activity of

Russell Dian

Fig. 2-4 Many salespeople are motivated to achievement by public recognition, such as awards.

each salesperson. People on the list get a feeling of satisfaction, and sometimes it spurs other employees to do a better job.

Money. Outstanding employees may receive bonuses or promotions for doing a good job.

Other Factors. Setting a goal, telling yourself you can do it, and then satisfying yourself by meeting your goal are other motivators. Some employees get satisfaction from increased job responsibility—a promotion or just more decision-making ability on the job. Increased responsibility means that management recognizes their ability. This feeling of being in charge makes you feel important and needed. Sometimes physical surroundings, such as a bigger office, motivate workers.

Everybody is motivated by different things. But what is important to one person is not important to another. As a manager, you need to realize that some motivators have more impact on some workers than on others. To achieve the most productive results from your workers, you must determine what incentives strongly motivate these employees.

You may wonder how you are going to find out what motivates your workers. When asked, most people can't say what really makes them work hard. People's motivations can only be estimated by observing and analyzing their behavior. For example, if a salesperson's sales increase by 25 percent every time there is a sales contest, it may be assumed that the employee is motivated by competition. During contests, other employees may be so "turned off" to the increased competition that their sales decrease. For these employees, contests are a negative motivation.

The only way managers can understand how to motivate others for best performance is to show an interest in the employees. By practicing effective human relations skills, managers should be able to get close to employees and find out "what really makes them tick."

Experience 2-7

Why You Do What You Do

1. Think about three goals you worked very hard to accomplish. On a separate sheet of paper, write what those goals were and what you think motivated you to achieve them. This paper will be private. Be honest with yourself.
2. Suppose you manage an apparel and accessory store. You are supposed to supervise a worker who is motivated by the same reasons that you wrote on your paper. Give three examples of how you, as a manager, would motivate this worker to do a better job of selling and working with customers.
3. Choose a friend that you know very well. Think about two times when this friend worked very hard to achieve a goal. On another sheet of paper, write down those goals and what reasons you think motivated your friend. Don't put your friend's name on the paper or tell others whom you are writing about.
4. Suppose your friend is a salesperson and is responsible for sales, stockkeeping, and display. You are the department manager. Your friend's work has not been up to standard. Write three examples of how you would motivate your friend to do a better job.

DEVELOPING A PLEASANT WORK ENVIRONMENT

Some factors that make up the **environment** of an apparel and accessory store are the building, the fixtures, the merchandise, and the other employees. Other factors are the store's atmosphere, the manager's leadership style, and employee morale.

Store Environment The store environment affects the way employees feel about their job. When employees feel comfortable in their environment, they will work to meet the goals of the store. If employees are dissatisfied with the work environment, they may spend their time complaining rather than working.

Apparel and accessory department managers usually don't have much voice in the physical surroundings of a store. But they certainly do have an impact on other parts of the store environment. For example, managers who encourage employees to keep the sales desk clean make it easier for salespeople to ring up sales. By making sure the selling area is well stocked with supplies, the

Fig. 2-5 Which one of these managers would you prefer to have for your supervisor? Why?

manager makes every person's job more efficient and less frustrating.

The Manager's Leadership Style How a manager plans the work, gives orders, and makes decisions also affect the working environment. For example, a manager who plans in advance eliminates the pressure that builds up when everything is left to the last minute. Managers who assign tasks by "ordering" rather than "asking" are a negative influence on their workers. No one likes being told what to do; people like to think that they make their own decisions. (See Figure 2-5.)

How a manager makes decisions influences the work environment. In a democratic leadership style, managers ask employees for their opinion before making a decision, which makes employees feel needed and a part of things. Managers who make all the decisions themselves, without consulting their employees, are called autocratic managers. These managers create an environment that limits employee creativity and initiative.

Employee Morale Employee morale is one of the most important factors in a pleasant work environment. When employees have a bad attitude about their job, their

Fig. 2-6 What kind of attitude do you think Jack has toward his job and his supervisor?

coworkers, and their supervisors, that attitude spreads to others. As a manager, you should watch for signs of poor employee morale: absenteeism, gossip, and tardiness. High turnover rate of employees is another sign of very poor employee morale. Look for employee morale problems and correct them before they spread.

A manager can improve employee morale by practicing good human relations. Often, if managers could learn the same skills that they want their employees to practice, employee morale could be improved. Cooperation and showing interest in and sensitivity to others are skills managers can use to improve morale. (See Figure 2-6.) Effective communications also improve employee morale. By recognizing problems and honestly talking about them, employees and managers can uncover reasons why the problems occurred and how they can be solved. This kind of communications makes for good morale.

Experience 2-8

Morale: The Invisible Force

1. Interview two apparel or accessory workers. These can be personal friends who work in a store now or have worked in a store in the past. Ask each person what he or she liked and didn't like about working in the store. Find out about the store's environment. On a separate sheet of paper, make a list of their responses. Analyze these responses. Write the changes you would propose to improve their work environment if you were the manager.
2. Form a small group with others who have also completed the above exercise. Think of yourselves as apparel and accessory department managers who are trying to improve employee morale. Assume you all work for the same store. On a separate sheet of paper, write your recommendations and the steps required to put your recommendations into effect. Evaluate each recommendation that each member of your group has suggested.

HANDLING EMPLOYEE CORRECTIONS AND GRIEVANCES

After a manager gives employees their initial training, the manager must follow up on the work of the employees to be certain they are knowledgeable about their duties. When employees are not doing their jobs well, it is also the manager's responsibility to correct the problems. As a manager, you may find this part of your job difficult. It's never easy to tell people their work is unsatisfactory, especially when they are trying to do a good job. When giving constructive criticism, you need to practice good human relations skills or you may make a bad situation worse.

As a manager, you will also have to handle employee grievances, or complaints. When handling employee corrections or grievances, some important concepts are important to remember.

Privacy. Discuss the situation with the involved parties in private so that other employees or customers are not listening. Your job is not to embarrass an employee; it is to solve a problem.
Clarity. Clearly explain to employees why their actions are causing a problem in the store or department. Be sure the employees realize that what they do affects the total operations of the store or department.
Fairness. Ask the employees if the facts you've presented are true. Ask for their side of the story.
Shared Responsibility. Ask the employees how you can help them solve the problem. Let employees share in the responsibility of correcting the problem.

When handling employee corrections or complaints, you have to be sensitive to employees' feelings. You shouldn't attack a person's intelligence, attitude, or character. Instead, you should talk about the employee's behavior and how it can be changed. You need to look into motivations for acting in a particular way. You may find that the situation was caused by your failure as a manager.

As manager, you must take responsibility for correcting your employee's inappropriate behavior. No matter how distasteful this task is, it's part of the manager's job.

ACCEPTING CRITICISM

Apparel and accessory store managers are criticized by their employees, coworkers, upper management, and customers. Because of this, unless you, as a manager, can accept criticism and turn it into a character-building asset, you may begin to dislike your job. When others criticize you, it is because they don't agree with the way you are doing your job or are not aware of all the facts.

There are two kinds of criticism, constructive and destructive. Suppose, for example, that your supervisor is concerned about your work. Rather than attacking you personally, your supervisor may offer suggestions for improvement to help you be more successful. Look upon these comments as constructive criticism, because they will improve your future performance.

When another person says something mean or cruel to intentionally hurt you, it is destructive criticism. Although little can take the "sting" out of destructive criticism, you should learn to look into why someone would try to hurt your feelings. Perhaps the person is jealous of your past successes. Even destructive criticism helps you, for it lets you see how what you do affects others. You can learn to use this information in your future interactions with others so that you will always improve your relationships.

Experience 2-9

Hardest Part of My Job: Employee Corrections

Suppose you are the manager of a women's shoe store. Have another classmate play the role of a salesperson, Sheila Roberts. Recently, an employee has told you that Sheila refuses to do any stock work in the department. All she wants to do is sell. She never puts away shoes after she shows them to customers and won't help check-in new shipments. This makes it hard on the other employees, who must do Sheila's share of this work to keep the department neat and well stocked. All of your salespeople receive salary and commission.

Role play how you, as manager, would correct this situation. If possible, use a tape recorder to record your conversation with Sheila. After role playing, answer the following questions on a separate sheet of paper.

1. Where would you discuss the problem with Sheila?
2. Based on the results of your role playing, how do you think Sheila feels about what happened?
3. How do you feel you handled the problem? What human relations skills do you think you need to improve on?
4. If the problem continues, what will you do?

Experience 2-10

How Can They Be So Cruel?

Assume you are the department manager of the Men's Suit Department at Cairo's, a specialty men's store. Today has not been one of your best. So far, you have heard the following comments:

From Your Supervisor. "You must not be pulling your weight in the department. Every week, you schedule more salespeople to work than any of our other managers. You simply budget for too many workers. You can't afford to continue this!"

From Your Coworker. "The store manager transferred that new trainee to my department this morning. Haven't you taught her anything? She can't even ring up a cash sale on the register. I used to have real confidence in the people you trained. I sure am disappointed in you!"

From Your Employee. "I just saw the work schedule for Friday night. I've had to work every Friday night for the past six weeks. How can you be so unfair?"

From Your Customer. "The selection and display of merchandise in this department is so poor I can't even find a plain white shirt. You know, when Bill was the manager here, everything was different. Is this your first job in retailing?"

On a separate sheet of paper, answer the following questions. Then carry out the instructions in 3:

1. How would you feel if you received criticisms such as these?
2. How do you think you would react to each of these criticisms?
3. All these criticisms are destructive criticisms. On a separate sheet of paper, reword each comment to make it a constructive criticism.

3 Communications

"Hello, Downtown Sportswear, Gerri speaking."

"Gerri, this is Pat at Olympus Hills Sportswear. Do you remember when I called and asked you to send me a size 12 pink shirt?"

"Sure. I filled out the transfer form to send it to your store. Haven't you received it yet?"

"We received it. The problem is that you sent a blue shirt, not a pink one. The customer is furious. She says she has never seen such irresponsible salespeople, and she just went to complain to the store manager."

"Oh, no!"

This is only one of the many communication mix-ups that may happen in an apparel and accessory store. Communications, or lack of it, affect every encounter you will have with customers, coworkers, and supervisors during your career.

COMMUNICATIONS IS A TWO-WAY PROCESS

Most of us think we are good communicators; after all, we've been communicating with people all our lives. But, is this really so? **Communications** deals with the way a message is transmitted to a person and the way that message is received. All communications include some common elements: (1) a **sender**, the person who sends the message; (2) a **message**, what is said and how it is said; (3) a **medium**, or how the message travels to the receiver; (4) a **receiver**, the person who receives the message; and (5) **feedback**, the signals sent back to the original sender by the receiver.

Let's examine these elements in a typical customer-salesperson communication. Suppose a salesperson is helping a customer choose a pair of slacks. The customer, who has tried on the slacks, is standing before a three-way mirror. The salesperson is checking the fit.

CUSTOMER: Karl, I don't feel comfortable with the waist so tight. Will you call the tailor?

SALESPERSON: Sure, Mr. Berkly. It will only take a minute to call him.

In this example, the sender is the customer and the receiver is the salesperson. The message is "I don't feel comfortable with the waist so tight. Will you call the tailor?" If the customer said this message in an angry tone, the anger would also become part of the message. The medium is both vocal and visual; that is the salesperson can both see and hear the customer. The feedback is the salesperson's reply to the customer "Sure, Mr. Berkly. It will only take a minute." This feedback helps the original sender, the customer, know that the message was received and correctly interpreted by the original receiver, the salesperson.

COMMUNICATION MIX-UPS

Even in the most skillfully constructed communications, it is easy for misinterpretations to develop. Some usual reasons for communication mix-ups follow.

The receiver is not paying attention:

SALESPERSON: You said you wanted a size 14. Here they are.

CUSTOMER: I said I need a size 10.

The sender is not using words the receiver understands:

BUYER: What season is that suit?

SALESPERSON: It's wool . . . it must be for winter.

BUYER: I meant what was the season code on the price ticket. I was referring to the season we received the suit at the store.

The sender may say one thing, but the tone of voice and facial expression say another:

MANAGER: Lindy, we need someone to work on Friday night. Would you be interested?
SALESPERSON: Uh . . . sure, Mrs. Naylor . . . I guess . . . I mean well, maybe I can.

EFFECTIVE COMMUNICATIONS

In apparel stores, communications are often verbal. At times, you will be the sender. When someone is speaking to you, you will be the receiver. In both situations, you will share responsibility in making communications effective and understood. When you are speaking, you want the receiver to understand what you mean, and it is your responsibility to use words the receiver understands. For example, when you talk with your buyer, you may use words like "open-to-buy" or "turnover." Buyers are familiar with these words. However, new salespeople may not understand these terms. Instead of "open-to-buy," you should say "the amount of money the buyer can use to purchase new merchandise." You are also responsible for speaking clearly in logical sentences. To be heard, you should face your listener.

To help your receiver understand what you mean, send a **consistent message**. This means that what you say should be the same as what you do. An example of a consistent message is saying, "I'm going to change the window display right now" and then changing the display. An example of an inconsistent message is saying, "I'm going to change the window display right now" and then going to lunch. In an **inconsistent message**—when you send one message verbally and then send a different message by your actions—the receiver becomes confused.

When you're the sender, try to get feedback from the receiver. This is a check to be sure that your message is being received the way you want it to be. You may say, "What do you think about that idea?" The person's reply, or feedback, lets you know if you both are talking about the same thing.

As a receiver, pay close attention to what a sender is saying. When you listen with "only one ear" or are thinking about something else, it is easy for you to miss the speaker's message. Some people are able to speak more clearly and more logically than others. If you are unable to understand a message, it is your responsibility to ask questions to clarify the subject. This will give the speaker feedback and will help the speaker clear up any misunderstandings.

There are so many factors that contribute to ineffective communications that it is remarkable any messages are understood. Try to eliminate the interferences that hurt communications. This will help you avoid missing or misinterpreting important messages from customers, coworkers, and management.

Experience 3-1

Feedback Lets Me Know That You Understand

Ask a classmate to send a message to you. Have the classmate choose a particular topic that he or she has definite ideas about and to communicate verbally these ideas to you for about 5 minutes. During this time, demonstrate how you would make sure you really understand what your classmate is saying. Ask questions and give appropriate feedback to show you understand the message. If possible, use a tape recorder to record your conversation. Play the tape back and evaluate your feedback in the conversation.

Experience 3-2

Are They Communicating?

Margie Hamilton is a salesperson at Creation's Best, a specialty clothing store. Although she has to work until 1:00 p.m., Margie has the afternoon off to move into a new apartment. Margie has been sizing clothing all morning, but her mind has been on her moving.

As Margie is resizing a group of slacks, her manager, Mrs. Wiley, comes up behind her and says, "I just received an important call from Mr. Henry, our buyer. He wants to send all the yellow and green seersucker pants and jackets to our South Town store. While I go to lunch, will you fill out a transfer form and get these garments ready for transfer? The delivery truck will make a special stop at 2 p.m. to pick up the merchandise."

By the time Margie realizes her manager was talking to her, Mrs. Wiley has gone. "If it's important, Mrs. Wiley will mention it to me again. I can't wait to get home to start packing!"

1. Was this communication effective? Give reasons to support your answer.

______

______

______

______

2. Identify the sender, receiver, message, medium, and feedback in this situation.

3. What could Mrs. Wiley and Margie have done to make this communication more effective?

THE STORE'S COMMUNICATION NETWORK

Many people are involved in the success of an apparel and accessory store. Management supervises the total store activities and the employees. Buyers work with the merchandise suppliers and the checking, receiving, and marking personnel. Salespeople work with the buyers, merchandise, and customers. Communication is the network that allows all these employees, in the many departments and divisions, to work together to achieve the goals of the store: customer satisfaction and profit.

A store's communication network consists of many forms: reports, instructions, and discussions among management, employees, and customers. Some of these communications, such as merchandise presentations, require good speaking and listening skills. Others, such as reading merchandise tags or writing sales reports, require reading and writing skills. These skills are important to a successful career in the apparel and accessories field.

CONFIDENTIAL INFORMATION

As an apparel or accessory store employee, you may come across confidential, or private, information. Such information should not be discussed with anyone outside the store. It should only be discussed with other authorized store employees, such as your manager. (See Figure 3-1.)

Examples of confidential information are (1) credit status of customers, (2) wages and commissions earned by other employees, (3) mark-up and mark-down percentages, (4) future store advertising or fashion promotions, and (5) store operation costs and budgets. As in all relationships where communications exist, you are trusted to use your common sense to know the difference between public and private information. Some stores view telling confidential information to unauthorized persons as reason for dismissal.

SPEAKING

In an apparel store, the spoken word is an important "tool of the trade." Let's examine some situations in which the spoken word is important.

Presenting Merchandise Many factors influence customers' buying decisions. One of these is the courtesy the salesperson shows the customer. Another is the salesperson's enthusiasm for the merchandise. Other reasons include the salesperson's tone of voice, vocabulary, and grammar. Examine the following.

SALESPERSON: Hey, Joe . . . you old fatso. How ya' doin'?

JOE: I'm fine, Clark. I need to pick up a blue shirt. Do you have something in a pinstripe?

SALESPERSON: Do I have something in a pinstripe? You come to the right place . . . I was just sayin' to Mel, the guy I work with, that I ain't never seen so many pinstripes in all my life. Let's see . . . you be about a 15 neck and 33 sleeve.

JOE: That's right.

SALESPERSON: Those shirts is over here.

JOE: I really didn't want an all-polyester shirt; they seem so hot. What do you have in a cotton-polyester blend?

SALESPERSON: You don't want none of those. I don't sell my friends those shirts. They cost almost $3 more. These here shirts will do the job for you.

JOE: I think I want to look around some more. Thanks for your help, Clark.

Fig. 3-1 How would you deal with gossip?

SALESPERSON: Darn it, Joe. Ever since you got that new job, you been so uppity. I was just tryin' to save you some bucks. Come in again when you want to buy some stuff.

This example is exaggerated. It does, however, bring out some important points.

All Customers Should Be Addressed in a Respectful Way. Many stores want their salespersons to call the customer Mr., Mrs., or Ms. If you know the customer well, you may call the customer by his or her first name.
Poor Grammar Lowers the Image of Store Personnel, the Store, and the Value of the Merchandise. Customers are not impressed with a salesperson's slang, swearing, or improper grammar. When customers find a salesperson who does not speak correctly, they often wonder to themselves, "Can I trust this person's merchandise knowledge and opinion?" Salespeople should remember that the way a person speaks is one of the factors that makes a first impression.
Salespeople's Enthusiasm Spreads to Customers. It's easy to see when people are enthusiastic about their jobs; their eyes sparkle and they seem to enjoy what they are doing. The tone of voice is pleasant and sincere which shows that they honestly want to be of service. It's no secret that customers enjoy dealing with enthusiastic salespeople.

Experience 3-3

What Is Correct?

Reword each sentence that follows to make it grammatically correct.

1. The store owners is Mr. and Mrs. Concord.

2. What's the retail prices on this group?

3. I'd rather have you make the display than me.

4. Who is this dress being sent to?

5. Lockers for all employees are provided four your personnel belongings.

Handling Customer Inquiries Customers often ask salespeople for information. For example, they may want to know how late the store stays open. They may want directions to the escalator. Salespeople should be just as courteous to customers when handling inquiries as they are when making a sales presentation.

When answering customer questions, it is important to understand what the customer is asking. Try to answer the customer in the simplest way possible, and make your answers clear and concise. Sometimes, you will meet people who are hard of hearing or who are unfamiliar with the English language. In these special situations, you need to speak clearly and distinctly. At all times, avoid the use of slang.

Experience 3-4

How Do I Get There from Here?

Suppose you are a salesperson in the Children's Department at the clothing store whose floor plan is shown on page 29. After examining the floor plan, answer the following customer inquiries. Write your directions in the space provided. Or, if possible, record your directions on a tape recorder.

1. How can I get to the down escalator?

2. How do I get to the mall parking lot?

3. Where is the women's restroom?

4. How do I get to the Men's Suit Department?

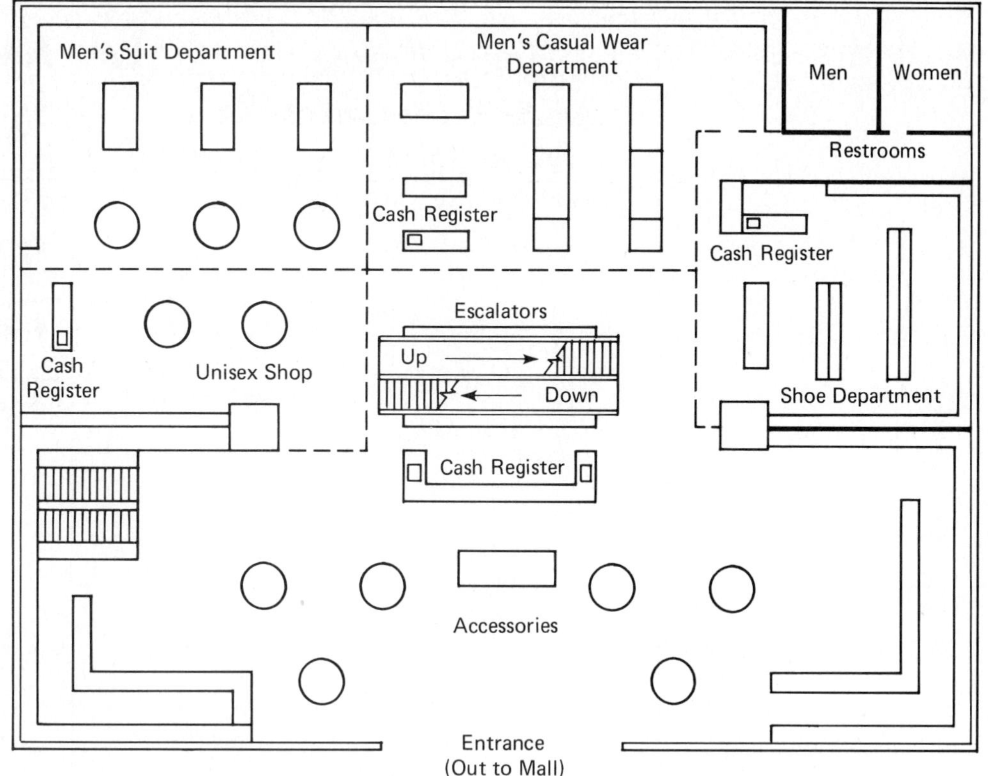

FIRST FLOOR

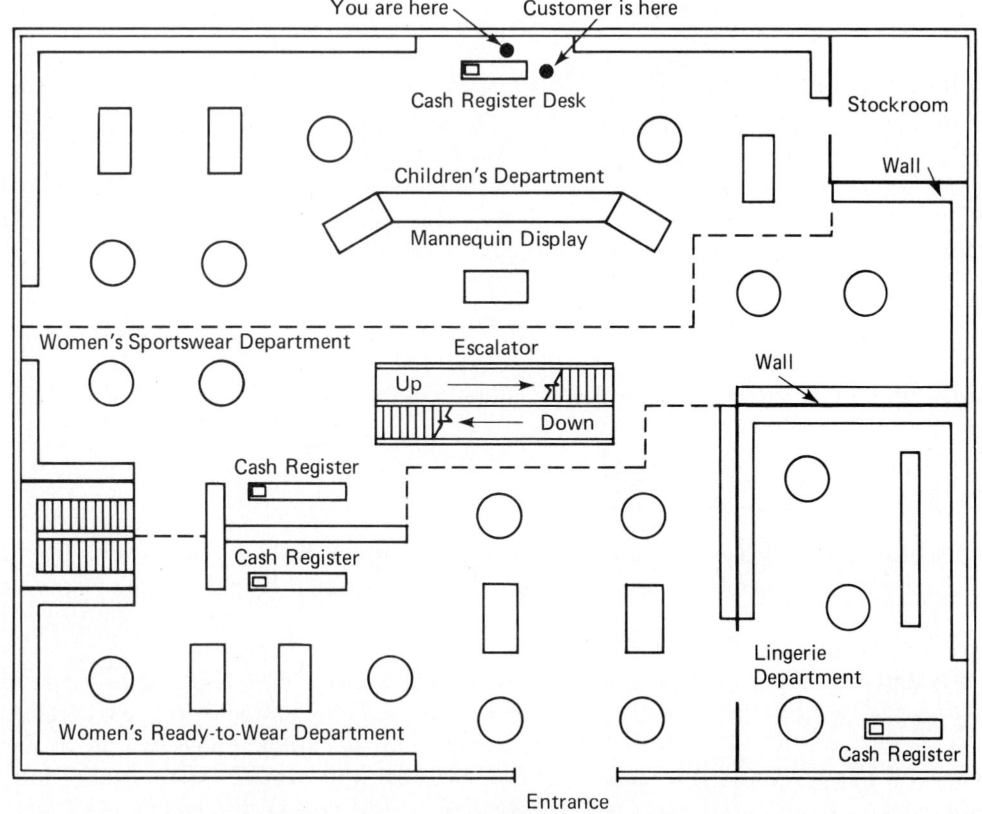

SECOND FLOOR

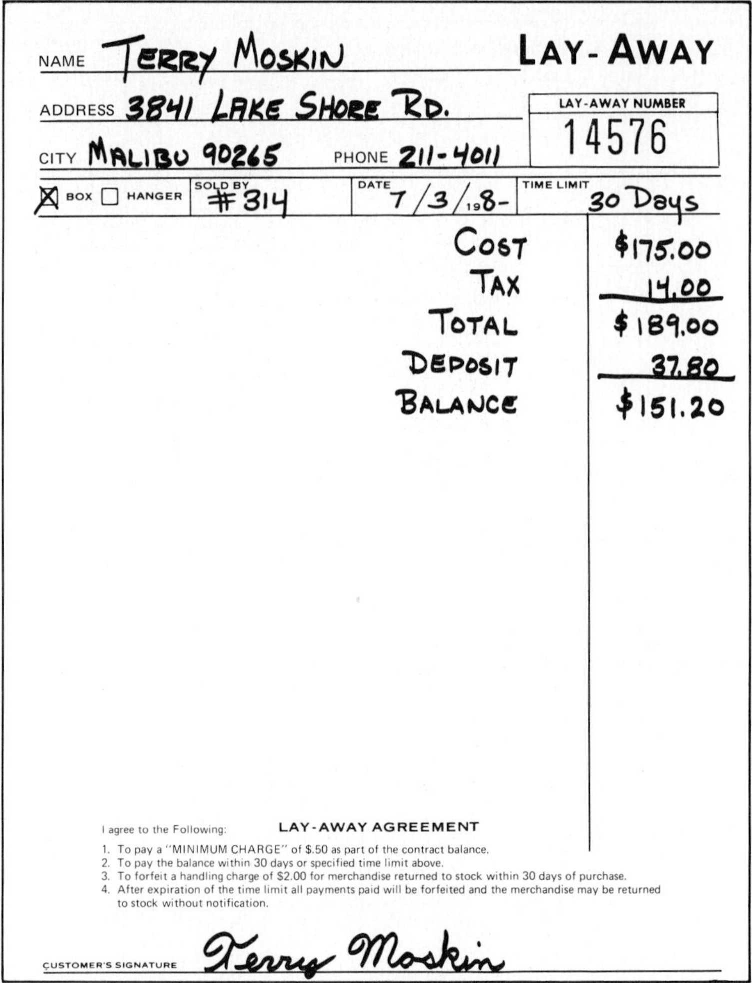

LAY-AWAY

NAME TERRY MOSKIN

ADDRESS 3841 LAKE SHORE RD.

CITY MALIBU 90265 PHONE 211-4011

LAY-AWAY NUMBER 14576

☒ BOX ☐ HANGER | SOLD BY #314 | DATE 7/3/198- | TIME LIMIT 30 Days

COST	$175.00
TAX	14.00
TOTAL	$189.00
DEPOSIT	37.80
BALANCE	$151.20

I agree to the Following: LAY-AWAY AGREEMENT

1. To pay a "MINIMUM CHARGE" of $.50 as part of the contract balance.
2. To pay the balance within 30 days or specified time limit above.
3. To forfeit a handling charge of $2.00 for merchandise returned to stock within 30 days of purchase.
4. After expiration of the time limit all payments paid will be forfeited and the merchandise may be returned to stock without notification.

CUSTOMER'S SIGNATURE Terry Moskin

Fig. 3-2 Here's a typical form that includes a store's layaway policy.

Interpreting Store Policies Stores establish policies and procedures as guidelines to help employees to respond in certain situations. For example, a store's policy might state that merchandise can be held in layaway for a maximum of 30 days. (See Figure 3-2) Many times, customers are confused about store policies and ask salespeople to explain the policies to them. They want to know how these policies affect them. They often will question why such a policy has been established. Customer problems occur when salespeople do not effectively communicate store policies.

When explaining store policies to customers, try to get feedback by asking questions to be sure the customer understands you.

If the customer still has questions, explain the policy again.

Experience 3-5

Can You Make Them Understand?

Suppose you are a salesperson at a specialty shoe store. Your store's policy on cashing checks is as follows:

Every customer who wishes to pay for a purchase by check must present two forms of proper identification. In accepting the identification, remember that you are looking for two things:

1. *The identity of the individual (a picture and signature are preferred).*
2. *A means of locating the individual if the check is returned (a phone number and current address).*

If you accept a check without recording two proper forms of ID, you will be held responsible if that check is returned.

A customer wants to purchase a pair of shoes by check. When you ask the customer for two forms of proper identification, the customer says they are at home. Demonstrate how you would explain your store's policy about accepting checks. If possible, use a tape recorder to record your explanation. If no tape recorder is available, write your explanation on a separate sheet.

Communicating over the Phone Many customers call a store to find out whether the store sells a certain brand of clothing. Salespeople at branch stores telephone to see if a particular size or color of merchandise is in stock at the main store. Salespeople, especially those who work in catalog sales, use the telephone to sell customers new merchandise. For these reasons and many others, a salesperson should be able to communicate clearly and distinctly on the telephone.

When using the telephone, you are relying on your voice to communicate the message. Because the listener cannot see you, you need to speak clearly and be exact.

When answering the phone, give an appropriate greeting, identify your store, your department (if any), and yourself. For example, you would say, "Good morning, The Small Shop, Ready-to-Wear, Janice Wong speaking." In a department store with other branch stores, the phone may be answered by a central answering service and then transferred to your department. In this case, you might say, "Good morning, Downtown Ready-to-Wear, Janice Wong speaking." Of course, you should always use telephone etiquette.

In the following situations you will need to use acceptable telephone communications.

Calling a Branch Store. In stores with more than one branch, salespeople may telephone other salespeople at different stores to find out about an item. To help salespeople discuss merchandise items, many stores include style numbers, class numbers, and vendor numbers on their price tickets. This information ensures that both people are talking about the same thing.

Answering Customer Phone Inquiries. When customers call a store about a particular garment, they may not be as specific as they should be. The salesperson should ask questions to find out about the merchandise needed by these customers.

Calling Customers. Some salespeople call their regular customers when a new item comes in that they think a particular customer will like. The purpose of the call is to "sell" the customer on coming into the store to see the merchandise.

Experience 3-6

Talking on the Phone

Assume that you work in the shoe department at Beckers. Beckers has several branch stores. When helping a customer, you find that you have the style and size the customer needs, but not the right color. You call the West Side store to locate the needed shoe.

Ask another classmate to play the part of the salesperson at the West Side store. Choose a particular shoe that someone in the room is wearing. Do not let your classmate know what shoe you have chosen. Pretend you are calling the other salesperson on the telephone to locate the shoe. Describe the shoe. Say that you need the shoe in black in size 8½B. (The shoe you've chosen may or may not be black.) After you have described the shoe, have the other salesperson identify it.

Repeat this exercise three more times. Each time, refer to a different apparel or accessory item. Trade places with your classmate and then repeat this exercise four more times.

Training Other Employees After you have gained experience on the job, you may be asked to help train new employees. When training others, it is important to give clear, precise instructions. After explaining each procedure step by step, ask for feedback. For example, after explaining how to ring up a cash sale, ask the trainee to use the cash register. Watch to see if the trainee understands the procedure. Clarify or reexplain any misunderstood points for the trainee. Refer to Chapter 16 of this manual, "Management and Administration," to find out more about how to go about training new employees.

Experience 3-7

Testing, Testing, How's Your Clarity?

Choose a particular task performed by apparel and accessory salespeople, such as ringing up a charge sale, making a display, making a sales presentation, or making change. (Each of these tasks is described in this manual. If necessary, refer to the section of the manual that describes how to do the task you've chosen.) In a logical, step-by-step manner explain to another classmate how to do the task. Then ask the classmate to perform the task you have described. Be sure to use any forms, equipment, or merchandise that you need to complete the task realistically. If possible, use a tape recorder.

After your classmate has completed the task and you have clarified any misunderstood points, ask the classmate to evaluate how well you give directions. On a separate sheet of paper, list what you did properly and the things you need to improve. If you taped your explanation, listen carefully to the tape to see how what you say comes across to other people.

WRITING

The managers at most apparel stores prepare many forms that salespersons must complete. Some of these forms, such as charge slips, return slips, and mark-down sheets, are for accounting purposes. Others are used to keep track of inventory or reorder merchandise items. Still others, such as layaway forms, are for the customer's benefit.

Usually, these forms are easy to understand. The columns are labeled so salespeople know what information is needed to complete each form. There may also be instructions on the form.

These forms are useless unless the written information is both correct and legible. Sometimes salespersons complete these forms when they are thinking about other things or in a rush. They may not be careful or their handwriting is sloppy.

Follow these two important guidelines:

Make Letters and Numbers Legible. Fancy handwriting is hard to read. Remember to write clearly so that others can read the information. If your handwriting is poor, print.

Double-check Written Information. Reread what you have written to make sure it is accurate and understandable. Look for misspelled words and transposed figures (15 instead of 51). Give customers an opportunity to read sales slips to verify that the information is correct. Many forms have a special place for supervisors to sign after double-checking employees.

Experience 3-8

Write on!

Using the following information, complete the sales ticket opposite. Mrs. Mary Bower purchased a straw purse for her niece, Linda Snow. Although Mrs. Bower charged the purse, she did not have her charge card with her. In cases like this, the store asks you to record the customer's address, which is 411 Van Dyke, Salem, Oregon 97308. After calling your store's credit office, you found out Mrs. Bower's account number is 383343373. Mrs. Bower wants the purse delivered to her niece, who lives at 28439 N.W. Clover, Portland, Oregon 97208. You work in Department 14. The purse costs $17.50; no sales tax is charged in Oregon. (The store has free delivery to Portland.)

CHARGE TO			ACCT. NO.
STREET			
CITY-STATE			
QUAN.	ARTICLE		AMOUNT
XX	XXXXXXXXXXXX	MDSE. TOTAL	
	15771-41	SALES TAX	
AUTHORIZED SIGNATURE		SHIP. CHG.	
X ______		TOTAL SALE	
SEND TO			
STREET			
CITY-STATE			
SENT BY			
SOLD BY	DEPT.	DATE	HOW SOLD

READING

Salespeople are usually trained by verbal instruction from supervisors and coworkers, but they also must read various materials. Many companies have pamphlets that explain fringe benefits, personnel policies, and employee regulations. (See Figure 3-3.) Stores also have written materials about store policies and procedures. Employees read fashion magazines and newspapers to be knowledgeable about new merchandise styles that are featured.

Sometimes employees may need only to skim written material, that is, read only the important facts. Often they may skim fashion magazines and newspapers to find out about new trends. Sometimes a person can **scan** the material, that is, read only specific information. Most employees scan sales charts or stock records because they may be interested in only a few items on the chart. Many times, however, an employee must read and understand nearly all of the written material. For example, a store policy on returns must be completely understood so as to be accurately explained to others. Although intensive reading takes more time than skimming and scanning, a careful reading of materials once can save rereading time in the future.

When you must remember information accurately, making notes on the important points is helpful. Always look up unfamiliar words in a dictionary. Although this takes additional time in the beginning, it will build your vocabulary and may save you time and embarrassment in the future.

Because reading materials just to gather facts is not too interesting or meaningful, learn to interpret the information you read into facts that are important to you. For example, if the store issues a memo on safety, try to think of ways you can put those safety procedures to work. This will help you to read with purpose and retain the written information.

PERSONNEL POLICIES: COMPENSATION

PAYROLL

Pay periods close every other Saturday and time cards are collected at that time. On the following Friday, paychecks are distributed. Therefore, you will receive your paycheck every other Friday.

1. Wages and commission rates are set up individually and by department respectively for reasons your manager or supervisor will discuss with you. Your wages and commissions are personal information and must never be discussed with fellow employees.
2. If questions arise, contact your store manager, who will notify the payroll office to review your pay.

Fig. 3-3 Here's a typical policy statement.

Reading Merchandise Hangtags Some of the most important reading you will do is attached to the merchandise you sell, such as hangtags or merchandise labels. (See Figure 3-4.) At some point, be sure to read the hangtags on new merchandise. If time does not permit you to read the tags while checking in the merchandise, be sure to read them at a slower time—perhaps while you are straightening merchandise items. These tags often contain important selling points.

Reading Mail Orders Some stores include merchandise order forms in their monthly credit statements or in newspaper ads. (See Figure 3-5.) Completed mail orders are distributed to particular departments and are filled in by salespeople.

When filling these orders, you will have to read the customer's name, address, and merchandise selection carefully. You will have to locate the correct merchandise item and ring up the sale. Pay attention to how the customer wants to pay for the merchandise.

Courtesy Celanese Fibers Marketing Co.

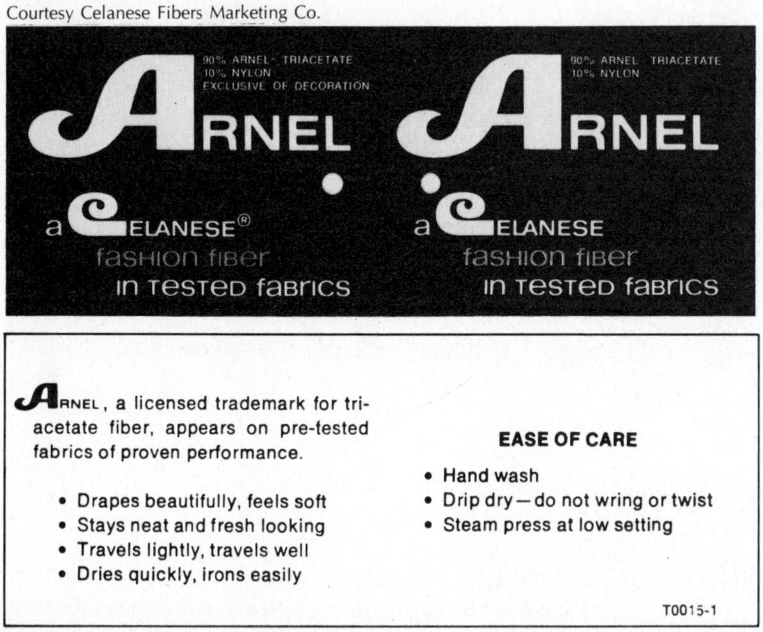

90% ARNEL TRIACETATE
10% NYLON
EXCLUSIVE OF DECORATION

ARNEL
a CELANESE®
fashion fiber
in tested fabrics

90% ARNEL TRIACETATE
10% NYLON

ARNEL
a CELANESE
fashion fiber
in tested fabrics

ARNEL, a licensed trademark for triacetate fiber, appears on pre-tested fabrics of proven performance.

- Drapes beautifully, feels soft
- Stays neat and fresh looking
- Travels lightly, travels well
- Dries quickly, irons easily

EASE OF CARE

- Hand wash
- Drip dry—do not wring or twist
- Steam press at low setting

T0015-1

Fig. 3-4 Merchandise hangtags contain important selling points that you can use in a sales presentation.

Courtesy B. Altman and Co.

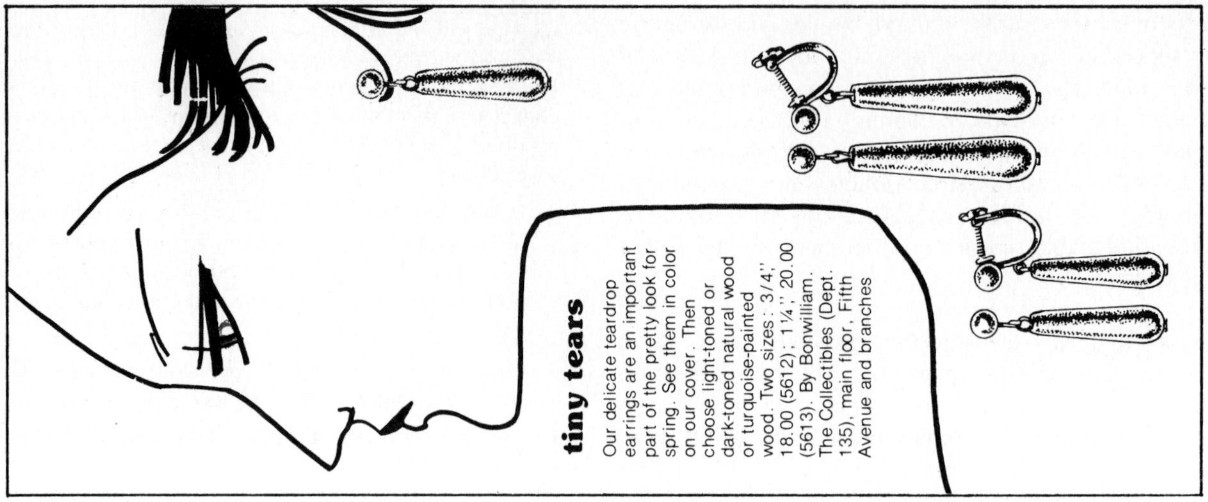

tiny tears

Our delicate teardrop earrings are an important part of the pretty look for spring. See them in color on our cover. Then choose light-toned or dark-toned natural wood or turquoise-painted wood. Two sizes: 3/4", 18.00 (5612); 1¼", 20.00 (5613). By Bonwilliam. The Collectibles (Dept. 135), main floor, Fifth Avenue and branches

FOLD HERE, FLAP IS GUMMED.
TEAR ALONG PERFORATION AND ENCLOSE ORDER BLANK IN ENVELOPE BELOW.

PLEASE DO NOT WRITE IN SHADED AREAS. FOR ALTMAN USE ONLY.	ORDER SEQUENCE	SOURCE	REMIT TOTAL	REV CODE	AUTH NO	PRE EDIT	SKU	POST EDIT

☒ charge my ALTMAN account no. A B 1 2 3 4 5 Z   ☐ check or M.O. NO C.O.D.'s.

All letters which contain cash should be registered
☐ Check here if this is change of address
if send to is same as purchaser, write (same as purchaser)

☐ Charge my AMERICAN EXPRESS CARD   Signature *Sara Simpson*   Date *4/10/—*

Your full American Express Card Account No. ______ VALIDATION DATES: From ______ To ______

PLEASE PRINT CLEARLY **Use Zip Code**

Purchased by SARA SIMPSON
Address 14 WILLOW ST. Apt. —
City, State, BROOKLYN, N.Y. Zip 11201
Telephone (area code 212) 919-1234

Send to ______
Address SAME AS Apt. ____
City, State, PURCHASER Zip ____
Delivery Instructions *Mail/Check enclosed*

ITEM NO.	SKU	HOW MANY	COLOR—PATTERN OR FRAGRANCE 1st choice	2nd choice	SIZE	ITEM NAME	PAGE NO.	MONOGRAMS INITIALS 1st	2nd	last	MONO COLOR	T C	E U C	S & H	AD CODE	UNIT PRICE	TOTAL $
5612		1 pr	light	dark	3/4"	earrings	—									18.00	18.00

B. ALTMAN & CO.
P.O. BOX 470
NEW YORK, N.Y. 10016
(361 5th Ave.)
(212) MU9-7000

DELIVERIES: Mail and phone orders filled on purchases over 10.00 (exclusive of tax) without charge within our motor delivery area. Under 10.00 add 1.00 for shipping and handling. **NO C.O.D.'s.** For shipments outside our motor delivery area but within continental limits of the United States add shipping and handling charges as follows: for orders up to 10.00 add 1.50, over 10.00 add 2.00. For foreign shipments, charges will be billed to you. Asterisked (*) items which exceed Parcel Post limitations are shipped within our motor delivery area only. **Call (212) MU9-7000 for our round-the-clock, 7-day-a-week phone order service. Please allow two weeks for processing and delivery of your order unless otherwise stated.**

Merchandise Total	18.00
Applicable Sales Tax	1.44
Shipping & Handling	—
GRAND TOTAL	19.44

Fig. 3-5 This illustration is an example of merchandise order forms which stores include in their monthly credit statements.

Experience 3-9

Sure You Read It, but Did You *Read* It?

Suppose your store is establishing a new policy on merchandise returns. This policy is shown on page 35. Read the policy very carefully. After you are sure you understand the policy, answer the questions below.

1. What type of credit will customers who are returning merchandise without proof of purchase receive?

____

2. What type of credit will customers who are returning gifts receive? Assume the customers do not have a sales slip.

______

3. Are all sales really final? Explain your answer.

______

______

______

______

______

4. A customer, Mr. Malloy, purchased merchandise at full price, $24. The merchandise item was the wrong size. During the next week, when he returned the merchandise, which had not been worn and was in good condition, he found the merchandise was on sale for $18.99. The customer has his sales slip. How much will the customer receive back? What kind of credit will he receive?

______

5. Suppose it is October 7. A customer enters the store and wants to return a swimsuit cover-up that was purchased in June. The customer has the sales ticket. How will you handle the return?

______

______

______

______

______

POLICY AND PROCEDURES

With few exceptions, a customer returning merchandise with which he or she is dissatisfied feels he has a justifiable complaint. The customer expects to encounter difficulty, so it is particularly important that he or she be put at ease and handled as courteously as possible. It is also extremely important that the matter be resolved quickly. The customer should not be passed from one person to another. With each delay or referral, the customer will become more upset. To the extent possible, adjustments should be handled promptly.

The following guidelines are set down in an effort to establish, so far as possible, a uniform adjustment policy at our store:

General: Merchandise that is current and salable is to be exchanged cheerfully, or, if necessary, a charge credit, merchandise credit, or cash credit is to be written.

Customers returning merchandise *without* proof of purchase will be given a charge credit or merchandise credit, but not a cash credit. The amount of the credit should be determined from the last retail price marked by the store.

Customers returning merchandise received as a gift will be given a charge credit or merchandise credit, but not a cash credit.

Sale Merchandise: Our policy regarding sale merchandise is that all sales are final; however, if, in your judgment, it will not harm the department and will accommodate the customer, an exchange of sale merchandise can be permitted.

Merchandise purchased recently, but put on sale after the customer's purchase, is to be redeemed at the customer's purchase price.

Fashion Merchandise: Merchandise that is completely out of season and not salable within the department is to be refused any allowance.

LISTENING

"Did you say blue or green?" "You want a size medium?" "What style did you say you like?" These are usual questions from apparel salespeople. Like most of us, salespeople are often guilty of not paying attention to what a customer is saying. They do not listen.

Listening is a skill that is just as important as reading, writing, and speaking. By becoming a good listener, you can decrease the amount of time it takes to do a job. This is because you won't have to ask questions to find out facts that you just didn't hear the first time. You can improve your listening skills by:

- Being an active listener by giving full attention to what is being said.
- Having an open mind by not making value judgments on what the speaker is saying.
- Minimizing interruptions and distractions, such as loud noises or two people talking at the same time.
- Being patient and not anticipating a speaker by interrupting or finishing sentences.
- Giving verbal and nonverbal feedback by asking relevant questions, keeping eye contact, and nodding your head.

As an apparel and accessory employee, you can practice your listening skills when you are on the telephone or in meetings. You will also need to listen carefully when you are making sales presentations or taking directions from supervisors.

When you are making your sales presentations, you will be able to increase the amount of sales you make by paying attention to your customers. And by making a sincere effort to understand your customers, you will make shopping a more pleasant experience for each one of them.

When you are taking directions from your supervisor, listen carefully. By doing so, you will know what you're expected to do and how to do it.

Experience 3-10

Are You Listening?

At the next meeting, class, or lecture you attend, test your listening power. Ask a friend or classmate who attends the speech or lecture to complete the following steps also. Use a separate sheet of paper for the following steps.

After the speaker has finished, make an outline of the major points of what was said. List all the distractions or interruptions that affected your listening. Identify things the speaker could have done to make it easier for you to listen and what you, as a listener, could do to make it easier to listen. Compare notes with your friend. Discuss three occasions when your lack of listening caused problems for each one of you, either at school or at work.

MANAGEMENT COMMUNICATIONS

An ability to communicate skillfully is necessary for management positions. All managers must be able to speak and write clearly, to communicate ideas effectively, to read and listen, and to hear and understand the ideas of others.

As a manager, you are a vital link in the store's communication process. It is your responsibility to give instructions and training to employees who work for you. You must make sure these employees understand the store's policies, procedures, and plans. You will also have to prepare reports on the progress of your department or store. You will need to keep stockholders or other management persons informed of aspects of your business. As a manager, you work to make communication a two-way process, flowing both upward and downward.

Managers come in contact with much more confidential information than salespeople. They know about their salespeople's past work history and salary. They know the amount of markup their store charges and if it makes a profit. Managers should never violate the trust a store places in them. They should never talk about confidential information to other unauthorized employees, such as another salesperson, or to anyone outside the store. They should set a good example for employees and show that confidential information really is private.

TRAINING AND ASSIGNING DUTIES

As a manager, you are responsible for the work of other employees. You train employees to do various tasks, assign work duties, and follow up to see that the work is done properly. These tasks require you to be a good communicator.

To help in training, many apparel and accessory managers use training manuals that explain how to complete various tasks. Instructions in the manual are written in a logical, step-by-step way. Notice the following instructions for ringing up a charge sale.

1. Ask customer for charge card.
2. Imprint charge card on charge sale slip.
3. Call Credit Department for charge approval on sales over $50.
4. Place charge slip in register.
5. Enter your employee number into register.
6. Enter code number (4) for charge sale.
7. Enter department, class, and price of each merchandise item.
8. Subtotal sale.
9. Add tax.
10. Total sale and tell customer total.
11. Take charge slip out of register.
12. Have customer sign charge slip.
13. Compare signature on charge slip with signature on charge card.
14. Give customer yellow copy of charge slip; put white copy in special box near cash register.
15. Thank customer for shopping at our store.

Managers also use follow-up sheets in order to be certain that various points have been covered during training. (See Figure 3-6.)

Policy manuals that give guidelines for employees are also part of the training program. These manuals include guidelines which state how a store employee is to respond in certain situations. For example, a policy manual may state that total customer satisfaction should be the outcome of every customer/salesperson meeting.

You may develop new training or policy manuals. Or you may be asked to revise outdated manuals. To write these materials, you will need to plan carefully what should be included in the manuals and decide how to organize it. You will need to write the information in an interesting and logical way in order to hold the reader's attention.

Besides writing manuals, you will prepare many written work schedules for your employees. Sometimes, you may prepare a written list of work tasks that your employees are to do. It is especially important that these written instructions are legible and easily understood.

You will often give employees verbal directions. Verbal directions are usually easier when telling one employee how to do a particular job or when explaining a one-time operation. If there are many employees who need to learn a store operation or procedure, you should call a meeting for all the employees. This procedure lets you explain the new information once, rather than once for each employee. It will save you time.

EMPLOYEE ORIENTATION RECORD

Employee Name______________________ Number__________

INSTRUCTIONS: This is a checklist to be followed in orienting new employees. Each item is to be checked to make sure that everything has been covered. General office orientation is completed during the employee's initial training session. Store orientation is to be completed at the time the employee first reports for work. On-the-job orientation is to be completed by the immediate supervisor within a few days after the new employee starts.

GENERAL OFFICE ORIENTATION: Training Director

____ Employee packages and belongings
____ Time card procedures
____ Scheduling and absenteeism
____ Employee conduct
____ Personal phone calls
____ Pay periods
____ Employee discount
____ Overtime
____ Checks, bank credit cards, charge procedures
____ Credit procedures
____ Cash register operations
____ Security
____ Sales techniques

STORE ORIENTATION: Store Manager

____ Introduction to store
____ Rate of pay
____ Store hours
____ Employee lockers
____ Appearance and dress
____ Attitude and initiative
____ Role of supervisor
____ Safety procedures

ON-THE-JOB ORIENTATION: Department Manager

____ Introduction to fellow employees
____ Work of the department
____ Line of supervision
____ Reporting in and out
____ Punctuality and attendance
____ Rest periods and lunch breaks
____ Commission
____ Use of equipment
____ Credit procedures
____ Shoplifting and security
____ Use of the telephone for sales
____ Transfer procedures
____ Stockkeeping duties
____ Promotional possibilities

TO THE NEW EMPLOYEE:

This form has been prepared as a guide to ensure that all information concerning your employment at this store has been explained to you. Check over the above items carefully and ask your supervisor to clarify anything you question.

______________________ ________
Signature of Employee Date

Fig. 3-6 Managers use forms such as this to follow up on an employee's training.

Training, assigning work, and following up on employee performance require good communication skills. Try to make all your communications clear, concise, and correct.

CONDUCTING MEETINGS

As a salesperson, you will attend many meetings. As a manager, you will attend even more meetings. Often, you will be responsible for conducting the meetings. Your organization and speaking skills will be evident to all who attend your meetings. Many managers rely on a written agenda to keep the meeting progressing. Usually, the most important matters are put on the top of the agenda, to make sure they are discussed before time runs out. Less important items are covered later in the meeting.

Often, visual aids are helpful in presentations. Graphs, charts, overhead transparencies, or handouts help your audience understand what you are trying to say and make listening to you more interesting.

At department meetings, you will spend some of your time interpreting management policies to employees. It will be your responsibility to clearly explain a management policy and get the employees to realize why that policy is important. By getting employees to see a problem and solution from management's point of view, you will win your employees' cooperation in following management policies.

When conducting department meetings, not all your time should be spent talking. You should also set aside some time to listen. Your employees will have questions. By encouraging employees to ask questions or tell how they handle certain situations, you will promote a feeling of friendship and cooperation among your staff. Also encourage employees to discuss their concerns.

When talking about their problems, many employees do not communicate effectively; they do not send clear messages. They tell only half the story because they don't want to embarrass others or themselves. Therefore, you need to listen with a sensitive ear so that you can uncover true sources of complaints or grievances among store personnel.

Experience 3-11

Try to See It Our Way

Suppose you are the store manager of a medium-sized apparel shop. The owner has started a new store policy that requires customers to present two forms of identification, as well as home and business phone numbers, when paying by check. This information should be written on the back of the check. The new check procedure will reduce the number of bad checks received by the store. In the past, your employees have been asked to record only a driver's license on the check.

You already realize that the new procedure will not be very popular with your employees because it will take more time at the cash register. Your employees have already told you that some customers feel as though their honesty is being questioned when they are asked for additional identification. It's your responsibility to explain this new procedure to your employees.

Ask two or three classmates to play the role of your employees. Demonstrate how you would explain this new management policy to these employees. Try to make these employees see the need for following the policy. If possible, use a tape recorder to record your department meeting. Play back the tape for self-evaluation of your demonstration of the new management policy to your classmates.

ATTENDING MEETINGS

As a manager, you will attend various kinds of meetings. At store management meetings, you will meet with the store manager or owner or the board of directors. You may be asked for your input concerning store operations and changes. Some of the time you will discuss problems you are having. Sometimes you will discuss the morale of your employees and try to get management to see things from the employees' viewpoint. Some other times, you will discuss your store or department's progress.

You will also have meetings with salespeople from other companies. Merchandise suppliers or advertising representatives will set up appointments to meet with you. During these meetings, suppliers or advertising representatives will try to sell you their products or services.

If your store is located in a mall, there will be mall association meetings for you to attend. If you are located downtown, there will be downtown merchant meetings. At these meetings, you and other retail merchants will talk about special promotions, such as sidewalk sales.

Besides business meetings, you may also attend educational meetings. At these meetings, you will have the opportunity to help students and teachers learn more about your industry. Many apparel and accessory managers are actively involved in working with local DECA (Distributive Education Clubs of America) chapters and meet frequently with students and DE coordinators. You may be asked to supervise a DE student's on-the-job performance or speak to a class of DE students. Or you may be asked to help a DE teacher-coordinator set up training plans for students who have a career goal of entering the apparel and accessory industry.

There are also civic organization meetings, such as the retail merchants association or the chamber of commerce. These organizations keep you aware of what is happening in your community and give you an opportunity to meet with other businesspeople in your area. You will have many opportunities to use your communication skills when you attend meetings. For example, you may be assigned to a committee that is supposed to study a particular problem and then recommend possible solutions.

During all phases of your job as manager, you will need to communicate your ideas effectively. The better you are at getting your ideas across and understanding the ideas of others, the more successful you will be in the apparel and accessory industry.

4 Mathematics

The ability to work accurately with numbers is an important skill for apparel and accessory employees. Mathematical skill is needed by almost every employee in this area. Salespersons must be able to total customer purchases, make change, take inventory, order basic stock, and mark prices on merchandise. Department managers calculate markdowns and keep records of merchandise units that are purchased, sold, in stock, on order, and returned. Buyers prepare buying plans, compute how much money they have available to buy merchandise, and complete purchase orders.

To do each of these tasks, and many more, employees must be able to add, subtract, multiply, and divide with speed and accuracy. They must be able to work with fractions, decimals, and percentages. And because apparel and accessory stores are often crowded with customers, workers sometimes have to complete their math computations under pressure.

WORKING WITH THE CASH REGISTER

Cash registers help stores keep track of their merchandise by recording merchandise sales, returns, exchanges, and layaways. There are various cash register models with many different features. Some models are mechanical and are similar to adding machines. Other models are electronic. Electronic cash registers, sometimes called point-of-sale (POS) terminals, may be connected to a computer that keeps track of inventory. (See Figure 4-1, page 40.)

No matter what model cash register an apparel and accessory store uses, the store employees follow some general cashiering procedures. The persons who use the registers must be able to:

- Open the register.
- Ring up sales, returns, exchanges, layaways, employee sales, mail or delivery charges, and alteration charges.
- Correct cash register errors.
- Replenish the change fund.
- Close out the register.

OPENING THE REGISTER

At the beginning of each day, the cashier, salesperson, or department manager must prepare the cash register to handle the day's business. One of the duties of the person in charge of "opening the register" is to put money in the cash drawer. This money is used to make change for the day's customers and is called the **change fund**.

Many apparel and accessory stores start the day with a $50 change fund in their registers. The actual breakdown of the change fund into bills and coins of different denominations varies upon the typical price of merchandise. For example, the men's furnishings department may have the following breakdown in its $50 change fund: one $10, four $5, twelve $1, sixteen quarters, thirty dimes, fifteen nickels, and twenty-five pennies. This money is arranged in the cash drawer in a numerical order with pennies and dollar bills on the right. Care is taken to keep all the pennies together, all the nickels together, and so on. (See Figure 4-2.)

The employee in charge of opening the register must get the change fund from the store's accounting office or bookkeeper before the start of business. This person must count the change fund to be sure the exact amount of money that is supposed to be in the change fund is really there. If the amounts do not agree, the employee immediately reports the disagreement to the manager or person in charge. Some apparel and accessory stores require that the person who opens a register complete a special form when the change fund is over or short. (See Figure 4-3, page 41.)

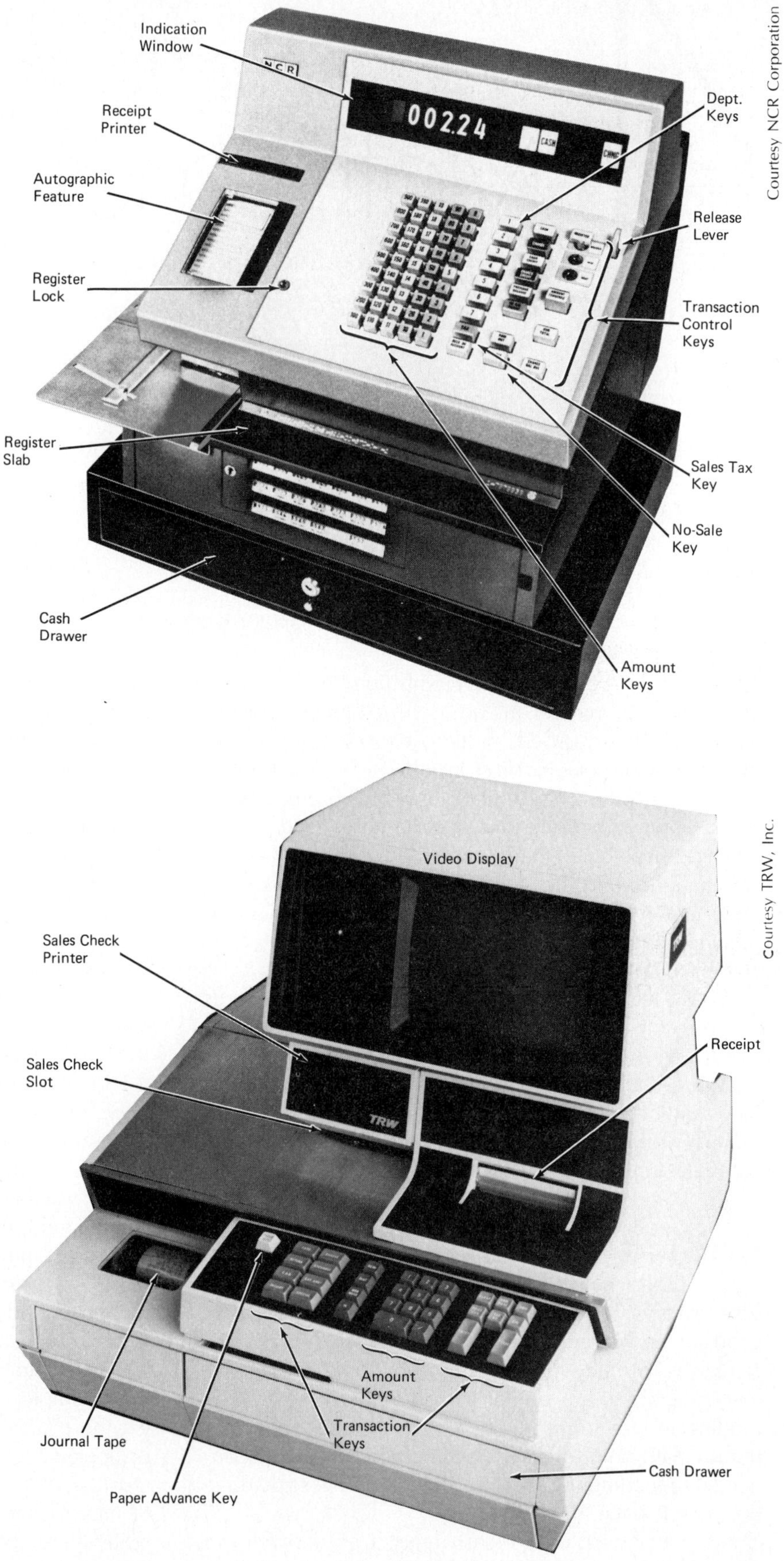

Fig. 4-1 The electric cash register (top) and the electronic cash register (bottom) are designed for accurate and efficient handling of sales transactions.

RINGING UP SALES

After a customer has decided to buy merchandise, the price of the item(s) is recorded on the cash register. The procedure used in ringing up sales will vary depending on the size of the store and the type of cash register used. Let's examine the cash register procedures at a

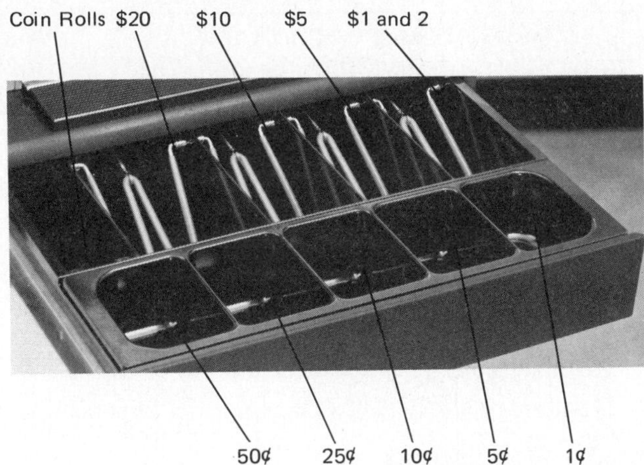

Fig. 4-2 Notice how bills and change are arranged carefully in this cash drawer.

children's wear specialty chain called Jasper's. Although this chain has six stores, it does not use electronic cash registers. In fact, Jasper's salespersons write up sales checks for each customer purchase. When a sales check is completed, the salesperson gives this check to a cashier who rings up the total price on the cash register. (See Figure 4-4, page 42.)

Lee Muller, manager of Jasper's outlet, explains, "For a cash sale, a salesperson should fill in the date, store number, his or her initials, merchandise quantity and description, the individual price of the merchandise items, and the amount. Accuracy is very important when completing the sales check. The prices on the sales check should correspond with the price tags on the merchandise. Numbers should be written clearly and in their correct columns. When customers purchase multiple quantities of merchandise, such as several pairs of socks, the salesperson should carefully count all items to be sure each has been included on the sales check.

"At the bottom of the sales check, the salesperson totals the amount column, adds tax, and computes the total amount due. Each salesperson is familiar with state tax charts, which are taped to the cashier counter. To use these charts, the salesperson locates the subtotal at the left of each column and reads across to find the corresponding tax amount. For example, on a purchase of $4.75, tax is 29 cents. (See Figure 4-5.)

"In our state, the tax is 6 percent on all apparel and accessory items. A salesperson could also compute the correct tax amount by multiplying the subtotal amount by .06 (6 percent). We try to discourage salespersons from doing their own tax computations. They are more accurate when they use the tax chart.

"All of our sales checks are written in duplicate. One copy is given to the customer as a receipt. The other copy stays at the store and is later used to compute the daily sales figures for each department."

Another system of recording sales is used at Weaver's Department Store. Each salesperson is responsible for ringing up his or her own sales on the cash register. The cash register prints a customer receipt that shows the price and total of the merchandise purchased. Manager Mike Garcia explains his store's system, "The salesperson helps the customer choose merchandise. The items sold are then recorded on a register. Our registers require the salesperson to punch in the class number of each merchandise item, the prices, and then depress the subtotal button. The salesperson reads the tax chart and enters the correct tax amount into the register. Finally, the salesperson depresses the total key.

"Our store, like most other apparel and accessory stores, honors bank credit cards, such as Visa and Master Charge. When customers present these cards for payment, the salesperson must complete a bank credit card sales slip. The salesperson must be careful that all information written on the slip is accurate and correctly added." (See Figure 4-6.)

High Castle is a chain of discount clothing stores that uses electronic cash registers and a computerized inventory system. Store owner Dorothy Lewis explains, "Our salespeople don't have to worry about adding the sales checks. Each merchandise item is assigned a special number that is coded onto its price ticket. When the item is purchased, the salesperson runs a wand over the price ticket. The computer finds the price of that item in its memory bank and records the price on the sales check. The computer automatically totals the items purchased, adds tax, and computes the change due. This system eliminates many human errors and has saved our store money. It also provides our buyers with reports of what merchandise has been sold, returned, or is still in stock."

OVER/SHORT REGISTER CHANGE FUND

Report of discrepancy in funds at beginning of day

Date 7/11/--

Change fund was:

☑ Over $ 26¢

☐ Short $ ______

Register No. 21

Salesperson # 3583

Errors in amount of change left in register must be recounted and approved by authorized O.K. Enclose this form in register detail envelope.

Store No. # 12

Authorized O.K. K. Ralston, mgr.

Fig. 4-3 When the change fund is over or short, it is reported on a form similar to this.

205397 DATE Feb. 14 19 —

NAME

STREET

CITY

SOLD BY	CASH	C. O. D.	CHARGE	ON ACCT.	MDSE RETD	PAID OUT	
TK	✓						

QUAN.		DESCRIPTION	PRICE	AMOUNT	
6	1	Socks	.69	4	14
1	2	Blouse	5.49	5	49
1	3	Jumper	7.99	7	99
	4			17	62
	5				
	6				
	7				
	8				
	9				
	10				
	11				
	12				
	13				
	14				
	15				
	16				
	17		Tax		88
	18		Total	18	50

CUSTOMER'S ORDER NO. — REC'D BY —

KEEP THIS SLIP FOR REFERENCE

519

Fig. 4-4 This is an example of a sales check that must be written up by a salesperson. This sales tax differs from that shown in Fig. 4-5.

6% TAX SCHEDULE

SALE	TAX	SALE	TAX	SALE	TAX	SALE	TAX
.11	.01	8.92	.54	17.75	1.07	26.59	1.60
.23	.02	9.09	.55	17.92	1.08	26.75	1.61
.40	.03	9.25	.56	18.09	1.09	26.92	1.62
.57	.04	9.42	.57	18.25	1.10	27.09	1.63
.74	.05	9.59	.58	18.42	1.11	27.25	1.64
.91	.06	9.75	.59	18.59	1.12	27.42	1.65
1.09	.07	9.92	.60	18.75	1.13	27.59	1.66
1.25	.08	10.09	.61	18.92	1.14	27.75	1.67
1.42	.09	10.25	.62	19.09	1.15	27.92	1.68
1.59	.10	10.42	.63	19.25	1.16	28.09	1.69
1.75	.11	10.59	.64	19.42	1.17	28.25	1.70
1.92	.12	10.75	.65	19.59	1.18	28.42	1.71
2.09	.13	10.92	.66	19.75	1.19	28.59	1.72
2.25	.14	11.09	.67	19.92	1.20	28.75	1.73
2.42	.15	11.25	.68	20.09	1.21	28.92	1.74
2.59	.16	11.42	.69	20.25	1.22	29.09	1.75
2.75	.17	11.59	.70	20.42	1.23	29.25	1.76
2.92	.18	11.75	.71	20.59	1.24	29.42	1.77
3.09	.19	11.92	.72	20.75	1.25	29.59	1.78
3.25	.20	12.09	.73	20.92	1.26	29.75	1.79
3.42	.21	12.25	.74	21.09	1.27	29.92	1.80
3.59	.22	12.42	.75	21.25	1.28	30.09	1.81
3.75	.23	12.59	.76	21.42	1.29	30.25	1.82
3.92	.24	12.75	.77	21.59	1.30	30.42	1.83
4.09	.25	12.92	.78	21.75	1.31	30.59	1.84
4.25	.26	13.09	.79	21.92	1.32	30.75	1.85
4.42	.27	13.25	.80	22.09	1.33	30.92	1.86
4.59	.28	13.42	.81	22.25	1.34	31.09	1.87
4.75	.29	13.59	.82	22.42	1.35	31.25	1.88
4.92	.30	13.75	.83	22.59	1.36	31.42	1.89
5.09	.31	13.92	.84	22.75	1.37	31.59	1.90
5.25	.32	14.09	.85	22.92	1.38	31.75	1.91
5.42	.33	14.25	.86	23.09	1.39	31.92	1.92
5.59	.34	14.42	.87	23.25	1.40	32.09	1.93
5.75	.35	14.59	.88	23.42	1.41	32.25	1.94
5.92	.36	14.75	.89	23.59	1.42	32.42	1.95
6.09	.37	14.92	.90	23.75	1.43	32.59	1.96
6.25	.38	15.09	.91	23.92	1.44	32.75	1.97
6.42	.39	15.25	.92	24.09	1.45	32.92	1.98
6.59	.40	15.42	.93	24.25	1.46	33.09	1.99
6.75	.41	15.59	.94	24.42	1.47	33.25	2.00
6.92	.42	15.75	.95	24.59	1.48	33.42	2.01
7.09	.43	15.92	.96	24.75	1.49	33.59	2.02
7.25	.44	16.09	.97	24.92	1.50	33.75	2.03
7.42	.45	16.25	.98	25.09	1.51	33.92	2.04
7.59	.46	16.42	.99	25.25	1.52	34.09	2.05
7.75	.47	16.59	1.00	25.42	1.53	34.25	2.06
7.92	.48	16.75	1.01	25.59	1.54	34.42	2.07
8.09	.49	16.92	1.02	25.75	1.55	34.59	2.08
8.25	.50	17.09	1.03	25.92	1.56	34.75	2.09
8.42	.51	17.25	1.04	26.09	1.57	34.92	2.10
8.59	.52	17.42	1.05	26.26	1.58	35.09	2.11
8.75	.53	17.59	1.06	26.42	1.59	35.25	2.12

Courtesy Magnetax, Bellevue, WA

Fig. 4-5 If the total does not appear on this sales tax chart, be sure to round up to the next number.

Courtesy Interbank Card Association

MASTER CHARGE 3 PT. SALES SLIP THE STANDARD REGISTER CO. FORM MC8013

5218 1134 602 711

1043 ESBC 09-77

KAREN LINDERS

WEAVER'S
1234-001-200-456

5129714

DATE	AUTHORIZATION NO.	IDENTIFICATION	CLERK	REG./DEPT.	TAKE / SEND
6 4 –			AP		☑ TAKE ☐ SEND

QTY.	CLASS	DESCRIPTION	UNIT COST	AMOUNT
1	A24	T-SHIRT		12 00

The Issuer of the card identified on this item is authorized to pay the amount shown as TOTAL upon proper presentation. I promise to pay such TOTAL (together with any other charges due thereon) subject to and in accordance with the agreement governing the use of such card. SUB TOTAL

X Karen Linders CUSTOMER SIGNATURE — TAX 60

SALES SLIP — TOTAL 12 60

MERCHANT COPY

Fig. 4-6 Here's a typical sales slip written for a bank credit card customer. Note that 5 percent sales tax is charged.

Experience 4-1

The Extra Cost: Tax

1. Using the tax chart in Figure 4-5, determine the tax on the following customer purchases.
   a. $2.89 ________
   b. $8.15 ________
   c. $10.40 ________
   d. $11.52 ________
   e. $11.72 ________

2. Suppose the state sales tax chart you are working with only goes up to $50. Compute the sales tax, at 4½ percent, for the following customer purchases.
   a. $51.49 ________
   b. $59.87 ________
   c. $62.70 ________
   d. $71.90 ________

Experience 4-2

What's the Total?

Suppose you are a salesperson at Jasper's, store Number 2. Complete each sales check below for the two customer purchases that follow. Because both sales are cash, it is not necessary for you to write the customer's name and address on each sales check. Use the sales tax chart in Figure 4-5.

1. The customer has purchased four items: two pair navy jeans at $9.95 each, one smock top at $7.95 each, and one tie-dyed knit top at $2.95 each. All items are from Department 8.
2. The customer has purchased two items: a wool sweater and flannel pajamas. The price tickets are in the opposite column.

JASPER'S	
DEPT.	CLASS
8	10
SIZE	PRICE
8	$11.50

Sweater

JASPER'S	
DEPT.	CLASS
8	20
SIZE	PRICE
8	$4.99

Pajamas

QUAN.	DESCRIPTION	PRICE	AMOUNT	

QUAN.	DESCRIPTION	PRICE	AMOUNT	

RINGING UP RETURNS AND EXCHANGES

Sometimes customers find that their purchases are the wrong size, color, or style. Most apparel and accessory stores allow customers who have their sales slip or sales check to bring back unsatisfactory merchandise and receive money or other merchandise in return. In a return or exchange, salespeople usually complete a credit slip or **refund check**. (See Figure 4-7.) When the return or exchange requires a salesperson to add or take out money in the cash drawer, the transaction must be entered into the cash register in order to keep the records straight.

MERCHANDISE CREDIT OR REFUND

NAME Hal Kramer
ADDRESS 820 Georgia Ave.
CITY & STATE Cambridge

SALES NO.	DEPT.	DATE	SOLD BY
214A6	6	4/12/8-	Andy

DATE OF PURCHASE	RECEIVED IN STOCK BY	AUTHORIZED BY
4/10/8-	HB	KM

REASON FOR RETURN split seam

QUAN.	DESCRIPTION		AMOUNT
1	returned shoes		65 00
		tax	3 09
	total of return		68 09
1	new purchase	44.95	
	tax	2.14	
	total	new	47 09
	cash	ref	21 00

P 10104

Becker's Shoes

Fig. 4-7 A refund slip such as this is used for a return or an exchange.

Andy Willis works at Becker's Fine Shoes. Recently, Mr. Kramer returned to the store with a pair of shoes he had purchased. Andy explains the situation as follows, "It seems as though the shoes, which were purchased a week ago, had a split seam on the instep and the customer wanted to exchange them. The customer decided on a pair of $44.95 shoes. He had his sales slip for the $65 shoes he wanted to return. Because the shoes he decided on were less expensive, I had to compute how much money the store owed Mr. Kramer.

"Our state has a 4¾ percent sales tax, so the total amount of the second shoe sale, with tax, came to $47.09. I figured I owed him $21 by working out this table. I realize this is a simple computation. But when I am under pressure, I get nervous and make mistakes. Since the store doesn't have calculators, I have to rely on my arithmetic skills."

Returned Merchandise	Exchange Merchandise	Amount of Refund
$65.00 Retail price	$44.95 Retail price	$68.09 Return total
+ 3.09 Tax	+ 2.14 Tax	−47.09 Exchange total
$68.09 Total	$47.09 Total	$21.00 Refund

Experience 4-3

I Owe You

Mrs. Henricks, a regular customer, says she wants to exchange two of the four pairs of slacks she purchased. The slacks she is returning cost $11.70 each. The slacks she wants in exchange cost $9 per pair. Compute the amount of the refund due this customer. Complete the quantity, description, and amount columns on the refund check in the opposite column. Use the tax chart in Figure 4-5.

MERCHANDISE CREDIT OR REFUND

NAME
ADDRESS
CITY & STATE

SALES NO.	DEPT.	DATE	SOLD BY

DATE OF PURCHASE	RECEIVED IN STOCK BY	AUTHORIZED BY

REASON FOR RETURN

QUAN.	DESCRIPTION		AMOUNT

P 10104

Philipsborn

RINGING UP LAYAWAYS

Many stores offer customers a service called **layaway.** With this service, customers can pay a small deposit to have merchandise put aside for them. The customers have a certain amount of time to pay the total price, plus tax, of the merchandise item. When the merchandise is completely paid for, the merchandise belongs to the customer. Although some stores charge a small service fee for holding the merchandise (often a percentage of the purchase price), there is no finance charge for layaway.

Customers who take advantage of a store's layaway service must pay a percentage of the total cost of the merchandise item at the time of the layaway, usually between 10 and 25 percent. The salesperson must compute the layaway deposit and balance due on the account.

For example, suppose a customer wants to layaway a $175 coat and the store requires a 20 percent layaway deposit. The salesperson would have to add tax to the purchase and compute the total amount of the sale. Assume that the tax is 8 percent, or $14. A 20 percent deposit on a total purchase of $189 ($175 + $14) is $37.80. The balance due is $151.20. The salesperson records all this information, including the customer's name, address, and the merchandise description on a layaway form. (See Figure 3-2, page 30.) Every time the customer pays on the account, the salesperson records the payment on a special form and computes a new balance.

Experience 4-4

You Say You Want This on Layaway?

1. A customer wants to layaway the following merchandise items: three pantyhose at $1.49 each, one leotard at $5.99 each, two batiste slips at $3.49 each, and one crinkle cloth smock at $8.99 each. Your store charges a 25 percent deposit on all layaway items. Complete the following layaway form. Compute the balance due after the deposit is paid. Use the tax chart in Figure 4-5.
2. On April 4, the customer paid $15 on the layaway balance. On April 15, the customer paid the balance. How much was the April 15 payment? Record both payments on the layaway form below.

LAY-AWAY

NAME ______

ADDRESS ______

CITY ______ PHONE ______

LAY-AWAY NUMBER 14576

☐ BOX ☐ HANGER	SOLD BY	DATE / / 19	TIME LIMIT

DATE	PAYMENTS	BALANCE DUE

RINGING UP EMPLOYEE DISCOUNTS

One of the benefits of working for an apparel and accessory store is that often employees receive a discount on the store's merchandise. Typical employee discounts range from 10 to 25 percent.

When an employee purchases an item, the salesperson computes the "employee cost" of the merchandise by multiplying the merchandise price by the amount of the discount. For example, suppose a customer purchased a shirt ($13.50) and a tie ($6.50) and received a 20 percent discount. The employee cost for these items would be $16 plus tax. See Figure 4-8 for an example of the sales check.

Many stores issue their employees and their employees' families a shopping pass called a **discount card**. If the cash register does not automatically record the employee's name and number, the salesperson should write this information on the sales check. Most stores ask employees to sign the sales check, even when it is a cash sale.

SOLD TO Philip Bell - Employee #403

CLERK	DATE		CHARGE	REC'D ON ACCT.
F. B.	11/5	Cash		

DEPT.	QUAN.	ARTICLE	AMOUNT	
	1	Tie	6	50
	1	Shirt	13	50
			20	00
		Employee Discount	4	00
			16	00
		TAX		80
		TOTAL	16	80

All claims and returned goods must be accompanied by this bill.

Philip Bell
CUSTOMER'S SIGNATURE

Thank You!

Fig. 4-8 Here's an employee discount on a sales check.

Experience 4-5

You Get a Discount

Record the following employee sale on the sales check below. The customer receives a 15 percent discount. Be sure to write the customer's name (Evelyn Johnson) and her employee number (411) on the ticket. Figure the sales tax at the rate of 4½ percent for the purchases shown on the tickets in the opposite column.

Jacket

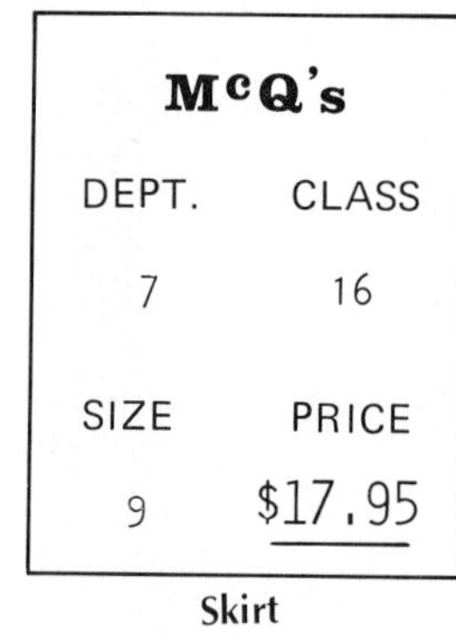

Skirt

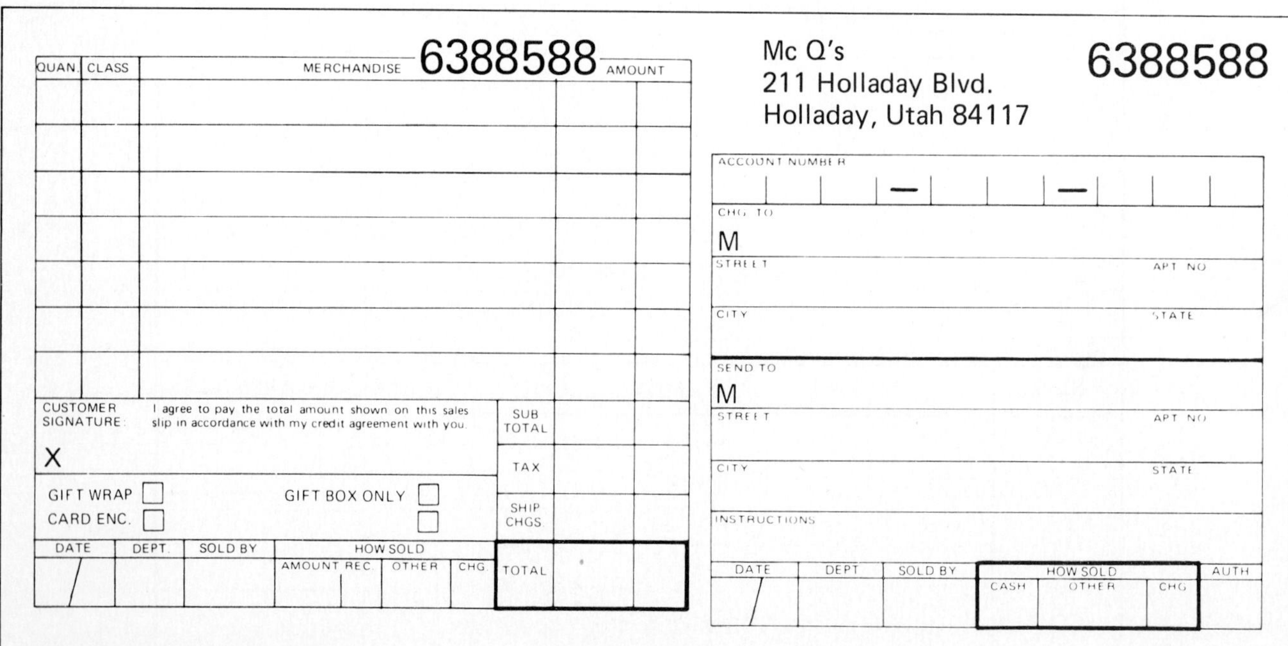
QUAN. | CLASS | MERCHANDISE 6388588 | AMOUNT

CUSTOMER SIGNATURE: I agree to pay the total amount shown on this sales slip in accordance with my credit agreement with you.

X

SUB TOTAL

TAX

GIFT WRAP ☐ GIFT BOX ONLY ☐

CARD ENC. ☐ ☐

SHIP CHGS

DATE | DEPT. | SOLD BY | HOW SOLD: AMOUNT REC. | OTHER | CHG. | TOTAL

Mc Q's
211 Holladay Blvd.
Holladay, Utah 84117
6388588

ACCOUNT NUMBER

CHG. TO
M
STREET | APT. NO.
CITY | STATE

SEND TO
M
STREET | APT. NO.
CITY | STATE

INSTRUCTIONS

DATE | DEPT. | SOLD BY | HOW SOLD: CASH | OTHER | CHG. | AUTH.

COMPUTING DELIVERY CHARGES

Large stores offer free merchandise delivery to customers in nearby areas. For delivery outside the store's delivery area, stores may provide customers with a mailing service. When merchandise is to be sent beyond free delivery points, the salesperson must compute the mailing charges and include them in the total sales price.

The cost of sending a package through the U.S. Postal Service depends on (1) the class of mail used, (2) the package's weight, and (3) the distance the package is being sent. Merchandise packages weighing less than 13 ounces are sent first class. Merchandise weighing over 13 ounces is sent either by a type of first class called priority mail or by fourth class (parcel post), depending on the customer's preference. **Priority mail** is more expensive than parcel post, but it is faster.

Stacy Schwartz works at McQ's Boutique in Holladay, Utah. A customer has purchased some merchandise and wants it shipped to Pittsburgh, Pennsylvania by first class mail.

Stacy places the wrapped package on the scales. It weighs 7¼ pounds. Because this odd weight amount is not listed on the priority mail chart, Stacy rounds the weight up to 8 pounds. (See Figure 4-9.) She refers to the Official Zone Chart and locates Pittsburgh in zone 7. Stacy locates the correct weight (8 pounds) and zone (7) on the priority mail chart. The mailing cost is $5.29.

The charge for mailing is not taxed (see Figure 4-10). It is added after the merchandise has been subtotaled and totaled. Notice that Stacy did not add tax to the total because customers do not pay state tax on merchandise shipped out of state.

Some apparel and accessory stores use UPS (United Parcel Service) or other transportation and delivery companies to send merchandise to their customers.

PRIORITY MAIL (Heavy Pieces)

Weight over 10 ounces and not exceeding (pounds)	Zones					
	To Local 1,2,3	4	5	6	7	8
1	$1.56	$1.58	$1.60	$1.62	$1.64	$1.67
1.5	1.73	1.77	1.84	1.90	1.97	2.07
2	1.89	1.96	2.07	2.18	2.29	2.46
2.5	2.05	2.15	2.29	2.43	2.59	2.78
3	2.21	2.33	2.50	2.68	2.88	3.09
3.5	2.37	2.51	2.70	2.91	3.15	3.38
4	2.53	2.69	2.90	3.14	3.41	3.67
4.5	2.68	2.86	3.09	3.35	3.65	3.94
5	2.83	3.03	3.27	3.56	3.88	4.20
6	3.13	3.37	3.64	3.98	4.35	4.72
7	3.43	3.71	4.01	4.40	4.82	5.24
8	3.73	4.05	4.38	4.82	5.29	5.76
9	4.03	4.39	4.75	5.24	5.76	6.28

FOURTH-CLASS (Parcel Post) ZONE RATES

Weight - 1 pound and not exceeding (pounds)	Zones							
	Local	1&2	3	4	5	6	7	8
2	$0.77	$0.90	$0.93	$1.04	$1.15	$1.28	$1.40	$1.48
3	.82	.97	1.02	1.15	1.29	1.46	1.62	1.74
4	.86	1.04	1.10	1.25	1.42	1.63	1.84	2.00
5	.91	1.11	1.19	1.36	1.56	1.81	2.06	2.26
6	.95	1.18	1.27	1.46	1.69	1.98	2.28	2.52
7	1.00	1.25	1.36	1.57	1.83	2.16	2.50	2.78
8	1.04	1.32	1.44	1.67	1.96	2.33	2.72	3.04
9	1.09	1.39	1.53	1.78	2.10	2.51	2.94	3.30

Fig. 4-9 Determine mail rates with these charts.

6388588

QUAN.	CLASS	MERCHANDISE	AMOUNT	
1	243	blue check pantsuit	89	00
1	437	blue blouse	20	00

CUSTOMER SIGNATURE — I agree to pay the total amount shown on this sales slip in accordance with my credit agreement with you. X

SUB TOTAL 109 00
TAX ——
GIFT WRAP ☑ GIFT BOX ONLY ☐
CARD ENC. ☑ ☐
SHIP CHGS 5 29
TOTAL 114 29

DATE	DEPT	SOLD BY	AMOUNT REC	OTHER	CHG
8/4	2	SS	120 -		

Mc Q's
211 Holladay Blvd.
Holladay, Utah 84117

6388588

ACCOUNT NUMBER
CHG TO: M James Lions
STREET: 439 Lincoln Lane APT NO
CITY: Holladay STATE: U
SEND TO: Ms Lisa Lions
STREET: 7244 Bryce Dr. APT NO
CITY: Pittsburgh, PA 16340 STATE
INSTRUCTIONS

DATE	DEPT	SOLD BY	CASH	OTHER	CHG	AUTH
8/4	2	SS	X			

Fig. 4-10 Here's the sales check Stacy Schwartz wrote up for the package sent to Pittsburgh.

Experience 4-6

The Cost of Getting It There

1. On a separate sheet of paper, compute the cost of mailing the following three packages from Holladay, Utah. Use the chart in Figure 4-9.
   a. Package A. Weight: 1 lb., 10 oz; mailing class: priority mail; destination: Albany, New York, zone 8. ______________
   b. Package B. Weight: $2\frac{1}{4}$ lb.; mailing class: parcel post; destination: Kansas City, Kansas, zone 5. ______________
   c. Package C. Weight: 8 lb., 8 oz; mailing class: parcel post; destination: Sacramento, California, zone 4. ______________

ADDING ALTERATION CHARGES

Some apparel and accessory stores provide free alterations; others charge an alteration fee if the garment was purchased on sale. When customers pay an alterations fee, the salesperson may refer to an alterations price list to determine the charge for such services, or the tailor or seamstress may set the fee. Customers are charged state tax on store alterations.

CORRECTING CASH REGISTER ERRORS

Even careful employees occasionally make mistakes when using the cash register. Usually, these mistakes involve entering the wrong price into the register. A salesperson makes an overring error when the amount entered is more than the actual price of the merchandise, for example, $3.95 rather than $2.95. When the amount entered into the register is less than the price of the merchandise, the salesperson has made an underring error, for example, $1 rather than $10.

The total daily sales rung up on a cash register are recorded on the cash register detail tape. These tapes are added together to determine the total sales of a department or store. During inventory, the store compares the merchandise that has moved through the department with the total sales figures. Cash register underrings and overrings cause the store management to have an inaccurate picture of the store's inventory levels and shoplifting problem.

How a cash register error is handled depends on store policy. Usually, if a mistake is made before a total or enter key is depressed, the salesperson can correct the error by pushing the clear key or correction lever. The salesperson can then enter the correct data into the register. If the error is recorded on the sales slip, the salesperson may have to void the slip with the incorrect information and complete another slip. Many stores give their salesperson a void form on which the salesperson records each void (mistake). The voided sales slips are attached to this form and turned in at the end of the day to the accountant or bookkeeper. Some stores require a head cashier or supervisor to void each error.

Other reasons for a salesperson to void a sales slip are (1) the customer decides to charge a purchase after the salesperson has rung up a cash sale and (2) the customer decides not to purchase an item after the sale is recorded on the cash register.

Experience 4-7

What to Do When You Make a Mistake

Visit a small specialty store and a department store. Explain to the management that you are planning to work in the apparel and accessory industry. Ask the following questions. Record your answers on a separate sheet.

1. What are some reasons a salesperson voids sales slips at your store?
2. How does a salesperson void a sales slip or correct a mistake? Ask to see how a slip is voided. If the manager uses a void form, ask for a copy of the form. Bring it to show to the class and your teacher.
3. What are some of the problems that occur when a salesperson incorrectly handles a void or cash register error?

MAKING CHANGE

Although electronic and many mechanical cash registers compute the change due customers, some salespersons may be required to calculate change. For example, if a customer's purchase totals $15.39 and the customer offers a $20 bill, the salesperson would have to subtract $15.39 from $20 to determine the customer's change, $4.61.

When making change, a salesperson should (1) tell the customer the total amount due, including tax. (For example, "That'll be $15.39, please.") And (2) take the customer's money, announce the amount, and place it on the change plate of the register. (For example, "Out of $20.")

Calculate the amount of change due by using the count up method. For example, the salesperson counts up from the total, $15.39, to the amount given, $20. The salesperson takes a penny out of the drawer, for $15.40, then a dime, for $15.50, then a half dollar, for

$16. The salesperson then takes one dollar out of the drawer, for $17, another dollar, for $18, another dollar, for $19, and another dollar, for $20.

Notice that when making change, the salesperson uses the least number of bills and coins possible. Instead of giving the customer a penny and six dimes or sixty-one pennies, the salesperson gives the customer a penny, one dime, and one half dollar. By using the least number of bills and coins, the salesperson is usually able to keep a good supply of coins and currency.

Count the change back to the customer while placing the bills and coins in the customer's hand. For example, say, "$15.39 from $20." While putting the change in the customer's hand, the salesperson should count up to the amount tendered like this:

Say to Customer	Give to Customer
$15.39	1 penny
$15.40	1 dime
$15.50	1 half dollar
$16.00	1 dollar
$17.00	1 dollar
$18.00	1 dollar
$19.00	1 dollar
$20.00	

When the cash register computes the amount of change due, the salesperson does not have to subtract the amount of the sale from the amount tendered. After the sale is totaled, the salesperson enters the amount tendered into the register. Change due the customer appears on the cash register read-out. For example, if the read-out says $2.89 CHG DUE, and the customer pays with a $5 bill, the salesperson takes two $1 bills, a half dollar, a quarter, a dime, and four pennies out of the register. Notice that the salesperson uses the least number of coins and bills to make change. The salesperson then says to the customer, "Your purchase totaled $2.11, out of $5, your change is $2.89." The salesperson then gives the customer change by following this procedure shown below:

Says to Customer	Gives to Customer
$2.00	two $1 bills
.50	one half dollar
.75	one quarter
.85	one dime
.89	four pennies

The salesperson always thanks the customer for shopping at the store. This is a courteous way to complete any sales transaction.

Experience 4-8

That Was $2.50 out of $3

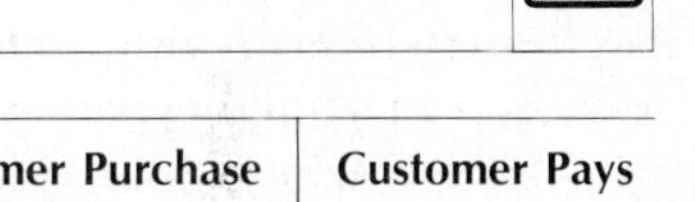

Have a classmate role-play a customer. You play the part of a salesperson. Assume your cash register does not tell you how much change is due. Using play money, demonstrate how you would make change using the count up method. Be sure to use the least number of coins and bills possible in making change for each of the situations in the opposite column:

Situation	Total Customer Purchase	Customer Pays
1	$4.89	$ 5.00
2	$6.13	$ 7.03
3	$2.73	$ 3.00
4	$5.15	$10.00
5	$3.51	$20.01

REPLENISHING THE CHANGE FUND

During the day, salespeople may find that they are almost out of a particular coin or currency in their change fund. Suppose, for example, that there are no $1 bills in the cash drawer. Because $1 bills are used so frequently in making change, the salesperson must replenish the supply. This process is called "buying change" because a salesperson must use other money in the cash drawer to buy the needed bills or coins. The salesperson could take a $20 bill, two $10 bills, or any other combination totaling $20 out of the cash drawer and buy twenty $1 bills. Change may be bought from the chief cashier or from another department's cash register. Notice that money is never taken out of one cash register and put into another register without an equal transfer of funds. When buying change, some stores require a change wanted form to be completed. (See Figure 4-11.)

CHANGE WANTED

Date 9/17/8-

Amount sent for change: 20.00

Please send change as follows:

Dollars and Cents		Bills	
Dollars		Twenties	
Halves		Tens	
Quarters		Fives	10.00
Dimes		Twos	
Nickels		Ones	10.00
Pennies			

John Doe

Cashier (Please sign in ink)

Fig. 4-11 Here's a typical form used for buying change.

Experience 4-9

When Money Changes Registers

Suppose you are a salesperson at Walker's Millinery. There are two cash registers in your store. Another salesperson, Jane Eskins, is ringing up a sale on cash register 1 and notices that she doesn't have enough $1 bills to make change. Jane comes back to you and asks you to give her five $1 bills from your register. Based on these facts, should you give Jane the money? Give reasons to support your answer.

CLOSING OUT THE REGISTER

At the end of the day, every apparel and accessory store follows certain closing procedures. The money from the day's sales and the charge and cash receipts are taken out of the cash drawer and turned into the accounting department or the bookkeeper. How each store "closes out" a department varies, but the general principles are the same.

Let's watch how the manager, Randy Tucker, explains the closing procedure to a new employee, Emily Hardy. Randy says, "Emily, you have worked here for a month and are fairly familiar with how the store operates. Next week you start on night shift and will need to learn how to close out the cash register. We have two cash registers in the department and both must be closed out. You can close out one register about 8:30 p.m. if it is slow. Close out the other cash register after 9:00 p.m. when all customers have left the department.

"To close out a register, you:

1. Open the cash register drawer.
2. Count the coins and paper money that will make up the next day's change fund. Because our change fund equals $50, you must count out $50 in coins and bills every night. Include as many coins and small bills, such as ones and fives, as possible.
3. Place the next day's change fund into a special money bag provided by the accounting office.
4. Count the remaining coins and bills and record them on the daily cash report. (See Figure 4-12A.)
5. Add the checks and record them on the daily cash report. (See Figure 4-12B.)
6. Add the bank credit card sales slips, such as Master Charge and Visa, and record them on the daily cash report. (See Figure 4-12C.)
7. Total the coins, bills, checks, and bank credit card sales slips and record the total on the daily cash report. (See Figure 4-12D.)
8. Add the paid-out vouchers (receipts for money that has been taken out of the cash drawer during the day) and record them on the daily cash report. (See Figure 4-12E.)

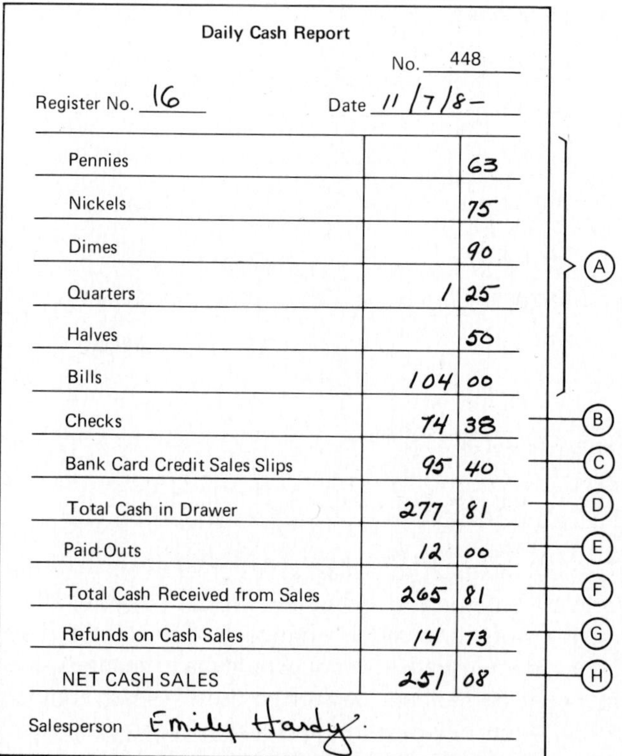

Daily Cash Report

No. 448

Register No. 16 Date 11/7/8–

Pennies		63	A
Nickels		75	A
Dimes		90	A
Quarters	1	25	A
Halves		50	A
Bills	104	00	A
Checks	74	38	B
Bank Card Credit Sales Slips	95	40	C
Total Cash in Drawer	277	81	D
Paid-Outs	12	00	E
Total Cash Received from Sales	265	81	F
Refunds on Cash Sales	14	73	G
NET CASH SALES	251	08	H

Salesperson Emily Hardy

Fig. 4-12 Here's a typical example of a daily cash report form.

9. Subtract the paid-out vouchers from the total cash in drawer and record the answer on the daily cash report. (See Figure 4-12F.)
10. Add all the refunds made during the day and record the total on the daily cash report. (See Figure 4-12G.)
11. Subtract the refunds from the total cash received from sales and record the net cash sales on the daily cash report. (See Figure 4-12H.)
12. Place the coins, bills, checks, bank credit card sales slips, paid-out vouchers, refund slips, and daily cash report in another money bag. Then deliver both money bags to the accounting office."

NAME ______________________ DATE ______________

Experience 4-10

Closing Time

Assume you are responsible for closing out cash register 14 in Department 12. Your salesperson number is 18. The change fund needs to be returned to $40.

1. In the cash drawer, you find the following. Complete the daily cash report in the opposite column.

Coins	Bills	Checks
34 Pennies 17 Nickels 15 Dimes 8 Quarters 1 Half Dollar	Fourteen $1 Seventeen $5 Seven $10 Four $20	$16.92 $17.85 $21.40

Bank Credit Card Sales Slips	Refunds
$12.18 $14.75	$ 5.85 17.40

2. Show the amount of coin and currency that will remain in the cash drawer.

Pennies ______ $ 1 Bills ______

Nickels ______ $ 5 Bills ______

Dimes______ $10 Bills ______

Quarters ______ $20 Bills ______

Half Dollars ______

Daily Cash Report

No. 448

Register No. ______ Date ______________

Pennies		
Nickels		
Dimes		
Quarters		
Halves		
Bills		
Checks		
Bank Card Credit Sales Slips		
Total Cash in Drawer		
Paid-Outs		
Total Cash Received from Sales		
Refunds on Cash Sales		
NET CASH SALES		

Salesperson ______________________

METRIC MEASUREMENTS

An apparel and accessory salesperson works with many different size ranges. In the past, all measurements in the United States were determined in inches, feet, and/or pounds. These measurements are part of the U.S. Customary System of Weights and Measures. At this time, however, the United States is in the process of changing from the U.S. Customary System to the metric system, sometimes called SI. Under the metric system, length is expressed in millimeters (one thousandth of a meter), centimeters (one hundredth of a meter), and meters. Weight is expressed in kilograms. Abbreviations for these measurements are millimeter = mm, meter = m, centimeter = cm, and kilogram = kg.

Apparel and accessory designers and manufacturers are finding that they are able to design clothing that gives a closer fit and cut clothing more precisely using the metric measurements. This system of measurements is also easier to use. The metric system will change some of the size markings for apparel and accessories. For example, instead of purchasing a pair of pants sized 32–34 (32-inch waist and 34-inch inseam), the pants may be sized 81–86 (81-centimeter waist and 86-centimeter inseam). Clothing whose sizes are not directly related to inches will not be changed. For example, a size 10 dress will remain a size 10.

As an apparel and accessory salesperson, some customers may ask you to convert metric measurements to the U.S. Customary System of measurements. Also, you may be asked to convert feet, inches, and pounds to centimeters and kilograms. It is easy to make these conversions. Look at the following charts.

From U.S. to Metric System

If You Know	You Can Convert to	If You Multiply by
inches	centimeters	2.54
feet	centimeters	30.5
feet	meters	3.3
pounds	kilograms	0.45

From Metric to U.S. System

If You Know	You Can Convert to	If You Multiply by
centimeters	inches	0.4
meters	feet	3.3
kilograms	pounds	2.2

Suppose that a customer, from another country which already uses the metric system, wants to purchase a pair of pantyhose. The size chart on the pantyhose has not yet been changed to metric measurements. The customer asks your help in finding out what size to buy.

You ask the customer her height and weight and find out that she is 165 centimeters and 53 kilograms. To convert these measurements to feet and pounds, you would multiply 165 centimeters by 0.4 (66 inches). Then divide 66 inches by 12 to determine the feet and inches (5 feet 6 inches height). And finally multiply 53 kilograms by 2.2 (116.6 or 117 pounds weight). Using this process, you could help the metric-oriented customer locate her size in the U.S. Customary System. Following this process in reverse, you could also help a customer who still thinks in feet, inches, and pounds to find the correct size in metric measurements.

Eventually, the measuring tape which apparel stores use to measure customers will be changed from inches and feet to centimeters and meters. The weight scales will be changed from pounds to kilograms. These changes, however, are slow in coming. It is estimated that clothing sizes, such as men's suits and shirts, will not be switched over to metric equivalents until the end of the conversion process. Until that time, manufacturers who use metric size ranges will include the U.S. Customary size equivalents on the merchandise tags.

Experience 4-11

Converting to Metric

Compute the answers to the following questions.

1. A customer wants to purchase a pair of pants for her son. His waist measures 23 inches. His inseam measurement is 23¼ inches. What are his equivalent metric measurements?

   ____

   ____

2. A customer wants to buy a shirt, size 15-inch neck and 33-inch arm length. What are the equivalent metric measurements?

   ____

3. A customer wants to buy footed sleepwear for a baby that weighs 26 pounds and is 31 inches high. What are the equivalent metric measurements?

   ____

MERCHANDISE COUNTS, REORDERS, AND MARKDOWNS

Apparel and accessories employees use their math skills when taking inventory counts, determining how much stock to reorder, and computing markdowns. Each of these tasks involves simple arithmetic: adding, multiplying, subtracting, and dividing. For example, although the buyer usually determines the percentage of the retail price that merchandise items are reduced, the salesperson often computes the exact mark-down reduction.

To compute a mark-down price, the salesperson multiplies the mark-down percentage by the original sales price and subtracts that amount from the original price.

The price of merchandise is also marked up, or increased, for various reasons. To compute a mark-up price, the salesperson multiplies the mark-up percentage by the original sales price and adds that amount to the original price.

Counting, reordering, and calculating prices of merchandise are discussed in detail in Chapter 11, "Buying and Pricing."

- **EXAMPLE OF MARKDOWN**

Mark-down percentage = 33⅓ percent
Original price = $24
Mark-down percentage × Original price = Amount of mark-down
33⅓ percent × $24 = $7.22
Original price − Amount of markdown = New sales price
$24 − $7.22 = $16.78

- **EXAMPLE OF MARKUP**

Mark-up percentage = 15 percent
Original price = $12.99
Markup percentage × Original price = Amount of mark-up
15 percent × $12.99 = $1.95
Original price + Amount of mark-up = New sales price
$12.99 + $1.95 = $14.94

Experience 4-12

What's This Selling for?

Your buyer has just handed you a list of merchandise markdowns. Compute the new sales price of each item.

Item	Markdown Percent	Regular Price	Reduced Price
1. Hooded sweaters	25	$14.99	________
2. Cotton sweatshirts	33	$15.99	________
3. Wool tunics	15	$10.99	________
4. Acrylic pullovers	33	$ 8.99	________
5. Nylon knit pullovers	20	$ 6.99	________

COMPUTING TURNOVER

The number of times stock is turned into sales is called **turnover**. It reflects the rate at which new merchandise enters a store or department. A constant flow of new goods into a department stimulates sales and makes for a sound profit because it creates enthusiasm in customers and salespersons. It creates more traffic also.

Retail is the merchandise price paid by customers. **Cost** is the price originally paid for the merchandise by the store. Most apparel and accessory stores use retail price figures. When working with retail or cost figures, the most important idea to remember is all the amounts must be expressed either as retail or at cost. The retail and cost figures cannot be mixed. Department managers or buyers may want to compute their rate of turnover. They can do this by following this formula:

$$\frac{\text{Net sales at retail}}{\text{Average stock at retail}} = \text{Rate of turnover}$$

Suppose Leon Chambers, owner of Chamber's Men's Furnishings, wants to compute his turnover rate for the 3-month period of February 1 to April 30. Before he can compute the turnover rate, he must first compute the average stock at retail. The average stock at retail is determined by adding all the inventory amounts and dividing by the number of inventories. For example, if the inventory figures are:

February 1 — $3,000 at retail
March 1 — $4,500 at retail
April 1 — $4,200 at retail
April 30 — $3,300 at retail

Then, the average stock, at retail, for this period is:

$$\text{Average stock at retail} = \frac{\$3{,}000 + \$4{,}500 + \$4{,}200 + \$3{,}300}{4} = \$3{,}750$$

The net sales for this three-month period are $6,200. Therefore, the turnover rate for this period is:

$$\text{Rate of turnover} = \frac{\$6{,}200}{\$3{,}750} = 1.65$$

After determining turnover rates for different time periods, these rates can be compared. The turnover rate provides management with a yardstick with which to measure performance. Although apparel and accessory stores want a high turnover rate, a turnover that is too high may reflect inadequate merchandise selection and out-of-stock conditions. Typical turnover rates for women dress shops are 5–7 turns; typical turnover rates for men's furnishings are 2–4 turns. Stores selling lower-priced merchandise have a high turnover rate.

Experience 4-13

Turnover

1. Compute the turnover rate for the 3-month period April–June. The net sales for this period is $13,550. The monthly inventory levels are April 1 $6,950 at retail, May 1 $5,845 at retail, June 1 $4,730 at retail, June 30 $3,970 at retail.

   Turnover rate ________

2. The turnover rate for last year's April–June period was 1.8. What conclusions can you draw when you compare last year's turnover rate with this year's rate?

   ____

   ____

RED·
YELLO

UNIT 3

Product Technology

Anyone who works in a marketing job must know about the products or services being sold. This unit discusses the products you may be working with in your apparel and accessories marketing career. First, in Chapter 5, you'll learn about the fabrics used to make today's clothing. In Chapters 6, 7, and 8, you will find out about the sizes and styles of women's, men's and children's clothing. You will also learn how to recognize apparel that fits properly and how to coordinate clothing and accessories to make a child, man, or woman look his or her very best. Chapter 9 presents information about fitting and selling all types of shoes. Other accessories, including gloves, handbags, hats, belts, and costume jewelry, are discussed in Chapter 10.

With this information you should be able to begin and advance in your apparel and accessories marketing career.

5 Fabrics

Working in the apparel industry, you will find that customers want information about the durability and care of the garments they purchase. Customers want to know if a garment will shrink, if it will wear well, and if the color will fade. They want to know how to launder the garment and if ironing is required. To answer their questions, you need to be able to identify certain fabrics and know something about how fabrics are made.

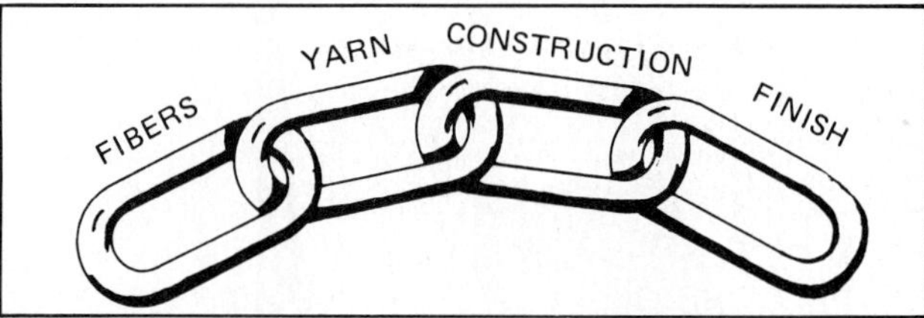

Fig. 5-1 Textile fabrics are made up of a combination of the four items shown here.

THE LANGUAGE OF FABRICS

In dealing with fabrics, there are many new words you will need to learn and understand. Some of these words are as follows:

Fiber is the smallest unit in a textile fabric.
Yarn is a continuous thread formed by twisting or spinning fibers together.
Finish is something done to a fabric, yarn, or fiber to change its appearance, performance, or feel.
Hand describes the texture or feel of a fabric, such as its softness or crispness.
Textiles are products made of natural fibers, such as cotton and wool, and of man-made fibers, such as rayon and polyester. These fibers can be woven, knitted, felted, braided, or bonded into cloth.
Textile fabrics are cloth made from fibers, such as denim and corduroy.

Most clothing is made from textile fabrics. Finished textile fabrics are a combination of four major items: fiber, yarn, construction, and finish. (See Figure 5-1.)

FIBERS

Your grandmother can probably remember back to when clothing was made from natural fibers, such as wool, cotton, silk, and linen. Natural fibers come from plants or animals. Much of today's clothing is made from man-made fibers, such as acetate, acrylic, nylon, and polyester. Man-made fibers, sometimes called synthetics, can look and feel like natural fibers.

There are also blends of man-made fibers and natural fibers. A **blend** is a combination of two or more fibers, natural and/or man-made, before they are spun into yarn. Blending combines the best features of each fiber. Any fabric may be made up of different fibers. For example, flannel can be blended from acetate and rayon, or acrylic and wool. The fibers used in a fabric affect its care and durability.

NATURAL FIBERS

Cotton, linen, wool, and silk are the commonest natural fibers. Cotton and linen come from plants; wool and silk come from animals. Table 1 provides specific characteristics and care details for cotton, linen, wool, and silk.

MAN-MADE FIBERS

Man-made fibers are made from liquid chemicals that pass through a disc called a spinnerette. (See Figure 5-2.) The chemicals harden into a long hairlike fiber called monofilaments. These monofilaments are twisted together to form yarn. The commonest man-made fibers

TABLE 1

FIBER	PROPERTIES	CARE INSTRUCTIONS[1]
COTTON Source: Boll of cotton plant The world's major textile fiber. Cotton is used alone or in blends. New wash-and-wear finishes have made cotton easier to care for. The finest quality cotton is Sea Island cotton. It is also the most expensive cotton. Another fine quality cotton is Pima cotton.	Is absorbent and colorfast (colors don't fade); is strong when wet or dry; takes dye nicely; is comfortable; shrinks unless treated with special finish; wrinkles, and needs pressing; has poor crease retention (cannot hold creases); does not melt, shrink, or stretch when ironed.	Usually, cotton can be machine-washed and tumble-dried. Sheer fabrics, or those with "doubtful" colorfastness should be hand-washed. Cotton can be bleached with chlorine or peroxide bleaches. However, cotton with a resin finish cannot be chlorine bleached (a resin finish makes a garment shrink resistant, wrinkle resistant, and easy to care for). Some finishes may cause the fabric to yellow when exposed to chlorine bleach. Medium- and heavy-weight cotton can be pressed with a hot iron. Use warm iron for thin or sheer cottons. Remove stains from cotton before washing. May mildew.
LINEN Source: Flax plant Flax that is processed into yarn or fabric is called linen. Because of its limited production and costly hand labor involved in producing it, linen is imported into the United States. Linen is more expensive than cotton.	Is highly absorbent, cool and comfortable in summer; is very durable (stronger than cotton); resists shrinking; soils less easily than cotton and is colorfast; wrinkles easily unless treated.	Most linens are machine-washable and can be tumble-dried. It is best to iron linen when damp; first on outside and then on inside. Linen will mildew if given the chance.
WOOL Source: Fleece of sheep, lamb, or hair of Angora or Cashmere goat, camel, alpaca, or llama Wool is classified into three groups (1) *Wool or virgin wool:* wool from live sheep that is being used for the first time. Virgin wool is the strongest and most resilient (ability to sprink back into shape after being crushed or wrinkled). (2) *Reprocessed wool:* wool that has been made into fabric before but never worn or used; such as mill end pieces. (3) *Reused wool:* wool that has been made into fabric before and worn or used. This wool is "reclaimed" and reprocessed. These classifications will appear on the label.	Insulates wearer against heat and cold; is absorbent; is colorfast; possesses elasticity (can stretch up to 30% of its length without strain); takes dye easily; resists wrinkles; is resilient but will pill (pills are balls of tangled fibers on the fabric's surface); poor resistance to bleach, friction, moths, perspiration, and strong soaps.	Most wool garments should be dry-cleaned. However, if the label says hand-wash, use cool water, mild detergent, and gentle action. Never soak, rub, or twist. Handle the garments carefully when wet or damp. Dry on a flat surface. Press with a cool iron and steam. By hanging wool garments in a steam-filled room, most set-in wrinkles can be removed. After wearing, wool garments should be brushed gently. Garments should be allowed to rest 24 hours before they are worn again.
SILK Source: Cocoon of silkworm Silk may be weighted or nonweighted. In their original state, silk filaments are covered by a gummy substance. When the gum is removed, the silk loses about 25% of its weight. This weight can be replaced by putting the silk in a solution of metallic salts. Pure silk, all silk, pure silk-dye, and silk are terms that describe an all-silk fabric that contains no metallic weightings and contains no more than 10% (by weight) of dyes or finished materials. Pure silk holds shape better and wrinkles less than weighted silk. Weighted silk has appearance and feel of pure silk, but is less expensive.	Is the strongest of the natural fibers; wears well and resists strain; is absorbent and warm; does not soil easily; resists wrinkles and is colorfast; has dimensional stability (ability of fabric to hold its shape and size after being worn, washed, and/or dry-cleaned); drapes nicely; takes dye well; luxurious hand and appearance.	Depending on the care label, silk should be hand-laundered or dry-cleaned. Iron with a warm iron on the wrong side. Use a press cloth to finish pressing seams, collars, and hems on the right side.

[1]These care instructions are general ones for the fibers listed. The care instructions on the garments' label should be followed closely.

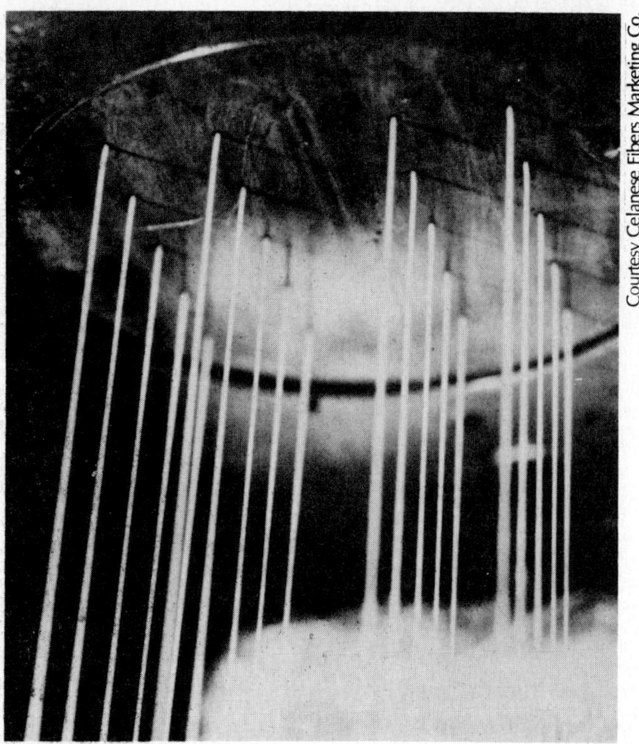

Fig. 5-2 Man-made fibers are passed through a spinnerette like the one pictured above.

used for apparel are acetate, acrylic, anidex, modacrylic, nylon, polyester, rayon, spandex, and triacetate.

There are two categories of man-made fibers: cellulose and noncellulose. Rayon, acetate, and triacetate are cellulose fibers and are made from natural substances, such as cotton linters or wood pulp. Cellulose fibers have characteristics similar to those of cotton and linen. Generally, these fibers are absorbent, easy to dye, have a high natural luster, and are economical. Table 2 details characteristics and care instructions for garments made of cellulose fibers.

Noncellulose fibers generally are thermoplastic (that is, able to be molded or shaped at high temperatures), able to withstand surface wear and rubbing, nonabsorbent, and resilient (can spring back into shape). They resist sunlight, mildew, and moths. These fibers are as strong when wet as they are when dry, and require little or no ironing after laundering. Table 3 details characteristics and care instructions for garments made of noncellulose fibers.

Today any garment can be made of either cellulose or noncellulose fibers. For example, many slips are made from rayon or triacetate or acetate, but many slips are also made from nylon and nylon/polyester blends nowadays.

TABLE 2

PRINCIPAL USES	PROPERTIES	CARE INSTRUCTIONS FOR CELLULOSE FIBERS	TRADE NAMES
ACETATE—A lustrous, silky fiber			
Dresses, blouses, foundation garments, lingerie, fashion fabrics (satin, jersey, tafetta, lace, faille, brocade, tricot, crepe)	Luxurious feel and silklike appearance; shrink-resistant; able to retain crispness; able to take beautiful color; drapes well; resists mildew and moths; fairly absorbent; wears out easily; fairly colorfast; ignites easily and not self-extinguishing; can be made flame resistant. Acetate melts at 500°. Nail polish, paint remover, and some perfumes dissolve acetate fibers.	Some acetate fabrics must be dry-cleaned. Others can be home laundered. If home laundered, hand-wash using warm water, mild soap, gentle agitation. Do not soak, wring out, or twist. Iron with cool iron; a safe ironing temperature is 250°-300°. Press garment while damp on wrong side. If pressed on right side, use a press cloth. If iron is too warm, may put a shine on the fabric. Let dry on nonrust hanger.	Acele Ariloft Avisco Celaloft Celanese Celaperm Celara Celatress Chromspun Estron Loftura
RAYON—Combines well with many other fibers (used extensively in blends)			
Dresses, blouses, suits, lingerie, coats, slacks, ties, lining fabrics	Very absorbent (cool); comfortable; drapes well; easy to dye; durable; not elastic (does not go back into shape when stretched); wrinkles easily unless it has resin finish; brushed or napped fabrics are flammable; can be made flame-resistant; will shrink unless has shrink-resistant finish.	Rayon can be washed by hand, machine-washed and tumble-dried, or dry-cleaned, depending on care label. If not handled carefully, may stretch when wet. Do not wring or twist when wet. It may shrink or lose finish if washed or dried at high temperatures. Rayon will scorch, but not melt if iron is too hot.	Avril Coloray Enkrome Fibro Jetspan Nupron Zantrel
TRIACETATE—Similar to acetate, but can withstand higher temperatures			
Bonded and tricot fabrics, permanently pleated garments	Resists heat and wrinkles and shrinking; holds pleats; wears out easily; easily washed; stronger than acetate; can withstand higher temperatures.	Most garments made of 100 percent triacetate can be machine-washed and -dried. If ironing is necesary, a hot iron can be used (450°).	Arnel

TABLE 3

PRINCIPAL USES	PROPERTIES	CARE INSTRUCTIONS FOR NON-CELLULOSE FIBERS	TRADE NAMES
ACRYLIC—A fiber with wool-like and easy care qualities			
Dresses, sweaters, skirts, suits, socks, fleece and pile fabrics	Soft; provides warmth without weight; shrink-resistant; strong; wrinkle-resistant; low absorbency; quick drying; subject to static buildup; ignites and burns easily; subject to pilling (little balls forming on surface).	Can be machine-washed and tumble-dried at low temperature. Remove garments from dryer as soon as tumbling is done. If ironing is necessary, use a moderately warm iron, not hot iron. Sweaters should be dried on a flat surface. Acrylic fabrics should be brushed if they get fuzzy.	Acrilan Anywear Colacril Creslon Orlon Zefran
ANIDEX—An elastic fiber commonly combined with other natural man-made fibers			
Dresses, suits, coats, shirts, blouses, sweaters, rainwear, jackets, slacks, lingerie, underwear, foundation garments	Permanent stretch and recovery; improves garment's fit and comfort while reducing sagging or bagging; no rubbery feeling; does not ignite easily, but will burn when ignited; flammability is dependent on other fibers with which it is combined.	Anidex is often blended with other fibers; follow care label for companion fibers. Can be home laundered or dry-cleaned. Machine-wash and tumble-dry at "normal" setting. Can use chlorine bleach. Safe ironing temperature is 320°F.	Anim/8
MODACRYLIC—A modified acrylic fiber with many properties similar to those of acrylic			
Deep pile coats, trims and linings, fleece fabrics	Soft and warm; long wearing; flame-resistant (generally self-extinguishing); quick drying; colorfast; softens at low temperatures; shrinks at 260°F.	Machine-wash in warm water and tumble-dry at low temperatures. Remove from dryer as soon as tumbling stops. Use low setting if ironing is necessary. Deep pile should be dry cleaned. No ironing for 100 percent modacrylic.	Dynel Elura SEF Verel
NYLON—A very versatile and strong fiber			
Hosiery, dresses, lingerie, underwear, suits, stretch fabrics	Exceptionally strong; keeps its shape; elastic; easily dyes; smooth; durable; low in moisture absorbency; dries fast; lustrous; easy to wash; woven fabrics sometimes hot and uncomfortable to wear; does not ignite easily, but when ignited will burn, melt, and drip.	Most items made from nylon can be machine-washed and tumble-dried at low temperature (fabric softener will prevent static cling); can be bleached with chlorine; requires little or no ironing; wash delicate items by hand in warm water and mild soap; wash whites separately.	Actionwear Anso Antron Bodyfree Cantrece Caprolan Celanelse Crepeset Enkaloft Nomex, Qiana
POLYESTER—Used extensively in blends with other fibers (especially wool and cotton)			
Permanent press apparel	Resists wrinkles; shrinkage, stretching, surface wear, and pilling; strong; holds pleats and creases well; easily washed; quick drying; colorfast; needs little or no ironing; does not ignite easily; but when ignited will burn, melt, and drip. Can look like wool, silk, cotton.	Wash delicate garments by hand in warm water and mild soap. Gently squeeze out water, smooth or shake out garment, and let dry on nonrust hanger; most polyester items can be machine-washed. Use warm water and add fabric softener to rinse cycle. Set dryer low and remove as soon as tumbling is done. Use warm iron, if ironing is necessary; may be dry-cleaned.	Avlin Dacron Encron Fortrel Kodel Trevira Vycron
SPANDEX—Few garments are made of 100 percent spandex; only small amount is needed to give garment necessary holding power			
Girdles, bras, swim suits, ski pants, support and surgical hose, elastic waist bands	Elasticity (recovers shape after being stretched); extremely strong; lightweight; yellows with age at temperatures above 300°F.	Can be hand- or machine-washed in warm water. Drip dry or tumble-dry low. Can be ironed at low temperature. Do not use chlorine bleach on any fabric containing spandex.	Glaspan Lycron Spandelle Unel Vyrene

GOVERNMENT REGULATION OF FIBER IDENTIFICATION

Until recently, it was difficult to determine the fibers in a fabric used to make a garment. That's why the government requires garment manufacturers to attach labels that state the fiber content in a garment. The Textile Fiber Products Identification Act (TFPIA), effective since 1960, requires all textile merchandise to carry a label that shows:

1. The generic names of the fibers in the fabric in the order of their proportion. (A **generic name** is a standard term describing the fiber.) Polyester (a man-made fiber) and cotton (a natural fiber) are examples of generic names. The companies that produce these fibers are also allowed to include their trade name on the label. For example, Dacron polyester is a polyester fiber made by Du Pont. Fortrel polyester is made by the Celanese Corporation. Dacron and Fortrel are trade names.
2. The percentage of each fiber in the fabric.

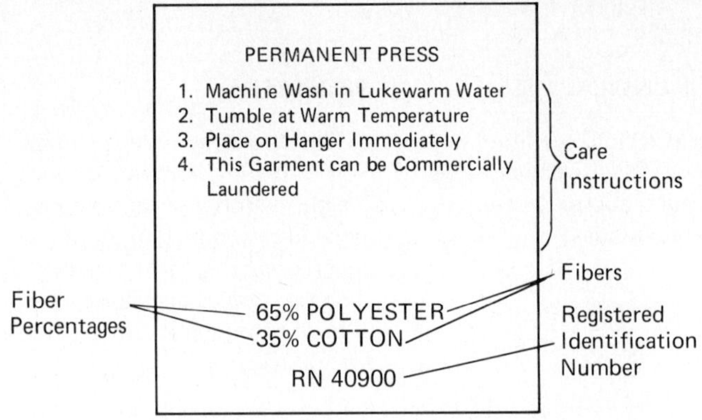

Fig. 5-3 Here's a typical apparel label.

3. The garment manufacturer's name, address, or registered identification number.
4. The country of origin of imported fibers.

The Federal Trade Commission's Trade Regulation Rule on Care Labeling requires apparel to have care and maintenance labels. (See Figure 5-3 and Table 4.)

TABLE 4

Explanation of care label instructions

WHEN LABEL READS:	IT MEANS:
MACHINE-WASHABLE	
Machine wash	Wash, bleach, dry, and press by any customary method including commercial laundering and dry cleaning.
Home launder only	Same as above but do not use commercial laundering.
No chlorine bleach	Do not use chlorine bleach. Oxygen bleach may be used.
No bleach	Do not use any type of bleach.
Cold wash Cold rinse	Use cold water from tap or cold washing machine setting.
Warm wash Warm rinse	Use warm water or warm washing machine setting.
Hot wash	Use hot water or hot washing machine setting.
No spin	Remove wash load before final machine spin cycle.
Delicate cycle Gentle cycle	Use appropriate machine setting; otherwise, wash by hand.
Durable press cycle Permanent press cycle	Use appropriate machine setting; otherwise, use warm wash, cold rinse, and short spin cycle.
Wash separately	Wash alone or with like colors.
NONMACHINE WASHING	
Hand-wash	Launder only by hand in lukewarm (hand comfortable) water. May be bleached. May be dry-cleaned.
Hand-wash only	Same as above, but do not dry-clean.
Hand-wash separately	Hand-wash alone or with like colors.
No bleach	Do not use bleach.
Damp wipe	Surface clean with damp cloth or sponge.

WHEN LABEL READS:	IT MEANS:
HOME DRYING	
Tumble dry	Dry in tumble dryer at specified setting—high, medium, low, or no heat.
Tumble dry Remove promptly	Same as above, but in absence of cool-down cycle remove at once when tumbling stops.
Drip dry	Hang wet and allow to dry with hand shaping only.
Line dry	Hang damp and allow to dry.
No wring No twist	Hang dry, drip dry, or dry flat only. Handle to prevent wrinkles and distortion.
Dry flat	Lay garment on flat surface.
Block to dry	Maintain original size and shape while drying.
IRONING OR PRESSING	
Cool iron	Set iron at lowest setting.
Warm iron	Set iron at medium setting.
Hot iron	Set iron at hot setting.
Do not iron	Do not iron or press with heat.
Steam iron	Iron or press with steam.
Iron damp	Dampen garment before ironing
MISCELLANEOUS	
Dry-clean only	Garment should be dry-cleaned only, including self-service.
Professionally dry-clean only	Do not use self-service dry cleaning.
No dry-clean	Use recommended care instructions. No dry-cleaning materials to be used.

(**Source:** *Consumer Affairs Committee, American Apparel Manufacturers Association, based on the Voluntary Guide of the Textile Industry Advisory Committee for Consumer Interests.*)

Experience 5-1

Naturals and Synthetics

1. With two to four classmates, visit a local fabric store when the store is not busy. Have one of the students explain to the manager that you are studying fabrics. Ask if you may have a small swatch of fabric made from each of the following fibers. Have another student attach each fabric to a separate sheet of paper and label each. Also ask the manager for the care labels for each fabric or copy the care information onto your papers. The care information is found on the top of each fabric bolt.

100 percent cotton	100 percent modacrylic
100 percent wool	100 percent nylon
100 percent silk	100 percent polyester
100 percent linen	100 percent rayon
100 percent acetate	100 percent spandex
100 percent acrylic	100 percent triacetate

2. In class, let all the students carefully examine the labeled fabric samples and care information. On a separate sheet of paper, describe each fabric.

Experience 5-2

Check the Label

Examine 13 different clothing items. Check the labels that describe the fiber content and care requirements. You may use your own clothing or visit an apparel store to locate these items. Complete the following chart.

Clothing Item	Fiber Content	Care Specifications
1.		
2.		
3.		
4.		
5.		
6.		
7.		
8.		
9.		
10.		
11.		
12.		
13.		

YARNS

The wear, appearance, and texture of a fabric depend upon the fabric's yarn. A yarn is a continuous thread formed by twisting or spinning strands of fibers together. (See Figure 5-4.) Yarns differ because of their twist, ply, and size.

TWIST OF THE YARN

Fibers are twisted into yarn. Yarn that is tightly twisted is stronger than yarn that is loosely twisted. Although tightly twisted yarn is more durable, it may also be more scratchy than loosely twisted yarn. Satin is an example of loosely twisted yarn; crepe yarn is an example of tightly twisted yarn.

PLY OF THE YARN

Ply refers to the number of strands that are twisted together to make the yarn. Single ply describes fibers twisted together to form a single yarn. By twisting together two single yarns, the yarn becomes two ply. A

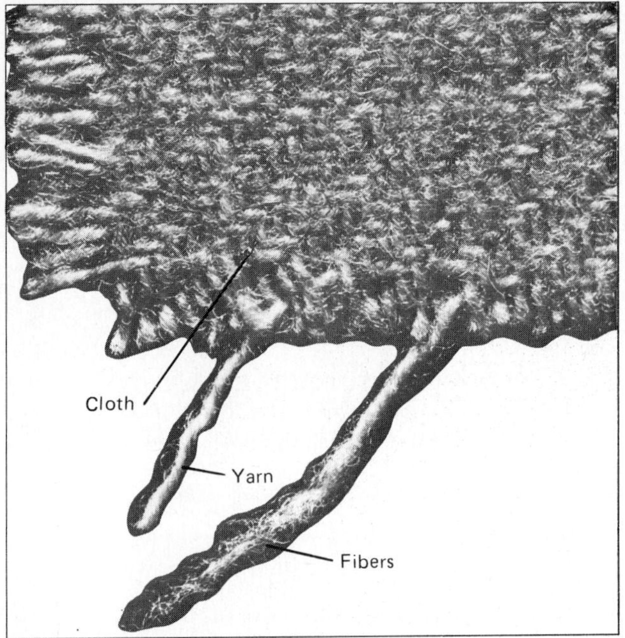

Fig. 5-4 Many strands of fibers twisted or spun together form a thread of yarn.

two-ply yarn is stronger than a single yarn of the same thickness and weight. Ply yarns are often used for fabrics that will get hard wear.

SIZE OF THE YARN

Denier and count refer to the size of yarn. **Denier** describes the thickness and diameter of longer-fibered, filament yarns. The finer the yarn, the smaller the denier number. For example, hosiery with a 10 denier is finer than hosiery with a 30 denier.

Count describes the thickness and diameter of short-fibered yarns, such as cotton. The higher the count number, the finer the yarn. For example, a 10S wool yarn is 10 times as fine as a 1S wool yarn. ("S" refers to single yarn.)

TYPES OF YARN

Yarn can be made from any fiber—natural, man-made, or a blend. How the yarn is constructed and the characteristics of the yarn depend on the fibers used.

Cotton Cotton comes from the cotton plant. Cotton fibers are the long strands attached to the seed inside the boll, or seed pod. When the boll reaches maturity, it bursts open and exposes the cotton, which is picked. The cotton gin removes the seeds from the cotton.

Before cotton fibers are spun or twisted into yarn, they are cleaned and carded. **Carding** is a process of straightening fibers. All cotton is carded. Some cotton goes through another process called **combing** to remove the short fibers. Combed yarns are finer and stronger than ones that are only carded and are used in higher-quality fabrics.

Linen Flax is a fiber that comes from the flax plant. Linen is the yarn or fabric processed from flax. Like the cotton plant, the flax plant produces both long and short fibers. Yarn that includes both the short and long fibers is called **tow linen**. Yarn that includes only the long fibers is called **line linen**. A tow-linen yarn is similar to a carded cotton; a line-linen yarn may be compared to a carded and combed cotton. Line linen is used for higher-quality linen fabrics.

Wool Wool, which comes from the fleece of sheep, is spun into two types of yarn: **worsted** and **woolen**. (See Figure 5-5.) Worsteds are produced by carding and combing wool fibers. Worsteds are firmer, more durable, and take a sharper crease than woolens. Woolens are made from wool yarns containing both long and short fibers. The fibers are carded but not combed. Woolens have a fuzzy surface, are soft, and resist wrinkling. They are warmer than worsteds but do not hold a sharp crease.

Silk Silk comes from the cocoons of silk worms. There are two kinds of silk fibers: reeled and spun. **Reeled silk** comes from unbroken silkworm cocoons. These long, strong, smooth fibers make the finest grade of silk. **Spun silk** is made from the shorter fibers and wastes of broken cocoons. Spun silk is not as smooth and does not have the elasticity, strength, or luster of reeled silk yarn. It has a "cottony" feel.

Man-Made Basically, there are two kinds of man-made fiber yarns: filament yarn and spun yarn. **Filament yarn** is made by twisting two or more strands of continuous monofilament fibers together. Filament yarn is smoother, more lustrous, and less inclined to pill—form small balls—than spun yarn. **Spun yarn** is made by twisting together shorter lengths of man-made fibers. Spun yarn is usually warmer than filament yarn because air is trapped in the short fibers. It has a fuzzy or fluffy surface. Spun yarn takes longer to dry than filament yarn.

Texturized yarns combine the good features of both filament and spun yarns. Texturized yarns are made from filament yarns, but they look like spun yarns. They have a rougher texture than spun yarns, but give greater weight and resist pilling because they have fewer fiber ends.

Fig. 5-5 Compare the woolen and worsted fibers illustrated above.

Experience 5-3

How to Make Yarn

1. Using the fibers in a cotton ball, make a two-ply yarn. Pull out four cotton fibers and loosely twist two of the fibers together. Tightly twist the other two fibers together. Break both yarns. Which yarn took the most strength to break?

   ____

2. Using the same cotton ball, make a two-ply, four-ply, and six-ply yarn. Tightly twist each yarn. Break each yarn. Which yarn took the most strength to break?

   ____

3. Locate the following yarns: single ply, two ply, four ply. (You can probably find these yarns at home or get them from a friend who knits or crochets.) Unravel a small section of each yarn and find the single fibers that make up the yarn. Break a small piece of each yarn. Which yarn was most difficult to break?

   ____

4. If you were purchasing a pair of work pants, would you want pants made of two-ply fabric or pants made of four-ply fabric? Why?

   ____

   ____

   If you were purchasing a lace blouse, would you buy a blouse made of single-ply yarn or a blouse made of eight-ply yarn? Why?

   ____

   ____

FABRIC CONSTRUCTION

In the construction process, yarns are made into fabrics. Yarns may be woven, knitted, felted, bonded, or laminated. Weaving and knitting are the two most popular methods.

WEAVING

Weaving, which is the interlacing of yarns at right angles, is done on a machine called a **loom**. The loom is prepared with lengthwise yarns, called warp yarns. Crosswise yarns, called woof, weft, or filling yarns, are interlaced over and under the warp yarns. (See Figure 5-6.) Woven fabrics are usually firm, strong, and keep their shape. They withstand friction, drape well, and launder well. There are three basic fabric weaves: plain, twill, and satin. All three weaves differ in appearance, even if they are made of the same fibers.

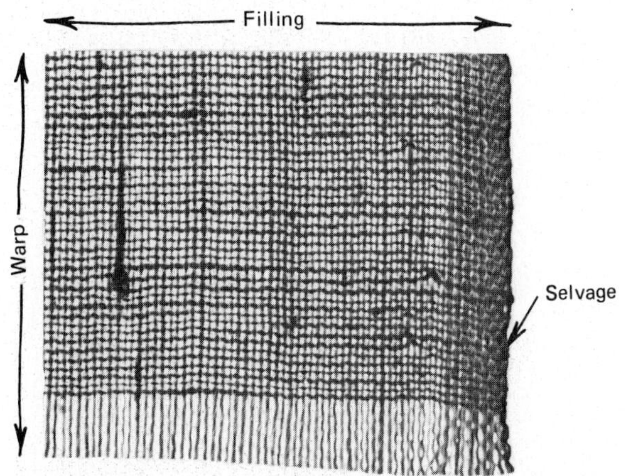

Fig. 5-6 Woven fabrics have warp (lengthwise) and filling (crosswise) yarns. Selvage is the finished edge.

Source: American Textile Manufacturers Institute, Inc.

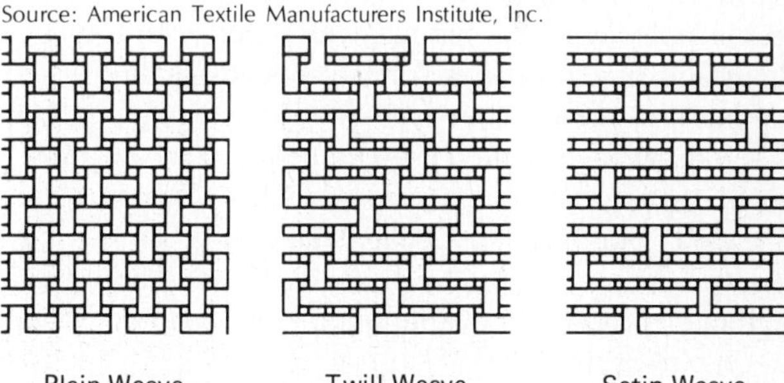

Fig. 5-7 Notice how the warp and filling yarns are interlaced in these three popular weaves.

Plain Weave The plain weave is the most basic of all weaves, with one filling yarn going over and under one warp yarn. Examples of fabrics with the plain weave are gingham, percale, chambray, chintz, and muslin. (See Figure 5-7.)

The basket weave and rib weave are variations of the plain weave. In the basket weave, two or more filling yarns are passed over one or more warp yarns. Oxford cloth, a fabric used for shirts, is an example of the basket weave. (See Figure 5-8.) In the rib weave, heavier yarns are used in the warp or filling or both. There is a ribbed, corded, or crossbar effect in the plain weave. Broadcloth and poplin are examples of fabrics with the rib weave. (See Figure 5-9.)

Twill Weave The design of the twill weave fabric has diagonal ridges, called "wales." The twill weave is formed by passing a filling yarn over and under one, two, or three warp yarns, lapping back one warp yarn in each line. The twill weave is very strong and resists

Fig. 5-8 In this basket weave, two filling yarns are passed over and under two warp yarns.

Fig. 5-9 Heavier yarns are used in a rib weave than in a basket weave as seen at left.

wear. Gabardine, flannel, and denim are examples of twill weave fabrics. Herringbone is a variation of the twill weave in which the twill reverses its direction. (See Figure 5-7.)

Satin Weave In the satin weave, either warp or filling yarns float over the surface. The satin weave reflects light and has a lustrous surface. Because satin weaves are easily snagged, they have limited wearing qualities. The satin weave is often used for coat linings and formal wear. Satin and sateen are examples of fabrics constructed with the satin weave. (See Figure 5-7.)

Other Weaves Other variations on the common weaves are as follows:

Pile. Formed by interlacing three sets of yarns. Two sets of yarn are used to form the background and a third set (cut or uncut) is used to give a three-dimensional quality. Examples of the pile weave are corduroy, terrycloth, velveteen, velvet, and velour.

Figured. Created when simple or complex designs are woven into the fabrics. Brocade, damask, and tapestry are examples of figured weaves.

Lino. Created by twisting warp yarns like a figure eight and passing a filling yarn through the loops made by the twisted warp yarns. The lino weave has an open, lacy appearance. Some fabrics constructed with the lino weave are gauze and marquisette.

Experience 5-4

A WEAVE . . . IS A WEAVE . . . IS A WEAVE?

1. Select two to four classmates to visit a local fabric store at a time when the store is not busy. Have one of the students explain to the manager that you are studying fabrics. Ask if you may have at least three different swatches of each of these types: a plain weave, a twill weave, a satin weave. Try to collect as many swatches as possible. Attach each swatch to a separate sheet of paper. Label each.
2. In class, let all the students carefully examine the labeled fabric samples. On a separate sheet of paper, each student should write a short description of how each fabric feels and looks.

KNITTING

Knitting is the looping of yarns together to form a fabric. For apparel use, knit fabrics are more popular than woven fabrics. Knits are known for their give; they are comfortable to wear because they stretch as the body moves. They are warmer than wovens of the same weight and are porous, lightweight, and absorbent. Knits are good for trips because they pack easily and resist wrinkles. To prevent stretching, they should be folded and stored in a drawer rather than on a hanger.

When washed, knits stretch and shrink more than wovens. They are also easier to snag and are subject to pilling. If the knit fabric is made of polyester, nylon, acrylic, or other heat-set fibers, it will usually return to its orginal shape when washed.

There are two basic categories of knits: warp knits and weft knits. Both knits are made on special knitting machines. Each type of knit can be identified by examining the fabric to see in which direction the yarn runs. (See Figure 5-10.)

Warp Knits In warp knitting, the yarns run down the length of the fabric. Warp knit fabrics stretch mainly in width. They are stronger, firmer, and more resistant to snags than filling knits. Warp knits do not easily run or ravel when a thread is broken. Lingerie and velour fabrics are often warp knit.

Weft Knits In weft or filling knits, yarns run across the width of the fabric. This knit creates fabrics that are very elastic and stretch in width and length. Hand-knitting, with the plain, purl, and rib stitches is a filling knit. Double-knit fabrics are a type of filling knit construction. In a double knit, there are two interlocked layers that cannot be separated. Double knits have a built-in stability and do not sag, stretch, or wrinkle easily.

Fig. 5-10 Compare the interlocking of the yarns in the weft knit (left) with those in the warp knit (right).

Experience 5-5

Knitting Versus Weaving: What Are the Benefits?

Bring to class a knit shirt and a woven shirt. Play the role of a shirt salesperson. Have another person role play a customer interested in buying a shirt. Explain to this customer the advantages of buying a knit shirt and the advantages of buying a woven shirt. Be prepared to answer the customer's questions. If possible, use a tape recorder to record the discussion about the knit shirt and the woven shirt.

OTHER FABRIC CONSTRUCTION METHODS

Some fabrics are made directly from fibers rather than yarns. Felting and bonding are some examples of these other fabric construction methods.

Felting Felting is the interlocking of fibers by heat, moisture, and pressure to form a compact fabric. Because the fibers are not securely fastened together, felted fabrics are not strong as woven or knitted fabrics. However, because they have no threads, felted fabrics do not ravel. Easily shaped, felted fabrics are used to make hats.

Bonding In bonding, fibers are joined together by adhesive. Natural fibers, man-made fibers, or blends may be made into bonded fabrics. Bonded fabrics are often used for interfacings, which add body and shape to collars, lapels, cuffs, pocket flaps, and waistbands.

FABRIC FINISHES

A fabric finish is a treatment that changes the fabric's behavior or appearance. Fabric finishes make cloth look better, feel better, give better service, and be easier to care for.

FINISHES THAT IMPROVE A FABRIC'S APPEARANCE

Some finishes that make a fabric more attractive are:

Bleaching. Makes a fabric white.
Brushing. Raises a fabric's fibers and gives the fabric a fuzzy look.
Calendering. Makes a fabric's surface flatter, smoother, and glossier, producing a satiny look.
Dyeing. Adds color to a fabric.
Embossing. Adds a surface design.
Mercerizing. Adds shine and luster to the fabric.
Moireing. Gives the fabric a watermarked appearance.
Singing. Removes the fabric's fuzz and makes the fabric smoother.

Man-made fibers can be dyed before they come out of the spinnerette; this is called solution dyeing. Stock dyeing is the dyeing of fibers while they are still loose fibers. Yarn dyeing is the dyeing of yarn before it is spun into cloth. Piece dyeing is the dyeing of an entire fabric after it is woven or knitted. Piece dyeing is the most used dyeing method today and the most economical.

Customers want the clothing they purchase to be colorfast, which means they want the color to be permanent and resist fading. Some garments are colorfast in soap and water, but may fade when exposed to sunlight, dry-cleaning fluids, perspiration, or certain chemicals. Solution-dyed garments are the most colorfast; piece-dyed garments are the least colorfast. Specific colorfast information should be listed on the garment label.

FINISHES THAT IMPROVE A FABRIC'S HAND

A fabric's **hand**, or feel, can be changed or improved by the following finishes:

Sizing. Adds weight, stiffness, and firmness to fabrics. (Sizing may not be permanent; many sizing finishes come out in laundering.)
Weighting. Adds a heavy feeling and stiffness to fabrics; silk and linen are often weighted.

FINISHES THAT MAKE A FABRIC MORE SERVICEABLE

Some finishes that help fabrics provide longer, more comfortable and safer wear are:

Antistatic. Controls or prevents static electricty "cling."
Flame-retardant. Makes fabrics ignite and burn slowly. (Children's sleepwear must pass government flame-retardant regulations.)
Insulating. Provides warmth or coolness, depending on the weather.
Mildew-resistant. Prevents mildew.
Moth-resistant. Makes wool fabrics immune to moths.
Water-repellent. Resists water but allows for the passage of air.
Waterproof. Allows no water or air to pass through the fabric.

Courtesy E. I. Du Pont de Nemours, Co., Inc.

Fig. 5-11 What are the special qualities of the fabric finish shown on this label?

FINISHES THAT MAKE A FABRIC "EASY CARE"

Some of the most well-known finishes today make it easier for consumers to care for their clothes:

Crease resistance. Helps such fabrics as linen, cotton, and rayon to resist creasing and lose their wrinkles after hanging.
Permanent Press. Allows a fabric to be machine-washed and dryed and worn without any ironing. Permanent press fabrics keep their sharp crease and do not wrinkle as easily as other fabrics without this finish. They shrink very little and do not get dirty as quickly as other fabrics. Permanent press fabrics are treated with special resin finishes. These fabrics cannot be washed in very hot water, dryed at high temperatures, chlorine bleached, or starched because the resin finish will be lost.
Shrinkage Control. Keeps a fabric from losing its shape. There are two types of shrinkage control; **preshrunk** and **Sanforized**. If a garment label says preshrunk, it means the fabric may shrink up to 3 percent of its size. This amount of shrinkage will affect the comfort and fit of the garment. (Shrunk and preshrunk mean the same thing.) A garment that carries a Sanforized label means the fabric was shrunk before it was made into a garment. This label is the manufacturer's guarantee that the fabric will not shrink more than 1 percent or one-third of an inch per yard. One percent shrinkage does not noticeably affect the fit of the garment either in the waist or the length.

Some fabric finishes, like embossing, are easily identified. Salespersons and customers may have a difficult time identifying many of the other less obvious fabric finishes, such as stain-repellent or fire-retardant finishes. Quality garments may mention the fabric finishes on their labels. (See Figure 5-11.) Often, however, garments only have care labels, with no exact description of the fabric finish. Only a few finishes are permanent; most can be destroyed through improper care and laundering. That's why it is important to read the care labels for all fabrics to learn how to care for them properly.

Experience 5-6

Investigation: Fabric Finishes

Visit an apparel shop or department store and locate ten hangtags on men's, women's, or children's clothes. On a separate sheet of paper, copy the hangtag information. Underline all information that refers to fabric finishes. Indicate whether the finish improves the fabric's appearance, hand, serviceability, or care.

Experience 5-7

What Should You Say When Customers Ask?

As an apparel salesperson, you will be expected to answer customer questions. The following are some typical customer questions about fabric finishes. Write your answers to these questions on a separate sheet of paper.

1. How much will these denim pants shrink? The label says preshrunk.
2. What's the difference between these two raincoats? The beige is water-repellent; the yellow one is waterproof.
3. The label on this silk blouse says it is weighted. What does that mean?
4. This tag says the sizing is permanent. Aren't all sizings permanent?
5. I've heard a lot about flame-retardant sleepwear for children. Does that mean the sleepwear won't burn?
6. This cotton fabric is so shiny that there must be a special finish on it. What do you think that finish could be?
7. How should I wash and dry this cotton/polyester shirt? The label says it's permanent press.
8. This brand of boys' pants cost $2 more than another brand and the only difference I can find is that the more expensive pants are Sanforized. Does that really make a difference?
9. This tag says the garment is colorfast. What does that mean?

THE FINISHED FABRIC

As was mentioned earlier in this chapter, a finished fabric has four characteristics: fiber, yarn, fabric construction, and finishes. For example, broadcloth is a finished fabric. It may be made of cotton *fiber,* the *yarn* may be two ply, and it is *woven* in a ribweave. Sometimes, this type of cloth is given a mercerized *finish* to increase the luster.

There are many fabrics in our wardrobes today. The list of common fabrics on page 68 gives many clothing fabrics and typical garments these fabrics are used to make. At any one time, not all these fabrics may be popular or fashionable. In the 1970s, for example, denim and chambray reached a high level of acceptance for many garments. At one time, these fabrics were used only for workclothes.

Experience 5-8

Spotting the Fashion Fabrics

1. Look through local clothing store catalogs or newspaper ads. Cut out ten descriptions of garments that mention a particular fabric. Attach them to a separate sheet of paper; underline the fabric's name.
2. Look through newspapers, fashion magazines, or clothing catalogs for the past winter and summer seasons. (You can find old newspapers and magazines at a local library.) On a separate sheet of paper, classify the fabrics in these ads. On this same sheet of paper, make a list of five winter fabrics and five summer fabrics. What were the three most popular fabrics of each season?

Experience 5-9

Your Own Fashion Vocabulary

Develop a vocabulary list of fabric terms. Using this chapter and other books or resources, prepare a list of words and definitions about fabrics. Organize your words and definitions into the following sections: (1) words about fibers, (2) words about yarn, (3) words about weaving, (4) words about knitting, (5) words about dyeing, (6) words about finishes, and (7) words about care of fabrics.

Arrange your list in alphabetical order. Refer to your list when you hear or see a fabric term that is unfamiliar. When you come across new fabric terms, add them to your list.

A LIST OF COMMON FABRICS

Batiste: A fine, thin, plain weave fabric. It generally has a soft texture, but it can have a crisper feel. It is usually made of cotton, but can be made of blends (polyester and cotton), wool, silk, rayon, polyester, and linen. It is used for linings, infant's wear, dresses, blouses, shirts, and lingerie.

Challis: A soft, lightweight, plain or perhaps twill weave fabric of wool, cotton, or man-made fibers. It usually has small floral designs. It is used for infants' wear for special occasions, pajamas, dresses, blouses, and shawls for infants and adults.

Chambray: A balanced, plain weave cotton fabric with a frosted appearance achieved by the use of colored warps and white filling. It is usually plain colored but may be striped or patterned. Fancy chambray may have small dobby designs (small figured designs) woven in the fabric. It is used for dresses, sportswear, pajamas, and shirting in lighter weights. The heavier weights are used for work clothes.

Chiffon: A soft, lightweight, sheer, plain weave silk or man-made fiber (often rayon) fabric. Fine, hard spun (highly twisted) yarns in a balanced weave are used. It is used for formal dresses.

Corduroy: A filling cut pile fabric with either narrow or wide wales of pile running the lengthwise direction of the fabric. The background weave may be either plain or twill weave. This was originally a cotton fabric, but man-made fibers are now sometimes used. Corduroy may be solid colored or printed. It is the traditional fall sportswear fabric for men, women, and children.

Covert: A medium-weight, closely woven, hard-surfaced twill fabric that has a mottled or mixed color effect in grays, tans, or blues. Cotton, wool, or wool blends are the fibers used. It is used for raincoats, work clothing, and sportswear.

Crepe: A large class of fabrics that have crinkled or grained surface effects. Most crepes are made in plain weave with highly twisted yarns used in either warp or filling directions or both. Rayon is the commonest fiber used, but silk, cotton, worsted, and man-made fibers may be used. True crepes usually require dry-cleaning to avoid excessive shrinkage.

Denim: A strong, yarn-dyed cotton fabric made in a warp-faced twill weave. Various colored yarns may be used for the warps, but white or unbleached yarns are commonly used for the fillings. Heavy denims are used for work clothes, while lighter-weight denims, called sport denims, are used for sportswear.

Double knit: A knit fabric made with two sets of needles, which gives a knit with a firm body and less stretchiness. A common stitch is the double pique stitch, which has a subtle diamond effect surface. Cotton, wool, acrylic, polyester, acetate, and silk have been used in double-knit fabrics. Double knits are used for women's suits, dresses, and sportswear.

Gabardine: A tightly woven, durable warp-faced twill fabric that has a steep twill line and a clear finish. It is made of wool, cotton, silk, and man-made staple fibers in solid colors. Gabardine is used for sportswear, suits, uniforms, and raincoats for men, women, children.

Jersey: A general term for a plain knitted fabric that does not have a distinct rib. It may be plain, printed, or embroidered. Jersey is used for dresses, coats, men's underwear, T-shirts, children's clothes, women's lingerie, and blouses.

Lace: An open-work fabric produced by a network of threads twisted or knotted together. It is made of linen, cotton, nylon, and other fibers. It is used for wedding or other formal dresses, lingerie, scarfs, and trimming.

Organdy: A fine, sheer, plain weave cotton fabric with a very crisp, clear finish. Most organdy has a permanent crisp finish that is done by a chemical treatment. It is used for women's and girls' summer blouses and dresses.

Satin: A smooth, usually lustrous fabric made of filament fibers, such as silk, acetate, or rayon, in a satin weave. It is used for evening dresses.

Seersucker: A medium-weight fabric with lengthwise, permanent, crinkle stripes woven into the fabric in a plain weave. It is made of 100 percent cotton or blends of cotton with man-made fibers, such as polyester, rayon, or acetate in stripes, checks, and plaids. Seersucker is used for men's and women's suits and for sportswear.

Serge: A clear-finished, even twill with a pronounced diagonal rib on both the right and wrong side. It is usually woolen or worsted but is also made of cotton, silk, man-mades, or blends. Serge is used for men's and women's suits and raincoats.

Terry cloth: An uncut pile weave fabric with loops on one or both sides of the fabric. It is made of all cotton or blends of cotton with man-made fibers, such as rayon or stretch nylon, and is used for beach wear and baby clothes.

*(Source: **Fibers & Fabrics,** University of Texas, Austin, Texas.)*

For more information about fabrics, see Chapter 7, page 90.

Experience 5-10

Fabric Details

Choose three fabrics mentioned in this chapter. Visit a clothing or fabric store and locate these fabrics. Complete the following chart.

Description	Fabric 1	Fabric 2	Fabric 3
Name			
Fiber content			
Weight (lightweight, etc.)			
Care instructions			
Available colors			
List five garments that could be made from this fabric			
List two main selling benefits for each of the fabrics (Example: easy care)			

6 Women's Wear

Suppose you've just started work as a sales trainee in women's apparel at a store called Manuel's. What information do you immediately need to meet your new responsibilities? Working with women's apparel requires knowledge of the many styles, sizes, and fabrics on the market. Customers will appreciate your suggestions on proper fit, garments that are attractive for their figure type, and how to coordinate accessories.

WOMEN'S APPAREL SIZES

As sales trainee, you need to learn much about women's apparel. You need to know that women's clothing is available in many size groupings—junior, misses, women's, and women's half sizes. You will soon find out that not all manufacturers produce clothing in a complete size range. Also, the sizes may vary by manufacturer. A size 8 for one manufacturer may be too tight on a customer, while a size 8 from another manufacturer may fit perfectly. Whatever size grouping a customer is in, proper fit is important.

CHOOSING THE RIGHT SIZE

When helping women choose apparel, you should know the "most important" measurement. If a garment fits the customer's "most important" measurement, it will be comfortable, attractive, and fit well. For example, for pants or skirts, the most important measurement is the hip measurement. If a customer has 35-inch hips, size 9 pants should fit her (see Table 1). For shirts, sweaters, jackets, vests, jumpers, or coats, the most important measurement is the bust measurement. The bust, waist, and hip measurements are all important when fitting a dress or suit.

When a customer is unsure of which size she wears, find out the item the customer wants to purchase. Next, determine the most important measurement for that particular apparel item. Because the most important measurement for a skirt is the hips, measure the customer's hips with a measuring tape. After measuring the customer, locate her measurement on a size chart (see Tables 1 to 4) and then show her that size clothing.

JUNIOR SIZES

Your store, Manuel's, has a special department for junior and junior petite clothing. This department sells sportswear, dresses, and coats for junior-sized customers.

Junior sizes usually range from 3 to 15, although some stores stock sizes 1 and 17. (See Table 1.) Junior sizes are for women who are between 5 feet 2 inches and 5 feet 5 inches, have a small waist and small, high bustline, and have a short shoulder-to-waist measurement. Junior petite sizes are for women and teenagers who are 5 feet 1½ inches or less in stocking feet. (See Table 1.) These garments are proportionately shorter in length than those for regular juniors.

MISSES SIZES

The store you are working in also has a dress and sportswear department for women who wear misses sizes. The most popular size grouping for women, misses sizes, range from 6 to 20. Misses sizes are for women who are between 5 feet 3 inches and 5 feet 7 inches in stocking feet and have a slender to medium build. (See Table 2.) Misses clothing is broader in the shoulders, bust, and hips than junior clothing.

There are misses petite sizes for women shorter than 5 feet 3 inches. These garments are shorter in total length, including shoulder to waist. However, they fit women of the same bust, waist, and hip measurements as shown in Table 2. The size tag will indicate a misses petite size. Misses tall sizes are available for women over 5 feet 7 inches. These garments are longer in total length and longer from shoulder to waist.

TABLE 1

JUNIOR SIZES

JUNIOR SIZES: Height is 5 feet 2 inches to 5 feet 6 inches in stocking feet; smaller, more defined waist; higher bustline; slightly shorter from shoulder to waist than misses.

PETITE JUNIOR SIZES: Height is 5 feet 1½ inches and under in stocking feet. Garments are proportionately shorter in length than regular juniors.

Order Size	**3**	**5**	**7**	**9**	**11**	**13**	**15**
If bust is (in inches)	29½–30	30½–31	31½–32	32½–33½	34–35	35½–36½	37–38
If waist is (in inches)	20–20½	21–21½	22–22½	23–24	24½–25½	26–27	27½–28½
If hips are (in inches)	31½–32	32½–33	33½–34	34½–35	35½–36½	37–38	38½–39½

(Source: Sears, Roebuck and Company)

TABLE 2

MISSES SIZES

MISSES SIZES Height is 5 feet 3 inches to 5 feet 7 inches in stocking feet. For the figure of average proportions.

PETITE MISSES SIZES: Height 5 feet 3 inches or under in stocking feet. Garments are proportionately shorter in length than regular misses.

Order Size	**6**	**8**	**10**	**12**	**14**	**16**	**18**	**20**
If bust is (in Inches)	31–31½	32–32½	33–34	34½–35½	36–37	37½–38½	39–40½	41–42½
If waist is (in Inches)	22–22½	23–23½	24–25	25½–26½	27–28	28½–29½	30–31½	32–33½
If hips are (in Inches)	33–33½	34–34½	35–35½	36–37	37½–38½	39–40	40½–42	42½–44

(Source: Sears, Roebuck and Company)

WOMEN'S SIZES

Women's sizes, for women with full hips, bust, and arms, range from 38 to 50. (See Table 3.) This size range is for women between 5 feet 4 inches and 5 feet 6½ inches with a medium to heavy build. Few stores stock a complete range of women's sizes, except specialty stores. Your store does not sell women's sizes, but you must know this size range.

TABLE 3

WOMEN'S SIZES

WOMEN'S SIZES: Height is 5 feet 4 inches to 5 feet 6½ inches in stocking feet for the fuller, more mature figure. Longer from shoulder to waist and waist to hemline than half sizes.

Order Size	**46**	**48**	**50**	**52**
If bust is (in Inches)	49–50½	51–52½	53–54½	55–56½
If waist is (in Inches)	42½–44½	45–47	47½–49½	50–52
If hips are (in Inches)	49½–51	51½–53	53½–55	55½–57

(Source: Sears, Roebuck and Company)

TABLE 4

HALF SIZES

HALF SIZES: Height is 5 feet 3½ inches and under in stocking feet; medium to heavy frame; shorter from shoulder to waist than women's sizes.

Order Size	12½	14½	16½	18½	20½	22½	24½	26½
If bust is (in inches)	35–36½	37–38½	39–40½	41–42½	43–44½	45–46½	47–48½	49–50½
If waist is (in inches)	27–28½	29–30½	31–32½	33–34½	35–37	37½–39½	40–42	42½–44½
If hips are (in inches)	36–37	37½–39	39½–41	41½–43	43½–45	45½–47	47½–49	49½–51

(Source: Sears, Roebuck and Company)

HALF SIZES

Half sizes are for shorter women (under 5 feet 4 inches) with medium to heavy frame. The garments, which range in size from 12½ to 26½, are cut shorter from shoulder to waist than women's sizes. (See Table 4.) Your store does not sell half sizes, but you must be familiar with this size range.

SMALL, MEDIUM, LARGE, AND EXTRA-LARGE SIZES

Sometimes, sweaters, blouses, and body shirts are sized according to small, medium, large, and extra large rather than numbered sizes. In junior sizes, small (S) is sizes 5–7, medium (M) is sizes 9–11, and large (L) is sizes 13–15. In misses sizes, small is 8–10, medium is 12–14, large is 16–18, and extra large is 20–22.

Experience 6-1

Size Them Up

1. Estimate the height and proportions of three female classmates. Record your estimates in the following chart. Then ask each for her actual measurements. If they are not sure, use a measuring tape and yardstick to determine the accurate measurements of your classmates.

Measurements	Classmate 1		Classmate 2		Classmate 3	
	Estimate	Actual	Estimate	Actual	Estimate	Actual
Height						
Bust						
Waist						
Hips						

2. Refer to the size charts in Tables 1 to 4. Based on your three classmates' actual measurements, decide which size pants, vest, coat, and dress each wears. Record the sizes in the following chart. Check with your classmates to see if the sizes determined from the size chart are the same sizes that they last purchased in each of the items listed in the chart below.

Item	Classmate 1		Classmate 2		Classmate 3	
	Size from Chart	Size from Classmate	Size from Chart	Size from Classmate	Size from Chart	Size from Classmate
Pants						
Vest						
Coat						
Dress						

Experience 6-2

An 8 Is an 8 Is an 8

(For Female Students)

Visit a store where you usually shop and choose three similarly styled dresses in your size. Be sure each dress is made by a different manufacturer. Ask if you may try on the dresses. Note differences in fit. Does each dress fit the same in the bustline, waist, and hips? Is one cut fuller?

On a separate sheet of paper, write a short description of the dress styles and sizes you tried. Explain differences in fit of the three different dresses that you tried on. Why is it important to try on garments before purchasing them?

WOMEN'S CLOTHING STYLES

As part of your sales training your assistant manager, Mr. Hershey, wants you to visit each department in the store and prepare a list of the basic apparel styles. He explains that it's important to recognize different styles because customers and other salespeople often refer to a particular garment by its style name.

You mention your difficulty in identifying different styles to your department manager, Kate Marks. Kate says that many people have problems at first.

COAT STYLES

Kate explains that the stock of coats includes princess coats, pea coats, wraparounds, Balmacaans, Chesterfields, capes, trench coats, cape coats, and polo coats. (See Figure 6-1.) Depending on the fabric used, these

Wraparound

Pea Coat

Trench Coat

Balmacaan

Box or Chesterfield or Boy

Capecoat

Princess

Polo

Fig. 6-1 Familiarize yourself with the basic women's coat styles shown in this illustration.

coats can be worn in winter or spring and fall. The coat fabric also determines whether or not the coat has a dressy or casual look.

DRESS, SHIRT, AND SKIRT STYLES

Kate tells you that there are three basic silhouettes, or shapes for women's dresses: the bouffant (bell-shaped), the bustle (back fullness), and the straight or tubular. Each of these silhouettes comes into fashion about once every 100 years. Today, many dresses have fuller, gathered skirts, such as **dirndls**. There are also dresses with a straight look, such as the shift. Other popular dress styles are the A-line, sheath, princess, and flare. (See Figure 6-2.)

Many salespeople and customers describe dresses, blouses, and skirts by referring to various details of the garment. For example, a customer may ask for a particular dress by saying it has a jewel neckline, dolman sleeves, and full skirt. The charts in Figures 6-3 and 6-4 will help you describe a garment (not every style name is included). When you hear a style name you're not familiar with, be sure to check this chart. Try to use these style words often. Remember, customers and coworkers respect salespersons who know clothing styles.

SPORTSWEAR STYLES

Pants, shorts, and swimwear are some of the many sportswear styles women wear. Basically, women's dress pants have a straight leg or flare leg with or without cuffs. The most popular style changes with a new fashion season. Shorts are an important part of many women's wardrobes, and they come in a variety of styles. (See Figure 6-4.) There are also many swimwear styles. (See Figure 6-5.)

UNDERWEAR AND SLEEPWEAR STYLES

In the hosiery department, pantyhose, stockings, knee-highs, footsocks, tights, and leg warmers are sold. They come in many textures and colors to coordinate with every fashion look.

The lingerie department sells body suits, slips, half-slips, panties, briefs, nightgowns, pajamas, robes, lounging clothes, bras, and girdles. These garments vary in size, fabric, and style. For example, full slips are fitted according to bust measurement. Half-slips are sized petite, small, medium, large, and extra large according to waist measurement.

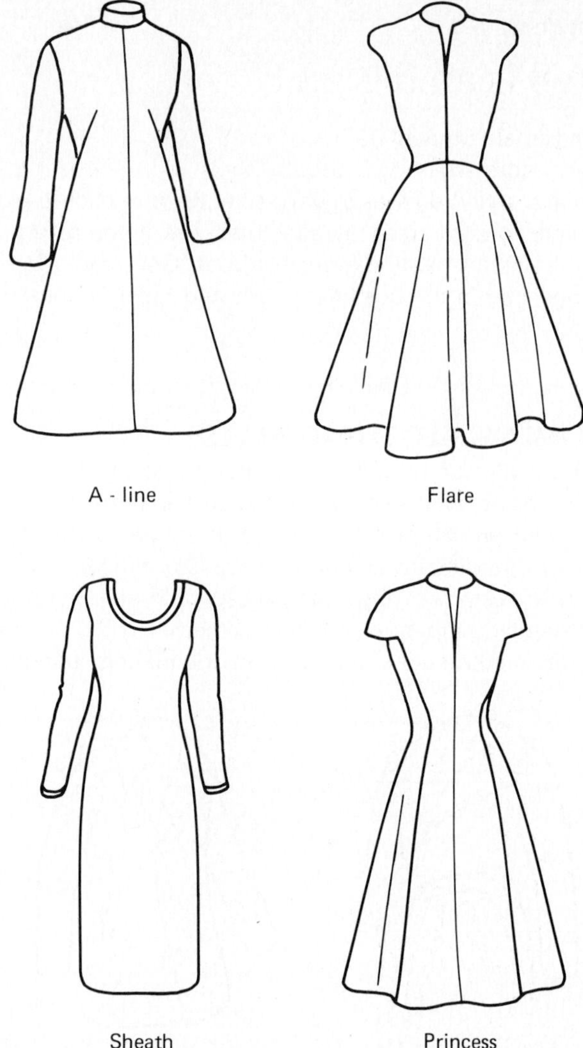

Fig. 6-2 Learn to recognize the four popular dress styles shown above.

Experience 6-3

Name that Style

1. Give a detailed description of one of your female classmate's clothing. Give the style name of the neckline or collar, sleeves, and skirt or pants. On a separate sheet of paper, write the description and sketch the garment.
2. Look through a fashion magazine or newspaper that displays women's apparel. Cut out five different items, such as a dress, shirt, skirt, shorts, or pants. Attach the pictures to a separate sheet of paper. Under each, describe in detail as many style features as possible.
3. Investigate different lingerie or sleepwear styles. Write to manufacturers or trade associations for information on popular styles of one type of garment you are especially interested in learning about. Write a short merchandise information report on this garment (robes, for example). Use illustrations from newspapers or fashion magazines.

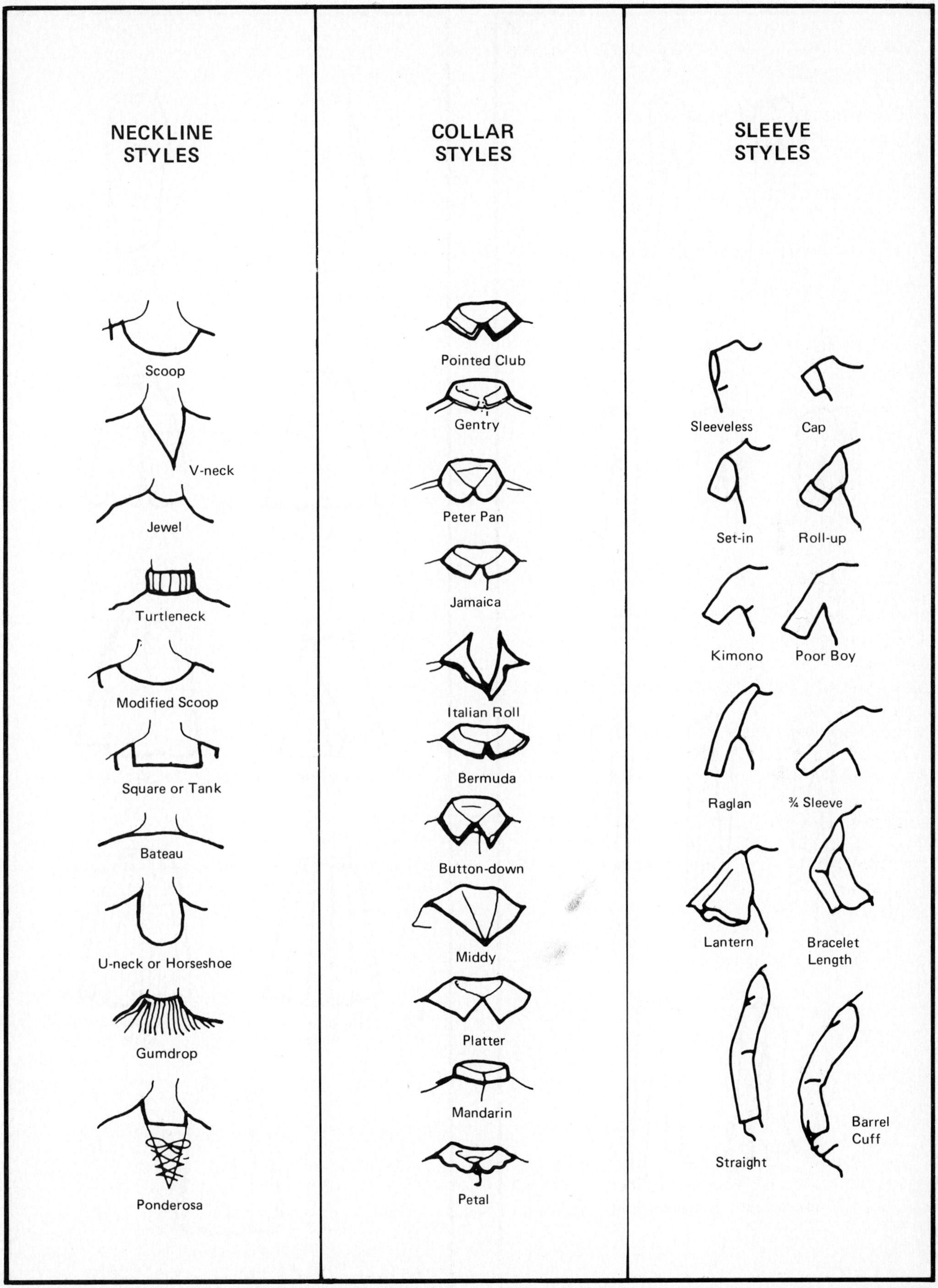
NECKLINE STYLES
Scoop
V-neck
Jewel
Turtleneck
Modified Scoop
Square or Tank
Bateau
U-neck or Horseshoe
Gumdrop
Ponderosa
COLLAR STYLES
Pointed Club
Gentry
Peter Pan
Jamaica
Italian Roll
Bermuda
Button-down
Middy
Platter
Mandarin
Petal
SLEEVE STYLES
Sleeveless
Cap
Set-in
Roll-up
Kimono
Poor Boy
Raglan
¾ Sleeve
Lantern
Bracelet Length
Straight
Barrel Cuff

Fig. 6-3 You can describe women's clothing if you know these details.

Courtesy Bobbie Brooks, Inc.

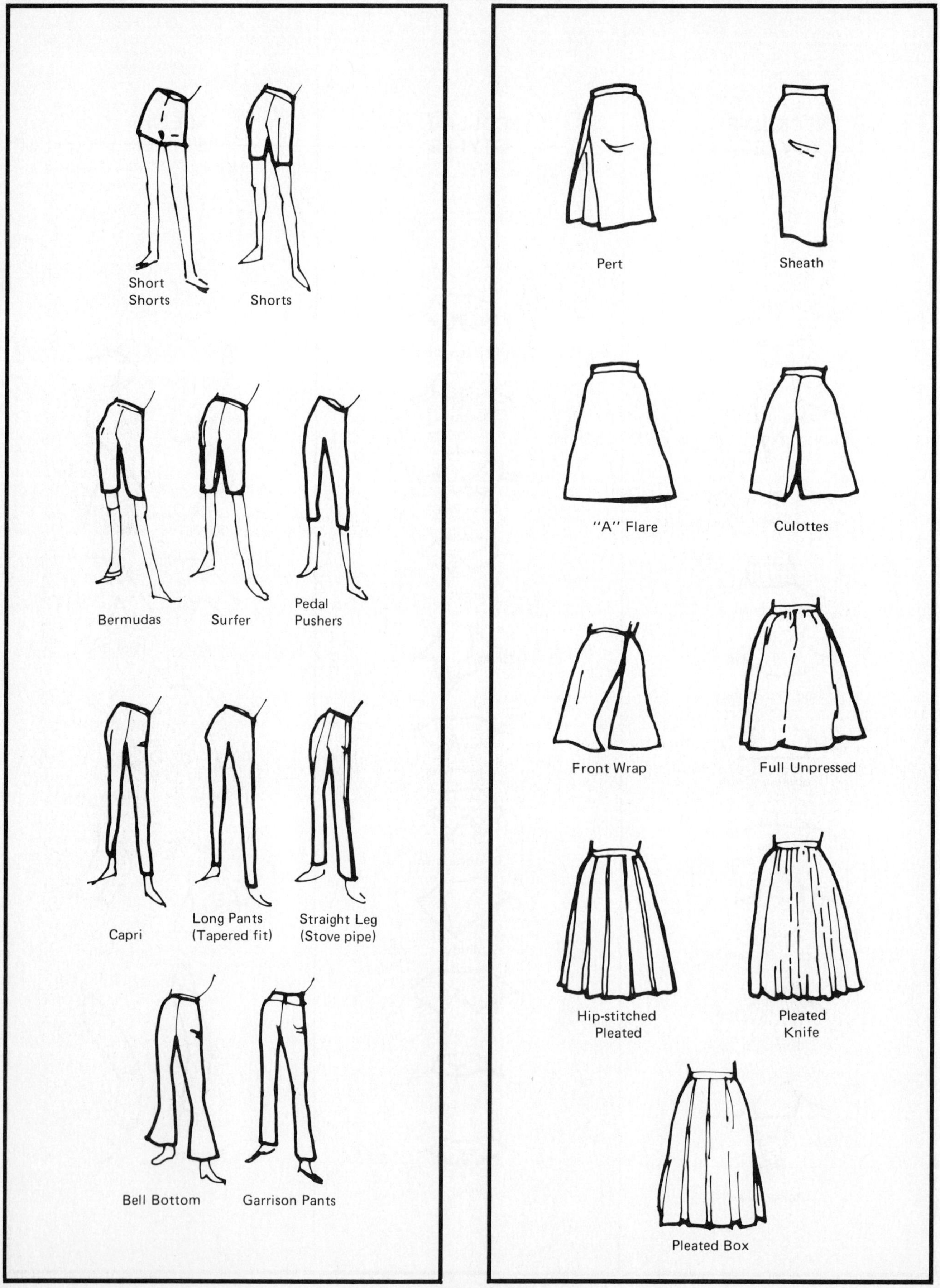

Short Shorts
Shorts
Bermudas
Surfer
Pedal Pushers
Capri
Long Pants (Tapered fit)
Straight Leg (Stove pipe)
Bell Bottom
Garrison Pants

Pert
Sheath
"A" Flare
Culottes
Front Wrap
Full Unpressed
Hip-stitched Pleated
Pleated Knife
Pleated Box

Courtesy Bobbie Brooks, Inc.

Fig. 6-4 Here are some basic styles of women's pants, shown at the left, and skirts, shown at the right.

Source: Sears, Roebuck and Company.

Fig. 6-5 Some of the many different styles of women's swimwear are illustrated above. Learn to recognize them.

BRIDAL ATTIRE AND FORMAL WEAR

When Manuel, the owner of your store, first started in business, he had a bridal and formal wear specialty store. Eventually, he expanded to include women's clothing and accessories in misses and junior sizes. Today, a large portion of his business still comes from the bridal and formal wear department.

Mrs. Williams is the store's bridal consultant. She helps to coordinate the entire bridal outfit. She also helps brides and their attendants choose the dresses and headpieces so that the wedding party is coordinated.

Mrs. Williams tells you that bridal gowns are sold differently than other apparel. Instead of buying a complete size range of a certain dress, the store stocks a sample dress in each style, usually size 10. Women look at the samples and try on the dresses they like best. When they decide which dress they want, that dress is special ordered in the size needed.

Bridal gowns are usually floor length. They may be styled to have a fitted waist, empire or raised waist, or no waist, such as the A-line. Because bridal gowns are special dresses for a special day, there are many style variations so that each dress looks unique or different. Luxurious fabrics—satin, tafetta, velvet, brocade, organdy, lace, and Qiana—are used.

Formal wear features floor-length dresses styled very much like street-length dresses. Luxurious fabrics and fancier looks are used for evening wear.

Experience 6-4

Special Dresses for Special Days

Visit a store that sells bridal gowns or formal wear for women. Choose three different dresses that you especially like. On a separate sheet of paper, describe in detail the style of each dress and its fabric. Next to each description, make a simple sketch of the dress. Choose accessories (jewelry, headpiece, shoes, and so on) that would turn this dress into a coordinated ensemble. Describe these accessories on your paper. If you are unable to visit a store, locate a copy of a bridal magazine and choose dresses and accessories from it.

FITTING WOMEN'S CLOTHING

In the short time you have worked at Manuel's, you hace found that how clothing fits is very important to customers. Becky, one of your coworkers, has a special talent for fitting customers. You ask Becky her secret.

"The most important idea to remember," Becky explains, "is that customers want clothing that is comfortable when sitting, standing, and moving around. They also want attractive clothing. Clothing that fits well will be comfortable and attractive.

"Customers will often ask your advice on whether or not a garment fits properly. Sometimes a customer is not used to seeing a particular style and has a difficult time recognizing proper fit. For example, if a customer is not used to raised waists, she may think a dress doesn't fit.

"You should check garments to determine how well they fit. For example, when fitting pants, look for horizontal wrinkles from the crotch to the hips. These wrinkles indicate that the fabric is pulling because the garment is too small at the hips or thighs. A coat, dress, or blouse collar should fit close to the neck at the back and sides. The sleeves should hang straight and, in most styles, the shoulder seam should be at the shoulder bone. **Darts**, which add fullness or taper the fit of a garment at the bust, shoulders, waist, or elbows, should make the garment fit better and look more attractive. Lengths go up and down with fashion. Check the hem on skirts and dresses to be sure it is straight.

"In general, look for too much fullness or unwanted wrinkles. These are signs that a garment does not fit properly. After you have identified a problem with fit, find the customer a larger or smaller size to correct the problem. For example, if a size 10 is too large in the waist, suggest the customer try a size 8.

"You will be able to help customers with fitting problems better when customers wear the same kind of undergarments and shoes as will normally be worn with the garment. The undergarments and shoes help you get the real picture of how a garment drapes on the customer's body and if the length is correct.

"When customers wear the wrong shoes or undergarments, I point out how the clothing will look with all of the proper accessories. Because we have a lingerie and a shoe department at Manuel's, I can get the right clothing and shoes for the customer. For example, a customer may need a strapless bra to wear with a strapless evening gown. Customers appreciate my effort to help them. And my efforts pay off in bigger sales."

Experience 6-5

It Doesn't Fit

1. Analyze the pictures on page 79. On a separate sheet, describe any problems with fit and explain how each problem can be corrected.
2. In a small group of students, discuss the problems each of you have in buying garments that fit. What alterations do these garments need to fit you properly? Discuss which brands of clothing seem to fit you best.

ANALYZING CUSTOMER FIGURE TYPES

At Manuel's, the sales personnel keep cards on their regular customers. These cards give each customer's name, address, phone number, sizes, and details about the customer's wardrobe. As you and Becky look through some of these cards, Becky explains how customers can compensate for figure problems.

Becky says, "A good figure is a matter of proportion. Each part of your figure is seen in relation to the other parts and to your entire body. Pleasing female proportions follow these guidelines:

- About two-fifths of the body height is above the waist and three-fifths of the body height is below the waist.
- The body can be cut in quarters at the bustline, hips, and knees (see Figure 6-6).
- The shoulders are slightly wider than the hips and the waist is narrow enough to complement both shoulders and hips.

"Few customers have a perfect figure and fewer still look the way they want to look. They want to be taller, thinner, fatter, or shorter. Sometimes they want to camouflage large hips or add to their hips. As a salesperson, you can help them achieve the look they want by analyzing their figures and choosing garments that compensate for their figure problems."

Source: *Dress,* Bennett Pub., 1975.

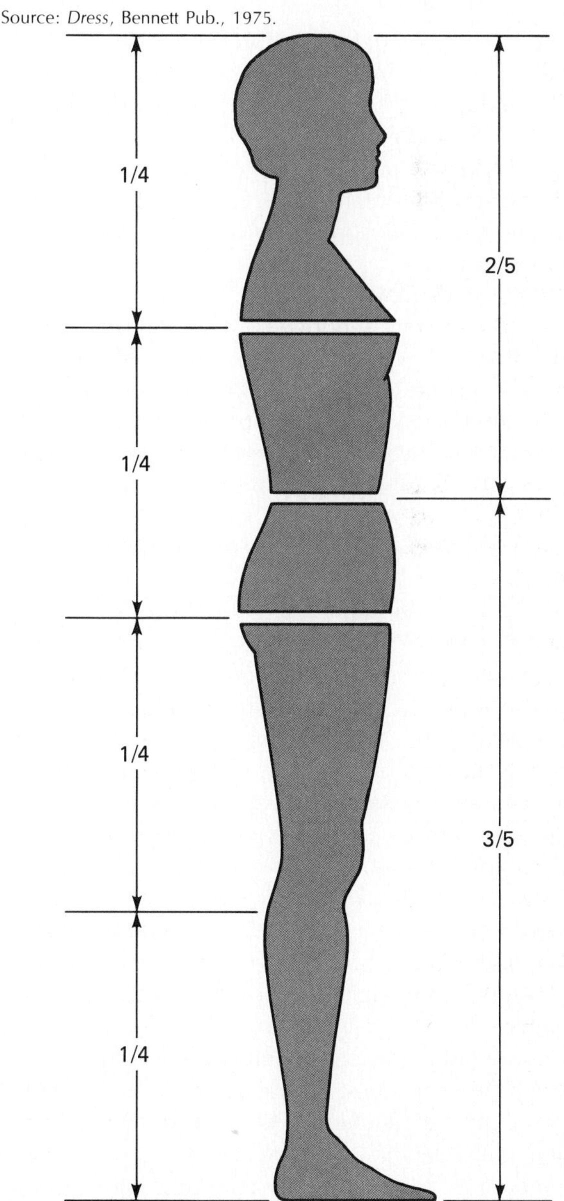

Fig. 6-6 The ideal female figure is proportioned according to the guidelines shown above.

COLOR, LINE, AND DESIGN

Well-chosen clothing calls attention to the customer's best features and away from her worst. Today, because of the large selection of clothing available in stores, women can experiment with lines, colors, and garment details to find an attractive look.

CLOTHING LINES

The lines of a garment can fool your eyes. For example, vertical lines, which carry your eyes upward, add height to a figure. Horizontal lines, which carry your eyes around the body, add weight and shorten a woman's figure. Curved lines add softness and fullness. When helping customers choose clothing, remember the following points:

- Garments with a single center vertical line add height and slim the figure.
- A series of vertical parallel lines, such as stripes or pleats, force the eyes to travel around the figure. These multivertical lines add height and width to the figure. The closer the parallel lines are, the less wide the figure appears to be.
- An asymmetrical or off-center vertical line adds height and cuts the weight of the figure.
- A T-line, a vertical line cut by a horizontal line, adds less height than a single vertical line; this line also adds width at the shoulders and makes the waist and hips look smaller. It is a good choice for a tall person.
- An arrow line adds height and narrows the shoulders. It is a good choice for a short, broad-shouldered woman.
- A Y-line adds height and width to narrow shoulders; also looks attractive on full figures.
- Diagonal lines do not change the figure's height and width, but do add interest and eye appeal and slenderize the figure. Diagonal lines look attractive on all but the very thin.
- Horizontal lines make any figure appear shorter and heavier. The lower the horizontal line, the shorter the woman looks. A low horizontal line, produced by wearing a long tunic or three-quarter length coat, may make a short woman look dumpy and a tall woman look more attractive. A short woman can wear a high horizontal line, such as an empire waist.

See Figure 6-7 for examples of the different dress lines discussed.

CLOTHING COLORS

Color is important in complementing or minimizing figure problems. Dark, cool colors, such as blue, green, or violet, make a figure look smaller. Grayed colors tend to decrease the size of a woman. Bright, warm colors, such as yellow, orange, and red, make a figure look larger. For example, a dark skirt with a bright blouse is a good choice for a woman who has large hips and a small bust.

Very dark colors, such as navy blue or black, tend to slim the figure. Grays and other medium colors make a figure blend into the background. Prints make a figure stand out.

Because bright colors call attention, they can be used to play up a woman's best features. For example, a colorful collar can call attention to the face and away from a bulging tummy. A shape will look longer and narrower if it is clothed in one color rather than two colors. Contrasting yokes, pockets, and belts can make a woman look shorter because contrasting colors interrupt the illusion of height.

The texture of a garment's fabric also tends to increase or decrease a woman's size. Shiny or glossy fabrics, such as satin, reflect light and make a figure appear larger. Stiff, bulky fabrics also make a figure look larger. Dull textures absorb the light and make a figure look smaller. Smooth or sheer fabrics make a figure smaller.

CLOTHING DETAILS

The various **details** of a garment also increase or decrease a woman's figure size. The details of a dress include its length, its outline or silhouette, its waistline including the belt, and its accents, such as pockets, collar, or trim. The following points should help you choose the most attractive clothing details:

- A short skirt makes a tall, slender woman look taller, and a short, plump woman look shorter.
- A fuller garment, one with ruffles or large sleeves, adds to the apparent body weight. Although some fullness can make a thin person look a bit heavier, too much fullness will dwarf the thin person.
- Long sleeves cover heavy upper arms and too thin arms.
- A low waistline, such as in a tunic or overblouse, helps a tall woman appear shorter. A high waistline, such as an empire waist, adds height.
- Narrow belts do not attract as much attention as wide belts. Belts in the same fabric as a garment are good for women with large waists and broad hips because they seem to blend into the garment.
- Narrow lapels, vertical darts, and long V-necklines are slenderizing because they add height. Broad V-necklines widen a figure.
- Fabrics with large patterns make a figure appear larger. Large designs on contrasting backgrounds, big checks, and bright plaids increase a woman's size.

Table 5 offers suggestions on clothing details for women of various figure types. Examine this table to learn how to compensate for figure problems.

COMPENSATING FOR FIGURE PROBLEMS

Becky continues to talk about line, color, and clothing details. She suggests applying these "figure compensation" ideas to some of the customers at Manuel's.

Becky says, "Mrs. Sawyer is short, 5 feet 2 inches, and a bit too plump, 140 pounds. To compensate for her figure problems, try to find clothing that makes her look taller and thinner. A solid color dress or suit, matching sweater and pants, or clothing with diagonal lines would make her look taller and thinner. If you choose a dress that has a belt, the belt should be narrow and of the same fabric as the dress. This way, the belt won't call attention to the size of her waist. A solid colored pantsuit with narrow lapels and vertical tucks would also have a tall, slenderizing effect. A dress with a V-neckline in a dark or grayed color would also tend to make a short, plump woman look taller and thinner. A pantsuit with pants and jacket of contrasting colors would tend to emphasize Mrs. Sawyer's short, stocky

Source: Whitcomb and Cochran, *The Modern Ms.*, McGraw-Hill Book Co., 1975.

Fig. 6-7 The proper dress lines emphasize one's best features. Study the many different dress lines shown above.

TABLE 5

CLOTHING FOR VARIOUS FIGURES

If you're tall and thin . . .

Wear	Avoid
Horizontal lines—tunics, two-piece outfits, wide belts, yokes, raglan shoulders	Vertical lines
Wide-panel fronts	Unbelted waistlines
Skirts—pleated, flared, draped, yoked	Narrow sheath styles
Sleeves—three-quarter length, bracelet length, full; wide cuffs	Deep V-necklines
Coats—full, three-quarter length, and belted; capes	Exaggerated shoulders
Tent silhouettes	Severely tailored suits
Full bodices, bloused tops	Pencil-slim skirts
Round necks, large collars	Angular necklines
Large accessories—big handbags and pieces of jewelry	Long, tight-fitting sleeves
Shoes with medium heels	Very high or very low heels
Pants—any length and cut	
Contrasting or bold colors	
Plaids, tweeds; large or bold prints	
Crisp, bulky, or shiny fabrics	

If you're tall and heavy . . .

Wear	Avoid
Vertical lines	Horizontal lines
Asymmetrical lines	Yokes, if bust is full
Diagonal lines	Princess lines
T-, Y-, and arrow lines	Wide-panel fronts
A-line or center-pleated skirts	Multiverticals
V-necklines	Wide belts
Pointed collars	Full or pleated skirts or very straight skirts
Self-belts (less than 1½ inches wide)	Round necklines
Moderate-length jackets	Tent silhouettes
Full-length coats	Bloused bodices
Set-in sleeves	Sleeveless dresses, cap or tight sleeves
Shoes with medium heels	Boleros or short jackets
Subdued colors	Jerseys, chiffon, satin, stiff materials
Pants—straight and simple in solid colors	Plaids or large prints
	Tight-fitting styles

If you're short and thin . . .

Wear	Avoid
Horizontal lines	Deep V-necklines
Modified vertical lines—T-, arrow, and Y-lines	Exaggerated lines of any kind
Narrow-panel and wide-panel fronts, princess lines	Very wide shoulders, capes
Multivertical lines	Wide belts
Pleated, full, flared, or draped skirts	Long jackets
Semifitted sheaths	Tunics
Bolero or short jackets	Tent silhouettes
Short V-necklines, round collars and necklines	Pencil-slim skirts
Bloused bodices	Tight-fitting sleeves
Empire waistlines	Heavy trimmings
Delicate trimmings	Large handbags and accessories
Bulky, shiny, or stiff fabrics	Chunky jewelry
Bold colors	Clinging fabrics
Small prints	
Pants—any cut	

If you're short and heavy . . .

Wear	Avoid
Vertical lines	Horizontal lines
Asymmetrical lines	Wide-panel fronts
Diagonal lines	Princess lines
Y-lines	Multiverticals
V-necklines	Wide belts
Set-in sleeves	Boleros and bulky tunics
Narrow, half- or self-belts or beltless styles	Extremely long jackets
A-line skirts	Draped skirts
Center-pleated skirts	Tent silhouettes
Jackets not much below hipbone	Pencil-slim skirts
Subdued colors	Full skirts
Shoes with medium heels	Capes and three-quarter-length coats
Medium-sized handbags	Blouson tops
Pants—straight cut in solid colors	Plaids and bold prints
	Bright colors
	Clinging or stiff fabrics, bulky or crisp textures, shiny finishes
	Hip-hugger pants

(Source: Helen Whitcomb and Laura S. Cochran, The Modern Ms., *New York: McGraw-Hill Book Co., 1975)*

size. So would tight waistlines, wide belts, and bright, shiny colors or large prints.

"Mrs. Northrup has a problem with her hips. They are fairly wide, out of proportion with the rest of her body. I suggest she wear bright blouses and neutral skirts. Flared skirts, like an A-line, are a good choice. They move your eyes away from her body and de-emphasize her hips. Wide collars or yokes that draw attention from her hips to her face are also a good choice for her. Mrs. Northrup should avoid plaid skirts or pants that draw attention to her hips. Skirts that taper toward the hem are also poor choices; they make her hips look even bigger. Also, tight fitting pants or skirts or those that have accents, like contrasting trim on the hips, should be avoided.

"Lena Stanton has a large build; she wants to look shorter and thinner. To achieve this desired look, she chooses tailored garments with simple lines. If she wears a belt, she chooses a narrow matching belt, not a wide one that would call attention to her waist. Ms. Stanton prefers 'grayed' colors; they help achieve that thinner look.

"Pat Cole wants to look shorter and a bit plumper; she's tall, 5 feet 7 inches, and very slender, 115 pounds. She chooses contrasting tops and bottoms, such as a solid blouse with patterned pants. Plaids, checks, and bright colors help her achieve a broader look. Horizontal lines, which carry the eye around the figure and seem to add weight, help Ms. Cole appear plumper. She has several blouses with ruffled collars and long, full sleeves. Long narrow skirts or pants and vertical lines would make her look even taller, so she avoids them."

Experience 6-6

Some Added Helps in Choosing Clothing

Examine each of the following statements. Circle any solution that would solve the figure problem.

1. A customer who wants to look thinner should wear:
   full sleeves — grayed colors
   matching colored belt — wide belts
   narrow lapels — shiny fabrics
2. A customer with large bust should wear:
   dark colored blouses — blouses with small prints
   double-breasted jackets — blouses with horizontal trims
   big checks
3. A customer who wants to look a bit plumper should avoid:
   large plaids — contrasting belts
   simple lines — full sleeves
   contrasting colors
4. A customer who wants to look taller should avoid:
   wide belts — solid colored dresses
   contrasting patch pockets — narrow vertical stripes
   diagonal lines — chunky jewelry

Experience 6-7

Solving Figure Problems

As an apparel salesperson, you will have to be able to analyze customers' figures and know which clothing items look best on certain figure types.

1. Examine the following descriptions of three female customers. On a separate sheet of paper, give three examples of clothing items that would minimize their figure problems. Also, give three examples of clothing items that would call attention to their figure problems.
   a. Loretta Rowe is 5 feet 1 inch and weighs 95 pounds. She has a well-proportioned figure.
   b. Marianne Zimmer is 5 feet 8½ inches and weighs 165 pounds. She has a well-proportioned figure.
   c. Daisy Eskay is 5 feet 5 inches and weighs 119 pounds. She has rather large hips and thighs and a small bust.
2. If you are female, complete the following to analyze your figure type. Use a separate sheet of paper for your answers.
   a. Look in a full-length mirror. Write your three most attractive features and three least attractive features.
   b. Have someone measure your height with a tape measure. Remove your shoes and stand against a wall or door. Is two fifths of your body height above your waist?
   c. Can your body height be cut in quarters at your bustline, hips, and knees?
   d. Based on the above information, what are your most attractive clothing lines? Colors? Textures? Garment details?
   e. Look through fashion magazines and cut out three clothing items that would look most attractive on you.

COORDINATING WOMEN'S CLOTHES

A complete, coordinated outfit includes many different clothing items—underwear, pantyhose, shoes, dress, coat, hat, jewelry, and scarf. All these items should add up to one "put together" look. Customers often ask for suggestions on "what goes with what." Salespeople usually suggest a coordinated look by combining colors or textures that are alike (complementary) or different (contrasting). For example, a woman who purchases a three-piece solid navy blue pantsuit may ask for suggestions on what blouses to wear. A navy blue plaid blouse or a white blouse with a bow are two possibilities that give the pantsuit different looks.

Clothing coordination is largely a matter of personal

taste. However, there is such a thing as being well-dressed. If your customers wear mismatched clothing or a garment too fancy or too casual for an occasion, they may be considered poorly dressed. Wearing clothing that is appropriate or fits the occasion, your customers will be considered well-dressed.

SELLING WOMEN'S CLOTHING

The principles involved in selling women's clothing are similar to those in selling any apparel and accessory items. Most of the merchandise is displayed on the sales floor on racks, fixtures, and tables where it is grouped by size or color.

WHAT'S APPROPRIATE?

After greeting a customer, a salesperson should determine what *type* clothing the customer wants. The type of clothing needed is usually determined by where the customer is wearing it. Find out if the customer is looking for something formal, dressy, businesslike, casual, or sporty. A customer who is going to vacation at the beach is looking for something different than a customer who wants something for business.

The salesperson should also be concerned about what size the customer needs. If the customer is shopping for clothing for herself, the good salesperson should be able to judge what size is needed. Of course, if the customer is shopping for clothing for another person, the salesperson must ask questions about the other person's height and weight.

Color is another important concern. A customer probably wants a new garment to fit into an already existing wardrobe. A customer will also want the color to show off her hair and skin coloring attractively. A color that complements a customer's build is important too.

Experience 6-8

Does Your Clothing Tell a Total Story?

1. Look through a current fashion magazine and cut out three pictures of coordinated women's outfits. Attach them to a separate sheet of paper. On each paper, write how each coordinated look was achieved. Also, name three occasions to which it would be appropriate to wear each outfit.
2. Put together your own coordinated outfit. Choose a particular occasion or event that you will be attending. Decide the type clothing that is appropriate to wear. Look through your wardrobe or, in a store, determine all of the clothing items that go together to make one coordinated look. Complete the following chart. Describe each clothing item in detail.

Occasion: ______________________

Type of Occasion (Circle One):
formal dressy business casual sporty

CLOTHING ITEM

coat ______________________

hat ______________________

dress ______________________

skirt ______________________

pants ______________________

blouse ______________________

jacket ______________________

jewelry ______________________

hosiery ______________________

underwear ______________________

shoes ______________________

purse ______________________

You need not include all these items.

PPRESENTING WOMEN'S CLOTHING

Suppose a customer has chosen some garments that especially appeal to her. The salesperson should suggest the customer try on these garments to check the fit. Having the customer try on the clothing is one way of involving the customer with the merchandise. Customers who try on merchandise and like what they see in the mirror are almost sure buyers.

Dressing Room Procedure The salesperson should carry the garments and lead the customer to an empty dressing room. To prevent shoplifting, the salesperson should keep track of how many garments have been taken into the dressing room. After hanging the garments on hooks, the salesperson should close the dressing room door and allow the customer enough time to try on the clothing. The salesperson should check back with the customer periodically. By seeing how the new clothing items look on the customer, the salesperson can tell if the customer needs a larger or smaller size.

Discussing the Benefits Benefits customers are interested in are suitability, comfort, attractiveness, easy care, fit, versatility, and workmanship. A salesperson should point out a garment's benefits while the customer is wearing the garment in the dressing room. An example of appropriate comments are as follows:

SALESPERSON: Mrs. Parker, those pants fit perfectly! Look how well they fit at the waist. And they're the perfect length. How do they feel?

CUSTOMER: They are comfortable. Do you think these beige pants would go with a pink jacket? I want to wear them to work.

SALESPERSON: Without seeing the jacket, it's hard to tell. But beige is a neutral, versatile color. Not only is beige attractive on you, it's also a big color this fall. These pants are dressy enough for work, yet they can look casual too.

OVERCOMING CUSTOMER OBJECTIONS

Customers may hesitate about purchasing a garment because of style, color, fit, or price. Even if garments look attractive and fit well, customers may decide they don't need something new.

For example, customers who are unsure about buying a new style or color should be shown fashion magazines featuring the style. They can then see the popularity of these new looks. Objections because of improper fit can be overcome by suggesting a different size or alterations. Price objections can be answered by stressing the value customers are receiving. If customers say they don't need a new dress or blouse, point out the special features of the garment that make it different from their other wardrobe items.

SUGGESTING RELATED ITEMS

Women's clothing salespersons have an opportunity to suggest related merchandise that can be worn with the merchandise the customer is buying. For example, pants need jackets and shirts. Customers appreciate related item suggestions.

Experience 6-9

Build a Wardrobe—Make It Appropriate

Suppose you work as a salesperson at a small women's shop that sells a wide range of clothing: business attire, formal wear, sportswear and casual clothes. Two of your best customers have asked you for advice in planning their summer wardrobes. Examine the following facts about the two customers. Look through fashion magazines and locate clothing items they should purchase. Cut out the items and attach them to a separate sheet of paper. Be sure to pay close attention to how much these customers can spend. You need to provide them with a total work-and-play wardrobe without going over their budgets. Do not include shoes, lingerie, or any kind of sleepwear.

1. Customer 1 is starting a new job as an accountant. She is 5 feet 5 inches and weighs 120 pounds. She has medium brown skin, and dark brown hair, and is fairly conservative. She has a budget of $300 to spend on her summer wardrobe.

2. Customer 2 is returning home from college for summer vacation. During the summer she works part time at a local florist, making deliveries. She likes to play tennis and go bike riding. She is 5 feet, weighs 110 pounds, and has red hair and fair skin. She likes to be casual. Her budget is $225 for her summer wardrobe.

Experience 6-10

Can You Sell It?

1. Choose four to five similar items and two to three related items. Hang these items on hangers and racks or place them on a table, similar to the merchandise arrangement in a woman's clothing store. (If you are unable to do this exercise in the classroom, make arrangements with the management of a woman's clothing store to do it there. Explain that you are studying selling women's clothing and would like to role play a typical sales situation with a "pretend" customer. Use a tape recorder to record your sales presentation in the store.)
2. Examine each of the merchandise items carefully. Be sure you are able to discuss details about care, style, and workmanship.
3. Play the part of a salesperson. Have another female classmate role play a customer. Role play a typical sales situation with the customer. Before beginning the role-playing experience, ask the customer to pretend to want to purchase a specific garment or something for a specific occasion. Try to make this sale as realistic as possible. Be sure to:

   a. Find out what the customer wants to purchase
   b. Suggest the customer try on the garment
   c. Point out the benefits of buying the garment
   d. Overcome any customer objections
   e. Close the sale
   f. Suggest related items

7 Menswear

"Good morning. I'm one of the department managers at Wacker's Men's Shop. Bill Melvin's my name. I was asked to show you around and introduce you to the merchandise. Menswear used to be always the same, but that's not so anymore. Today men have almost as many apparel choices as women, and they are becoming fashion conscious. They often rely on their salesperson to help them fit and coordinate their clothes.

"Let's start with the most detailed and expensive merchandising area in the store—the Suit, Jacket, and Dress Slacks Department."

SUITS, JACKETS, AND DRESS SLACKS

A man's suit consists of a coat and pants that the manufacturer specifically intended to be worn together. When selling suits, you will hear customers and other salespeople talk about duos, trios, and quads. A **duo** is a two-piece outfit, usually a coat and pants in contrasting colors. A **trio** is a three-piece outfit that can be worn together, such as a coat, vest, and pants. A **quad** has four pieces, such as a coat, vest, and two pairs of pants. Three-piece vested suits, which consist of a coat, pants, and vest, were very popular in the late 1970s. (See Figure 7-1.)

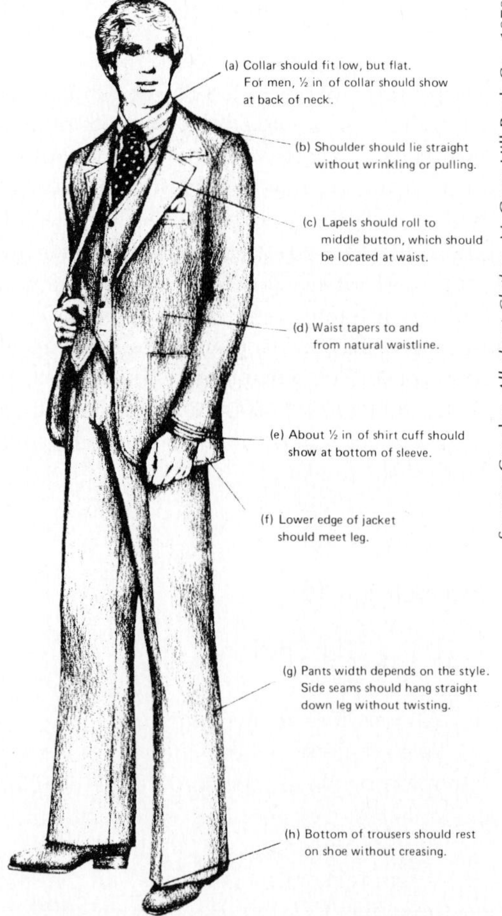

Source: Crowley, *All about Clothes*, McGraw-Hill Book Co., 1978.

Fig. 7-1 Some pointers for fitting a man's three-piece suit are shown above.

Customers who purchase duos, trios, or quads get more clothing combinations for the money spent than customers who buy suits. Most often, the suit offers men one look, because men do not usually wear a suit coat without the suit pants. A quad with two pairs of pants, one matching and one contrasting the coat, offers many different looks. The coat may be worn with or without the vest with either pair of pants. And the coat of a duo, trio, or quad can usually be worn with other trousers and still make an attractive outfit.

Blazer suits are popular men's attire. These suits consist of a blazer with, most often, matching pants. A **blazer** can be identified by its metal buttons on the front closing and cuffs. Blazer suits offer versatility because the blazer can be worn with the suit pants or with other matching or contrasting pants.

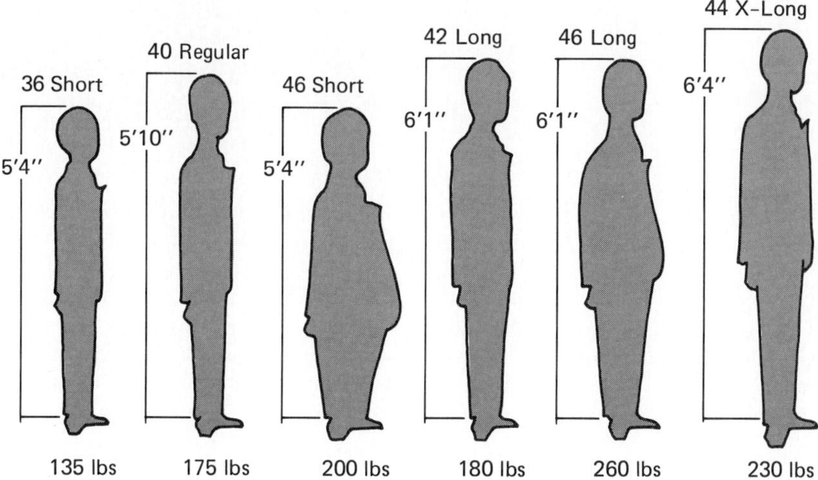

Fig. 7-2 A man's suit size is related to his height and weight.

Sport jackets are more casual than suit coats, and they offer versatility in clothing coordination. They often have patch pockets and are in solids, plaid, checked, or other patterned designs. Depending on the color and pattern of the jacket, these coats may be worn with a variety of matching or contrasting pants. Today, men wear sport jackets to almost any function.

Dress slacks are available in a wide range of colors and patterns. Also versatile, they can be worn with blazers, sport coats, or with a shirt and/or sweater without a coat.

SIZES

A man's size is determined by his chest measurement and height. Suits and sport coats are sized the same way. Men between 5 feet 3 inches and 5 feet 6 inches wear a short. Men between 5 feet 7 inches and 5 feet 11 inches wear a regular. Men between 5 feet 11 inches and 6 feet 3 inches wear a long.

Many men's apparel stores stock suits and jackets in even sizes ranging from 36 to 46 short, regular, long, and extra long. Some stores include odd sizes (37, 39, 41, and 43) and larger sizes (48, 50, and 52). Some stores also carry stouts or portly sizes, to fit the short, heavyset customer. (See Figure 7-2.) The suit or coat size is usually written on a tag attached to the left coat sleeve.

As a menswear salesperson, it is your responsibility to determine what suit or coat size a customer wears. To measure a customer for a suit or coat, wrap a measuring tape around his chest, under his arms, and over his shoulder blades. Hold the tape snugly, but not too tightly. This will give you the customer's chest measurement. Then estimate the customer's height or ask him. Depending on the customer's height and chest measurement, you can then choose the appropriate size. For example, a man who has a chest measurement of 39½ inches and is 5 feet 10 inches would wear a size 40 regular.

Another way to determine suit or coat size is to estimate the size needed and try that size coat on the customer. If the coat is too large, locate a smaller size; if it is too small, choose a larger size. After some experience and practice, a salesperson finds it easy to estimate the correct size.

The size of suit trousers depends on the size of the suit coat. Usually suit trousers have a 6-inch drop, which means the waist of the suit pants is 6 inches less than the chest measurement. For example, the trousers of a size 40 regular suit, with a 6-inch drop, have a 34-inch waist.

Dress slacks are sized in inches according to the waist and inseam measurement. The inseam is the measurement from the crotch to the bottom of the pants. (See Figure 7-3.) Slacks that are sized 30–33 will fit a person with a 30-inch waist and 33 inch inseam measurement. The size is usually on a tag attached to the waist.

Most men's shops sell slacks in sizes 28, 29, 30, 31, 32, 33, 34, 36, 38, 40, and 42. More expensive slacks have not been hemmed or cuffed.

Although many customers know what size slacks they wear, a men's clothing salesperson should measure the customer's waist before he tries on slacks. To measure the waist, wrap the measuring tape around the waistline, just above the hip bones. To measure the inseam, place the tape measure below the zipper and measure the length according to the customer's preference. Be sure to ask the customer the length he prefers. Some men like slacks about ½ inch above the floor, some prefer slacks to "break" the foot, and others prefer slacks to come to the ankle.

Source: Crowley, *All about Clothes*, McGraw-Hill Book Co., 1978.

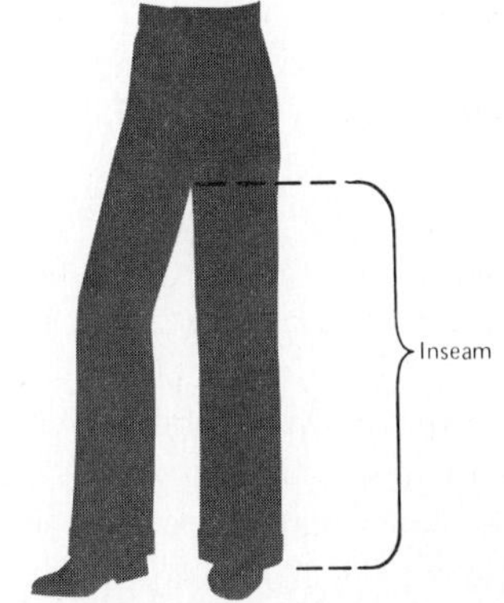

Fig. 7-3 The inseam of men's slacks is measured from the crotch to the bottom of the pants leg.

Experience 7-1

Size Them Up

FOR MALES ONLY

1. Estimate the height and chest and waist measurements of three male classmates. Record your estimates in the following chart. After you have made your estimates, use a measuring tape and yardstick to determine their accurate measurements.

	Classmate 1		Classmate 2		Classmate 3	
Measurements	Estimate	Actual	Estimate	Actual	Estimate	Actual
Height						
Chest						
Waist						

2. Based on the actual measurements of your classmates, decide what size suit, sport coat, and dress slacks each would wear. Record the sizes below. Check with your classmates to see if the sizes you estimated are the sizes they last purchased in each item.

	Classmate 1		Classmate 2		Classmate 3	
Item	Estimate	Actual	Estimate	Actual	Estimate	Actual
Suit						
Sport jacket						
Dress slacks						

STYLES

Suit styles are often referred to as **models**. Some common models that have been popular in the recent past are the traditional or business model, the contemporary or tapered model, and the European model. Fashion dictates which styles are popular; therefore, not all styles may be featured at one time.

The traditional model (see Figure 7-4) can be identified by the following features:

Coat. Natural shoulders do not look padded or raised; two-button closing; center vent; lower flap pockets; breast welt pocket.

Pants. Plain front with regular rise (the distance from the crotch to the waist, a regular rise is about 11 inches); straight or stovepipe leg; belt loop.

The contemporary model (see Figure 7-5) can be identified by the following features:

Coat. Natural shoulders; shaped waist; center or side vents; two-button closing; lower flap, slant, or patch pockets (sportier models have patch pockets); breast welt pocket.

Pants. Plain or pleated front with a shorter rise than traditional model; flare leg; belt loops.

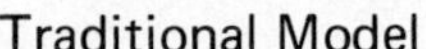

Traditional Model

Contemporary Model

Source: Hart, Schaffner, & Marx, Chicago.

Figs. 7-4 and 7-5 The features of a traditional suit model are illustrated at the left. Compare them with those of the contemporary model shown at the right.

See Figure 7-6 for the European model features:

Coat. Rope or peaked shoulder; high armholes; tailored waist; two-button closing; side vents; trim cut; lower patch or flap pockets; breast welt pocket.
Pants. Plain front; short rise (about 9 to 10 inches); flared leg; slant pockets; belt loops.

Sport jackets are styled similarly to suit coats. Dress slacks are styled basically the same as suit pants. Some slacks have a continuous elasticized waistband with no belt loops, called a continental waistband. Slacks usually have inset, scoop, or quarter front pockets, and welt or flap back pockets. (See Figure 7-7.) For example, an inset pocket with a welt may sometimes be used as a watch pocket. Often a basic style stays fashionable for a long time. Designers may make slight detail changes, however. Some details are shown in Figure 7-8.

Fig. 7-6 What are the features of the coat in European suit models?

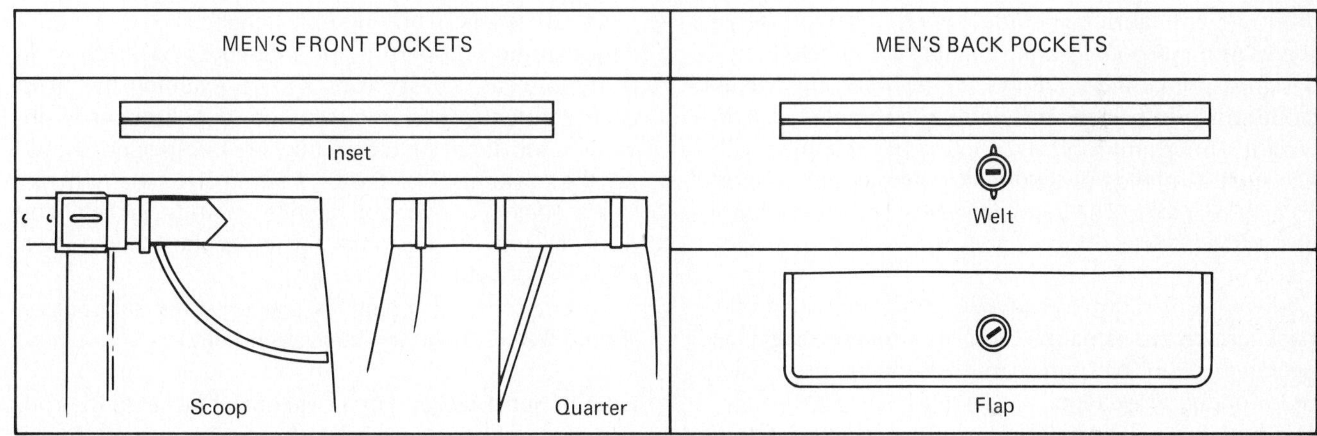

Fig. 7-7 Men's pant styles can vary according to the use of the pocket details illustrated here.

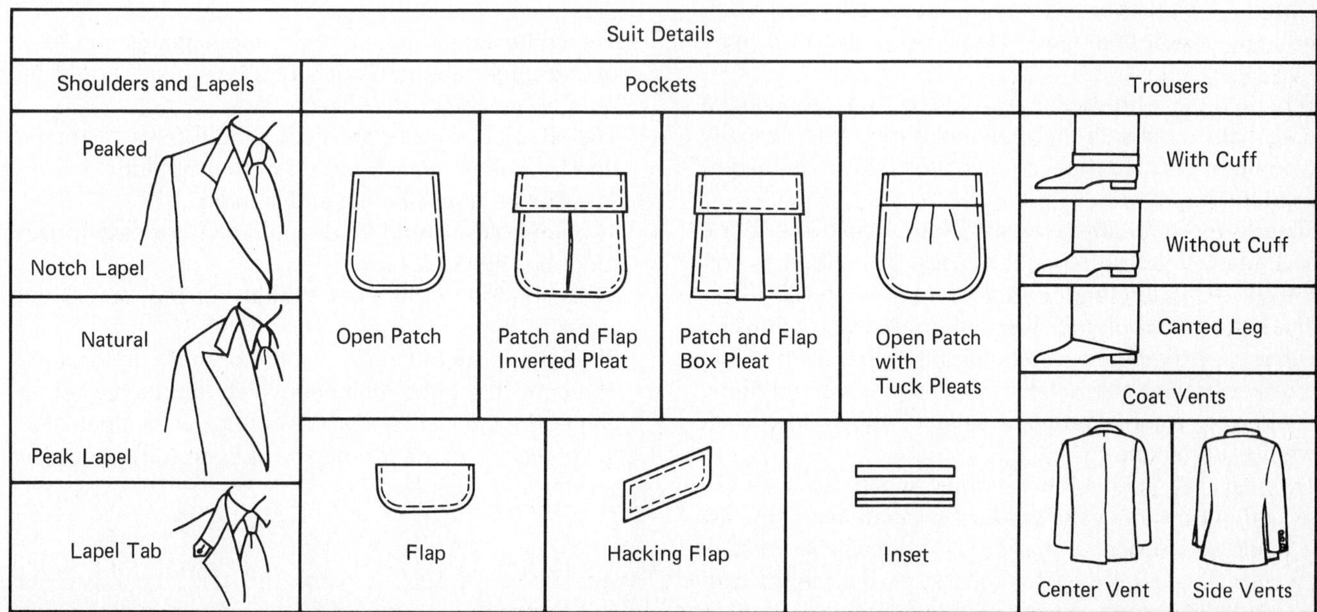

Fig. 7-8 Men's suits can be varied with these shoulder and lapel, pocket, vent, and trouser details.

Experience 7-2

Style Details: Can You Describe Them?

In a men's fashion magazine, such as *Men's Wear* or *Gentlemen's Quarterly,* or in your newspaper, locate two advertisements of suits with different style features. If possible, bring the pictures to class with you.

1. Examine the style features of each suit. On a separate sheet of paper, write a detailed description of the style features.
2. Without showing a classmate the advertisements, read the descriptions of both suits to your classmate. Ask the classmate to sketch both suits on a separate sheet of paper based on your descriptions that you read about.
3. Compare the classmate's sketches to the advertisements. What additional information should you have provided your classmate to get a better likeness of both suits? Write your answer on a separate sheet of paper.

FABRICS

Suits, jackets, and slacks are made from different weight fabrics. A suit may be made from regular weight, lightweight, or year-round fabrics. Regular weight or medium-weight fabrics include tweed, cheviot, serge, sharkskin, and double knit. Regular weight clothing is designed primarily for fall and winter wear; lightweight clothing is worn in warm weather. Examples of lightweight fabrics are tropicals, poplin, and shantung. Fabrics such as blends of wool and polyester are comfortable all year long. The following gives a brief description of several fabrics:

Cheviot. A medium- to heavyweight fabric with a compact surface that is napped to give a rough, shaggy appearance; wool or spun man-made fibers, plain, twill, or herringbone weaves.
Double Knit. A knit fabric made with two sets of needles, which gives a knit with a firm body and less stretchiness; cotton, wool, acrylic, polyester, acetate, or silk.
Poplin. A plain weave fabric with a crosswise rib; cotton, silk, wool, man-made fibers; or of blends of these fibers.
Serge. A clear-finished even twill with a pronounced diagonal rib on both the right and wrong sides, usually woolen or worsted, but can be cotton, silk, man-mades, or blends.
Shantung. Originally a rough, plain weave silk fabric with uneven yarns in the filling; now such fibers as cotton, rayon, nylon, and acetate in addition to silk.
Sharkskin. A woolen or worsted in an even twill using yarns of two different colors (usually white with black, blue, or brown) alternately in both the warp and filling directions; smooth and flat surface; other fibers, but wool is commonest.
Tropicals. A lightweight summer suiting using high-twist fine yarn in a variety of weaves and fiber contents; if made of worsted, it may be called tropical worsted.
Tweed. A general term for rough-textured fabrics with mixed-color effects; plain, twill, or herringbone twill weave in practically any fiber or blend; Harris and Donegal tweeds are famous.

CHECKING THE FIT

Good fit is important to men. They want to add, not detract, from their appearance. Menswear salespeople must be able to recognize good fit and point it out to their customers. This increases the customer's confidence in the salesperson and influences him to buy. In ready-to-wear, salespersons should examine the fit of each garment a customer tries on. If a garment is obviously too large or too small, the salesperson should get the customer into the best fitting size. Many men's stores offer free alteration service for suits, jackets, and pants to provide customers with the best fitting merchandise possible.

To determine if a suit fits properly, the salesperson should follow the guidelines given here.

Coat or Sport Jacket For a coat or suit jacket to fit properly, it should have the following features:

- The garment should hang smoothly with no wrinkles or bulges at the neck and no pulling across the shoulders.
- The collar should lie flat and smooth against the back of the neck; about ½-inch of shirt collar should be seen above the coat collar in back.
- The shoulder line of the coat should form a straight line from the collar to the tip of the shoulder.
- The lapels should lie flat and smooth.
- The armholes should be deep enough for easy movement but not look baggy.
- When buttoned, the coat should not pull across the chest.
- The sleeves should allow ½-inch of shirt cuff to show.
- The coat should be long enough so that the customer can curl his fingers under the bottom of the coat. (Adjustments are made for men whose arms are longer or shorter than average.)

Pants To determine if pants fit well, the customer should wear the same type of shoe that he will usually wear with the pants. If your menswear store sells shoes, suggest that he try on a pair of shoes that match the suit or pants. This practice will oftentimes increase your sales. If the pants have belt loops, the customer should wear a belt for the fitting. Provide a belt if necessary. When fitting pants, notice the following:

- The proper positioning of the waist for men's pants is slightly above the hips. Because this position is uncomfortable to some men, ask customers to position the waistband where it feels most comfortable.
- The waistband of the pants should be horizontal to the ground, not higher in the front than in the back. The waist should fit snugly; however, the customer should be able to slip the flat of his hand in and out of the waistband.
- The seat and crotch of the pants should not look baggy or wrinkled. The pants should look smooth and feel comfortable when the customer is sitting and standing.
- The length of the pants is a matter of customer preference. Many men like the slacks to "break" the foot, that is, have a slight break over the instep. Most pants are finished so that the front is ½-inch to ¾-inch shorter than the back.

Vest When a customer buys a suit with a vest, the jacket should be fitted with the vest on. Because a vest should fit close to the body, it is important that the customer wear the same weight shirt he will wear under the vest. Notice the following when fitting a vest:

- The vest should fit with no pulling or sagging.
- The armholes should be open enough for comfort but should not sag.
- The back should have no wrinkles and should not ride up when the customer moves his arms.

Experience 7-3

Is It a Good Fit?

Pretend you are a menswear salesperson. Have a male classmate play the part of a customer. (Ask the classmate to wear slacks, sport coat, and shirt to class to complete this exercise.) Point out to the customer why his slacks and coat are a good fit. If possible, use a tape recorder to record your conversation.

ALTERATIONS

Even though men's suits, jackets, and slacks are available in many sizes, some men need their clothing shortened, lengthened, taken in, or let out. These changes are called **alterations**. At many finer stores alterations are made free of charge.

Some men's apparel stores or departments have tailors who mark garments for alterations. Besides marking the garments, the tailors also make the needed changes. At other men's stores or departments, the menswear salespeople mark the alterations. After the garments are marked, the salespeople send the clothing to the tailor, who makes the alterations.

Most stores require their tailors or salespeople to complete an alteration ticket when any garment needs to be altered. Information about the customer, the garment, and alterations needed are written on this ticket. Usually, the ticket is perforated so the customer can use the bottom part as a "claim check," to claim the altered merchandise. (See Figure 7-9.)

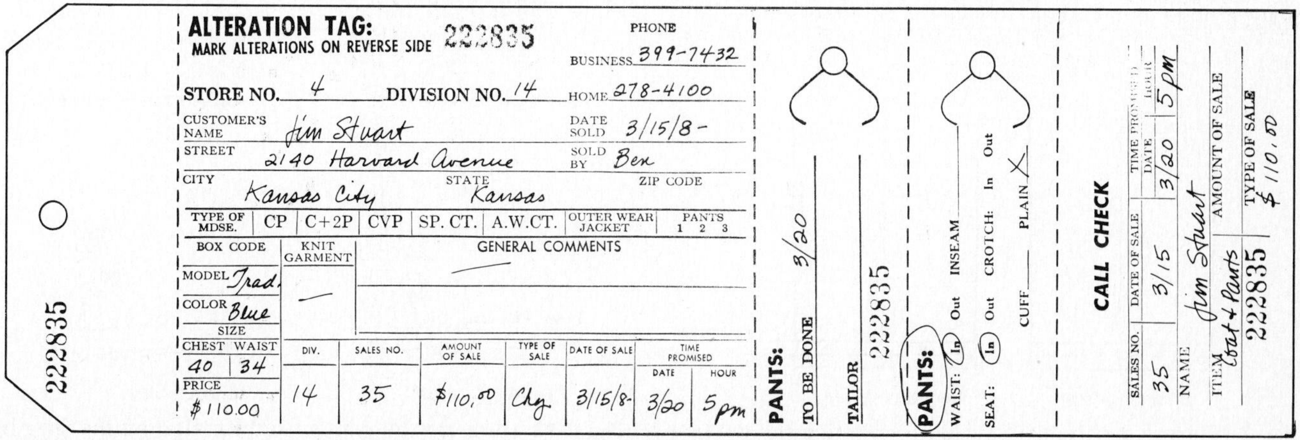

222835

ALTERATION TAG: 222835
MARK ALTERATIONS ON REVERSE SIDE

PHONE
BUSINESS 399-7432
STORE NO. 4 DIVISION NO. 14 HOME 278-4100
CUSTOMER'S NAME Jim Stuart DATE SOLD 3/15/8-
STREET 2140 Harvard Avenue SOLD BY Ben
CITY Kansas City STATE Kansas ZIP CODE

TYPE OF MDSE.	CP	C+2P	CVP	SP. CT.	A.W.CT.	OUTER WEAR JACKET	PANTS 1 2 3

BOX CODE | KNIT GARMENT | GENERAL COMMENTS
MODEL Trad.
COLOR Blue
SIZE: CHEST 40 WAIST 34
PRICE $110.00

DIV.	SALES NO.	AMOUNT OF SALE	TYPE OF SALE	DATE OF SALE	TIME PROMISED DATE	TIME PROMISED HOUR
14	35	$110.00	Chg	3/15/8-	3/20	5pm

PANTS:
TO BE DONE 3/20
TAILOR 222835

PANTS:
WAIST: In Out INSEAM
SEAT: In Out CROTCH: In Out
CUFF ____ PLAIN X

CALL CHECK

SALES NO.	DATE OF SALE	TIME PROMISED DATE	TIME PROMISED HOUR
35	3/15	3/20	5 pm

NAME Jim Stuart
ITEM Coat + Pants | AMOUNT OF SALE $110.00 | TYPE OF SALE
222835

Fig. 7-9 Here's an example of a perforated alteration ticket with a customer's "claim check" attached.

Alterations Symbols The tailors or salespeople who mark alterations use certain symbols. For example, a row of short, unconnected lines means the garment should be shortened or taken in. A row of unconnected, slashed lines means the garment needs to be lengthened or let out. When marking alterations, the salesperson uses marking chalk. Even though this chalk comes out when the garment is steam pressed, the chalk should be used sparingly. On light-colored clothing, pins are used to mark the alterations, because chalk lines do not show up on light colors.

Pant Alterations Before making any alteration marks, the customer should be sure the pants are positioned where he likes to wear them on his hips. If the pants have belt loops, the customer should be wearing a belt. The customer should also be wearing the same type shoes he will normally wear with the pants.

The commonest pant alterations are shortening or lengthening the pant leg and taking in or letting out the waist. Some stores use pins to hold the pants temporarily at certain lengths. When the customer has decided on the correct length, the salesperson marks the pants with marking chalk. Only one leg is marked for alterations. If the customer has one hip lower than the other or one leg shorter than the other, both legs should be marked.

If the pants are too long, use the chalk to mark where the finished bottom of the pant leg should be. Fold the excess material inside and determine the correct length. Mark the length by using a horizontal, dotted line. Some stores make the mark on the inseam, some at the heel, and some mark the pants at the front crease. (See Figure 7-10.) If the pants are to be cuffed, the excess material is turned up and the pant leg is marked at the center crease to show the correct length with cuffs.

If the pant legs are too short, use a measuring tape or ruler to determine how much the legs should be lengthened. Measure from the customer's instep to the bottom of the pant leg. Measure that same distance up the leg and mark a horizontal dotted line with vertical slashes.

To alter the waist, ask the customer to position the pants at his waist. The customer should not be wearing a belt. If the waist is too loose, pinch the pants at the waist along the backseam to take up the excess material.

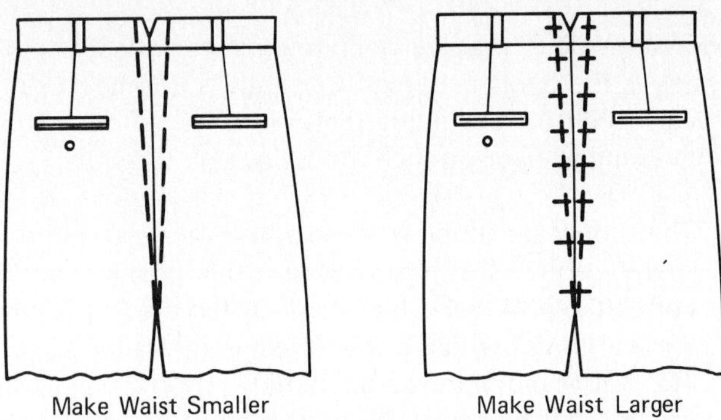

Fig. 7-11 Here are the marks used for altering the waists of men's pants.

Taper the excess material downward in a wedge shape toward the crotch. Be sure the amount of material on both sides of the backseam is equal. Mark the sides of the wedge with a dotted line on both sides of the backseam. The width of this wedge tells the tailor how much material should be taken in. (See Figure 7-11.)

Letting out the waist calls for more experience and skill than taking it in. The best way to determine how much to let out is to have the customer open the waistband to the point where the pants feel comfortable. Then measure the width of the distance the pants lack. Mark this distance along both sides of the backseam with slashed lines. (See Figure 7-11.) Another way is to measure the customer's waist. Then take the difference between this measurement and the waist size on the pants. The difference is the number of inches the wasit should be let out. If the waist is taken in or let out more than 2 inches the pockets and seams will be out of position.

Other alterations, such as letting out or taking in the crotch and leg width, may also improve the fit of the pants. Because these alterations require skill and experience, their measurements should be made by a tailor.

Coat or Jacket Alterations The commonest coat or jacket alterations are lengthening or shortening the sleeves. The same procedure as lengthening or shortening pant legs is used for these sleeve alterations. (See Figure 7-12.) Other coat alterations are lowering the collar, letting out the armholes, and taking wrinkles from the shoulder. These alterations are complicated and require skill in marking.

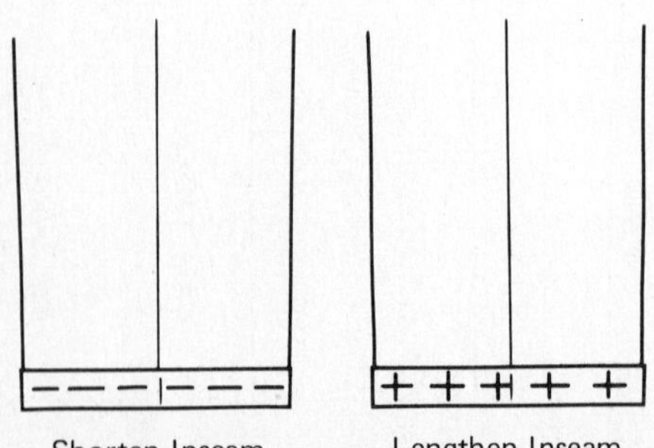

Fig. 7-10 Here are the marks used for altering the length of men's pant legs.

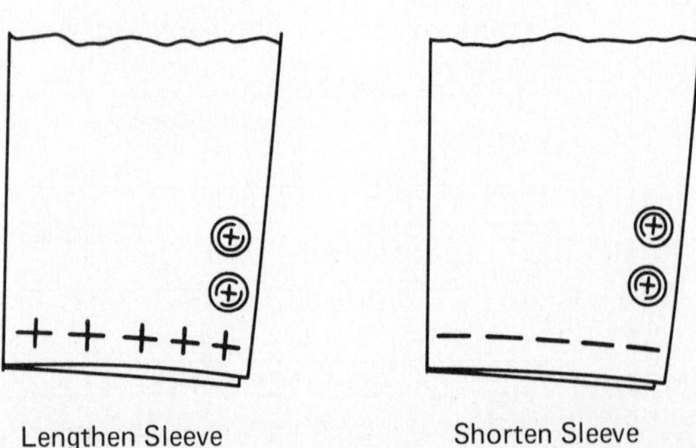

Fig. 7-12 Here are the marks used for altering the length of men's coat sleeves.

Experience 7-4

Change the Fit: Alter It!

1. In the space provided, make the alteration marks for shortening and lengthening the sleeve.
   a. Shortening sleeve ____________
   b. Lengthening sleeve ____________
2. Assume you are a men's clothing salesperson. Ask a male classmate to bring a pair of old slacks or an old jacket to class that is too long or too short. Have the classmate try on the garment. Using a piece of chalk, check the fit of the garment and mark the necessary alterations during class. Complete the alterations ticket following. Use factual information about the classmate. Assume the classmate can pick up the garment, which costs $25, in 4 days from the time the ticket is written.

222835

ALTERATION TAG: 222835
MARK ALTERATIONS ON REVERSE SIDE

PHONE
BUSINESS ________
STORE NO. ________ DIVISION NO. ________ HOME ________
CUSTOMER'S NAME ________ DATE SOLD ________
STREET ________ SOLD BY ________
CITY ________ STATE ________ ZIP CODE ________

TYPE OF MDSE.	CP	C+2P	CVP	SP. CT.	A.W.CT.	OUTER WEAR JACKET	PANTS 1 2 3

BOX CODE | KNIT GARMENT | GENERAL COMMENTS
MODEL
COLOR
SIZE: CHEST WAIST
PRICE

DIV.	SALES NO.	AMOUNT OF SALE	TYPE OF SALE	DATE OF SALE	TIME PROMISED DATE	HOUR

PANTS: TO BE DONE
TAILOR
222835

PANTS: WAIST: In Out INSEAM
SEAT: In Out CROTCH: In Out
CUFF ____ PLAIN ____

CALL CHECK
SALES NO. | DATE OF SALE | TIME PROMISED DATE HOUR
NAME
ITEM | AMOUNT OF SALE
222835 | TYPE OF SALE

ANALYZING CUSTOMER BUILDS

Men's clothing salespeople should be able to determine the size and style that will look best on each customer. A man of average build will look good in almost any style, pattern, and color of suit, slacks, or jacket. A man who is tall, short, thin, or heavy may not be able to wear all styles and colors. Menswear salespeople should help customers choose garments that help them look their best.

A short, slender man will look best in clothing that makes him appear taller. A suit with vertical stripes and no contrasting colors will look good on him. Slacks that are tapered at the bottom will help him look taller. Jackets with lapels that form a deep V will also add height. Jackets and slacks in contrasting colors, as well as slacks with cuffs, will cut the man's height.

A short, stout man will look good in vertical stripes and tapered pant legs because they make him appear taller and slimmer. He should wear a single-breasted jacket rather than a double-breasted jacket. And he should avoid checks, plaids, contrasting colors, cuffs, and patch pockets.

A tall, thin man should wear clothes that make him appear broader. A suit with horizontal lines or a jacket with wide lapels and patch pockets gives the impression of more weight. Jackets full at the waist and padded or raised at the shoulders will also add weight. Double-breasted jackets are a good choice for the tall, slender man. This body build can easily wear cuffs and contrasting colors because of his height. A tall, slender man should avoid garments that make him appear taller and thinner, such as jackets with deep lapels and vertical stripes.

A man with a tall, heavyset build should wear garments that make him look slimmer. Plaids, checks, horizontal stripes, and contrasting colors should be avoided.

Experience 7-5

What to Wear?

Read the descriptions of the following two men. In the space provided, describe the style and pattern (solid, plaid, striped) of jacket and slacks each should wear and avoid wearing. In magazines, newspapers, or clothing catalogs, locate pictures of men's jackets and slacks you would recommend for each man. If possible, cut out or copy one recommended outfit for each man. Attach or sketch your recommendations on a separate sheet of paper.

1. Mr. Harper is short, 5 feet 6 inches in height, and fairly heavy.

2. Mr. Miller is very tall and slender.

MR. HARPER

Garment	Recommended	Not Recommended
a. Jacket		
b. Slacks		

MR. MILLER

Garment	Recommended	Not Recommended
a. Jacket		
b. Slacks		

SELLING

Generally, men have a fairly specific idea of what they want to buy. If they are not browsing, they should be approached promptly. Because suits, sport jackets, and dress slacks are often expensive, the menswear salesperson must be professional and use selling skills.

Approaching the Customer Many menswear stores encourage salespeople to approach customers, introduce themselves, and shake the customer's hand. For example, "Good morning. My name is Timothy Henricks. Welcome to our store." Customers often respond to this approach by telling the salesperson their name.

If the male customer is accompanied by a woman, it's very important to pay attention to her. After greeting the man and woman, find out what merchandise they are interested in and get the woman comfortably seated near where the man will be trying on garments.

What's Appropriate? The customer's build will give clues to what sizes and styles will look best on him. If the customer is wearing a suit, sport coat, or dress slacks, the salesperson should observe them. This gives the salesperson a clue to the quality of clothing the customer is used to wearing.

By asking questions, the salesperson can find out what type of clothing the customer wants to purchase. If the man says he wants to purchase a suit, the salesperson should ask more questions to find out where the man will be wearing the suit. Men buy suits for many reasons. Men who wear suits to work will probably have between four and seven suits in their wardrobe. Men who do not wear suits regularly will probably own only one or two. For a man who does not wear many suits, a dark-colored suit will be the most versatile. Men who own many suits will probably want a different color or style than they already own, but one that is appropriate for the stated occasion.

Presenting the Merchandise When selling a sport coat or suit, the salesperson should offer to help the customer remove his coat so that he can try on one of the store's coats. Seeing the merchandise on him arouses the customer's interest.

Help the customer off with his coat and carefully hang it up or drape it over a chair. It's important to treat the customer's clothing with respect. When selling a coat or suit, proceed as follows:

Putting on the Coat. When helping a customer into a coat or jacket, make sure the customer's shirt sleeves are rolled down. Hold the coat by the collar, lift it high on the customer's neck, and drop it forward to the collar line. Starting at the neck, smooth the coat over the customer's shoulders.

At the Mirror. If the coat fits well, take the customer to a three-way mirror. Position the customer in front of the center glass so that he can get an overall view of the front of the coat and how the sleeves fit. Position the customer in front of the left mirror so that he will see the reflection of his side by turning his head and looking in the center mirror. He will see the reflection of his back in the right mirror.

If the customer is with a woman, take him over to her for her approval. Usually her approval is a must for completion of the sale.

Suggest to the customer that he also try on the matching pants to get an idea of the overall look of the suit. Select dress slacks for customers who are trying on sport coats and encourage them to try on the slacks with the jacket. Show the customer to the dressing room. When he comes out, take him to the three-way mirror and point out the benefits of the suit.

Talk about Comfort and Appearance Customers are interested in comfort and appearance. While in front of the mirror, ask the customer to move around to see how the coat or suit feels. Point out why the coat or suit looks good on him. Talk about the color. Make your sales demonstration stronger by actually pointing out specific fit features, such as the way the lapels and collar lie flat and smooth. If the garment needs alterations, say so and explain how the suit will look after it is altered.

Talk about Quality Before he will make a purchase, the customer must be convinced that he is getting his money's worth. Point out the quality features, such as fabric, styling, and workmanship, that make the garment worth its price. Some quality workmanship features of a well-made suit are:

- Hand-finished seams, which prevent raveling.
- Wide seams, which make alterations easy.
- Reinforced points of stress, such as the crotch.
- Good grade, nonchip buttons.
- Well-bound and firmly sewn buttonholes, which prevent raveling.
- Interfacings, which help garments keep their shape and hang better.
- A lining, which helps prevent wrinkles or stretching of the fabric and protects the outer part of the coat or suit from perspiration and wear. Hand-stitched linings create softer lines and prevent irregular bulges.

Meeting Objections The commonest objection customers make is price. Like everything else, clothing prices have risen in the past few years because materials and labor costs have increased. The best way to meet the customer's price objection is to point out the quality features of a garment. Fabrics that keep their texture and color, tailoring that keeps a garment's fit and shape, and styling that always looks fashionable are three reasons to pay more for menswear.

Suggestion Selling Suits, sport coats, or slacks are not worn alone. Shirts, ties, sweaters, socks, and shoes are only a few of the many additional items a menswear salesperson can suggest to customers. Many customers appreciate a salesperson who chooses accessories that complete an outfit or increase the number of possible clothing combinations.

Experience 7-6

Mirror Maneuvers

Play the part of a men's clothing salesperson. Have a male classmate play the part of a customer who is looking for a sport jacket. Visit a local store that has a three-way mirror.

If the customer is wearing a coat, demonstrate how you would help him take off his coat. Then demonstrate how you would help him try on the sport jacket.

1. Choose a sport coat that would complement the customer's appearance. (If you have a three-way mirror in your classroom, you can complete the experience at school. Have the classmate who is playing the part of the customer bring a sport coat from home.)
2. If the coat fits well, position the customer in front of the three-way mirror and proceed to point out the fit of the jacket.

Experience 7-7

Sell Quality, Not Price

Assume you are a men's clothing salesperson. You have been showing a customer a high-quality, expensive traditional business suit. Some of the features of the suit are 100 percent worsted wool, full hand-stitched lining, reinforced seams, and hand-sewn buttonholes. The customer has objected to buying the suit because "It's too expensive."

Give the customer two reasons why the suit is well worth its price. Write your explanation on a separate sheet. Or role play the situation with another student.

DRESS SHIRTS

Dress shirts, which are designed to be worn with a tie, are sized by the man's neck and sleeve measurement, in inches. They're in a variety of sizes, fabrics, and colors.

SIZES

Most men's stores stock shirts in sizes 14½, 15, 15½, 16, 16½, 17, and 17½. The sleeve length includes even sizes 32 through 36 inches. Some dress shirt manufacturers are using a new sizing system in which the sleeves are designed to fit two arm lengths, such as 15½ neck and 32–33 sleeve.

Shirt collar size and sleeve length are marked in the back of the collarband with two numbers. The number 15–33 means the collar size is 15 inches and the sleeve length is 33 inches. Half sizes in collars are sometimes marked 15^2 or 16^2 rather than 15½ and 16½. Naturally, short-sleeve shirts do not include a sleeve length. Therefore, the size printed on the collar is a single number, such as 14½ or 15.

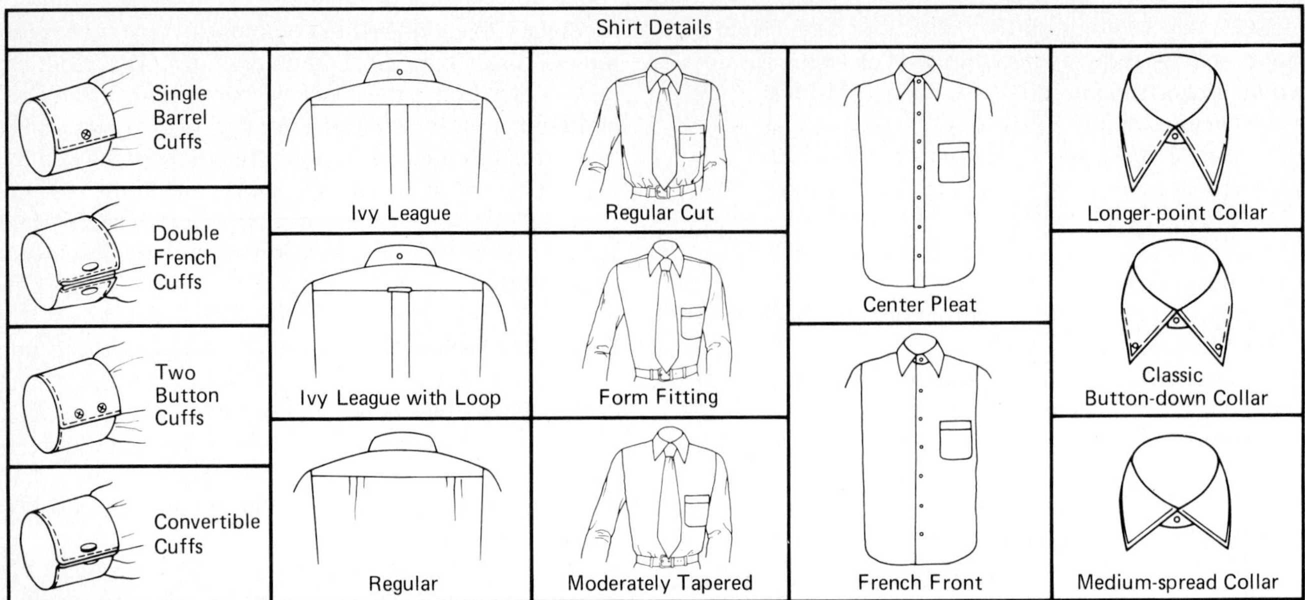

Fig. 7-13 Men's dress shirts come in a variety of styles as these cuff, cut, and collar details show.

To measure a man for a dress shirt, measure around the base of the neck with a measuring tape. The measurement should be taken to the nearest half inch. If the neck size falls between sizes, show the customer the larger size shirt. To determine the sleeve length, have the customer hold his arm at shoulder level and bend the elbow at a 45-degree angle. Measure from the back of the customer's neck, at the spine, to the wrist joint.

STYLES

Dress shirts are available in a variety of collar styles, cuff styles, and cuts. (See Figure 7-13.) There are three basic collar styles: button-down, spread, and long point. As a general rule, the button-down collar is the most versatile and can be worn by most facial shapes. The spread collar flatters a thin, narrow face. The long point is most flattering to a broad, round face.

Some important "shirt" words for menswear salespeople to know are:

Collar Stays. The plastic or metal strips inside the collar that help keep the points of the shirt collar straight and keep the collar down on the shirt front. Stays can be removable or permanent.
Points. The distance from the neckband to the collar's tips.
Placket. The opening in a garment that allows for ease in dressing at the throat or cuffs.
Shirttail Bottom. The part of the shirt below the waist, short at the seams and longer in the front and back.
Spread. The distance between the collar tips.
Yoke. The fitted or shaped piece at the top of a shirt over the shoulders.

FABRICS

The commonest dress shirt fabrics are broadcloth, oxford cloth, and various knits, such as jersey. A broadcloth is a tightly woven plain weave fabric that has very fine crosswise ribs. Oxford cloth is a soft but sturdy basket weave fabric made of cotton, rayon, and polyester. Jersey is a plain knitted fabric that does not have a distinct rib.

CHECKING THE FIT

Most men know their shirt size; however, as a man gains or loses weight, his size may change. It's a good idea to measure a regular customer about once a year to determine the proper size. A salesperson should check the following areas to determine if a shirt is a good fit:

- The waist should be smooth, with no bagginess or bunching of material. It should be loose enough so the material does not pull at the buttons when the customer moves.
- The shirt should be long enough so it does not pull out of the pants when the customer moves.
- The collar should not wrinkle because of tightness.
- The armholes should be open enough for easy movement, but the sleeves should not look baggy.
- The shoulder seams should fall slightly over the edge of the shoulder bone.
- The shirt sleeves should stop just below the wrist bone, about ½-inch below the jacket.
- Buttoned cuffs should fit close to the wrist and still allow movement.

TIES

Two popular tie styles are the long tie and the bow tie. The long tie is worn for business and many social occasions. The bow tie, most often worn for formal occasions, also passes in and out of fashion for streetwear. A variation of the bow tie is the string tie, sometimes worn in the South and parts of the West.

Long ties are available in different lengths. The standard length is 55 to 56 inches; better ties tend to be longer than lesser quality ties. Long ties may be tied in a Windsor knot, half-Windsor, or four-in hand. The Windsor, a wide knot, is best worn with wide-spread collar shirts; the four-in-hand knot with the long point.

The width of a tie should be harmonious with the width of the suit lapels. A wide tie should be worn with a suit with wide lapels.

Ties are made from silk, polyester, wool, cotton, acetate, rayon, wool challis, and various blends of these fibers.

Experience 7-8

All about Shirts

1. Identify the lettered sections of the dress shirt shown below.
2. Analyze the fit of the dress shirt pictured. Identify areas that show the garment is a good fit if any. Also identify any areas of poor fit.

a. ______

b. ______

c. ______

d. ______

e. ______

a. Areas of good fit ______________________

____

____

____

____

____

b. Areas of poor fit ______________________

____

____

____

____

____

COORDINATING SUITS, SHIRTS, AND TIES

Because there are so many colors, textures, and styles of men's clothing, a menswear salesperson must be able to coordinate the customer's wardrobe. The clothing a customer buys should match his hair, eye, and skin coloring. As a general rule, men with light hair, blue eyes, and fair complexions look best in cool colors or soft, grayed colors. Men with darker skin tones, dark hair, and brown eyes can wear warm, more intense colors.

A customer's build also plays a role in color selection. Cool colors make a shape look smaller. Warm colors stand out and make a silhouette appear larger. A man who is 6 feet 4 inches tall and weighs 240 pounds would appear larger in bright yellow slacks with a yellow-orange shirt.

The easiest clothing coordination is achieved by combining solids. For example, a solid navy blue suit may be worn with a white shirt and maroon tie. A basic rule for coordinating patterns is if one garment is patterned (checked, plaid, striped), another garment should be solid. For example, a pair of bold brown, gold, and green pants should be worn with a solid shirt. The color of the shirt should pick up one of the colors in the pants, such as gold.

Many men wear a combination of patterns. A person needs talent for combining two patterns so that they do not clash. When combining patterns, the salesperson should pick out the boldest garment first. This bold garment should serve as the focal point. The other patterned garments should be less bold and not clash with the bold garment. It is easy to combine two patterns when the patterns are separated by a solid and one pattern stands out. For example, a plaid suit may be combined with a solid shirt and a paisley tie.

Apparel salespeople should not recommend a particular color to a customer just because it is in fashion; a color should be recommended to enhance the customer's appearance. Some guidelines for coordinating men's apparel are given on the next page.

- When combining a suit, shirt, and tie or any apparel combination, avoid colors that clash or colors that are so similar they fade into each other.
- Patterns of the various garments should be harmonious. A pattern that travels in one direction should not be placed next to a pattern in another direction. For example, a pinstripe suit with a vertical pattern will clash with a plaid shirt that has an obvious horizontal pattern.
- Similar style clothing should be worn together. For example, clothing that has a conservative style, such as a traditional suit, looks mismatched when worn with a sport shirt.

The four most popular menswear colors are blue, brown, gray, and green. The color combination chart in Table 1 (shown below) may help you coordinate customers' clothing.

TABLE 1:

COLOR COORDINATOR FOR MENSWEAR

SUIT	GRAY	BLUE	BLACK	BROWN	OLIVE
Shirt (Solid or Stripe)	1. Blue 2. Off white/yellow 3. Gray	1. Blue 2. Off-white 3. Gray	1. Gray 2. Rose 3. Yellow	1. Tan/green 2. Off-white/yellow 3. Blue	1. Yellow 2. Blue 3. Off-white
Tie	1. Red/navy 2. Black/gold 3. Green/red	1. Red/gold 2. Blue/yellow 3. Blue/green	1. Red/burgundy 2. Black 3. Black/green	1. Brown/green 2. Brown/yellow 3. Blue/brown	1. Yellow/green 2. Blue/green 3. Red/green
Silk Square or Scarf	1. Blue 2. Black/gold 3. Green or red	1. Red/gold 2. Yellow 3. Blue/green	1. Gray 2. Burgundy 3. Green	1. Green 2. Yellow 3. Blue	1. Yellow 2. Blue/green 3. Red or green
Jewelry	1. Silver finish 2. Gold finish 3. Gold or silver finish	1. Silver Finish 2. Gold finish 3. Silver finish	1. Gold finish 2. Silver finish 3. Gold finish	1. 2. Gold finish 3.	1. Gold or 2. Silver finish 3.
Belt	1. Cordovan 2. Black 3. Brown or black	1. Black 2. Cordovan 3. Black	1. Gray 2. or 3. Black	1. Brown 2. or 3. Cordovan	1. Brown 2. Cordovan 3. Brown
Socks	1. Navy or gray 2. Black 3. Green	1. 2. Navy 3.	1. Black 2. Burgundy 3. Black	1. Green 2. Brown 3. Brown	1. Olive 2. Green 3. Brown
Shoes	1. Cordovan 2. Black 3. Brown or black	1. Black 2. Cordovan 3. Black	1. 2. Black 3.	1. Brown 2. or 3. Cordovan	1. Brown 2. Cordovan 3. Brown
Hat	1. Medium gray 2. Black 3. Olive	1. Gray 2. Blue 3. Camel	1. Black 2. Gray 3. Olive	1. Green 2. Brown 3. Brown	1. Olive 2. Brown 3. Bronze
Outercoat	1. Gray or black 2. Black or Covert 3. Gray or camel	1. Gray 2. Blue 3. Camel	1. Gray or 2. Black 3. Olive	1. Brown, Tan, 2. Olive 3.	1. Olive 2. Olive or Brown 3. Olive or Tan
Gloves	1. Gray suede 2. Black/gray 3. Capeskin	1. Gray 2. Black 3. Cape or mocha	1. Gray suede 2. or 3. Black cape	1. Brown cape 2. Natural pigskin 3. Olive leather	1. Brown, tan, 2. or Olive 3. Leather

(Source: Hart Schaffner and Marx, Chicago)

Experience 7-9

Which Colors Are Right?

1. On the following chart, record details about your personal coloring. Then identify three colors you think will look best on you. Also, identify three colors you think you should avoid.

Personal Coloring	Colors to Wear	Colors to Avoid
Hair color		
Eye color		
Complexion		

2. Visit a clothing store and locate a shirt in each color you should wear. Also locate a shirt in each color you should avoid. Try on each shirt and notice the difference each color makes. Explain the difference you observed in the space provided.

Experience 7-10

Suits + Shirts + Ties

In this exercise, you will coordinate suits, shirts, and ties. To complete the exercise properly, you will need a camera. If you do not have a camera, use pictures from magazines or catalogs.

Visit a men's clothing store. Explain to the manager that you are studying men's apparel and would like permission to coordinate three men's suit, shirt, and tie ensembles. Choose a solid colored suit, a striped suit, and a plaid suit. Next choose a shirt and tie to match each suit. You may choose patterned or solid shirts and ties as long as each combination looks attractive. Place the tie on top of the shirt and place the shirt inside the suit coat. When the suit, shirt, and tie are arranged, take a picture of your three clothing combinations.

SELLING SHIRTS AND TIES

Selling shirts and ties is basically the same as selling other apparel items. Color coordination is the most important skill, as shirts and ties should harmonize or pleasantly contrast.

Because shirt selections are large, a customer may have a difficult time choosing a shirt. A salesperson can help the customer by limiting the merchandise selection. The salesperson should identify three or four shirts in the customer's size and lay them on the counter. This practice focuses the customer's attention on a few shirts and makes the choice easier. If the customer is buying a suit or sport coat, the salesperson may slip the packaged shirt inside the coat front to show how the shirt complements the jacket.

When selling ties, choose three or four suitable ties and lay them on the counter. This will focus the customer's attention. Many salespeople present ties to the customer by holding them in their hands, tied in the salesperson's knot. To make the salesperson's knot, follow these steps:

1. Drape the tie, folded in half, over the palm of your hand. The narrow end should extend half way down your hand.
2. Draw the narrow end between your first and second fingers, over the wide end.
3. Bring the narrow end around behind the thumb. Hold the knot in place with your thumb. Form a dimple in the tie right under the knot.

Shirts and ties are natural go-together sales items. If a customer has decided on a shirt, suggest a tie to go with it. Using the salesperson's knot, place the tie on top of the shirt, near the collar. This will help your customer see how attractive the shirt and tie are together.

Experience 7-11

Shirts and Ties: They're a Natural

1. With a tie, demonstrate how you would make the salesperson's knot.

2. Why is it important to choose a few shirts and ties and present them to the customer?

OUTERWEAR

There are four basic types of men's **outerwear**: overcoats, topcoats, three-quarter length coats, and all-weather coats. Overcoats are heavy coats worn in cold weather. Topcoats are full-length coats worn in the spring and fall made of lightweight fabrics. Both overcoats and topcoats are designed to be worn over a suit. Their actual length is determined by fashion. Lapel styes follow the current fashion of suit coat lapels.

Three-quarter length coats are shorter and more casual. All-weather coats usually have a water-repellent or water-resistant finish. They usually have a zip-out lining that makes them warm enough to be worn in the cold weather. Without the lining, they can be worn in the chilly spring and fall weather. An example of an all-weather coat is a trench coat. (See Figure 7-14.)

Men's outerwear is sized the same as men's suits, by chest sizes (36 to 46) and height (short, regular, long, extra long). Thus, for example, the label for a coat may read 38L, meaning the coat should be worn by a person 5 feet 11 inches to 6 feet 2 inches who has a 38-inch chest.

Most of the sales principles that apply when selling a suit also apply to selling a coat. Asking the customer to try on the coat, positioning him at the mirror, checking the fit, and pointing out the quality features and benefits are techniques that should be used when selling a coat.

CASUAL WEAR

Casual wear—slacks, jeans, shorts, sport shirts, and sweaters—is a major part of a man's wardrobe. The popularity of casual wear has grown because of its comfort.

SLACKS, JEANS, AND SHORTS

Casual slacks, jeans, and shorts are popular menswear items. They are worn for sports or leisure. They are comfortable clothes. When worn for active sports, they must allow room for freedom of movement.

Casual slacks are styled like dress slacks; however, they are often in more casual fabrics, such as corduroy or cotton-polyester blends. Jeans are most often made of denim. Casual slacks and jeans are sized by waist and inseam measurement. Men's shorts vary in length from just above the knee, as in walking shorts, to high on the thigh, as in tennis shorts. Shorts are sized by waist measurement only.

SPORT SHIRTS AND SWEATERS

Sport shirts are short or long sleeve shirts that are not designed to be worn with a tie. Most woven and knit sport shirts are sized by a man's neck measurement into four categories. These sizes and their corresponding neck measurement are: small (S) 14 to 14½ inches, medium (M) 15 to 15½ inches, large (L) 16 to 16½ inches, and extra large (XL) 17 to 17½ inches.

Sport shirts may be button up the front or pullover style. The neckline may be scoop, V, round, or crew. Sport shirts are usually made from easy-care, comfortable fabrics, such as polyester/cotton blends.

Sweaters are sized by chest measurements. These sizes and measurements are: small (34 to 36 inches), medium (38 to 40 inches), large (42 to 44 inches), and extra large (46 to 48 inches). They come in two classic styles, pullovers and cardigans. The pullover sweater may have a V-neck, turtleneck, or crew neck. Sleeveless V-neck sweaters are called sweater vests. Cardigan sweaters button down the front. They may or may not have a collar, and they may or may not be belted.

Sweaters are available in a variety of colors and patterns. They are chosen to match or contrast with slacks. They are made of natural fibers, or man-made fibers, or a combination of fibers.

Experience 7-12

Mix and Match a Wardrobe

1. Create a casual wear wardrobe for a customer who is going on a three-day vacation to San Diego, California. The temperature there is usually mild, in the upper 60s. This man plans on playing some golf and sightseeing in southern California. The customer wants to take as few clothing items with him as possible. He has just purchased a 100 percent worsted wool navy blue blazer to wear on formal occasions.

   Look through magazines or newspapers and locate two pair of slacks and three shirts the customer could mix and match with the blazer. Cut out or copy these clothing items and attach them to a separate sheet of paper. On that same paper, explain why you chose the clothing items. Discuss the texture, colors, and versatility of each item. What other casual wear would you suggest he take?

2. Look through your wardrobe and identify all the casual wear. On a separate sheet of paper, describe these items by style, color, texture. Determine how many different looks you can create by mixing and matching these casual wear items. Write all the combinations on the paper.

Fig. 7-14 Men's coats are available in a variety of styles. Learn to recognize these basic styles.

FORMAL WEAR

Men wear formal wear to weddings, evening social events, and semiformal functions, such as dances. Many men's stores sell or rent men's formal wear, including tuxedos and dinner jackets.

There is a wide variation of formal wear available to men. The classic tuxedo or "tux" is a finely tailored black suit with faille (a ribbed silk or rayon fabric) or satin lapels, black vest, pleated shirt, and black bow tie. Contemporary tuxedos are colorful variations of the

Fig. 7-15 Learn the elements that go to make up these two popular looks in men's formal wear.

black tuxedo, such as pastel blue, sunshine yellow, and wine. The trim on the ruffled shirt and the bow tie usually match the tux color. Grooms often choose white or light colors in summer and dark colors for fall. Two men's formal wear styles you should be familiar with are shown in Figure 7-15.

Experience 7-13

Checking Out a Formal Look

Visit a local store that sells or rents men's formal wear. Make a list of the various styles and colors of formal wear. Find out what accessories (shirt, shoes, tie, and so on) would give each suit a total formal wear look.

If there are no formal wear stores near you, locate a copy of a bridal magazine. Usually these magazines feature formal wear for grooms. List the men's formal wear styles and accessories featured in the magazine.

HOSIERY

Most men's hosiery is one size that stretches to fit all sizes. These are called stretch socks. Nonstretch hosiery sizes run in half sizes from 9½ to 13. Nonstretch sock sizes do not correspond to shoe sizes. See Table 2.

TABLE 2

SHOE AND SOCK SIZES

If shoe size is	7–8	8½–9½	10–11½	11½–13
Nonstretch hosiery size is	10½	11	12	13

The most popular hosiery colors are black, navy, brown, gray, green, and olive. Usually, the sock color matches or blends with the man's slacks. Black socks are worn with black or gray slacks. Navy socks are worn with blue. Brown, green, or olive socks are worn with brown, green, or olive slacks.

UNDERWEAR

Undershirts and undershorts make up a man's underwear wardrobe. Customers look for fit, comfort, absorbency, and easy care when buying underwear.

Undershirts are in two styles—T-shirts and athletic shirts. T-shirts have short sleeves and either a V-neck or crew neck. Athletic shirts have a scoop neck and no sleeves. Undershirts are sized by chest measurement: small (30 to 34 inches), medium (36 to 40 inches), large (42 to 44 inches), and extra large (46 to 52 inches). They are available in a range of colors, but white is the most preferred.

Two styles of undershorts are briefs and boxer shorts. Briefs have an elasticized waistband and legs. And boxer shorts have an elasticized waist and hemmed legs. Undershorts are sized by waist measurement, 28 to 44, in even inches. They are available in many colors and different patterns.

PAJAMAS AND ROBES

Sleepwear, such as pajamas and robes, are available in a wide range of colors and patterns. Popular sleepwear fabrics are flannel and broadcloth. Pajamas and robes are sized by chest measurement: small (34 to 36 inches), medium (38 to 40 inches), large (42 to 44 inches), and extra large (46 to 48 inches). Pajamas are also sized by letters A, B, C, and D. Size A pajamas are small; B are medium; C, large; and D, extra large.

Two popular pajama styles are the pullover with a V-neck or crew neck and the coat style, which buttons up the front. For hot weather, some men wear short pajamas with pants above the knee. Others prefer nightshirts.

Men's robes are usually the wraparound style. Often, robes are made of terry cloth. More luxurious robes are made of velour or "silky" fabrics. For warmth, men wear flannel robes.

SELLING MEN'S FURNISHINGS

Selling men's furnishings, including casual wear, underwear, and hosiery, requires product knowledge and selling know-how. Both men and women purchase men's clothing. Sometimes you will see the person and be able to draw your own conclusions about the best styles and colors. When waiting on women customers, you will need to rely on skillful questioning to decide on the appropriate merchandise. Men's furnishings is a profitable sales area for salespeople who know their product and understand their customers.

Experience 7-14

Making a Sale

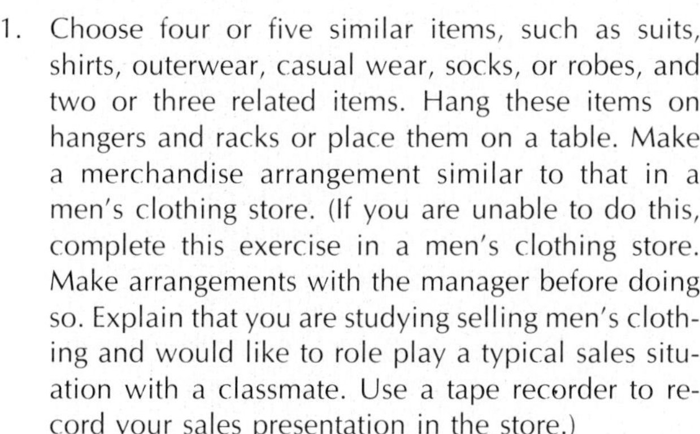

1. Choose four or five similar items, such as suits, shirts, outerwear, casual wear, socks, or robes, and two or three related items. Hang these items on hangers and racks or place them on a table. Make a merchandise arrangement similar to that in a men's clothing store. (If you are unable to do this, complete this exercise in a men's clothing store. Make arrangements with the manager before doing so. Explain that you are studying selling men's clothing and would like to role play a typical sales situation with a classmate. Use a tape recorder to record your sales presentation in the store.)
2. Examine each of the merchandise items carefully. Be sure you are able to discuss details about the style, care requirements, and construction of each garment.
3. Take the part of a salesperson and have a male classmate take the part of a customer. Role play a typical sales situation. Be sure to:
   a. Find out what the customer wants to purchase.
   b. If appropriate, suggest the customer try on the garment.
   c. Point out the benefits of buying the garment; talk about the color, line, style, fit, and quality of the garment.
   d. Overcome any customer objections.
   e. Close the sale.
   f. Suggest related items.
4. Before beginning the role playing experience, ask the customer to pretend to want to purchase a specific garment or something for a specific occasion. Try to make this sale as realistic as possible.

8 Infants' and Children's Wear

Selling infants' and children's apparel is somewhat different from selling men's or women's clothing. Unlike men and women, children seldom purchase clothing for themselves. In fact, much of a child's wardrobe is purchased when the child is not with the customer. Most buyers of children's clothing are usually parents, grandparents, and other relatives.

Children's wear customers are interested in fashion, durability, care, fit, and style. Because children are hard on their clothes, customers demand quality garments.

CHILDREN'S WEAR SIZES

Children's wear is classified into various size groups: infants, toddlers, children or preschool, girls, boys, subteen, and prep. These size groups reflect the growth stages of children. Although there is some overlap between size groups, and some manufacturers may use different sizing standards, children's sizes are usually based on height and weight.

Children's sizes sometimes relate to the age of the child. Many 4-year-olds do wear a size 4, for example. However, there are many variations in the body build of children. A 6-year-old may not wear a size 6 because children of the same age often vary in height and weight.

When a customer asks, "What size do I need for my nephew? He's 6" you do not have enough information to determine the correct size. Also, "He's big for his age" will not help you, because you will not know how big. Try to find out the child's height and weight and then refer to the size charts for the merchandise your store sells. Many manufacturers print sizing guides for their clothing on merchandise boxes or bags. Let's examine infants' and children's size groups.

INFANTS' SIZES

Infants' clothing is for babies from birth until the time they begin to walk. Two methods are used to size infants' clothing. Both methods are based on a baby's height and weight. (See Table 1.) One method uses the following sizes: 3 months, 6 months, 12 months, 18 months, 24 months, and 36 months. The other uses these sizes: newborn, small, medium, large, and extra large.

TABLE 1

INFANTS' SIZES

Size	Height (in Inches)	Approx. Weight (in Pounds)	Size	Height (in Inches)	Approx. Weight (in Pounds)
3 mo.	24	13	Newborn	24	up to 14
6 mo.	26½	18	Small (S)	24½–28	15–20
12 mo.	29	22	Medium (M)	28½–32	21–26
18 mo.	31½	26	Large (L)	32½–36	27–32
24 mo.	34	29	Extra Large (XL)	36½–38	33–36
36 mo.	36½	32			

TODDLERS' SIZES

A toddler is a young child who is learning to walk. Clothes for the toddler are shorter in the legs and wider at the waist than clothing for older children. Toddler sizes range from T1 to T4. (The T stands for toddler.) The sizes are based on height and weight. (See Table 2.)

CHILDREN'S SIZES

Children's sizes, or preschool sizes, are mostly worn by boys and girls between the ages of 3 and 6. These children have "round" figures and have not developed waistlines. Many children's wear manufacturers produce sizes 4, 5, 6, and 6x for girls and sizes 3, 4, 5, 6, and 7 for boys. (See Table 3.) There is some overlap between toddlers' and children's sizes. For example, a T3 has the same height and weight measurements as a children's size 3.

GIRLS' SIZES

Girls' sizes are for school-aged girls who have slimmer, longer figures than those in the earlier groups. The U.S. Department of Commerce, National Bureau of Standards, has proposed 18 sizes for girls' clothing. Each size is based on height and girth (broadness). The height and weight, plus bust, waist, and hip measurements, for girls' clothing are shown in Table 4.

TABLE 2

TODDLERS' SIZES

Size	Height (in Inches)	Approx. Weight (in Pounds)
T1	31	25
T2	34	29
T3	37	34
T4	40	38

TABLE 3

CHILDREN'S SIZES

Size	Height (in Inches)	Approx. Weight (in Pounds)
3	37	34
4	40	38
5	43	44
6	46	49
6x	48	(girls) 54
7	48	(boys) 54

TABLE 4

GIRLS' SIZES

1. Find the girl's height on the top line of the chart.
2. Look through the groups of measurements labeled Group A, B, or C.
3. Find the group that best matches the girl's measurements.

Height (in Inches)	49–51½	52–53½	54–55½	56–58	58½–60½	61–63
REGULAR						
GROUP A (Regular)	7R	8R	10R	12R	14R	16R
Bust (in Inches)	25½–26½	26½–27½	28–29	29½–30½	31–32	32½–33½
Waist (in Inches)	22½–23	23–23½	24–24½	25–25½	26–26½	27–27½
Hip (in Inches)	27½–28	28–29	29½–30½	31–32½	33–34½	35–36½
Weight (in Pounds)	60	66	74	84	96	112
SLIM						
GROUP B (Slim)	7S	8S	10S	12S	14S	16S
Bust (in Inches)	24–25	25–26	26½–27½	28–29	29½–30½	31–32
Waist (in Inches)	20½–21	21–21½	22–22½	23–23½	24–24½	25–25½
Hip (in Inches)	25½–26	26–27	27½–28½	29–30½	31–32½	33–34½
Weight (in Pounds)	53	57	67	77	89	103
CHUBBY						
GROUP C (Chubby)	7½	8½	10½	12½	14½	16½
Bust (in Inches)	28–29	29–30	30½–31½	32–33	33½–34½	35–36
Waist (in Inches)	26–26½	26½–27	27½–28	28½–29	29½–30	30½–31
Hip (in Inches)	30½–31	31–32	32½–33½	34–35½	36–37½	38–39½
Weight (in Pounds)	71	79	89	102	116	132

(Source: Voluntary Product Standard PS 54-72, Body Measurements for the Sizing of Girls' Apparel, *US Department of Commerce, National Bureau of Standards.)*

The numbers in each size correspond with the height of the girl in her stocking feet. Weight and body measurements determine whether she wears a slim, regular, or chubby size. For example, a girl who wears a size 10 is 55 inches. If she weighs 69, she will wear a 10 slim.

BOYS' SIZES

Boys' sizes range in even numbers from 8 through 20. Some boyswear manufacturers produce clothing in sizes 6 and 22 through 26. Boys' clothing is classified into three size groups: regular (R), slim (S), and husky (H). (See Table 5.) The height of the boy in his stocking feet is the primary guide to size. Chest, waist, and hip measurements determine whether the boy wears a slim, regular, or husky. For example, all boys 4 feet 2 inches tall wear a size 8. A boy 4 feet 2 inches tall with a 26 inch waist and 28 inch hips would wear 8H (husky) pants.

TABLE 5

BOYS' SIZES

Slim (S)

SIZE	6	7	8	10	12	14
Height (in Inches)	44–46½	47–48½	49–50½	51–54½	55–58½	59–61½
Chest (in Inches)	23½–24	24–24½	25–25½	26–27	27½–29	29½–30½
Waist (in Inches)	20–20½	20½–21	21½–22	22½–23	23½–24	24½–25
Hip (in Inches)	23½–24	24–24½	25–25½	26–27½	28–29½	30–31
Approx. Weight (in Pounds)	43	48	53	65	77	90
SIZE	**16**	**18**	**20**	**22**	**24**	
Height (in Inches)	62–64½	65–66½	67–68½	69–70½	71–72½	
Chest (in Inches)	31–32	32½–33½	34–35	35½–36½	37–38	
Waist (in Inches)	25½–26	26½–27	27½–28	28½–29	29½–30	
Hip (in Inches)	31½–33	33½–34½	35–36	36½–37½	38–39	
Approx. Weight (in Pounds)	104	115	126	138	152	

Regular (R)

SIZE	6	7	8	10	12	14
Height (in Inches)	44–46½	47–48½	49–50½	51–54½	55–58½	59–61½
Chest (in Inches)	24½–25	25½–26	26½–27	27½–28½	29–30	30½–32
Waist (in Inches)	22–22½	22½–23	23½–24	24½–25	25½–26	26½–27
Hip (in Inches)	24½–25	25½–26	26½–27	27½–28½	29–30½	31–32½
Approx. Weight (in Pounds)	49	54	59	73	87	100
SIZE	**16**	**18**	**20**	**22**	**24**	
Height (in Inches)	62–64½	65–66½	67–68½	69–70½	71–72½	
Chest (in Inches)	32½–33½	34–35	35½–36½	37–38	38½–39½	
Waist (in Inches)	27½–28	28–29	29½–30	30½–31	31½–32	
Hip (in Inches)	33–34½	35–36	36½–37½	38–38½	39–40	
Approx. Weight (in Pounds)	115	126	138	152	168	

Husky (H)

SIZE	6	7	8	10	12	14
Height (in Inches)	44–46½	47–48½	49–50½	51–54½	55–58½	59–61½
Chest (in Inches)	25½–26	26–27	27½–28	28½–29½	30–31½	32–33½
Waist (in Inches)	24–24½	24½–25	25½–26	26½–27	27½–28	28½–29½
Hip (in Inches)	26–26½	27–27½	28–29	29½–30½	31–32½	33–35
Approx. Weight (in Pounds)	55	61	67	81	95	112

BOYS' SIZES (CONTINUED)

SIZE	16	18	20	22	24	
Height (in Inches)	62–64½	65–66½	67–68½	69–70½	71–72½	
Chest (in Inches)	34–35½	36–37	37½–38½	39–40	40½–41½	
Waist (in Inches)	30–30½	30½–31½	32–32½	33–33½	34–34½	
Hip (in Inches)	35½–36½	37–38	38½–39½	40–40½	41–42	
Approx. Weight (in Pounds)	130	143	156	170	186	

Note: This chart represents a range of measurements for each size for each key measurement. It is included only to assist the consumer in identifying boys' body types and sizes, and is not a requirement of the standard. 1 inch equals 2.54 centimeters, 1 pound equals 0.45 kilograms.
(Source: Voluntary Product Standard PS 36-70. Body Measurements for Sizing Boys' Apparel, *US Department of Commerce, National Bureau of Standards.)*

Experience 8-1

What's the Size?

Using Tables 5 and 6, determine the correct size clothing for the following boys and girls. In the space provided, write the size that will best fit each child.

1. Boy, age 8, height 53 in., weight 66 lb. ____
2. Girl, age 9, height 57½ in., weight 100 lb. ____
3. Girl, age 7, height 51 in., weight 55 lb. ____
4. Boy, age 11, height 60 in., weight 109 lb. ____
5. Boy, age 14, height 60 in., weight 94 lb. ____
6. Girl, age 13, height 62½ in., weight 102 lb. ____

SUBTEEN SIZES
Subteen sizes, for girls whose figures are beginning to mature, range from 6 through 14. These sizes are determined mainly by height and bust, waist, and hip measurements. (See Table 6.) When girls outgrow subteen sizes, they move into the junior sizes described in Chapter 6.

PREP SIZES
Prep sizes are for young men, usually between the ages of 12 and 16, whose bodies are maturing. Often there is a separate young men's, student, or prep department for these customers. Prep sizes are determined in the same way as men's clothing: pant sizes by waist and inseam (see Table 7); shirts and jackets by chest measurement. (See Table 8.)

TABLE 6

SUBTEEN SIZES

Size	Height (in Inches)	Weight (in Pounds)	Bust (in Inches)	Waist (in Inches)	Hips (in Inches)
6	57½	69	27	22½	28
8	58½	79	28½	23½	30
10	59½	89	30	24½	32
12	60½	99	31½	25½	34
14	61½	109	33	26½	36

TABLE 7

PREP SIZES

Waist (in Inches)	25	26	27	28	29	30
Short Inseam (in Inches)	27	28	28	28	29	29
Medium Inseam (in Inches)	28	29	29	29	30	30
Long Inseam (in Inches)	29	30	30	30	31	31
Extra long Inseam (in Inches)			31	31	32	32

TABLE 8

PREP SIZES

Size Chest (in Inches)	14 35¼	16 37¼	18 39¼	20 41¼	22 41¾	24 42¼

MEASURING CHILDREN

The best way to fit children's clothing is to know their measurements. Many parents know their children's height and weight when they are infants. For toddlers and young children, salespeople should use a tape measure to determine their measurements. To measure a child's waist, hips, chest or bust, follow the procedure described in the chapters on women's and men's apparel. (See Figure 8-1.)

To determine a child's height, many stores use a measuring stick attached to the wall. Ask the child to stand next to the measuring stick in stocking feet to measure his or her height. Some stores have scales, however, most stores rely on their salespeople to estimate each child's weight.

When determining clothing sizes for children, other measurements besides height and weight are important. For example, the chest measurement is important to determine coat, jacket, sweater, shirt, or blouse sizes. Both height and waist measurements are important for determining the size slacks, underwear briefs, and swimwear a boy wears. A girl's height, waist, and hip measurements are needed to determine sizes for her pants and skirts.

Experience 8-2

Size Them Up

1. Choose three children. (If possible, they should be 6 months old, 12 years old, and somewhere in between.) Estimate the height and weight of each child. Record your estimates in the space provided. After you have made your estimates, use a yardstick or measuring tape to determine each child's height. Weigh each child on a scale. For children over 5 years old, also estimate and then measure their chest, waist, and hips. Record the measurements in the space provided.

Measurements	Child 1: Age ____		Child 2: Age ____		Child 3: Age ____	
	Estimate	Actual	Estimate	Actual	Estimate	Actual
Height						
Weight						
Chest						
Waist						
Hips						

2. Based on the actual measurements you took, decide what size coat, slacks, and shirts or blouse each child should wear. Refer to the size charts in Tables 1 through 8. Record the sizes in the space provided. Check with the children or their parents to see if the sizes you determined from Tables 1 through 8 are the same sizes they last bought in each of the items.

Item	CHILD 1		CHILD 2		CHILD 3	
	Size From Table	Actual Last Size	Size From Table	Actual Last Size	Size From Table	Actual Last Size
Coat						
Slacks						
Shirt or blouse						

Source: Sears, Roebuck and Company.

How to Measure for Girls' and Teens' Apparel

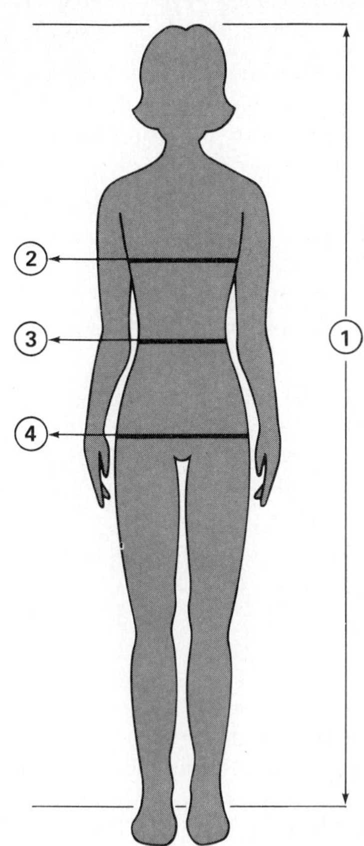

(1) **Height:** Have girl stand against the wall without shoes. Make a mark level with the top of her head. Measure from this point down to the floor.

(2) **Chest or Bust:** Measure around girl's body at fullest part of her chest or bust. Hold tape firm but not tight. Keep the tape straight across her back. Be sure girl is standing naturally.

(3) **Waist:** Measure around the smallest part of girl's natural waistline. Hold the tape firm but not tight.

(4) **Hips:** Have girl stand naturally with her feet together. Measure in a straight line around body at fullest part of hips. Hold the tape firm but not tight.

Fig. 8-1 When measuring girls and teenagers, follow the guidelines shown here.

CHILDREN'S CLOTHING FABRICS

Children like soft, comfortable fabrics. Parents like children's clothing to be easy to care for, especially those

FLAME-RESISTANT
U.S. STANDARD FF5-74
AND DOC FF3-71
GPU 8410-001
SIZE 1
MADE IN U.S.A.
RN 14600
65% MODACRYLIC
35% POLYESTER
MACHINE WASH WARM
NO BLEACH
TUMBLE DRY LOW
NO IRON

Courtesy Nazareth Mills, Inc. A Division of Kayser-Roth Corp.

Fig. 8-2 Here's a typical example of a label from a garment made of a flame-resistant fabric.

worn for school or play. This means clothing that can be machine-washed and -dried and requires no ironing. Delicate fabrics, such as organdy, which must be washed by hand or dry-cleaned, are popular for "dress up" occasions.

The most widely used fabric for children's clothing is cotton. Because it is cool, soft, lightweight, and absorbent, it is comfortable. Cotton is also washable and needs no ironing if it is knitted or permanent press. Much infant clothing is made from combed cotton because it is very soft and does not irritate a baby's skin.

Children's clothing is often made from blends of man-made and natural fibers; cotton and polyester is the commonest blend. This blend combines the long-wearing, easy-care features of man-made fibers with the coolness, absorbency, and natural look of the natural fibers.

Many children's apparel items are also made from wool. Wool is warm and can insulate the child from cold, damp weather. It is often used for children's outerwear, such as sweaters and coats, and is long-wearing and always in fashion.

Children's sleepwear must be made of fabrics that can pass current government flammability standards. Today, apparel stores sell flame-resistant sleepwear that is self-extinguishing when removed from the flame. (See Figure 8-2.)

Experience 8-3

What's the Fabric?

Visit a store that sells children's clothing. Locate ten different articles of children's clothing. On a separate sheet of paper, make a list of the items, the fiber content of each, and the fabric of each. Also list an advantage of each fabric for children's clothing. If necessary, ask a salesperson to help you determine the fabric and the advantages of that fabric for each of the items that you selected.

FITTING CHILDREN'S CLOTHING

When fitting children's clothing, it is very important to consider comfort. Each garment should allow the child to move around, sit, stoop, stand, run, and jump. Clothing that is too tight or too large restricts a child's movement. Uncomfortable, ill-fitting clothing may cause a child to be irritable or to have an accident.

When possible, the child should be taken shopping to try on clothing. The child gets the best fit, and parents do not have to return poorly fitting clothing to the store.

When the child tries on clothing, the salesperson should check for proper fit. Note how the "Check List for Proper Fit," prepared by Sears, Roebuck and Company, will help you identify the proper fit for children's clothing. If you can answer yes to each question on the check list, the garment fits the child well.

Customers who shop alone for children's clothing should know their children's height, weight, and other measurements. Many parents solve this problem by bringing along a clothing article that fits the child. The salesperson can then measure the article or check the label for size and choose the corresponding size in the store.

If you sell infants' clothing, you will often wait on customers who are buying gifts for new or expected babies. Because this clothing is usually for future use, help them select garments that will be appropriate to the season when the baby will be large enough to wear them.

CHECK LIST FOR PROPER FIT

YES	NO	
☐	☐	Can the child move freely? Ask the child to sit, bend, stoop, reach, stretch.
☐	☐	Does garment fit smoothly, neither bagging nor binding?
☐	☐	Do clothes hang from the shoulders rather than the neck?
☐	☐	Do necklines and collars fit well without binding or rubbing and yet go over the head easily?
☐	☐	Are armholes and sleeves roomy enough for action?
☐	☐	Are separate tops long enough to stay tucked in as child moves and plays?
☐	☐	Are pant legs and dresses short enough to prevent the child from stepping on hems and tripping as he or she moves?
☐	☐	Are coats, jackets, snowsuits, large enough to fit comfortably over other clothing?

(Source: Sears, Roebuck and Co.)

When you are helping customers buy clothing, remind them that it is important to buy the right size. Clothing that is too large may be worn out by the time the child actually grows into it, or the child may never grow into that exact size. It is a safety hazard because it may trip the child. Also, garments that are too large will not be comfortable or look attractive.

Experience 8-4

How Does It Fit?

Take a small child between the ages of 3 and 8 shopping at an apparel store. Choose three different clothing items the child could wear. (Try to estimate accurately the size the child needs.) Help the child try on all three items and analyze the fit of each. Use the "Check List for Proper Fit" to help you. On a separate sheet of paper, describe the clothing items the child tried on and the good and poor fitting features of each.

SELLING CHILDREN'S CLOTHING

In selling children's apparel, you will often work with two shoppers: the parent, who pays for the merchandise, and the child, who is a strong influence on the parent's decision of what to buy. When selling to a parent and child, try to determine who is the decision maker and gear your sales approach to that person.

Many children dislike shopping trips, even when the purpose of the trip is to buy them new clothes. They don't like waiting around or looking at so many items. They get bored listening to salespeople talk about styles, fit, or construction details in language they don't understand. When the salesperson gears the total sales presentation to the "grown up," young shoppers probably wish they were out playing.

It takes a skillful salesperson to make shopping fun for both parents and children. Successful children's wear salespeople have to know the merchandise they sell, as well as how to work with children. They need to understand that children try to "show off" for strangers. They must realize that children who are looking for attention will do almost anything to get it.

Successful children's wear salespeople show a real interest in children, which makes both children and adults feel good. These salespeople pay attention to their young customers and talk to them in words they understand. Often they crouch down so that they are on the eye level with a child. They do everything possible to make the child feel as though he or she has a part in the sale.

GREETING CUSTOMERS

As a children's wear salesperson, you should start the sale by greeting both the child and the customer. Many children's wear salespeople greet the child first to make the youngster feel important. Talk about things that interest the child to begin a good relationship with the child and adult as soon as you greet them.

Suppose a woman and young boy in a Little League baseball suit enter your store. You may say to the child, "What position do you play?" This greeting will probably lead you into a conversation about baseball. And you know that this is a subject that the boy is eager to talk about.

Children like salespeople who make them feel important. If you know how to make the child feel important, the child will probably like you and be cooperative. If the child likes you, the sale is half made!

Experience 8-5

Selling to Children: It's a Challenge!

1. Visit two stores that sell children's wear. At each store, speak with a salesperson who specializes in selling children's wear. Explain to the salespeople that you are studying children's wear in school. Ask them the following questions and record their answers in the space provided.
   a. In what ways is selling to children different from selling to adults?

      Store 1: ______________________

      ____

      ____

      Store 2: ______________________

      ____

      ____

   b. What special sales techniques do you use that appeal to children?

      Store 1: ______________________

      ____

      Store 2: ______________________

      ____

   c. How do you handle difficult children?

      Store 1: ______________________

      ____

      ____

      Store 2: ______________________

      ____

      ____

      ____

2. After you have visited both stores, form into a small group with other classmates who have completed this experience. Discuss your findings. If you are unable to visit a store, form into a small group with three or four classmates. Discuss the following questions. Record your answers on a separate piece of paper.
   a. In what ways do you think selling to children will be different from selling to adults?
   b. What special sales techniques do you think would appeal to children? Discuss any special techniques that you have seen.
   c. How would you handle difficult children? Be realistic in your answer.

DETERMINING NEEDS

Some children's wear customers have very specific ideas about the merchandise they want to buy. They may tell the salesperson what items they are looking for or the salesperson may ask questions to determine their needs. Other children's wear customers, especially those shopping for gifts, have few ideas about what to buy for children. These customers often rely on the salesperson to recommend attractive and appropriate merchandise.

As a children's wear salesperson, you will need to be familiar with the types of children's clothing sold. You also need to know about the activities children do at different ages so that you can suggest appropriate clothing. For example, you should know that infants mainly wear only diapers, undershirts, and sleepers. Toddlers are usually dressed in play clothes, and school-aged children need clothes for play, dress, and school.

Ask customers questions about the child's measurements and weight so that you can choose the right size and style clothing. Also you need to find out about the child's personal coloring so that you can choose attractive colors.

Let's examine some of the many types of children's clothing. Because preschool and school-aged children's clothing is similar to men's and women's clothing, the emphasis is on infants' and toddler's apparel.

Infants' Clothing If you work in the infants' department, you will often be asked to help choose a layette. A **layette** is a combination of articles a newborn baby needs: diapers, waterproof pants, shirts, nightgowns, sweaters, crib sheets, and blankets. Sometimes bottles, scales, and infant carriers are included.

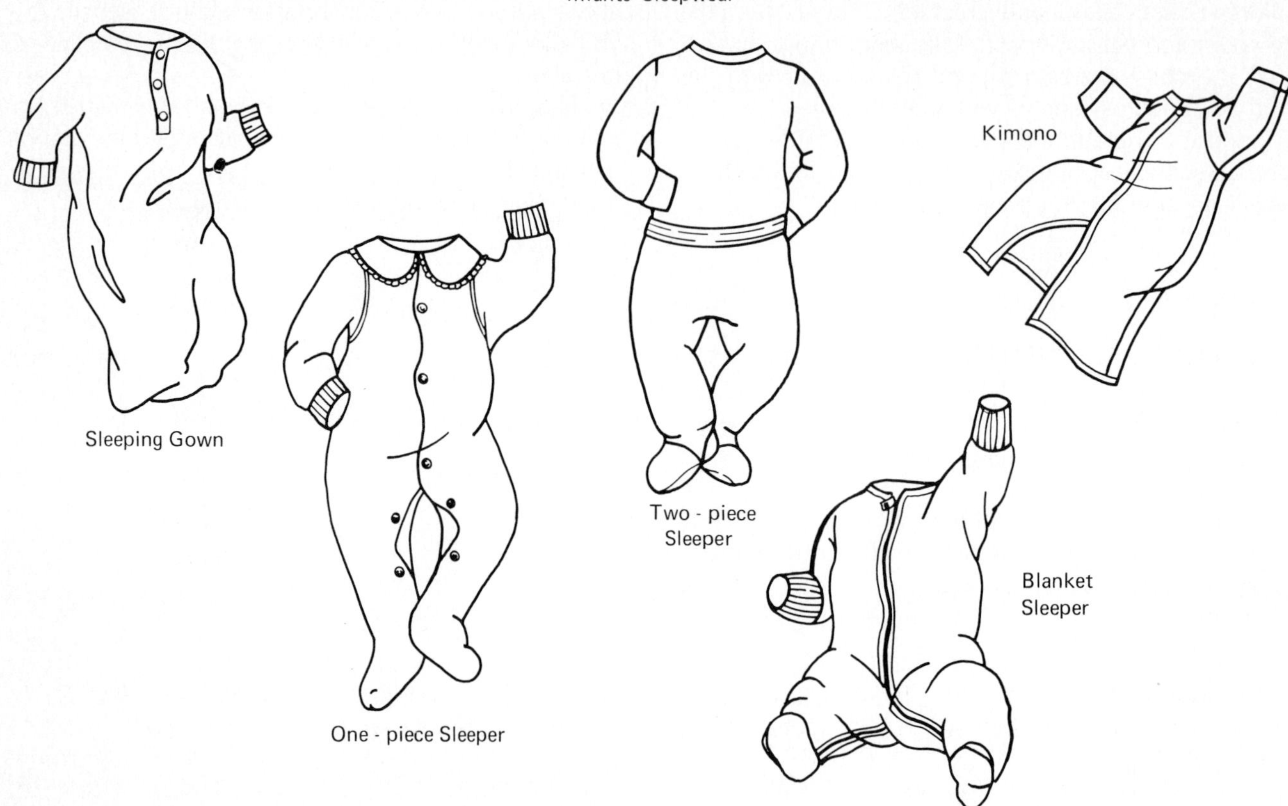

Fig. 8-3 As this illustration shows, there are many sleepwear styles available for babies.

Many types of diapers are available for infants. Diapers may be prefolded, shaped to look like pants, made of birdseye for older infants, and disposable. Waterproof pants are worn over cloth diapers.

Infant shirts are designed for warmth. Two popular styles are slip-on and snap. Snap shirts are convenient because they open down the front and do not have to be slipped over the baby's head. Both types of shirts are worn under other clothing or alone.

There are many sleepwear styles for babies. **Sleepers**, usually made of a stretch fabric with raglan sleeves, are one-piece suits that cover the baby's feet. They also have snaps down the front, crotch, and legs for easy dressing and changing. **Sleeping gowns** have set-in sleeves with a cuff that can be turned back to cover the baby's hands and a drawstring bottom that covers the baby's legs and feet. **Kimonos** are the length of sleeping gowns, have long sleeves, and close at the neck with two snaps or ties so that they are open around the feet. **Two-piece sleepers** include a pullover top and bottoms that snap together at the waist and may have snaps down the crotch and legs. (See Figure 8-3.)

Because newborn babies sleep much of the time, they are often dressed in sleepwear. These sleepwear styles keep babies warm even when they kick off the covers. For dress up, baby girls wear dresses and baby boys wear suits.

During the winter, infants wear a bunting bag or bootie suit when out of doors. The **bunting bag**, shaped like a bag, covers the baby's hands, legs, feet, and head. The **bootie suit** has separate legs. Older babies wear a **snowsuit**, which covers their arms and legs but not their feet. (See Figure 8-4.)

Infants beyond the newborn stage wear coveralls, overalls, pants, and shirts for casual occasions or for play. Coveralls have long pants, long sleeves, and a high neck. Overalls have long pants and shoulder straps. In cooler weather, babies wear a knit shirt under their overalls for warmth. (See Figure 8-5.) Snaps along the inseam make it possible to change diapers without completely undressing the infant.

Baby's clothing styles appeal to the purchaser, not the wearer. Adults choose clothing that is washable and requires no ironing. They want clothing that is styled for baby's comfort and easy movement.

Toddlers' Clothing Toddlers are just beginning to walk. They need clothing styled for maximum freedom of movement. Clothing with baggy legs or big cuffs can impair movement or cause accidents. Also toddlers need clothing that is easy to take off, because this period is when most children are toilet trained. Because toddlers don't have a definite waist, their clothing should have elasticized waists or adjustable straps.

Toddlers' clothing is similar to infants' clothing. Boys and girls usually wear sleepers with gripper feet to bed for warmth. They wear training pants, rather than diapers, and undershirts for warmth. Toddlers often wear

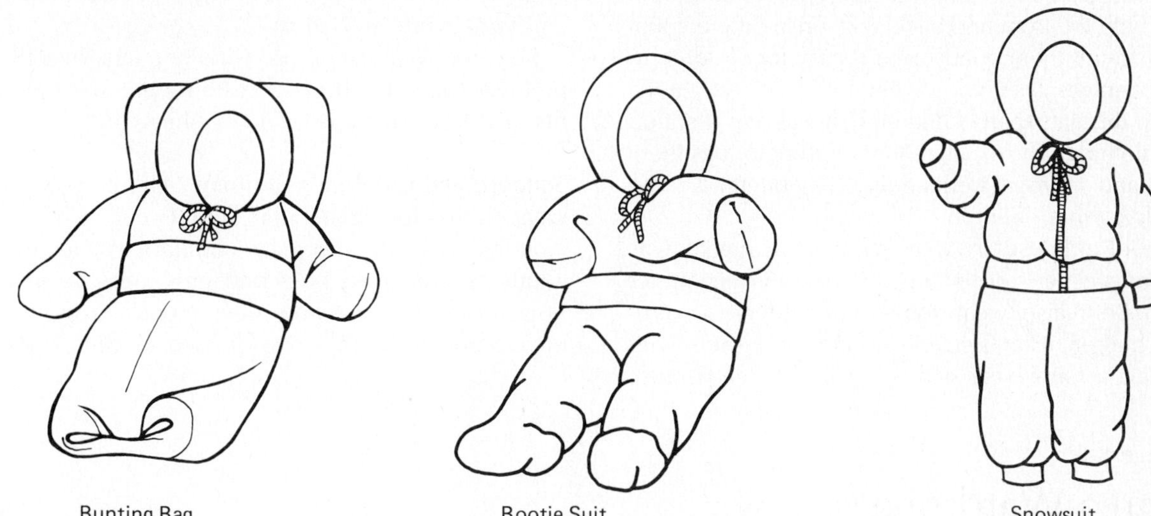

Fig. 8-4 Become familiar with the three basic styles of infants' outerwear pictured above.

pants and pullover shirts or overalls for play. Overalls often have adjustable suspenders or straps that button on the waist. Usually straps and suspenders are adjustable and can be changed as the toddler grows. They hold up the toddler's pants.

Girls' play clothes often have puffed or ruffled sleeves, round collars, and flowery designs. Boys' play clothes usually have squared collars, tailored sleeves, and flat trimmings. For dress occasions, little girls wear short dresses, smocks, a jumper and blouse, or a dress with a pinafore. A **pinafore** is a sleeveless garment that looks like an apron. Boys usually wear long or short pants with a shirt and jacket. Both boys' and girls' clothing often includes **appliques**, special designs that are sewn or ironed on the garment.

Preschoolers' Clothing Most children begin to wear preschool children's sizes when they are 2½ or 3 years

Fig. 8-5 Learn to recognize the different garments available for infants' and toddlers' play wear.

old. At this age, children begin to learn to dress themselves. Large armholes, front openings, big buttons, and clothing with the front and back alike or so different that it is easy to tell them apart make it easy for children to dress themselves.

Around this age, many children begin to pay attention to their clothing. They realize that clothing brings them attention and approval from adults. They often ask to be dressed like other children.

Preschool girls usually wear pajamas or nightgowns rather than sleepers for bedtime. Boys at this age prefer pajamas. Both also wear robes. For underwear, preschool children wear sleeveless shirts or T-shirts with short sleeves. Girls wear banded or ruffled leg panties, sometimes trimmed in lace. They wear slips under their dresses. Boys wear knitted briefs or woven undershorts and undershirts or T-shirts.

Playtime wear usually consists of pants, overalls, and pullover shirts. For dress occasions, girls wear pant outfits or dresses; boys wear pants, shirts, and jackets.

School-Aged Children's Clothing School-aged children wear clothes for school, play, and dressy occasions. The clothing styles they wear are similar to styles worn by adults. School-aged boys and girls are very aware of how they dress and how their friends dress. It is not uncommon to see a group dressed in almost identical clothing.

Experience 8-6

Design a Wardrobe

Choose items from a clothing catalog or store for an infant, toddler, preschool, or school-aged child. Plan one wardrobe for a boy and one for a girl. They can be for different ages. For example, you may plan a layette for a boy and a wardrobe for a school-aged girl.

1. Choose the age, height, weight; and other measurements of the two children for which you will be planning a wardrobe. If necessary, refer to Tables 1 through 6 to help you determine average sizes.

Measurements	Boy	Girl
Age		
Height		
Weight		
Chest		
Waist		
Hips		

2. Determine what sizes you will need for both of the children.

Garment	Boy	Girl
Sleepwear		
Underwear		
Pants		
Shirts		
Jackets		
Outerwear		
Dresses	xxxxx	

3. On a separate sheet of paper, make a list of the clothing items for each child. Then visit a store that sells these items or locate the items in a clothing catalog. Make a list of each item, its description, fiber content, needed size, color, and price. You cannot spend more than $75 for either child.

Choosing Clothing Styles When selling children's wear, it is important to determine the type clothing a customer wants to purchase. It is also important for a salesperson to choose a style that will emphasize the child's desirable features and minimize the undesirable ones. Chubby or skinny children can be made to look different by choosing clothing with certain lines. For example, a high yoke dress will give fullness to a very slender girl.

Choosing Clothing Colors Children's clothing should be chosen so that the colors suit the child's coloring. For example, a child with warm coloring, such as dark hair, eyes, and skin, will look good in warm colors, such as red. Children with light complexions, blue eyes, and blond hair look best in cool colors. Most children like bright colors; red is a favorite. If bright colors "wash out" a child's color, they may be used for accents.

Experience 8-7

Choosing Outfits

Follow the principles of color and line and choose outfits for play and dress occasions for the following two children:

1. A boy, age 7, who is tall and slender with dark skin, hair, and eyes.
2. A girl, age 10, who is medium height and chubby with fair skin, brown eyes, and light brown hair.

You may find these outfits in children's wear catalogs, magazines, or stores. Either cut out pictures of these outfits or describe them on a separate sheet of paper.

PRESENTING THE MERCHANDISE

After the clothing size, style, and color have been decided, the salesperson's next task is to present the merchandise in an attention-getting way. For example, the salesperson may ask a young child to come over to the three-way mirror to see a magic trick. While at the mirror, where the child is fascinated by seeing three images of himself or herself, the salesperson can be helping the child try on a new coat or sweater. While the child is occupied, the salesperson can point out the benefits of the garment to the adult.

Talking about the Benefits Children's wear customers want clothing that is comfortable, durable, good fitting, and fashionable. Help customers decide to purchase children's apparel by pointing out the advantages or benefits of children's wear. Try to point out the following features and benefits:

Comfort. Some styles and fabrics are more comfortable than others. For example, clothing that hangs from the shoulders is usually more comfortable than clothing that hangs from the waist. Nonbinding clothing with simple designs and minimum trim are comfortable. Stretch fabrics and knits, as well as soft, lightweight fabrics, are comfortable. Clothing that fits the child well is also comfortable.

Ease in Self-Dressing. Parents appreciate clothing that children can put on and take off by themselves. For example, front buttons or zippers can be opened and closed by a child.

Room for Growth. Because children outgrow their clothing quickly, parents look for clothing that has room for growth. These features allow a child to wear apparel for a long period of time. Some of these features are:

- Raglan sleeves, which have no definite shoulder line
- Adjustable shoulder straps
- Deep hems
- Deep cuffs
- A set-in band across the front of a dress rather than a seamed waistline
- Undefined waistline
- Stretch fabrics
- Two rows of buttons or snaps for attaching tops and bottoms

Easy Care. Because children get dirty so often, clothing that can be machine-washed and -dried and requires no ironing will appeal to customers. Soil-resistant or soil-release finishes will keep the clothing clean longer and cut down on washings. Care labels attached to children's wear provide information on how to take care of the garment.

Clothing Coordination. Part of growing up involves learning how to coordinate clothes. When young children begin to dress themselves, they often combine garments that do not go together. They may wear clothing that clashes, or they may combine a dressy blouse with casual pants. To help children learn how to coordinate clothing, many manufacturers produce clothing that has the same design or color pattern on the slacks and shirt. This helps children learn "what goes with what" at a young age.

OVERCOMING OBJECTIONS

Customers may refuse to buy children's wear because it is too expensive, the wrong style or color, or just "doesn't fit right." Some customers hesitate to buy certain items because they think the child will outgrow them too quickly.

As a salesperson, you should be able to anticipate customer objections and be prepared to overcome them. For example, suppose a customer says, "I like the dress, but I'm afraid my daughter would outgrow it before the end of the summer." You may be able to overcome this customer's objection by showing the customer another dress that has "room for growth" style features.

SUGGESTING RELATED ITEMS

A children's wear salesperson should practice suggestion selling with all customers. Suggest a matching shirt when the customer buys a pair of slacks or a sweater to the customer who is buying a skirt. Remember that additional sales for the store and commission for the salesperson can be made by suggesting appropriate merchandise to customers.

Experience 8-8

Make the Sale

1. Choose a particular children's clothing garment and three related apparel or accessory items.
2. Play the role of a children's wear salesperson and ask a classmate to play the role of a customer. Demonstrate how you would sell a children's garment to the customer. Determine the appropriate size, style, and color needed for the child. Point out the features and benefits of the garment. Discuss such benefits as comfort, self-dressing features, room for growth, easy care, and easy clothing coordination. Overcome any objections, close the sale, and suggestion sell a related item to the customer. If you can, use a tape recorder to record your sales presentation as you role play a salesperson.

Information to Customer Before beginning this role-playing experience, think about the child for whom you are buying. Decide on the child's age, sex, size, and coloring. Try to make this sales presentation as realistic as possible.

9 Shoes

Rogers Department Store has regular training meetings for salespeople and department managers. These training sessions, which are conducted by the store's buyers and sales representatives from apparel and accessory manufacturers, provide employees with information on new products.

Lillian Day, buyer for the Women's Shoe Department, kicks off the session. "Over and over again you have heard that product knowledge is important. Have you ever asked yourself why? One proven reason is that merchandise information enables salespeople to increase their sales and their earning capacity. Does that surprise you? It shouldn't. Merchandise knowledge creates enthusiasm for what you sell and it adds to your self-confidence. When you talk knowledgeably about your product, you build the customer's confidence in you, the merchandise, and the store.

"There's much merchandise information new shoe salespeople need to know. Some of you may be working in men's shoes, some in women's and some in children's. Much of the information we will be discussing about shoes applies to all three customer groups."

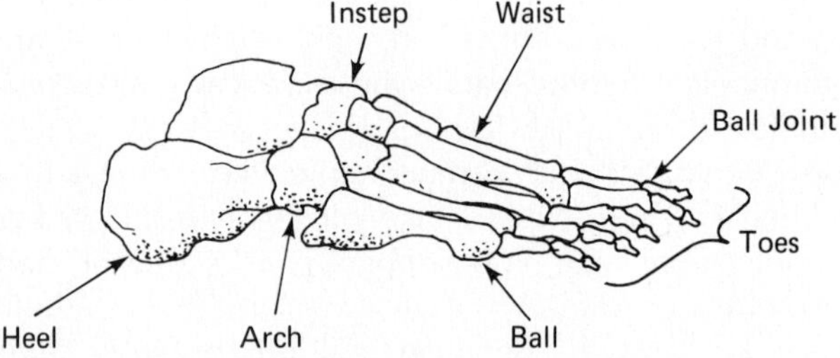

Fig. 9-1 You should learn the various parts of the foot as illustrated here. Courtesy National Retailers Assoc.

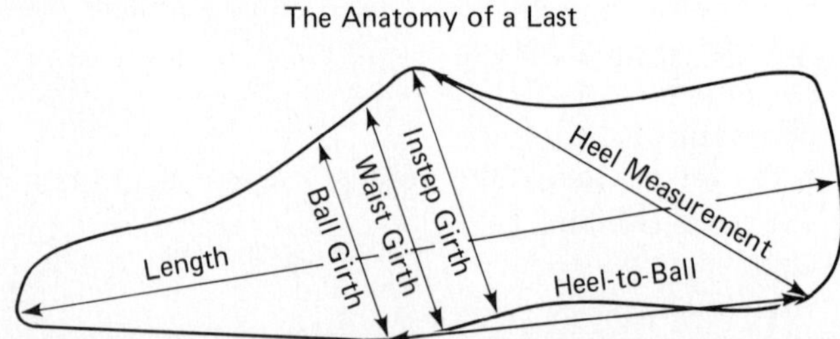

Fig. 9-2 A shoe's shape, size, and fit is determined by its last. A last's dimensions are pointed out above. Courtesy National Retailers Assoc.

PARTS OF A SHOE

Shoes provide protection, comfort, and fashion for feet. They are made to fit the various parts of the foot: toes, ball, instep, arch, heel, ball joint, and waist. (See Figure 9-1.) Basically, a shoe consists of three parts: sole, heel, and upper. The "sole" is the bottom of the footwear. The "heel" is the raised part of the shoe under the heel of the foot. The "upper" includes all the upper parts of a shoe, including the outside of the shoe and its linings. These shoe parts are joined together on a **last**, a plastic or wooden form that determines a shoe's shape, size, and fit. (See Figure 9-2.)

As you sell shoes, you may hear other salespeople refer to counter, shank, and tongue. They are using specific names for parts of the shoe. To familiarize yourself with specific shoe parts, see Figure 9-3 as you carefully examine the following list:

Quarter. Back portion of a shoe upper; covers the heel and sides of the heel
Topline. Top edge of the quarter
Quarter Lining. Lining for the quarter or back part of the shoe

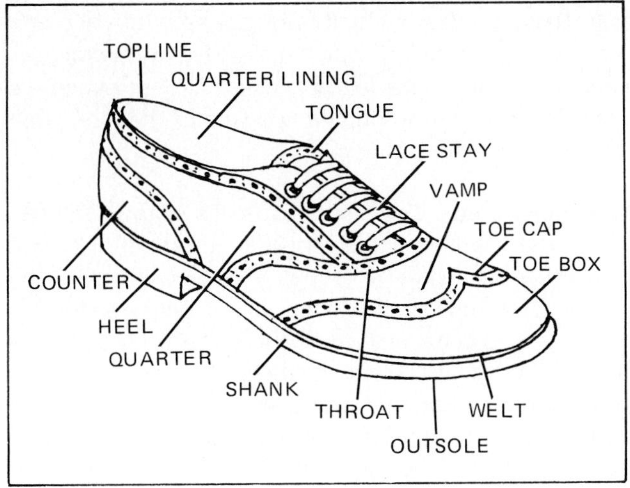

Fig. 9-3 By studying this diagram, you can learn the parts of a shoe. These parts are described in more detail in the list beginning at the bottom of the page opposite. Adapted from Wingate et al., *Know Your Merchandise for Retailers and Consumers,* 4th ed., McGraw-Hill Book Co., 1975, p. 272; based on National Shoe Retailers Association information

Counter. Piece of stiff material between the outside and lining; prevents shoe from sagging and losing shape
Heel. Raised part of the shoe under the heel of the foot
Outsole. Bottom of the shoe that comes in contact with the ground
Shank. Part of the outsole under the arch of the foot
Throat. Top line of the vamp in front of the instep
Welt. Narrow strip of leather stitched to the top edge surface of the sole
Toe cap. Tip of a shoe at the toe
Vamp. Complete forepart of a shoe upper that is stitched or otherwise attached to the sole
Tongue. Shoe section attached inside the throat of a laced shoe

Experience 9-1

Shoes and Feet—Name Those Parts

1. Identify the lettered parts of the shoe in the space provided.

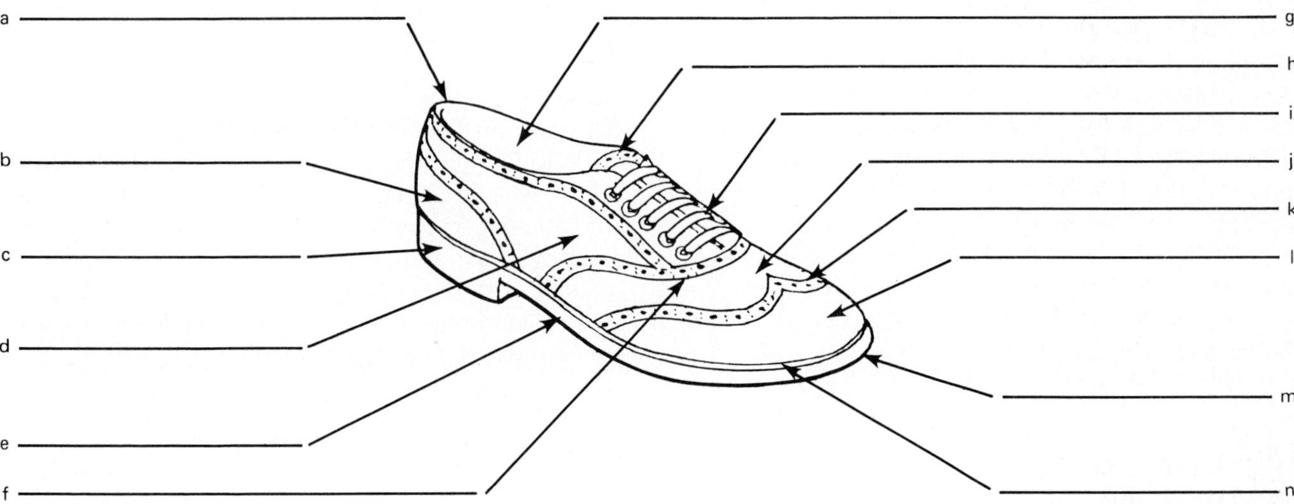

2. Identify the lettered parts of the foot in the space provided.

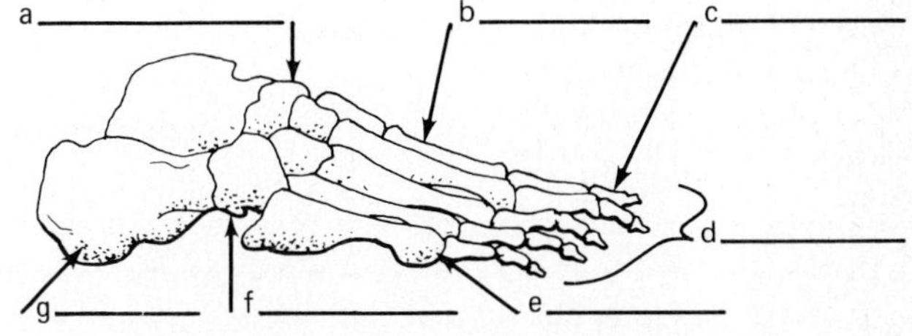

SHOE MATERIALS: THE UPPER

Shoe uppers are made from leathers, man-made materials, or fabrics. For example, men's oxfords may be made with calfskin or cordovan uppers. Vinyl uppers are featured in dress, casual, and sport shoes for men, women, and children. Linen and satin uppers are preferred for women's shoes for dyeing.

LEATHER

Leather comes from the hides and skins of cows and calves (cowhide and calfskin), pigs (pigskin), goats and kids (goatskin and kidskin), sheep (sheepskin), and horses (cordovan). The raw skins are converted into finished shoe leather by a process known as tanning. Leather, used for the shoe upper and sole, has the following characteristics:

1. *Leather is flexible.* Leather stretches to fit the shape of the foot and returns to its original shape so the shoe does not lose its style. This flexibility makes for a very comfortable fit.
2. *Leather is porous.* Pores allow air to pass through the upper of the shoe, keeping the foot cool, and permits moisture to evaporate, keeping the foot dry.
3. *Leather is renewable with polish or creams.* Properly cared for leather shoes can provide customers with years of attractive wear.

Types of Leather As you read product literature about leather shoes, you will come across the following words to describe various types of leather:

Side Leather. Side leather refers to all cowhides. A cowhide is so large that it is cut down the center, along the spine, into two parts. Cowhide is a durable, pliable shoe leather.

Top Grain Leather. The hair side of an animal's skin is called the grain side. The side next to the flesh of an animal is called the flesh side. The grain side is more attractive, durable, firmer, and smoother than the flesh side. If the grain side of the leather has not been altered, the leather is called top grain. Top grain leather is the finest quality leather. It is the most attractive and wears the longest.

Split Leather. Heavy, thick hides are split into two layers. The under layer, which has no grain surface, is called the split. Split leather, which is less expensive than top grain, has a rougher appearance than top grain and does not wear as well.

Questions about Leather Because so many synthetic materials look like leather, it is difficult to tell if a shoe is made from leather or vinyl. One way to tell is by smelling the new shoe. Leather has a unique smell.

The best way to determine the material in a shoe is by reading the label inside the heel. If the label says "all leather sole and upper," the entire shoe is made of top grain leather, except for the heel, inside stiffenings, and ornamentation. If the shoe is made of split leather, it will be labeled as such. If the upper is made from one kind of leather, for example, split cowhide, but is made to look like another, such as snakeskin, the label must say so. It would say "simulated snakeskin made of split cowhide." Shoes not made of leather should say "all parts man-made."

VINYL

Vinyl is the most popular synthetic material for shoes. A vinyl upper can be made to resemble any type of leather. The texture of vinyl can range from shiny patent leather to suede.

Originally, shoes made with vinyl had a reputation for being very hot because vinyls could not "breathe" like leather. However, a new synthetic material, called **poromeric**, is now being used. Like leather, poromeric can breathe. The label inside the heel or on the sole of a vinyl shoe will say "man-made."

The features and benefits of good quality vinyl shoes are listed in Table 1.

FABRICS

The upper material of adult's or children's shoes may be made of fabrics. The decision regarding which fabrics to use as shoe uppers is influenced by fashion. Linen and satin uppers can be easily dyed and are popular for weddings. Jute and strawcloth are popular uppers for summer shoes, as is canvas for sneakers and sports shoes. One disadvantage of fabric uppers is that they are hard to keep clean and looking attractive.

Table 1

VINYL SHOES

Features	Benefits
Vinyl can breathe	Offers the wearer a cool, dry, comfortable foot
Vinyl will stretch while wearing and bounce back to its original shape after wearing	Offers the wearer a good fit and comfort
Vinyl can be cleaned with a damp cloth	Easy to keep clean, no polish required
Vinyl shoes usually cost less than leather shoes	Offers customers a price savings
Vinyl shoes can resemble leather shoes	Fashion conscious customers can still get the look of leather at a reduced cost

Experience 9-2

What's It Made of?

1. Visit a shoe store and examine an interior women's shoe display. Locate two shoes with leather uppers, two shoes made of synthetic materials, and one shoe made from a fabric. Complete the following chart after you have examined the shoes in an interior display.

Leather Uppers	Synthetic Uppers	Fabric Uppers
a. Type of leather ________ Price ________ b. Type of leather ________ Price ________	a. Price ________ b. Price ________	a. Type of fabric ________ Price ________

2. Explain how you identified the leather and man-made shoes.

____

____

____

Table 2

MATERIALS USED IN SHOE SOLES

Quality	Crepe	Leather	Neolite	Wood
Durability	Very durable, but will darken	Not as durable as crepe, will wear out	Most durable	Not as durable as crepe, leather, or neolite
Comfort	Most comfortable, is flexible and offers give	Comfortable, flexible, and offers give; let's foot breathe	Does not give, not very comfortable, hot	Not as comfortable as leather, does give somewhat
Fashion	Presently very fashionable	Top grain leather very fashionable	Not as fashionable as leather	Fashionable
Price	Ten to 15 percent more than leather	Costs more than neolite	Least expensive	Costs about same as leather

SHOE MATERIALS: THE SOLE

The commonest materials used for shoe soles are leather, neolite (hard plastic), crepe, and wood. Each material has distinct qualities. These soles are compared in Table 2 above. For example, crepe soles are tops in comfort and fashion. They are close to the top in durability, but they are expensive.

SHOE MATERIALS: THE HEEL

Common materials for shoe heels are crepe, leather, plastic, rubber, and wood. The durability and comfort of these materials are ranked in Table 3. The most durable and comfortable heel is made of crepe. Although leather is comfortable, it wears down quickly. Today, most shoes have plastic or rubber heels.

Table 3

COMPARISON OF DIFFERENT SHOE HEELS

Durability

1. Crepe (most durable)
2. Rubber
3. Plastic
4. Wood
5. Leather (least durable)

Comfort

1. Crepe (most comfortable)
2. Leather
3. Rubber
4. Wood
5. Plastic (least comfortable)

Experience 9-3

Find the Customer Benefits

1. What are three customer benefits of leather uppers?

2. What are three customer benefits of leather soles?

3. What are three customer benefits of vinyl uppers?

SHOE CONSTRUCTION

As is true with most apparel and accessories products, a new shoe begins in the designer's office. After the shoe is designed and priced, marketing research is conducted to determine if the shoe will sell. If the shoe appears to be profitable, the assembly-line process begins.

A cardboard pattern of the shoe is made. **Dies**, or steel cutting forms, are made from the patterns. There must be a die for every style and size of the shoe. In the cutting room, shoe parts are cut from large pieces of leather, man-made materials, or fabric. The pieces are tied and bundled by size and type.

In the stitching room, the quarter, lining and upper are sewn together. The completed upper then goes to the lasting room. The upper is attached to the innersole and nailed to the last, a form that resembles a human foot. A heat setter is used to make the upper conform to the shape of the last.

Next, the outersole is attached to the innersole by sewing, cementing, or nailing. One well-known method of attaching the upper to the sole is the Goodyear Welt Construction. (A welt is a narrow strip of leather or plastic stitched to a shoe between the upper and the sole.) Shoes made by this method are durable, flexible, comfortable, and eaily repaired.

Most shoe factories use heeling machines to attach the heel to the outersole. Sock lining and heel pads are added to the shoe. Finally, heels are dyed and uppers are polished. If necessary, laces are added.

SHOE STYLES, TEXTURES, FINISHES, AND COLORS

People buy shoes with a certain purpose in mind. Shoe salespeople hear customers ask for dress shoes, casual shoes, school shoes, work shoes, and so on. Many shoe stores and departments stock sport shoes, such as hiking boots, tennis shoes, golf shoes, and after-ski boots. During the late summer, shoe stores receive their boot order: fashion boots in smooth leathers, vinyls, and suedes and the more functional rubbers and galoshes. Christmastime is when most customers purchase house slippers. There are many shoe styles, textures, finishes, and colors to fit people's needs.

STYLES

Shoe styles can be loosely grouped as oxfords, slip-ons, boots, or sandals. Most styles have specific names. See Figures 9-4, 9-5, 9-6 and 9-7 for some popular shoe styles and their names. Salespeople in larger shoe stores

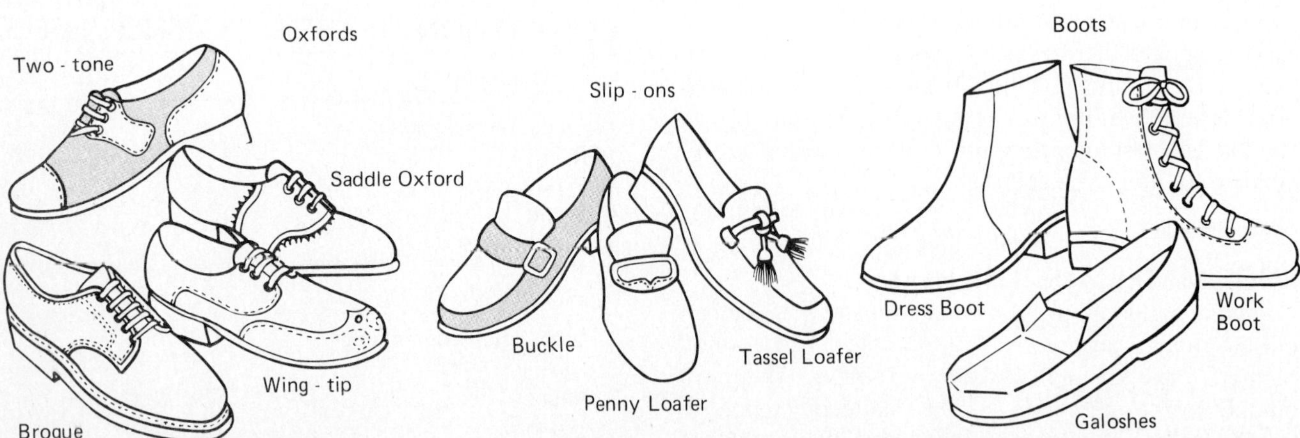

Fig. 9-4 Become familiar with the names for these popular men's shoe styles of oxfords, slip-ons, and boots.

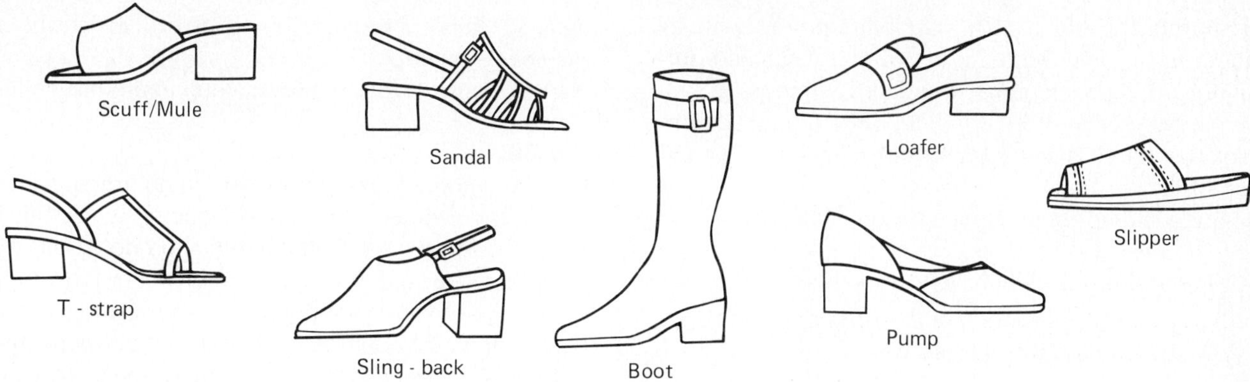

Fig. 9-5 Know and be able to identify by name the popular women's shoe styles illustrated above.

may need to know something about **orthopedic** shoes also. Not a particular style of shoe, orthopedic shoes are special shoes to correct or maintain the natural way of walking or standing. Usually these shoes are built according to a podiatrist's, or foot doctor's, specifications. Not every shoe store handles orthopedic shoes.

Fig. 9-6 Learn to identify the popular children's shoe styles pictured opposite.

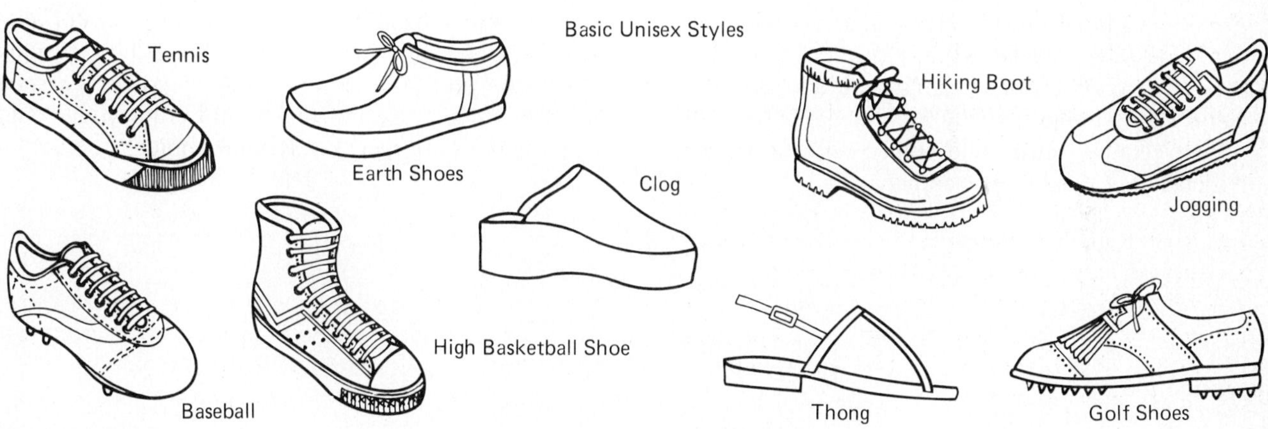

Fig. 9-7 The basic unisex shoe styles illustrated above are popular with men and women.

Experience 9-4

What Style?

Visit a local men's, women's, or children's shoe store or a department or specialty store that carries shoes for all. Find out from the salesperson what the most popular shoe styles for men, women, and children are this season. On a separate sheet of paper, sketch and label the three most popular shoe styles for each.

SURFACE TEXTURES AND FINISHES

Surface texture refers to the appearance and touch of a shoe's upper materials. Some textures are smooth, such as kidskin. Others, such as pigskin, have a grained surface. Suede is a buffed leather surface that has a fine **nap**. Brushed leather has a coarser nap than suede.

The same style shoe, but with different textures and finishes, can serve two completely different functions.

For example, a kid leather sling-back pump, with its smooth finish, may be worn to a party. A grained **aniline**-finish sling-back pump, with its casual look, can be worn to the grocery store. (Aniline, a dye produced from a coal-tar base, is transparent and allows the natural grain of leather to show.)
Some guidelines about surface textures follow:

1. Dressy shoes usually have a smooth surface.
2. Napped shoes (suedes and brushed leather) are usually for casual or leisure wear.
3. Grained textures can be worn for daytime, business, or casual wear.

Various finishes are applied to shoe uppers to give them different looks. A shoe can have a patent finish (shiny and mirrorlike) or matte finish (flat and dull). Other shoe finishes are the following:

Aniline. Polished, mirrored look achieved by using aniline dyes
Antique. Burnished, weathered, dual-toned look
Metallic. Glistening gold, silver, or bronze finish; not as shiny as patent
Pearl. Opaque finish, between a dull and polished look

COLOR

Because color is important in fashion coordination, it is one of a customer's first considerations when buying shoes. Customers buy certain colors to coordinate with apparel, relate to a season, or follow a fashion trend. For example, pastels are popular in spring and summer; darker colors are popular in fall and winter. Many times, customers are more concerned with a shoe's color than with its style or finish.

Black shoes for men can be worn with nearly any color suit or sportcoat-slacks outfit. However, brown shoes should only be worn with brown, olive, or white clothing. White shoes should be worn during warm months or in a warm climate. Navy shoes can be coordinated with blue and black; gray shoes with gray, black, and shades of green. Women's shoe colors depend on the season and fashion. Some women try to match their shoes to the color of their clothing.

Experience 9-5

Different Shoes Fit Different Needs

1. A male customer wants a dress shoe to coordinate with his brown and olive suit. He works as a salesperson in a high-fashion men's store and is on his feet for long hours. Identify a particular shoe style, surface texture, finish, and color you would show the customer. Justify your choice.

____

____

____

2. A female customer wants a casual, comfortable shoe. She wants to wear the shoe when running errands and shopping. Identify a particular shoe style, surface texture, finish, and color you would show the customer. Justify your choice.

____

____

____

Experience 9-6

Shoe Analysis

Visit a men's, women's, or children's shoe store. Choose three shoes displayed in the store. Analyze each shoe and complete the following chart. (Use refers to where the shoes would probably be worn: dressy occasions, business, and so on.)

Considerations	Shoe 1	Shoe 2	Shoe 3
1. Upper material			
2. Sole material			
3. Style			
4. Surface texture			
5. Finish			
6. Color			
7. Use			

FITTING SHOES

Shoes are sized according to length and width. For infants and children, sizes range from zero to 13. For adults, length begins at size 1 and continues to about size 14 or 15. Each full size is one-third inch longer than the previous full size. Each half size is one-sixth inch longer than the previous full size. Widths for shoes range from the very narrow AAAA (quadruple A) to the very wide EEE (triple E). Each width amounts to one-quarter inch. Not all shoe stores stock all these sizes. The commonest size range for men is 8½ to 11C and D. The commonest for women are 6½ to 8½ A and B.

As a shoe salesperson, you have the responsibility of properly fitting customers. To help you determine a customer's correct shoe size, many stores use the Brannock device. The **Brannock device** can take three foot measurements: heel-to-toe, heel-to-ball (arch length), and width. All three of these measurements are needed to determine the proper size shoe. There is a Brannock measuring device for children, men, and women. (See Figure 9-8.)

MEASURING

Once the customer is seated, carefully take off both shoes. When measuring infants' and children's feet, be especially gentle. Always measure both feet because one foot is usually larger than the other. The larger foot determines the shoe size needed.

To measure the customer's foot, place the customer's right foot on the Brannock device with heel firmly against the right heel cup. Then ask the customer to stand. When the customer stands, the foot spreads out and lets you see the foot's true width and length.

To determine the shoe length needed, find out the customer's heel-to-toe measurement and arch length. Determine the **heel-to-toe measurement** by locating the number at the end of the customer's longest toe. For example, in Figure 9-9, the customer's longest toe comes to the number 9. Therefore, the heel-to-toe length of the customer's foot is 9. (See Figure 9-9, letter A.) Then determine the **arch length** by placing the arch measure against the bone of the ball of the customer's foot and reading the number of the arch measure. For example, in Figure 9-9, letter B, the arch length is 8.

To determine the shoe width needed, move the width indicator against the side of the customer's foot. For example, the width of the foot in Figure 9-9, letter C, is D. The customer in Figure 9-9 wears a size 9D shoe. Use this process to measure the customer's left foot.

When the heel-to-toe measurement is greater than the arch length, use the heel-to-toe measurement to determine the shoe length needed. For example, suppose a customer's heel-to-toe measurement is 10 and arch length is 9, and the foot width is C. The customer would wear a size 10C shoe. When the arch length is greater than the heel-to-toe measurement, but not more than two sizes greater, the arch length determines the shoe length needed. For example, suppose the heel-to-toe measurement is 9, the arch length is 10, and the foot width is C. The customer wears a size 10C shoe.

When the arch length is two sizes greater than the heel-to-toe measurement, subtract the heel-to-toe measurement from the arch length. Divide your answer by 2 and add this number to the heel-to-toe measurement. For example, suppose the heel-to-toe measurement is 8 and the arch length is 11, and the foot width is D. Following the formula, subtract 8 from 11. Divide the answer, 3, by 2. Add this answer, 1½, to the heel-to-toe length. The size needed is 9½D.

Courtesy The Brannock Device Co., Syracuse, NY

Courtesy The Brannock Device Co., Syracuse, NY

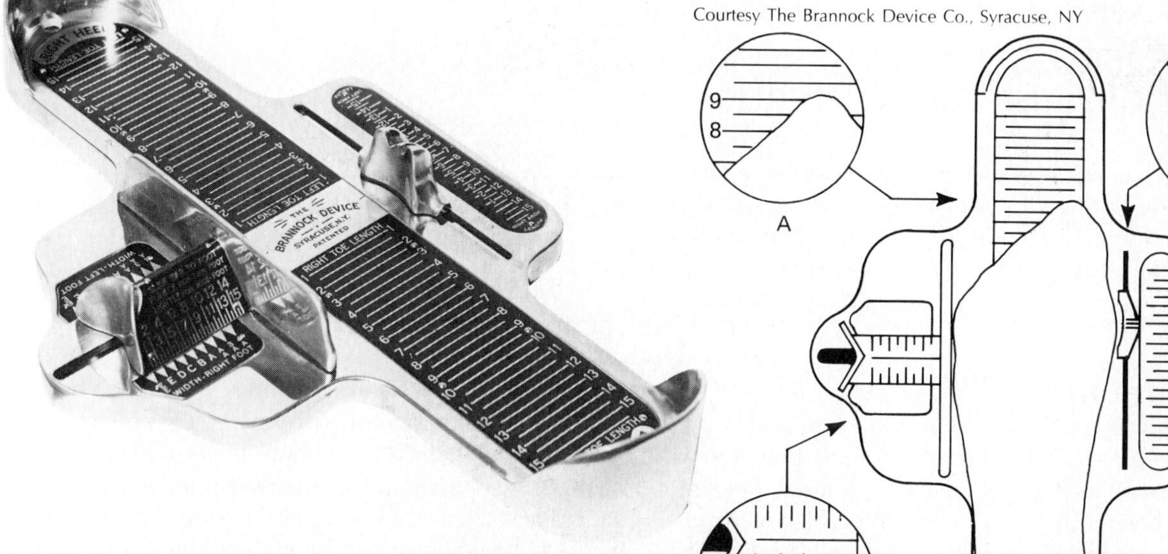

Fig. 9-8 The Brannock device, a measuring tool for fitting shoes, measures length and width at the same time.

Fig. 9-9 The foot being measured at the right needs a size 9D shoe. Read this page and find out why.

Measuring a foot gives you a good indication of shoe size. However, you may find that a customer does not wear the shoe size the measurements say. Shoe sizes vary by manufacturer, the shape of the last, shoe style, and heel height. A customer may wear a 9½D in one style and a 10C in another. After you have measured a customer's foot, avoid saying, "You take a 9C" or a specific size. Leave yourself an opening just in case the measured size is not correct.

You may have a customer who refuses to let you measure the feet. In situations like this, the old shoe size is a rough guide of what size is needed. Rather than argue with the customer, bring out the size requested. Then check the shoes for proper fit.

Experience 9-7

Can You Measure a Foot?

Obtain a Brannock device. Form into a group of six students, including males and females. In the following chart, write the name of each student on the first row and first column. For example, the student's name in the spaces labeled 1 should be the same and so on.

One at a time, each student should play the part of a shoe salesperson and measure the other five students' feet. Each student should record the measurements of the other students' feet in the column under his or her name. Have each student write the shoe size he or she actually wears in the far right column of the chart. Compare the shoe measurements that were taken in the classroom with your five classmates' actual shoe measurements.

Measurement Chart

							Correct Size
	1	2	3	4	5	6	
1							
2							
3							
4							
5							
6							

Experience 9-8

Answering Customer Questions

Suppose you are a shoe salesperson. A female shoe customer wants to know why she wears an 8B one time, an 8½A another time, and a 9AA the next time. Write in the opposite column what you would tell her.

CHECKING THE FIT

To check the fit, watch the shoe when the customer walks. Watch to see if the shoe slips on the heel. On a flat shoe, a small amount of slippage is natural, but see if the shoe opens too much when the foot is bent. A customer should be able to move his or her heel slightly. If the heel is too snug, it will cause blisters. The topline should fit snugly and not rub against the ankle bone.

With your hand, check the shoe length. There should be about a half inch space beyond the big toe for adults. Children should be fitted with shoes ¾ to 1 inch beyond the big toe to allow room for growth.

With your thumb and middle finger, check the ball fit. The big toe should fit the ball joint pocket of the shoe. Press against the sides of the shoe. The ball of the foot and the shoe should be wide at the same place. If there are creases that form lengthwise around the ball of the foot, the shoe is too short.

Customers are the best judges of how a shoe really fits. Ask customers how shoes feel when they are sitting down and how they feel when they are walking. If the customer says the shoes are too tight, get another pair of the same shoes in a larger size. If the larger size shoes are still too tight, the shoe style may be wrong. Get another style shoe in the customer's true size. The same procedure applies to shoes that are too loose.

Experience 9-9

Check the Fit

Assume that you are a shoe salesperson. Have a classmate pose as a customer. Demonstrate how you would check the classmate's shoe for proper fit. On a separate sheet of paper, explain the steps you followed to check whether or not your classmate's shoe fitted him or her properly.

Experience 9-10

Is This a Bad Fit?

Analyze the following shoe fits. Read each of the following statements and decide if the statement describes a proper or improper fit. Place a check mark in the appropriate space provided.

Statement	Proper Fit	Improper Fit
1. There are 1½ inches of space beyond the big toe.		
2. The big toe joint fits the ball joint pocket of the shoe.		
3 The topline rubs against the ankle bone.		
4. The customer can move the heel slightly.		
5. There is 1 inch of toe room in a child's shoes.		

LOCATING SHOES IN THE STOCKROOM

A shoe department has a large inventory. For example, the women's shoe department of Rogers Department Store stocks 36 pairs of women's shoes in different sizes for just one style and color. The store keeps the shoes in the back room because it could never keep track of merchandise if all of the shoes were on the sales floor.

In the women's shoe stockroom at Rogers Department Store, the department manager arranges the shoes by color, manufacturer, style, and size. There are eight color sections. In each color section, shoes are grouped according to style and then by size. The shoes are stocked vertically with the smallest size at the bottom of the stack and the largest size at the top. (See Figure 9-10.)

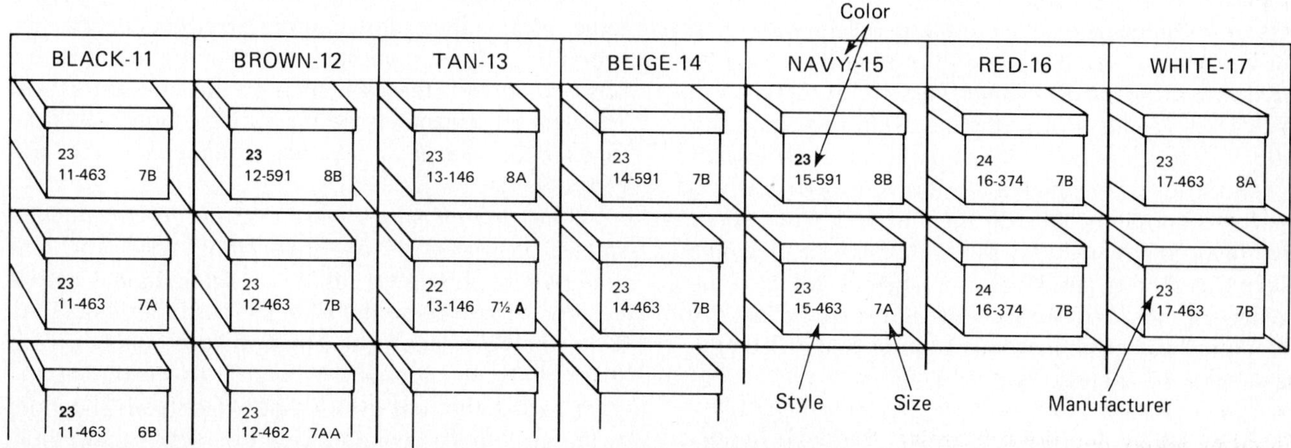

Fig. 9-10 This illustration shows how shoes in a stockroom are arranged by color, manufacturer, style, and size.

This store has many interior shoe displays that help customers get an idea of what type shoe they want. To prevent shoplifting, the department manager puts only the right shoe on display, not the pair. Customers will usually point to a shoe or hold the shoe they want in their hand. It's the shoe salesperson's job to find the same style shoe in the correct size and color in the stockroom.

The shoe style number is located inside the shoe near the heel. The style number in the shoe will correspond with the style number on the shoe box. See below:

5½B 17-432-24

The customer may want a different color, so salespersons should ask questions and carefully listen.

Experience 9-11

Can You Find the Shoe?

1. A woman and a young girl approach you. The woman hands you a black patent leather Mary Jane shoe and asks if you have it in white in her daughter's size. You measure the girl's feet and determine she wears a size 2C. Refer to the shoe number (a) and stockroom (b) on page 127. Draw an arrow to show where the correct size white shoes would be located.
2. Draw arrows to show where you should restock the shoe boxes (c) on page 127 in the stockroom shown on that page.

SELLING SHOES

Selling in a shoe department is very different than in other apparel departments. Only display stock is on the sales floor, customers are seated during the sales process, the salesperson always measures the customer, and the stock is brought to the customer rather than the customer going to the stock. Let's follow some typical shoe sales to get an idea of how to sell shoes.

GREETING THE CUSTOMER

Customers may examine the many window or interior displays to determine the stock a shoe department carries. Salespeople should greet customers promptly, by name if possible, and invite them to have a seat.

WHAT KIND OF SHOE?

Customers usually have some idea of the type of shoe they want. Some customers tell salespeople what kind of shoe they are looking for; others wait for the salesperson to ask questions. Shoe salespeople need to find out information about what kind of shoe the customer wants, its color, and its style. Possible questions are: "What will you be wearing the shoe with?" "What color did you have in mind?" "What particular style appeals to you most?" "How high a heel do you want?" As you ask these questions, take off the customer's two shoes and measure both feet. Try to have a fairly specific idea about the shoe a customer wants before going to the stockroom. You must locate shoes in the stockroom, try them on a customer's feet, check the fit, and explain the benefits of the shoes.

Choosing Shoes in the Stockroom Bring out two or three variations of the type of shoe the customer wants. For example, if a woman asks for a dressy, black patent leather shoe, you may bring out a mid-high heeled pump, a sling-back with a closed toe, and a T-strap in black patent. This gives the customer a choice. It also saves time in running back and forth from the stockroom to the customer.

A good way to increase shoe sales is to bring out additional shoe styles the customer may not have mentioned. While you are in the stockroom, locate another shoe style for the customer to see. For example, bring out a fast-selling fashion item, a traditional style in a new color, or shoes that your store is trying to close out (eliminate from stock). These other styles are shown later in the sales presentation.

Before coming out of the stockroom, open all the shoe boxes to be sure both shoes are in the box. If the shoes are dirty or dusty, wipe them off so they will make a better impression.

Trying on Shoes Present the shoe selection to your customer. With a little showmanship, one-by-one, open the shoe boxes of the requested style. Put the lid under the box and support the right shoe on the side of the box. This lets the customer see the various shoes you have to offer for sale. It also builds customer interest. (See Figure 9-11.)

While putting shoes on the customer's foot, you should be seated on the shoe fitting stool. The customer's foot should be resting on the diagonal part of the stool. First put on the shoe the customer requested. If the shoe has laces insert them before putting on the shoe. Hold the shoe under the arch or shank. Slip the front part of the foot in the shoe. Place your shoehorn at the customer's heel and slide the foot into the shoe. If the shoes are sling-backs, you do not need to use your shoehorn.

1B
13–872 (a)

BLACK - 11	BROWN - 12	TAN - 13	WHITE - 14	MISC - 15
11 42-117 11½D	12 13-211 1B	13 12-872 2B	14 42-117 2D	15 8-73 3B
11 13-211 11½C	12 8-73 1B	13 10-384 2B	14 13-872 2C	15 13-211 2½D
11 42-117 11B	12 42-117 12D	13 28-134 12C	14 13-872 2B	15 16-384 2B
11 8-73 11B	12 13-872 12C	13 8-73 12B	14 16-384 12C	15 13-211 1D
11 13-872 10½D	12 8-73 11B	13 16-384 10½C	14 13-211 11½D	15 13-872 1C

(b)

These shoe boxes are arranged by color and by size.

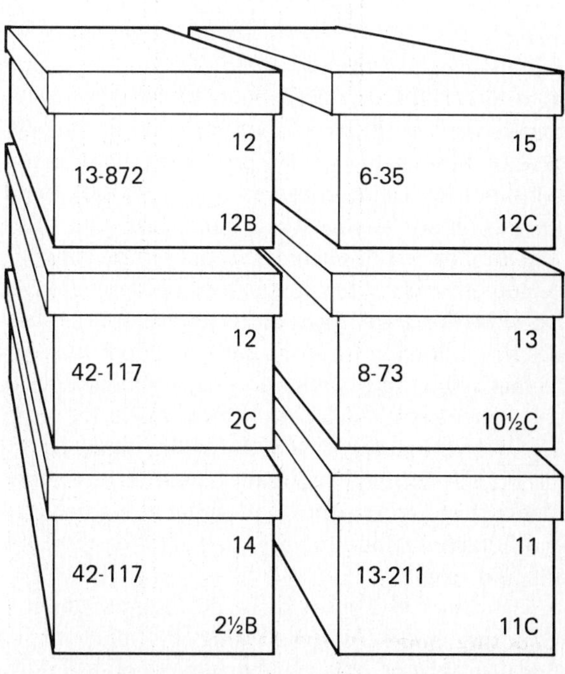

(c)

Tie the laces or adjust the shoe strap so that the shoe fits firmly. Check the fit of the one shoe. If it seems a good fit, try on the other shoe. Again check the fit.

Ask the customer to stand and take a few steps. Observe the shoe as the customer walks. A salesperson cannot always see an incorrect fit. Be sure to ask the customer how they feel. Get the customer to walk over to a mirror to see how the shoes look.

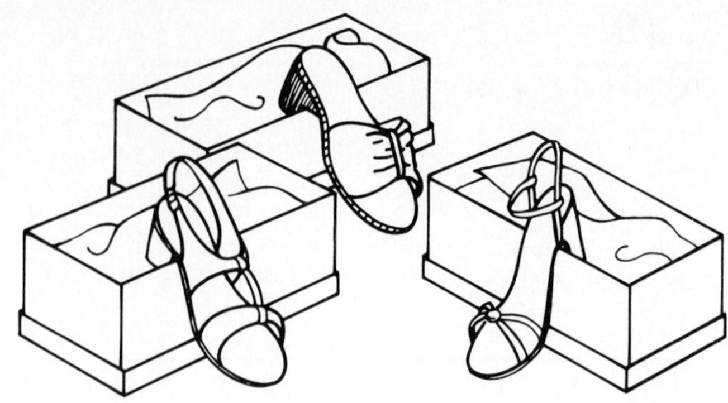

Fig. 9-11 If you use some shoe showmanship, customers will take more interest in the styles being offered.

Experience 9-12

What Kind of Shoe?

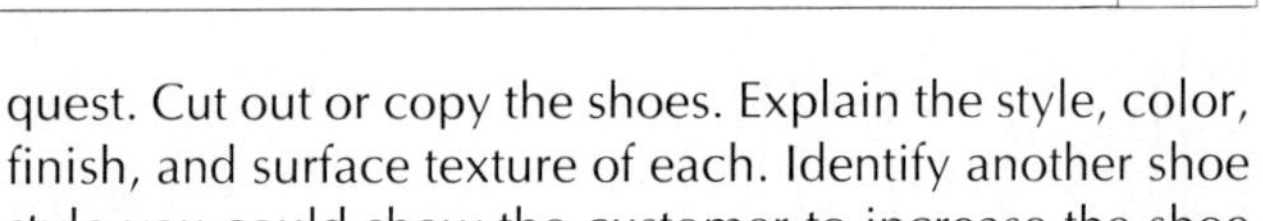

Suppose you are a shoe salesperson. A male customer has asked to see a casual shoe, something in dark brown. Look through men's fashion magazines and identify three shoes that would fill the customer's request. Cut out or copy the shoes. Explain the style, color, finish, and surface texture of each. Identify another shoe style you could show the customer to increase the shoe sale.

Experience 9-13

Try It On

1. Suppose you are a shoe salesperson. Ask a classmate to pose as a shoe customer. Demonstrate how you would try a pair of shoes on the customer's foot. You may use the classmate's shoes. To make this more real, you need a shoe fitting stool and a shoehorn.
2. Suppose you have identified four pairs of shoes to show this customer. Using four shoe boxes with four pairs of shoes inside, demonstrate how you would present the shoe selection you have identified to the customer.

Discussing the Benefits While you are trying shoes on a customer, discuss the benefits of the shoe. Shoe customers look for fashion, comfort, good fit, and quality. One of these features is the primary motivation for buying shoes. As a shoe salesperson, it is your job to identify the customer's strongest need and gear your sales presentation to it. For example, suppose you have a male customer who is interested in a comfortable, long-wearing shoe. You are about to try on his foot a shoe that has the following features: calfskin upper leather, fully leather lined, half leather and half rubber heel, leather sole, and steel shank. You could make the customer aware of the comfort benefits of the shoes by saying: "The shoe you will be trying is one of our finest. It is made of calfskin, a most comfortable leather. Calfskin is a durable leather and does not scuff easily. Feel how soft it is."

Then hand the shoe to the customer to involve him with the shoe. "Feel the lining. It's made of leather. Because leather can breathe, your foot will stay cool and dry. The leather lining adds to your comfort.

"The shoe has a steel shank. This is a metal support that runs from the center of the heel to the ball. It adds support to your foot. It also has a leather sole that flexes and adds to your walking comfort. The heel, which is half leather and half rubber, is designed to resist wear, making your shoes a longer lasting and very economical investment.

"This shoe will keep its shape and fit longer than many other shoes. It will continue to look attractive for a long time."

If the shoe customer seems brand-conscious, mention the shoe manufacturer. Explain that the manufacturer stands for fashion leadership, quality construction, and well-fitting shoes. If the customer seems fashion-conscious, point out the style, detailing, and finish of a shoe.

Salespeople need product information to build interesting, factual sales dialogs. Once they know the facts about a shoe, they can adapt what they know to the customer and his or her primary buying motives. Product analysis sheets, like the one in Table 4, help salespeople analyze the shoe and its benefits.

Table 4

PRODUCT ANALYSIS SHEET

Sales Features—Facts	Selling Points—Benefits
Calfskin leather	One of the most comfortable leathers; durable and does not scuff easily
Leather lining	Adds to the shoe's comfort because it allows the foot to breathe
Steel shank	Adds support for the foot and helps keep the shape of the shoe
Half leather, half rubber heel	Heel resists wear and lasts longer
Brown color	Brown is a very versatile color that can be coordinated with many clothing colors
Ball joint of the foot fits the ball pocket of the shoe; there is about a half-inch of room beyond the longest toe; heel fits snugly but does not rub	Shoe fits properly and will be comfortable to wear; will not damage the foot
Style: slip-on Surface texture: grained Finish: aniline dyed	Style is very fashionable Grained surface adds to appearance Aniline dye does not rub off easily; shoe can be worn for daytime, business, or casual wear

Experience 9-14

Analyze the Product

1. Choose a pair of quality men's, women's, or children's shoes. Complete the following product analysis sheet. Write facts about the shoes on the left side of the sheet; write benefits or reasons why those facts are important to customers on the right side of the sheet. You may want to talk to a professional shoe salesperson to help you complete the sheet shown below.

PRODUCT ANALYSIS SHEET

Sales Features: Facts	Selling Points: Benefits
Type of upper	
Type of sole	
Type of heel	
Important construction features	
Color	
Style	
Finish	
Brand	
Price	
Other important facts	

2. Using the information from your product analysis sheet, prepare a sales presentation about those shoes. Assume you will be talking to a customer who is interested in the comfort and the durability of those shoes.
   a. On a separate sheet of paper, outline the important points you want to bring to your customer's attention.
   b. Using a tape recorder, record a 2-minute sales presentation for the shoes.

COMMON OBJECTIONS TO SHOES

Customers may refuse to purchase shoes because they are an incorrect fit, color, style, or price. Shoe salespeople need to be able to overcome these objections. For example, if the shoes are the wrong fit, the salesperson should bring out the correct size. If the new size still does not fit properly, the salesperson should suggest a different style. If the style is wrong, the salesperson should show another style. Many styles can be worn for casual, dress, or daytime wear. (See Table 5.)

Shoes are available in so many colors that a shoe salesperson should have an easy time overcoming this objection. If the customer is trying to match a particularly difficult color, the salesperson could suggest the customer purchase a fabric shoe and dye it. If the price is too high, the salesperson should point out the quality features of the shoe that justify the price. If the customer cannot afford a high-priced shoe, the salesperson should show a lower-priced shoe in the same style.

MULTIPLE SALES

A shoe salesperson can increase a customer's purchase by selling another pair of shoes in a similar style, another pair of shoes in a different style, or a related item.

Selling Two Similar Styles When customers have difficulty deciding between two pairs of shoes, shoe salespeople may suggest that they buy both pairs. The salesperson should point out the advantage of buying both pairs—longer life for both shoes.

Selling Two Different Styles When customers have decided on a particular pair of shoes, the shoe salesperson should call the customer's attention to another shoe style. The salesperson should have located this other style in the stockroom when getting the original shoes the customer wanted. These shoes, in the customer's size, should be next to the salesperson on the sales floor. The salesperson could call attention to the second style by saying, "I want to show you one of our newest arrivals. Would you like to try it on to check the fit?"

Selling Related Items Related items are handbags, hosiery, leather goods, and shoe-care products. These related items are located in the shoe department or shoe store. Notice how each of these may be presented to a customer.

Handbags. Customers often need a new handbag to match their new shoes. As the customer is in front of the mirror examining the shoes, go to the handbag rack and choose two or three handbags in the same, or complementary, color and material to go with the shoes. As you present the handbag, you may say, "Here's a fashionable new bag that will complement your shoes and complete your outfit."

Hosiery. Point out the hosiery selection. Nylon hose, knee socks, over-the-knee socks, midcalf socks, and pantyhose are related items that the customer may need to purchase. The shoe salesperson is offering customer service by bringing these related items to a customer's attention.

Leather Goods. Many shoe stores also feature belts. Locate a belt in the same color or complementary shade and material to coordinate with the new shoes.

Shoe-Care Products. Keeping new shoes looking attractive and well fitting requires shoe maintenance. Leather shoes, like skin, have pores that need to be cleaned and moisturized. Saddle soap is used on all finished leather except suede. Saddle soap cleans, softens, and polishes leather. Shoe cream that has a lanolin base softens and conditions leather. Shoe polish, good for all finished leathers except suede, restores the shine. It also preserves the leather by adding moisture to the shoes. For suede shoes or boots, be sure to mention suede brushes and water-repellent spray. The suede brush raises the nap and cleans the leather. The spray keeps water from soaking in and ruining the nap. Another shoe-care product is shoe trees. This product, which is sold in pairs, is shaped similar to a foot. Shoe trees absorb the moisture in the shoes and help keep the shoes in shape when the shoes are not being worn.

Table 5

MEN'S SHOE STYLES

Daytime
Oxfords
Brogues
Cordovans
Slip-ons
Monk straps
Boots
After-Six
Slip-ons
Formal wear
Active Sport and Utility
Work shoes
Sport boots
Golf shoes
Athletic shoes
Casual, Sport, Leisure
Casual shoes
Casual boots
Loafer types
Handsewns
Moccasins
Sandals
Spectator sport
Special Footwear
Slippers
Canvas
Comfort or prescription
Rubber
Summer types

(Source: National Shoe Retailers Association)

Experience 9-15

Related Items

1. Visit a women's shoe store or department. On a separate sheet of paper, list the related shoe items available.
2. Visit a men's shoe store or department. On a separate sheet of paper, list the related shoe items available for purchase.
3. Visit a children's shoe store or department. On a separate sheet, list the related shoe items.

Experience 9-16

Handbag Coordination

1. You have shown a customer a pair of black patent leather pumps. Look through a women's fashion magazine and identify three handbags that you could coordinate with the new shoes. Cut out or copy pictures of the handbags and paste on a separate sheet of paper.
2. You have shown the customer a pair of brushed suede low-heeled boots. Look through a women's fashion magazine and identify three handbags that you could coordinate with the new shoes. Cut out or copy pictures of the handbags and paste them on a separate sheet of paper.

Experience 9-17

Shoe-Care Products: What Do They All Mean?

Shoes need care. Visit a shoe store and examine the shoe maintenance products. Complete the following chart.

Shoe-Care Products	Used for Type of Shoe	Advantages of Using the Product
1.		
2.		
3.		
4.		
5.		
6.		
7.		
8.		

10 Accessories

Accessories are an important part of the total fashion picture. Accessories can enhance or detract from any clothing **ensemble** or outfit of harmonizing pieces. They can minimize bad features and play up good ones. They can help the wearer create a special mood, or they can express individuality.

Accessories and apparel work together to carry out a fashion theme. For example, one of the themes of the 1970s was the "Natural Look." This look was seen in clothing with natural, earthtone colors and fibers. To emphasize this fashion trend, the fashion industry saw the emergence of "Natural Look" accessories, such as macrame handbags and belts.

To be successful in working with accessories, you need to know how they are made, the properties of the materials they are made from, and how to care for them. Customers will appreciate your suggestions on what styles and colors look most attractive on them. By being able to combine individual apparel and accessory items into a coordinated look, you will increase your sales and earnings. Your sales ability and product knowledge will also help you increase your self-confidence and gain the confidence of customers. Knowing more about the merchandise you sell will make your job more interesting and enjoyable.

There are many popular accessory items that men, women, and children wear. In this chapter, only six types of accessories will be discussed in detail; gloves, bags, hats, belts, umbrellas, and costume jewelry.

GLOVES

Gloves are both functional and decorative. They keep hands warm and complement coats, boots, and scarves. Golf gloves give a better grip on the golf club, as well as a sporty, coordinated look. Formal-wear gloves add the finishing touch to an evening gown or tuxedo.

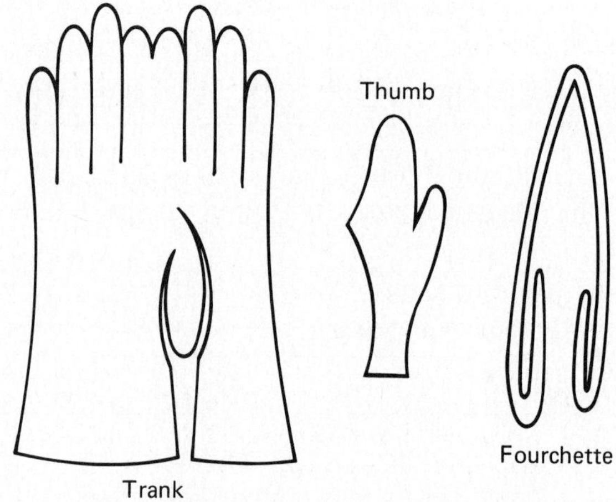

Fig. 10-1 Glove salespeople should know the names for the parts of a glove pictured here.

PARTS OF A GLOVE

When you sell gloves to customers or, as a buyer, purchase gloves for your store, you will need to know the different parts of a glove. Examine Figure 10-1 as you study the following terms.

The **trank** is the general outline that forms the palm, back, and fingers of the glove. The **thumb** is made from a separate piece of material that is stitched around a hole cut in the glove trank. Two types of thumbs are the **Bolton thumb** and the **quirk thumb**. The Bolton thumb is bulkier in appearance but provides freedom of movement. The quirk thumb makes the thumb appear thinner but somewhat restricts movement of the hand. Men's and women's driving gloves usually have a Bolton thumb. Dress gloves usually have the quirk thumb.

The **fourchettes** are the side pieces of the glove fingers. When the glove fingers are made in four sections, the trank provides the front and back of the fingers. The fourchettes provide the space for the finger width. The

quirks are the tiny, triangular sections at the base of the fourchettes. They provide extra "give" between the fingers. Not all gloves have quirks; those that do have quality workmanship.

Some gloves have a **lining**, which is a material used to cover the inner surface of the glove. Fur and acrylic linings make the gloves warm. Silk or nylon linings make the gloves easy to put on and take off. Skeleton linings cover only the trank. Full linings cover the fingers and wrists and are really gloves within gloves.

GLOVE CONSTRUCTION

Knitted gloves are made differently than leather or woven-fabric gloves. Knitted gloves are knitted by hand or, more usually, by knitting machines. After the gloves are knitted, the tips of the fingers are closed. Because knitted gloves stretch to fit the shape of the hand, they are comfortable to wear. Knitted gloves are also warm because air is trapped between the fibers. Usually, knitted gloves can be machine-washed.

Leather or woven-fabric gloves are cut from the skin of an animal or from a woven fabric using one of three methods: table cut, pull-down cut, and die cut. In the **table-cut method**, which is the most expensive way of cutting tranks, the leather is dampened slightly and then pulled and stretched by hand to ensure the right amount of stretch. Each piece is cut with scissors according to accurate measurements. Each pair of gloves is cut from the same piece of leather. Two advantages of table-cut gloves are (1) they fit the hand well and (2) they give the wearer flexibility of movement. These gloves can usually be identified by the words "table cut" stamped on the inside.

The **pull-down cut** is a variation on the table cut. In this cut, no attempt is made to achieve a perfect fit. These gloves are less expensive to cut and buy.

Inexpensive leather, work, and fabric gloves are cut by a metal die that is shaped like the trank of the glove. This is similar to cutting cookies with a cookie cutter. Unlike the table cut, the **die-cut method** often scars the leather or fabric. The advantage of this method is that the manufacturing process is easier. The gloves are cheaper than those cut by the other two methods.

After the trank, thumb, fourchettes, and quirks are cut, **finger slitting** is done. In this step, the trank is cut for the fingers, the holes for the thumbs, and the quirks that fit at the base between the fingers. The next step is adding any decorations, such as stitches, beads, or braid, to the trank. Decorative seams or stitching on gloves is called **pointing**.

Stitching the glove parts together is the next step. The stitching should be small and regularly spaced. The closing stitches close the fingers and sides of the gloves, and attach the thumb, fourchettes, and quirks. There are different types of closing stitches; each type affects the appearance, durability, and price of the glove. (See Figure 10-2.)

The least expensive and easiest closing stitch is called the **inseam stitch**. With this stitch, the outside surfaces of the tranks are placed face-to-face. The tranks are sewn around the fingers and then turned inside out so that the finished surfaces are facing the outside. Although this stitching method is easy to do, the stitch is not as durable as other stitches.

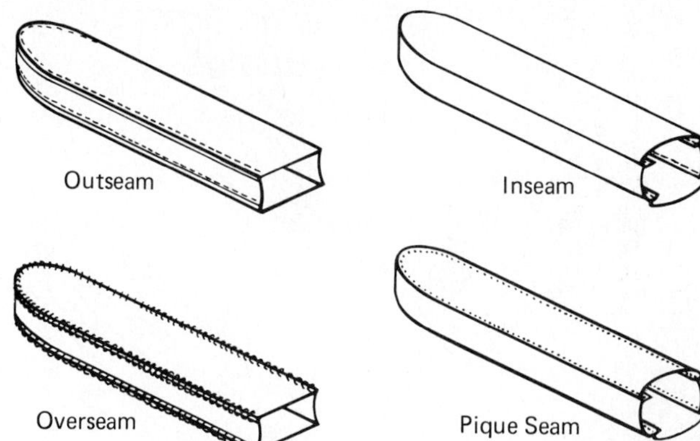

Fig. 10-2 Here are four popular closing stitches used in glove making.

The **outseam stitch** is the opposite of the inseam in appearance. Both raw edges of the material and the seam holding the edges together are visible on the outside of the glove. This stitch gives the fingers a bulky appearance. It is used mainly on men's gloves and women's sport gloves. It is more durable and more expensive than the inseam stitch.

With the **overseam stitch**, both raw edges of the leather are seen on the outside of the glove, but the stitches lap over the edges. This stitch is attractive and more durable than the other two stitches.

The **pique**, or P.K., **seam** is made by lapping one edge over the other so that only one raw edge shows on the outside. The advantage of this stitch is that it is the most finger slimming and durable stitch for street and dress gloves. Because this is the most difficult stitch to make, it is found on fine quality, expensive gloves.

GLOVE STYLES

When you work in the accessory section of a store, you may sell any of the following glove styles (see Figure 10-3):

Slip-on. These gloves have no fasteners or openings; they just slip over the hand. Although these gloves usually extend to the wrist, they are also available in lengths that extend up the arm.

Shorty. These gloves are wrist-length with either a side or center vent or center fastening with clasps or buttons.

Gauntlets. These gloves have a wide flare above the wrist made by a separate triangular-shaped piece set into the side section. Some ski gloves have gauntlets.

Mittens. These gloves have one section for the thumb and a larger section for the fingers and hand. Children and skiers wear mittens for warmth.

Formal. These gloves are worn by women and men to formal events. Women wear elbow-length or shoulder-length formal gloves. Men wear wrist-length white gloves for very formal "white tie and tail" events.

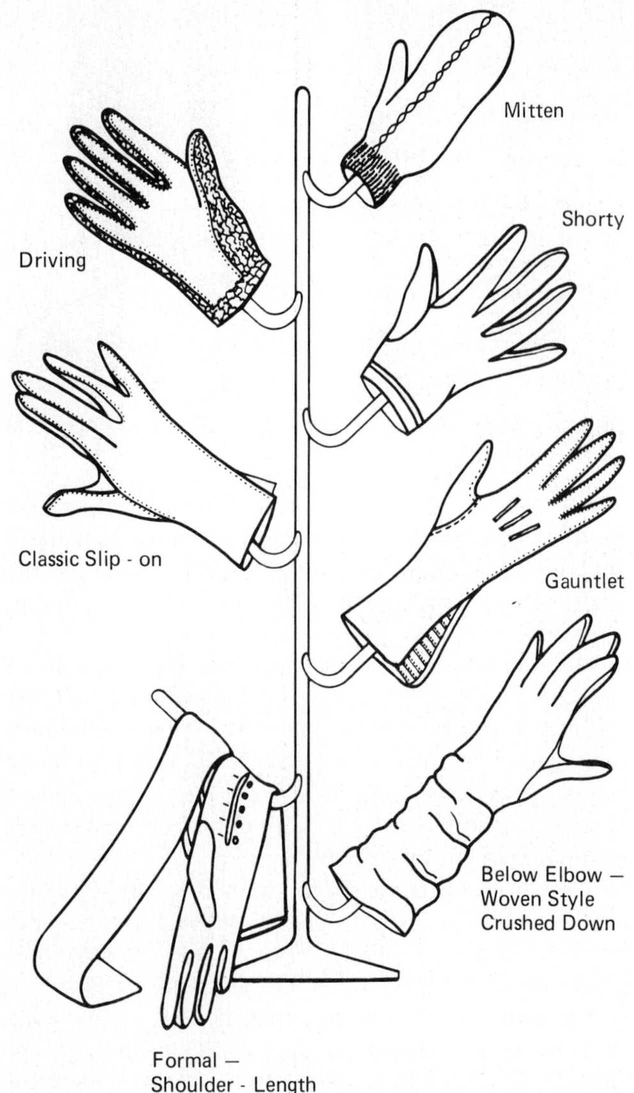

Fig. 10-3 For almost every occasion, formal and informal, there's an appropriate glove style.

Driving. These gloves have a leather palm. Some have a cutaway section on the back of the hand with a clasp fastening.

There are also specially designed gloves for sports and for work. These gloves have special characteristics. For example, ski gloves are designed for warmth and are insulated. Work gloves are designed to protect the wearer's hands from callouses. Gloves used for sports are usually found in the sporting goods department of a store. The work gloves are usually found with work clothes.

GLOVE SIZES

Sizes in men's and women's leather gloves run in quarter inches. Sizes in fabric gloves run in half inches. Women's glove sizes range from 5½ to 8, with the average 6½. Some women's gloves and mittens are sized small (5–6), medium (6½–7), and large (7½–8). Children's glove sizes are usually half the child's age. A 6-year-old would wear a size 3, a 10-year-old would wear a size 5, and so on. Men's glove sizes range from 8 to 11½ or small (8–8½), medium (9–9½), large 10–10½), and extra large (11–11½). Stretch gloves fit all sizes.

Lengths of women's gloves are measured in buttons. Each button equals 1 inch of length from the base of the thumb up the arm. A one-button glove is wrist-length; a four-button glove is above the wrist; and eight-button glove is to the middle of the arm. The most popular length glove for women is the two-button glove. The one-button glove is used for daytime and evening wear. A four-button glove is for three-quarter-length sleeves. Sixteen-button gloves come between the elbow and shoulders. They're only for very formal occasions.

The wrong size glove can be uncomfortable and wear out quickly. To determine proper glove size, use a tape measure to measure the customer's hand around the knuckles at the widest part.' Do not include the thumb. Suppose a woman customer's hand measures 6¾. If the customer is buying a leather glove, which stretches somewhat, she should buy a size smaller, or 6½. If she is buying lined gloves or washable doeskin gloves, the customer should buy a size larger. Because glove sizes vary with different materials and different manufacturers, always ask the customer to try on the gloves.

CARE OF GLOVES

Customers should be told that gloves should be eased on gently and smoothed out immediately after removing them. Salespeople should explain that gloves labeled "washable" can be washed in mild soap and water and rinsed and then shaped while still damp. Gloves marked "nonwashable" should be dry-cleaned.

COLOR, LINE, AND DESIGN OF GLOVES

Gloves attract attention to a person's hands. A person with large arms or hands may want to wear the same color gloves as clothing so as to minimize attention to the hands. Persons with long arms should wear gloves that are slightly longer than wrist-length to make the arms look shorter. Decorative stitching on the back of the glove can make the hand appear narrower. The pique seam will make broad fingers appear slimmer. The outseam stitch will cause fingers to appear broader.

Experience 10-1

Everything You Always Wanted to Know about Gloves

1. Visit a store that sells men's leather gloves, children's knitted mittens, and women's fabric gloves. Find out the styles, sizes, brands, colors, and prices available for these three types of gloves. Write information about the men's gloves on the comparison shopping report, on page 135. Record that

COMPARISON SHOPPING REPORT

Description	Our Reg. Price	Competitor A Name ________ Price, Brand, Comments	Competitor B Name ________ Price, Brand, Comments

information in the first box under the head "Description." Write the information about the women's gloves and children's mittens in the next two boxes.

2. Next, visit two other stores that also sell men's leather gloves, women's fabric gloves, and children's knitted mittens. Write information about the styles, sizes, brands, colors, and prices of these gloves in the columns labeled "Competitor A" and "Competitor B."
3. On a separate sheet of paper, answer the following:
   a. Which store offered the largest selection?
   b. In your opinion, which store appeals to the quality-minded customer? In your opinion, which store appeals to the price-conscious customer? Give reasons to support your answers.

Experience 10-2

The Facts about Gloves

Role play a salesperson in a glove department and have a classmate play the part of a customer who is interested in buying a pair of gloves. Using a real pair of gloves, demonstrate how you would point out the parts of the glove, how the gloves were made, and how to care for the gloves. If possible, use a tape recorder to record your presentation. After recording your presentation, play the tape back and evaluate it.

Experience 10-3

Size Them Up

Using a measuring tape, measure the hands of five of your classmates, both men and women. What size leather glove would fit each? What size lined glove? Record your answers on a separate sheet.

HANDBAGS

Handbags, also called purses, bags, or carrying cases, have long been an important accessory in the well-dressed person's wardrobe. Today, both men and women use handbags to carry their personal belongings, such as keys, wallets, glasses, and appointment books. These handbags vary in size, color, style, and material.

Fig. 10-4 You should be able to recognize and name these handbags, which are grouped into the three most popular styles.

PARTS OF A HANDBAG

A handbag consists of many parts, including outer material, filler, frame, fastener, lining, and handle. The outer material may be made of leather, such as calfskin. Many are made from a fabric, such as velvet or canvas. Vinyl handbags are very popular also.

Filler is the material or substance that helps the bag hold its shape. The frame also helps to give the bag a distinct shape. Handbag fasteners may be snaps, turn locks, latches, buckles, drawstrings, or zippers. The lining and interlinings give the inside of the bag an attractive, neat appearance by hiding the filler. The handle, which is used to carry the bag, comes in a variety of sizes—small for holding in the hand, medium length to fit over the arm, and shoulder length.

HANDBAG STYLES

Some popular handbag styles are shown in Figure 10-4. Some of the most popular styles are as follows:

Envelope. Resembles an envelope with a top flap. This style may or may not have handles. Some shoulder bags are envelope styles. Clutch purses may also be envelope-styled.

Box. Shaped like a square or rectangular box. This bag is rigid and does not expand. It may have small, medium, or shoulder-length handles. An example of a box is a brief case.

Pouch. Has a top closing, a frame, or a top handle. This bag is usually soft and is pleated or gathered to a top opening. Examples of this bag are the duffle and tote.

CARE OF HANDBAGS

Customers want to know how to keep their handbags looking attractive. Explain that handbags that are not overloaded will last longer than bags that are overflowing with items. Overloading a bag weakens seams, stretches the handbag out of shape, and pulls the material away from the frame or handle.

Vinyl handbags should be wiped clean with a damp cloth. Suede handbags should be brushed with a suede brush. Leather handbags should be polished with a good leather cream. Frabric handbags should be cleaned by brushing, spot cleaning, or dry cleaning. The handbag lining should be kept clean by brushing or vacuuming.

Stored handbags should be filled with paper to keep their shape, and wrapped in plastic. Vinyl handbags should be wrapped in tissue paper.

COLOR, LINE, AND DESIGN OF HANDBAGS

To achieve a fashion look, handbags should either blend with the wearer's clothing or provide a pleasing contrast. Many people choose their handbags to coordinate with their shoes so that the textures, colors, and designs of both harmonize. The right handbag can make a person look "put together"; the wrong handbag can ruin the best looking ensemble.

When helping customers select the right handbag, remember that the handbag should be scaled to the size of the wearer. When a handbag and wearer are not in scale, (1) a small person looks dwarfed by an oversized bag, (2) a tall person looks even taller with a small bag, and (3) a large person makes a tiny bag look as if it were a child's.

A small person should carry a small to medium-sized handbag. A large person should carry a medium to large handbag. You should also be aware that shoulder handbags call attention to the wearer's hips. A thick shoulder handbag that is parallel with a person's hips can make that person look broader.

Although a wide variety of handbags is available, many customers buy only one bag to coordinate with all their clothing. Customers who buy only one or two bags for their wardrobe should choose bags in neutral tones, such as light brown or deep beige.

OTHER HANDBAG ACCESSORIES

Handbag salespeople, department managers, and buyers usually work with other small accessories. As an accessory salesperson, you may also sell wallets, cigarette cases, cosmetic cases, keycases, and eyeglass cases. These items are often coordinated to give the customer a total look.

Experience 10-4

This Style Is Called a . . .

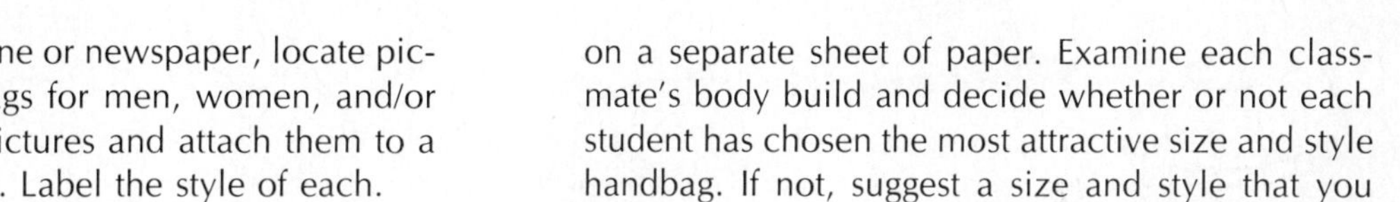

1. Using a fashion magazine or newspaper, locate pictures of 10 different bags for men, women, and/or children. Cut out the pictures and attach them to a separate sheet of paper. Label the style of each.
2. Identify the style of handbags your classmates are carrying. Write the style and the classmate's name on a separate sheet of paper. Examine each classmate's body build and decide whether or not each student has chosen the most attractive size and style handbag. If not, suggest a size and style that you think would be more appropriate. Write your comments on your paper.

HATS

Some time ago, a person would not be considered well dressed without wearing a hat. That's not the way it is today. Although most of the hats sold today are functional, many people still wear hats to achieve a different, special look or just for fun.

HAT MATERIALS

Hats are made from almost any material. Felt, straw, wool, and fur have all been part of the hat fashion scene. Feathers, ribbons, lace, artificial flowers, veiling, and metal and stone clips or pins have been used for trim.

HAT CONSTRUCTION

There are many ways to make a hat. Felt hats are usually blocked on a wooden block, steamed, and molded into shape. Fabric hats are generally draped and cover a stiff hat body that has been previously shaped. Some hats, especially those for winter wear, often are knitted or crocheted.

The materials used, workmanship, and hat designer affect the price of hats. Hats made of a rare fabric or trim, require a special construction process, or are "original" creations and are more expensive than mass-produced hats. Good quality hats have linings and are hand-stitched. They may have sweatbands, sometimes made of ribbon, at the base of the crown.

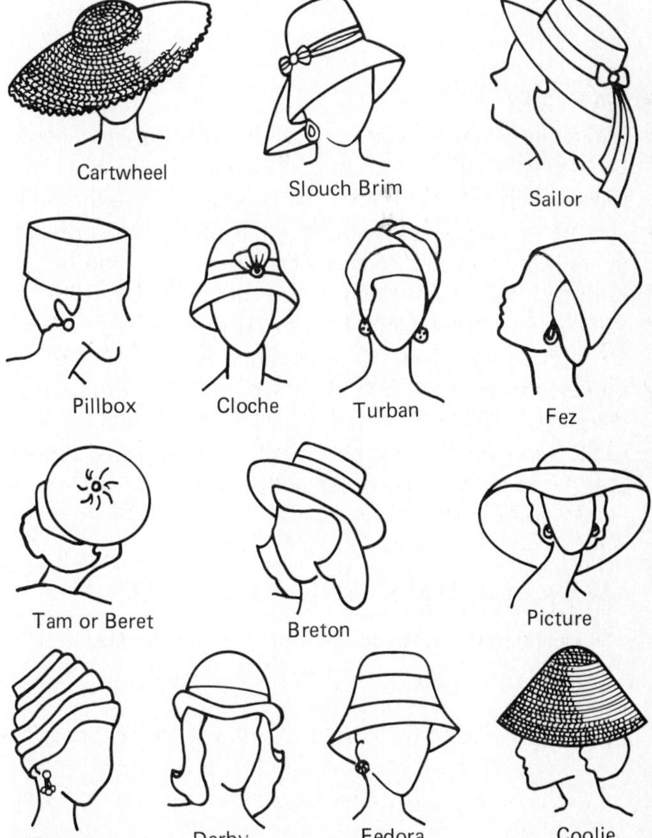

Fig. 10-5A Here are some popular women's hat styles.

HAT STYLES

Hat styles change with fashion trends. There are many popular hat styles that keep recurring throughout fashion history. As a salesperson, you should be acquainted with these styles and their names. Customers often refer to a hat by using its style name. Popular hat styles for women, men, and children are shown on pages 137 and 138.

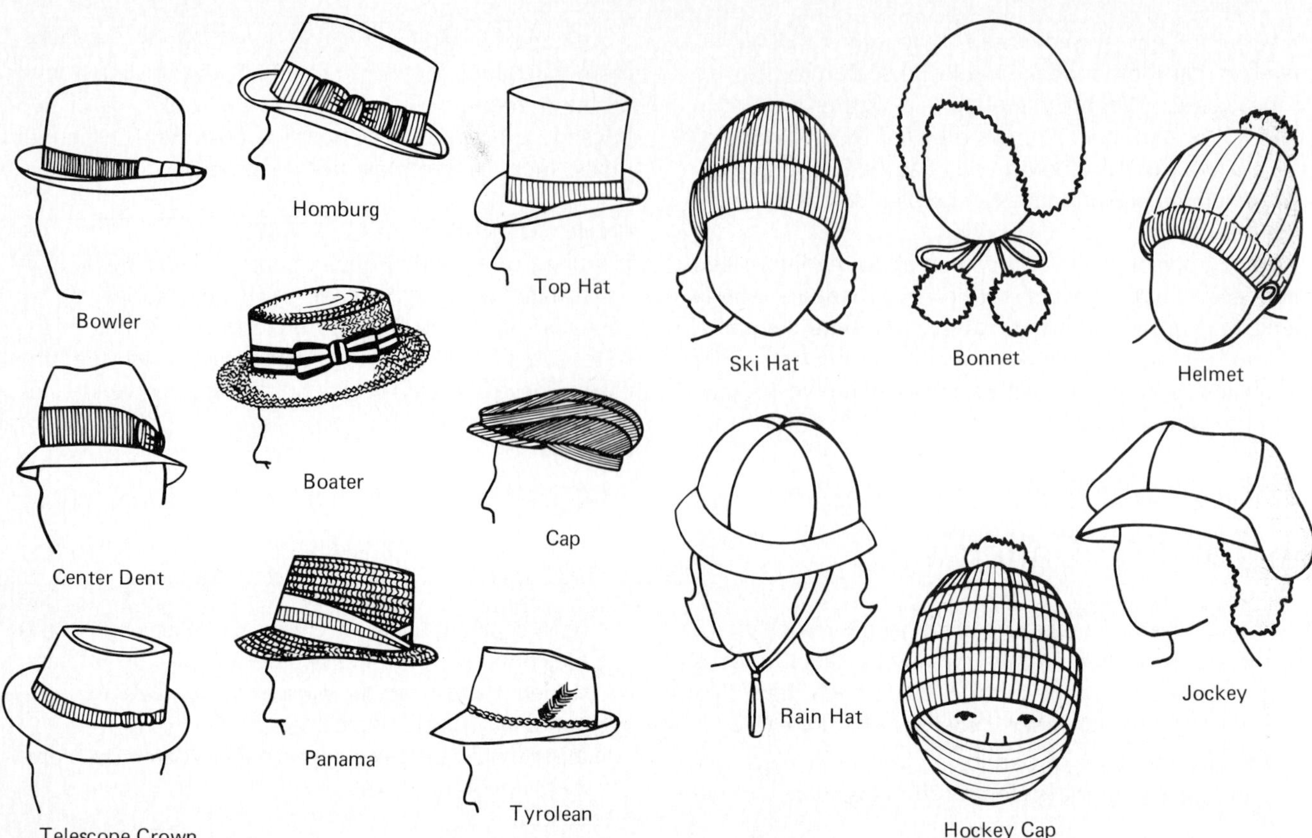

Fig. 10-5B Can you identify the popular men's hat styles shown above?

Fig. 10-5C Can you identify the popular children's hat styles shown above?

HAT SIZES

Infant hat sizes generally coincide with the age: newborn to 6 months, 6 months to 1 year, and so on. Hats for children age 3 to 6 are usually adjustable so that one size fits all. Girls' and women's hat sizes are expressed in inches according to the circumference of the head. Girls age 6 to 12 wear hat sizes ranging from 19½ to 21½ inches. Teenagers' hats usually range from 21 to 22 inches. Women's hat sizes range from 21¾ to 23½ inches, with 22 to 22½ inches being the commonest size. Many styles of women's hats, such as knitted caps, fit all head sizes. Boys' and men's hats are sized differently than girls' and women's. (See Table 1.)

Table 1

SIZING OF BOYS' AND MEN'S HATS

Circumference of Head (Inches)	Hat Size
19½	6¼
20½	6½
20¾	6⅝
21⅛	6¾
21½	6⅞
21⅞	7
22¼	7⅛
22⅝	7¼
23	7⅜
23½	7½
24⅜	7¾

To measure a hat size, place a tape measure around the head just over the eyebrows. After determining the size needed, have the customer try on the hat. The customer will want a hat that is comfortable to wear. If the hat slips or binds, it is the wrong size. Ask customers to wear the hat for a short time to see how it feels.

CARE OF HATS

Hats should be stuffed with tissue paper to hold their shape and then stored in a hatbox. Some hats, such as knitted ski caps, are washable. Others must be professionally cleaned and blocked.

COLOR, LINE, AND DESIGN OF HATS

A hat frames the face. It should complement, not detract from, the wearer's face and silhouette. Remember the following points when helping customers choose hats:

- A viewer's eye can be carried up or down depending on the type of hat. Hats with high crowns give the illusion of height and are good choices for short customers. Hats with wide brims give the appearance of width and are good choices for customers with thin, long faces.
- The size of the hat should be scaled to the size of the wearer. A large person who wears a tiny hat will look even larger; this individual should wear a medium to large hat. A small person may be overpowered by hats with medium to large brims. Overly tall hats will make

the small person look even smaller by creating a stovepipe appearance.

- The shape of the hat should complement the shape of the customer's face. An oblong face needs extra width. A square-shaped face will want a hat that appears to add length. A round face needs a hat with a tall crown or uplifted brim to lengthen the chubby look.
- Most people look best in hats that are tilted at a slight angle. When placing a hat on the customer's head, position the hat first in front and then in back. Then position it at the most attractive angle.
- Give customers a mirror so they can view the hat from all angles.
- Many women match their hat color with the color of their gloves. This gives them a coordinated look. The color of any hat should harmonize with a customer's clothing.

Choosing the right hat can definitely improve a customer's appearance. Use your knowledge of color, line, and design principles to call attention to the customer's best features.

Experience 10-5

What's the Latest in Hats?

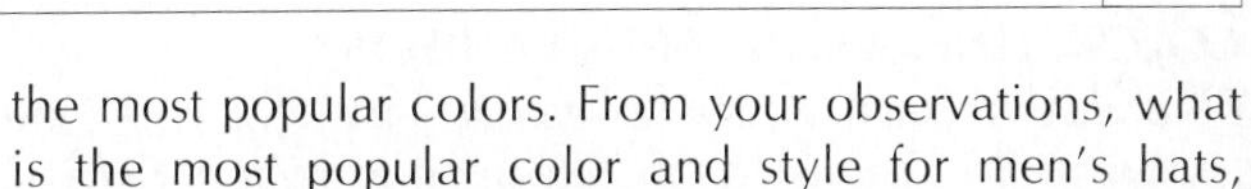

Visit a store that sells a wide variety of hats for men, women, and children. On a separate sheet of paper, make a list of the hat styles available for sale. Also list the most popular colors. From your observations, what is the most popular color and style for men's hats, women's hats, and children's hats?

BELTS

Like gloves, bags, and hats, belts may be functional or decorative. They may be used to hold up pants or add a splash of color or interest at the waist. Fashion trends determine the types of belts worn and whether or not you wear them.

BELT MATERIALS

The most popular belt materials are leather, suede, plastic, straw, macrame, and metallic fabrics. Some belts are made of fabric to match a particular garment. Belts are made by cutting the material to the desired length and width, stitching the edges, adding buckles, and punching holes. Some belts also have a backing.

BELT STYLES

Customers may use the following style terms when buying a belt (see Figure 10-6):

Cinch Belt. Tight, stretch elastic belt or a wide belt that laces up the front to accent the waist
Cummerbund. Wide sashlike fabric belt usually worn by men with evening clothes
Link Belt. Belt made of interlocking links, such as a chain belt
Metallic Belt. Any metal belt
Rope Belt. Cord belt that can be wrapped and tied
Sash Belt. Soft fabric or ribbon worn around the waist
Self-Belt. Belt made of the same fabric as the garment with which it will be worn

BELT SIZES

Belts are sized according to waist measurements. Women's belts are sized 22 to 32 inches. Men's belts are sized from 28 to 50 inches. Belts are also sized small, medium, and large, and some are adjustable.

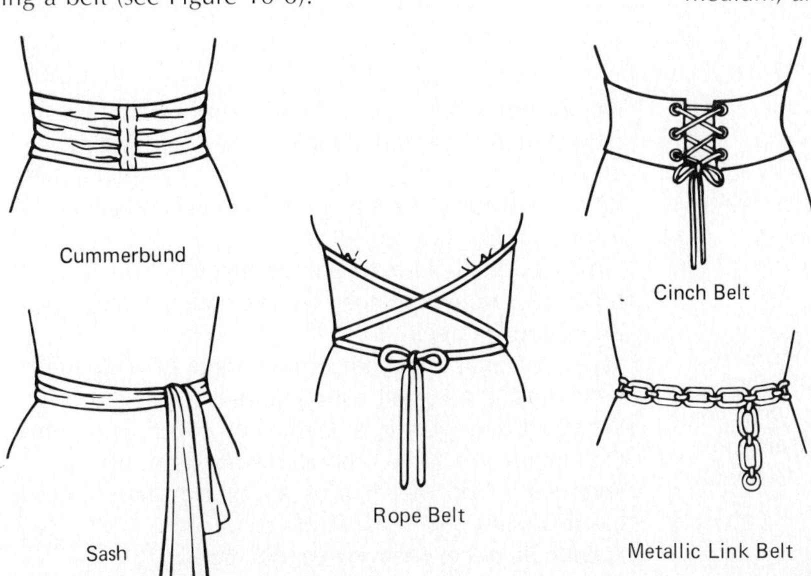

Fig. 10-6 Be able to identify these decorative belt styles.

To measure a customer for a belt to wear with slacks, place a measuring tape through the belt loops of the customer's slacks. If the customer is buying the belt for a blouse or dress, wrap the measuring tape around the customer's waist.

CARE OF BELTS

When belts are not used, they should be rolled or hung. Leather belts should be polished with wax shoe polish. Patent leather belts should be wiped with a damp cloth. For fabric belts, follow the care instructions for the entire garment if the belt does not have a leather, vinyl, or cardboard backing. Fabric belts with these backings should be dry-cleaned so that the belt keeps its shape and appearance.

COLOR, LINE, AND DESIGN OF BELTS

Belts can make a waistline appear smaller, higher, or lower. They can make a tall person appear shorter. They can add interest and give a "different" look to an ordinary outfit.

Belts that match clothing do not attract as much attention as belts that contrast with clothing. Narrow belts of the same fabric as the rest of the customer's clothing, called **self-belts**, are especially becoming for customers with broad hips and large waists. Belts in a contrasting color or design call attention to the waist and, if the customer is short, tend to cut the customer's height. Customers of average height and with trim, slender waists can wear almost any style and color belt.

Tall people often use belts to give the appearance of a shorter waistline. Some tall people place the belt above the waist to look like they have a shorter torso. They also use wide belts to make their waistlines appear higher. Likewise, many short people wear belts to achieve the look of a longer torso. By wearing a belt on the hips with hip-hugger pants or a hip-hugger skirt, a short-waisted, long-legged person will look much more attractive.

Clothing that has belt loops requires a belt; however, many people wear belts with clothing that has no belt loops. Besides traditional belts, some people wrap colorful scarves around their waists to add interest to an otherwise plain garment. People who do not want to emphasize their waists should avoid colorful, unique-looking belts.

Experience 10-6

A Look Around the Waist

Belts attract attention to a person's waist. What type belt would you recommend for the following customers:

1. Customer A has a slim waist and is of average height and weight.

   ____

2. Customer B has a large waist and broad hips. She is of average height.

   ____

3. Customer C is tall and is very long-waisted.

   ____

4. Customer D is very short and of average weight.

   ____

5. Customer E is of average height but very short-waisted.

   ____

UMBRELLAS

Umbrellas are used as protection against the sun and rain. Although they are basically a functional accessory, umbrellas add to an attractive appearance. Umbrellas are available in a wide range of colors and styles.

PARTS OF AN UMBRELLA

When selling umbrellas or purchasing umbrellas, as a store buyer, you will gain the confidence of others if you use the correct terminology when talking about this accessory item (see Figure 10-7). During a sales presentation, you may demonstrate any of the following umbrella parts:

Canopy. Part of the umbrella that spreads and protects the user from rain or sun. It is made from water-repellent fabrics such as treated nylon or cotton, or plastics, such as vinyl. (1)

Ribs. Thin metal strips that arch radially and give shape to the canopy. (2)

Tips. Rounded plastic pieces at the end of the ribs; tips hold the canopy in place and are a safety feature when the canopy is open. (3)

Tape. Material attached to the canopy that is used to wind around and fasten the umbrella. (4)

Sheath. Cloth, plastic, or leatherette covering to protect the canopy when the umbrella is not used. (5)

Spreaders. Thin metal strips attached to the center of the ribs that open or close the canopy. (6)

Shank. Shaft between the canopy and handle. (7)

Sleeve. Metal shaft that slides over the shank and is

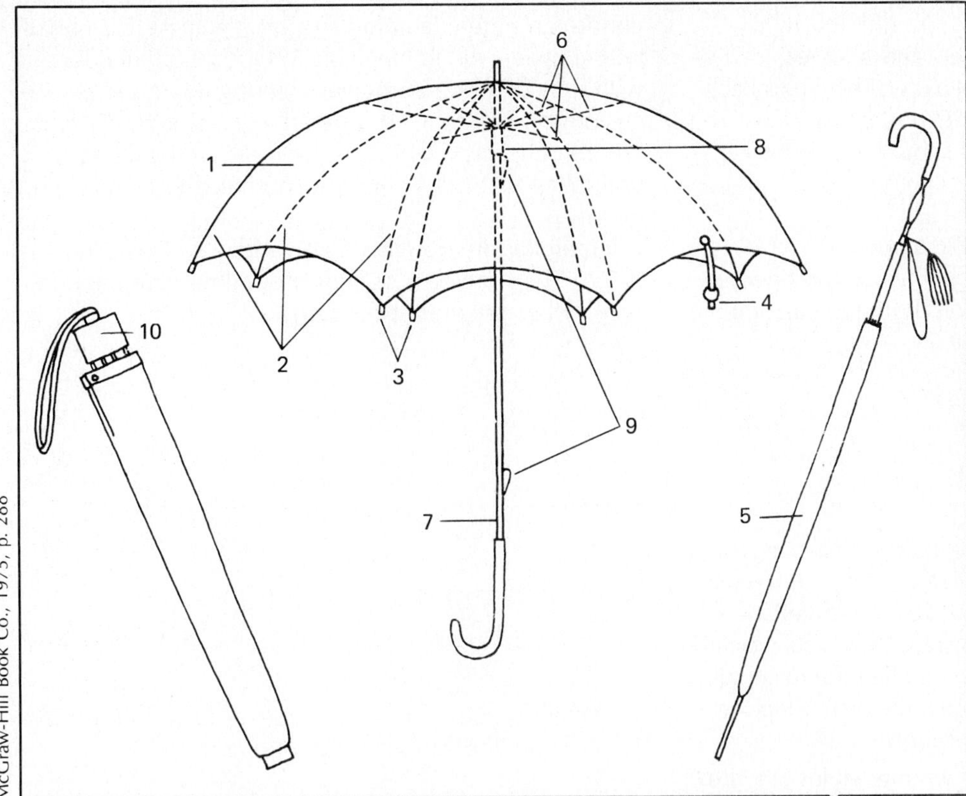

Adapted from Wingate et al., *Know Your Merchandise for Retailers and Consumers*, 4th ed., McGraw-Hill Book Co., 1975, p. 288

Fig. 10-7 Since correct terminology is important when making a sales presentation, this diagram should help you come to terms with umbrellas: (1) canopy, (2) ribs, (3) tips, (4) tape, (5) sheath, (6) spreaders, (7) shank, (8) sleeve, (9) springs, and (10) handle.

attached to the spreaders; when the sleeve is pushed toward the spreaders, the canopy opens. (8)

Springs. Two metal pieces that hold the sleeve in position when the canopy is opened or closed. (9)

Handle. Device at the end of the shank used to hold onto the umbrella when opened or closed. Handles are made of many materials, such as plastic, wood, leather, bone, or cane. (10)

UMBRELLA STYLES

Customers may refer to the style terms in Table 2 when choosing an umbrella. Children's umbrellas have a shorter shaft and smaller canopy than adult-sized umbrellas. Women's umbrellas generally have a smaller canopy spread than men's. The number of ribs in an umbrella varies depending on the umbrella's size, shape, and construction.

Table 2

UMBRELLA STYLES

Style	Description
Ballerina	Has dainty appearance with ruffled edge that resembles ballerina's skirt.
Beach	Made from waterproof materials; has gaily colored stripes or figured patterns. Center pole is usually made of wood or aluminum and is pointed on one end to fit easily into sand or soil. Size varies from 5 to 8 feet in diameter.
Bubble-shape or bird cage	Deeply domed to cover the head and shoulders of user; must be made of transparent material, such as clear vinyl (the most commonly used), in order for user to see.
Folding	Ribs fold to permit umbrella to be reduced in size for ease in carrying or packing.
Parasol	Light umbrella used as sun shade.
Regular	Approximately 24 inches in length, with 8, 10, or 16 ribs.
Stadium	Same as bubble-shape, except large enough to fit over two people.
Self-opening	Push button works hidden spring that releases sleeve, pushing ribs into place. When closed, tip ends of ribs are held in place in metal cup.
Windproof	Can be snapped back into shape if blown inside out. May have spring between spreaders and ribs just under canopy that helps to keep umbrella in shape or may have hinges at point where spreaders and ribs join that permit ribs to be turned back without bending out of shape.

(Source: Isabel B. Wingate, Karen R. Gillespie, and Betty G. Milgram, Know Your Merchandise for Retailers and Consumers, *4th ed., New York: McGraw-Hill Book Co., Inc., 1975.)*

CARE OF UMBRELLAS

Wet umbrellas should be opened and allowed to dry before they are rolled up and put away. This helps keep the fabric from spotting and wrinkling excessively. To prevent melting, vinyl umbrellas should not be near direct heat.

COLOR AND DESIGN OF UMBRELLAS

Because umbrellas are basically functional, most people have only one umbrella. When helping customers choose an umbrella color, suggest a neutral that blends with a variety of clothing colors. Or match the umbrella with the color of a particular clothing item, such as the customer's raincoat. The traditional color for a man's umbrella is black. Children often carry brightly colored umbrellas that allow them to be more easily seen by motorists.

Umbrellas are designed in a variety of ways. (See Table 2.) The sturdiness of their ribs, rather than the number of ribs, determines their quality.

Experience 10-7

All about Umbrellas

1. Role play a salesperson in the accessory department of a local store. Have a classmate pose as a customer who is interested in buying an umbrella. Using a real umbrella, demonstrate how you would point out the parts of an umbrella and the materials the umbrella is made of. If possible, use a tape recorder to record your conversation.
2. Umbrellas are available in various styles. In the space provided, identify and describe four of those styles.

____

____

____

____

____

3. Why do you think it is important for a salesperson to know the various styles of umbrellas?

____

____

____

____

COSTUME JEWELRY

Costume jewelry is worn to decorate or add interest to an outfit. It differs from fine jewelry in that it is not made from precious metals and gems, such as gold or rubies. It is made from base metals, such as aluminum or tin. Often, these base metals are covered with a thin coating of gold or silver to give the jewelry a richer look. Costume jewelry is also made from plastic.

JEWELRY STYLES

Fashion trends greatly influence the look of costume jewelry each season. Sometimes the styles are delicate; sometimes they look heavy. Customers may refer to the following style terms when buying jewelry:

Barette. Clamplike device that holds hair in place

Bracelet. Arm bands of various types

- *Bangles.* Round hoops of varied width that slip over the hand
- *Charm bracelet.* Bracelet with tiny curios of metal or stone that dangle from a metal chain
- *Identification bracelet.* Bracelet with the wearer's name engraved on a piece of metal

Brooch. Ornamental pin

Charm. Small ornament hung from bracelets or chains

Clip. Ornament with a clip backing

Collar pin. Straight, bar, or looped pin worn between collar points

Cuff links. Ornaments on stems that are used to fasten French cuffs

Earrings. Ornaments worn in the ears with screw backs or clips or posts and screw heads for pierced ears

- *Ball earrings.* Earrings round in shape, like a ball
- *Button earrings.* Round, flat earrings that fit against the earlobe
- *Drop earrings.* Earrings with a pendant or hoop that dangles
- *Hoop earrings.* Earrings circular in shape that resemble a hoop

Fob chains. Chains that connect pocket watches to a garment

Key chains or rings. Chains or rings that hold a group of keys together

Necklace. Jewelry worn around the neck

- *Amulet.* Pendant worn on a neck chain
- *Bib.* Multistrand necklace that hugs the base of the neck

Choker. Single or multistrand necklace that fits the neck snugly
Collar. Flat necklace that fits the neck just atop the collarbone
Lavaliere. Pendant or ornament that hangs from a chain or cord
Locket. Small case hanging from a chain, cord, or ribbon that holds a picture or other mementos
Matinee length necklace. Pearl or bead necklace 30 to 35 inches long
Opera length necklace. Pearl or bead necklace 48 to 120 inches long
Rope. Long chain or bead necklace, matinee or opera length

Ring. Ornament worn on the finger
Cluster ring. Ring with stones set in groups
Cocktail ring. Ring in fancy shapes and fitted with stones
Dinner ring. Long, narrow ring usually worn on fingers of the right hand
Signet ring. Ring with a crest or initials

Studs. Tiny disc or ball on a stem; used instead of buttons on a formal shirt
Tie bar Bar with hinged back worn to hold a tie in place
Tie tack. Small ornament set on a short, straight pin that pierces the tie and holds it in place
Watch. Timepiece worn on a bracelet or chain

COLOR, LINE, AND DESIGN OF JEWELRY

When choosing jewelry colors, it is easier to design an outfit around two colors rather than three or more. If an ensemble is a solid color, jewelry in a contrasting color may give the outfit added appeal. Jewelry for clothing that is multicolored should repeat one of the strong colors in the garment.

Jewelry should be chosen in relation to a customer's figure, personality, and age. A small person will look most attractive wearing small jewelry, whereas a large person can successfully wear large jewelry.

Necklaces call attention to the neck and throat. Bracelets and rings call attention to the hands. Earrings call attention to the face. Customers who do not want to emphasize a particular feature or part of their body should refrain from wearing certain jewelry items.

When helping customers choose jewelry, keep the shape of the face and body in mind. Long necklaces that make a "V" are more slenderizing and a better choice than large, round beads for a person with a short, thick neck. A pin centered on a customer's sweater or dress will have a slenderizing effect on the face and neck. Two pins, one on each side, will add breadth to a thin person. A pin worn high on the shoulder will make a short person appear taller.

When helping a customer choose earrings, remember that round earrings accentuate a round face and drop earrings accentuate a long face. A person with a long face should consider ball or button earrings to add width to the face. Likewise, the round-faced person would look more attractive when wearing drop earrings that add length.

People with heavy arms should wear wide bracelets, not delicate ones, or several narrow ones. People with thin arms should not wear bulky bracelets or watches; these will make the arms look thinner. Large hands can wear large rings. Small hands need delicate rings.

The purpose of jewelry is to decorate the body, to make it look more attractive. Choose jewelry that emphasizes each customer's best features and minimizes the most undesirable ones. Customers will appreciate your suggestions of what jewelry styles and colors help them look their best.

Experience 10-8

The Many Looks of Jewelry

1. Look through a fashion magazine or catalog and locate a basic apparel garment for either men or women. For example, you may choose a knit sweater dress with long sleeves and round neck. Cut out or copy the garment you choose and attach it to a separate sheet of paper.
2. In magazines, catalogs, or newspapers, locate costume jewelry that gives the garment you chose three different looks. Choose jewelry combinations that can be worn with the garment at work, school, and on a date. Cut out or copy the jewelry and attach it to your paper. Label the jewelry "work," "school," or "dressy" depending on the occasion.
3. Form into a small group with other classmates who completed this exercise. One by one, present your jewelry and clothing choices to the others and ask for comments. After the presentations, discuss the guidelines you followed in choosing your jewelry items.

Experience 10-9

What Looks Best?

Jewelry should be chosen in relation to a person's size. It should call attention to a customer's best features. Read each of the following descriptions of customers and answer the questions on the next page.

1. The customer has a short, thick neck. What style necklace would you suggest?

___

2. The customer has a very round face. What style earrings would you suggest?

___

3. The customer has very slender arms. What style bracelets would you suggest?

___

4. The customer has a very long face. What style earrings would you suggest?

___

5. The customer is very slender. How would you suggest the customer wear two matching pins?

___

6. The customer has very small, delicate hands. What size rings would you suggest?

___

OTHER FASHION ACCESSORIES

Other fashion accessories sold in apparel and accessory stores include wigs, scarves, shawls, handkerchiefs, and sunglasses. Each of these accessories may fill a functional need. For example, scarves may be used to hold back the hair, shawls may provide warmth. However, when customers are buying these accessories, they give most consideration to how that item looks on them. If they feel the item is unattractive, customers will refuse to buy it.

When selling these accessories, find out the purpose the customer has in mind for the item. Shades, tints, and color hues are very important when helping customers select wigs, scarves, or shawls. Shape is the more important consideration when helping customers choose sunglasses. When working with these accessory items, suggest a color and style that will highlight the customer's best features.

SELLING ACCESSORIES

Accessories are combined with clothing and other accessory items to make the customer look well dressed and coordinated. Although selling accessories is similar to selling clothing, there are some unique differences.

WHAT KIND OF ACCESSORIES?

After greeting the customer, it is important for the salesperson to find out what the customer will be wearing with the accessory item to be purchased. This information will help the salesperson determine the color and texture of the item needed. By analyzing the customer's figure or body build, the salesperson will be better able to suggest a style that complements the customer. When choosing accessories, the salesperson should remember the principle of scale and choose the size of the accessories based on the size of the wearer. For example, a dainty, petite customer should wear or carry small accessories. A larger customer will look best with large accessories.

Color schemes are very important when choosing accessory items. A two-color outfit is easier to design than more complicated color schemes. If the customer has a real talent for combining colors, three- or four-color outfits may look very appealing.

Some accessory items, such as wigs and pierced earrings, are not returnable. Therefore, salespeople should make a special effort to help customers choose the correct merchandise. Customers should also be told before purchasing merchandise that certain items cannot be returned.

DEMONSTRATE THE MERCHANDISE

Salespeople should demonstrate all accessory items as well as let customers handle the merchandise for themselves. A handbag, for example, can easily be demonstrated. The salesperson should have the customer open the fastener so that he or she can see how it works. When a salesperson points out the well-made, roomy interior and extra compartments, the customer realizes the value of the bag. By offering the bag to the customer for inspection, the salesperson is letting the customer experience a feeling of ownership. When the customer holds the bag next to his or her body and looks in a mirror, the customer can actually see how attractive the bag is.

The salesperson who encourages a customer to try on hats is demonstrating the product. The salesperson is giving the customer a firsthand experience with how the hat looks and feels. By having the customer look in the mirror, the salesperson is providing the customer with proof that the hat looks attractive. Many salespeople discover that if they properly demonstrate products, customers often convince themselves to buy.

SUGGEST OTHER ACCESSORIES

In selling accessories, you will have many opportunities for suggestion selling. Take advantage of these opportunities. For example, when a customer buys a necklace, suggest the matching earrings. Suggest the matching knit scarf and gloves to customers who buy a knit hat. You will find that customers appreciate these thoughtful suggestions when you give them.

Experience 10-10

Accessorize!

Choose three different clothing groups for yourself—for dress, work, and casual wear. Locate these clothing items in a fashion magazine or catalog and cut out or copy the pictures. Accessorize each of these outfits. Choose such accessories as gloves, hats, jewelry, belts, scarfs, umbrellas, or any other appropriate items. Find pictures of these accessories in magazines and/or newspapers and cut them out or locate the accessories in local apparel stores and take photographs of them. Arrange the clothing items and accessories on separate sheets, one for each group. List all merchandise below.

When completing this exercise, pay special attention to the color schemes. Choose clothing and accessories that will make you look most attractive.

Group 1: Dress Outfit	Group 2: Work Outfit	Group 3: Casual Outfit
1. ______	1. ______	1. ______
2. ______	2. ______	2. ______
3. ______	3. ______	3. ______
4. ______	4. ______	4. ______
5. ______	5. ______	5. ______
6. ______	6. ______	6. ______
7. ______	7. ______	7. ______
8. ______	8. ______	8. ______
9. ______	9. ______	9. ______
10. ______	10. ______	10. ______
11. ______	11. ______	11. ______
12. ______	12. ______	12. ______
13. ______	13. ______	13. ______
14. ______	14. ______	14. ______
15. ______	15. ______	15. ______

ACE
T-SHIRT
COMPANY

UNIT 4

Marketing Skills

One of the largest employment areas in the apparel and accessories industry is retailing. Apparel and accessories retailers buy clothing and accessories from suppliers. They transport the merchandise to their stores, check it in, display it, advertise it, and sell it to you—the consumer.

This unit discusses the marketing skills involved in apparel and accessories retailing. It also discusses the special management skills required of an apparel and accessories retail manager, including recruiting and hiring workers, training and supervising employees, controlling shoplifting, preparing budgets, and handling expenses.

After reading this unit, you will be ready for a job in apparel and accessories marketing. You can look forward to an exciting career with many rewards. Good luck!

11 Buying and Pricing

A major merchandising responsibility, buying the right merchandise and selling it at the right price, belongs to the apparel and accessory buyer. This is no easy task. Customers are the determining factor in a store's success, and each person is different. How do buyers know what merchandise is right? How do they know what sizes, colors, and styles customers want?

If you climb the career ladder to become an apparel and accessory buyer, you will face these questions. To help you handle this merchandise responsibility, put yourself in the role of a buyer.

PLANNING YOUR PURCHASES

"Good morning. I just dropped in to discuss any questions you may have before you leave on your spring buying trip," says Ms. Martin, your merchandise manager at Crawford & Murphy's Department Store. You are the new buyer of the Dress Down Shop. Your department sells casual pants, shirts, sweaters, and jackets to young adults.

"It's a bit frightening to be going to New York on your first big buy," Ms. Martin says. "You're responsible for a large sum of money and your success as a buyer depends on the buying decisions you make. I'll be going on the trip with you, but I also have to supervise four other buyers. That's why I want to be certain that you are as organized and prepared as possible."

PREPARING A SEASONAL MERCHANDISE PLAN

Ms. Martin hands you a form filled with numbers. It's titled Six-Month Merchandise Plan. (See Figure 11-1.) You remember the first time you saw this form. It was the week after you became the buyer of the Dress Down Shop, almost 3 months ago. Ms. Martin gave you the blank form and asked you to complete it and submit it to her for review.

You had many meetings with Ms. Martin, trying to understand what each column meant and how it was to be completed. Ms. Martin told you, "Our store, like other clothing stores, prepares a six-month merchandise plan twice a year, once for the spring/summer season, February 1 through July 31, and once for the fall/winter season, August 1 through January 31. This plan helps buyers control the amount of money they invest in inventory. Notice that it includes information about sales, retail stock, markdowns, and retail purchases. All the numbers on the form represent dollars."

You still remember how Ms. Martin explained each of the four sections of the plan to you. She was so patient, and you had so many questions.

Sales All the activities of a store are dependent on sales. Therefore, when a store does its planning, it plans its sales first. To determine what sales will be for the coming year, a buyer looks at last year's sales figures, as well as other previous years' figures. Usually, there is an upward or downward trend. For example, if sales have been increasing by 5 percent every year for the last 5 years, they will probably continue to increase by 5 percent next year. Of course, this depends on whether or not conditions during the coming year are similar to conditions in the past.

After many hours of examining past sales records, you and Ms. Martin forecast the planned sales for the coming year. The planned sales are listed on the second line of the six-month merchandise plan. (See Figure 11-1, letter A on the opposite page.)

Stock There is a direct relationship between the amount of sales and the amount of stock in a store, called the

CRAWFORD & MURPHY'S

Department Name Dress Down Shop Department No. 17

SIX MONTH MERCHANDISE PLAN

SPRING 198–		Feb.	Mar.	Apr.	May	June	July	Season Total
Sales	Last Year	7300	5400	4700	5600	6700	4900	34,600
	Plan	8500**	6700	5800	6600	7800	5800	41,200
	Revised							
	Actual							
Retail Stock (Bom)	Last Year	27,100	23,900	23,400	25,100	26,500	24,400	150,400
	Plan	31,500	29,700	28,800	29,600	30,800	28,800	179,200
	Revised							
	Actual							
Markdowns	Last Year	1400	1300	1250	1350	1450	1500	8250
	Plan (dollars)	1250	1200	1150	1200	1300	1350	7450
	Revised							
	Actual							
Retail Purchases	Last Year	5400	4700	5600	6700	4900	3900	31,200
	Plan	6700	5800	6600	7800	5800	4700	37,400
	Revised							
	Actual							

Comments

*Represents stock end of period **All numbers rounded up to nearest $50

Merchandise Manager R. Martin Buyer Your Name

Controller ______________________

(A → Sales Plan, Feb.; B → Retail Stock Plan, Mar.)

Fig. 11-1 In this six-month merchandise plan, A indicates planned sales for February and B points out planned retail stock for the beginning of March.

stock-sales ratio. It tells buyers that if they plan to sell a certain amount of merchandise, they must have a certain amount of stock in the store. The stock-sales ratio is determined over a period of time. The ratio is calculated by dividing the stock, in dollars, by the sales. For example, a department that, during the month of April, has a stock or inventory of merchandise amounting to $20,000 and sales amounting to $10,000 has a stock-sales ratio of 2.

$$\frac{\$20{,}000}{10{,}000} = 2$$

The monthly stock-sales ratios for the Dress Down Shop are shown in Table 1.

You used your stock-sales ratios to determine the dollar volume of merchandise you need in stock at the beginning of every month. For example, the six-month merchandise plan shows that the planned sales for March are $6,700. The stock-sales ratio for that month is 4.43. By multiplying 4.43 by $6,700, you determine that you need planned retail stock amounting to $29,681 for the beginning of the month (BOM). This is rounded up to $29,700. (See Figure 11-1, letter B.) By multiplying the stock-sales ratio for each month by the planned sales for that month, buyers can determine the retail stock needed at the beginning of each month. The stock-sales ratios help buyers keep their stock in balance with their sales.

Table 1

DRESS DOWN SHOP: Monthly Stock-Sales Ratios

Month	Ratio
January	3.64
February	3.71
March	4.43
April	4.97
May	4.48
June	3.95
July	4.97
August	4.42
September	4.21
October	4.18
November	4.28
December	4.92

Markdowns The next section of the six-month merchandise plan lists past and future markdowns for the Dress Down Shop. Markdowns reduce the dollar value of inventory in the store or department, just as sales do. No buyer can avoid taking markdowns, as they are a necessary part of merchandising. They move out damaged, out-of-season, and slow-selling merchandise and make room for new purchases.

Last year, the markdowns in the Dress Down Shop were high. Poor buying decisions were made and markdowns were necessary to move out the merchandise. This year, a 10 percent reduction in markdowns is planned.

Retail Purchases The retail purchases section of the six-month merchandise plan shows the dollar amount of merchandise that a buyer may purchase for 1 month without going over the planned inventory level. The formula for computing planned purchases is:

Planned purchases = Planned sales + Planned EOM inventory − Planned BOM inventory

For example, the planned purchases for February = $8,500 + 29,700 − 31,500 = $6,700

Notice that the end of month (EOM) inventory for February is equal to the beginning of month (BOM) inventory for March.

Open-to-Buy Although the open-to-buy figures are not listed on the six-month merchandise plan, they are derived from retail purchases. "In the merchandise plan, buyers are allotted certain amounts of money for retail purchases," Ms. Martin told you. "When buyers place orders for any new merchandise, they decrease the total amount of money available for retail purchases. Because most merchandise orders are not received the same month they are ordered, buyers have to keep track of what they have spent and what is still available to spend. **Open-to-buy** refers to the available amount of money a buyer can spend at any particular time."

Buyers can calculate their open-to-buy amount by using a formula:

Open-to-buy = Planned purchases − Merchandise on order

For example, in February, the planned purchases for the Dress Down Shop equal $6,700. There are outstanding orders for February totaling $1,040. This merchandise has already been ordered but not yet received. The open-to-buy for February equals $5,660.

Open-to-buy = $6,700 − $1,040 = $5,660

When buyers spend more money than there is available, the store or department is in an "overbought" situation. Overbought departments do not have the proper balance between stock and sales. Buyers in overbought departments or stores are usually in trouble.

Retail versus Cost All figures on the Dress Down Shop six-month merchandise plan are expressed in retail, not cost, amounts. **Retail** is what the store charges for the merchandise. **Cost** is what the store pays for the merchandise it has for sale.

In reality, the buyer does not have $5,660 to spend on purchases in February. To determine the actual amount of money the buyer can spend, or the **open-to-buy at cost**, multiply the open-to-buy at retail by the store's mark-up complement. The mark-up complement is equal to 100 percent minus the mark-up percentage. Suppose, for example, that the buyer marks up all merchandise by 40 percent. The open-to-buy at cost for February would equal $3,396.

Open-to-buy at cost = Open-to-buy at Retail
× (100 percent − mark-up percentage)
= $5,660 × (100 percent − 40 percent)
= $5,660 × 60 percent = $3,396

Completing the Merchandise Plan The six-month merchandise plan is one of the buyer's most important tools. Because it shows the specific amount of sales, stock, and purchases for a store or department, the merchandise plan helps buyers to buy an adequate assortment.

Also there are spaces in the merchandise plan for revisions. When a store or department does not meet its planned sales, or exceeds its planned sales, the buyer can adjust the other figures on the plan. At the end of each month, the buyer records the actual sales, retail stock, markdowns, and planned purchases on the form. This helps to determine how closely the planned figures are to the actual figures.

Experience 11-1

How Much Can I Buy?

Ms. Martin, your merchandise manager, asks all her buyers to complete a six-month merchandise plan for the upcoming season. Complete the fall merchandise plan seen on page 151. Ms. Martin has already forecast the planned sales. You estimate that you can reduce each month's markdowns by 15 percent. Refer to Table 1 for the monthly stock-sales ratios. The retail stock BOM for February equals $17,300. When completing the merchandise plan, round off each number to the nearest $50.

CRAWFORD & MURPHY'S

Department Name Dress Down Shop Department No. 17

SIX MONTH MERCHANDISE PLAN

FALL 198–		Aug.	Sep.	Oct.	Nov.	Dec.	Jan.	Season Total
Sales	Last Year	3500	4000	5000	4500	8500	4500	30,000
	Plan	4000	6000	7000	6500	12,800	7200	43,500
	Revised							
	Actual							
Retail Stock (Bom)	Last Year	15,450	16,850	20,900	19,250	24,650	16,400	113,500
	Plan							
	Revised							
	Actual							
Markdowns	Last Year	350	400	450	400	350	400	2350
	Plan (dollars)							
	Revised							
	Actual							
Retail Purchases	Last Year	4900	8050	3350	13,900	250	7600	38,050
	Plan							
	Revised							
	Actual							

Comments

*Represents stock end of period

Merchandise Manager R. Martin Buyer Your Name

Controller ______

Experience 11-2

How Much Can I Spend?

Compute the open-to-buy at retail and open-to-buy at cost for the following merchandise items. Assume the store's markup is 50 percent.

Merchandise Item	Planned Purchases	Merchandise on Order	Open-to-Buy at Retail	Open-to-Buy at Cost
Boys' elasticized belts	$1,750	$ 380		
Boys' polo shirts	6,720	2,500		
Boys' socks	9,460	4,800		
Boys' T-shirts	600	220		

ANALYZING UNIT-CONTROL RECORDS

Once a buyer has determined planned sales and needed inventory levels, the buyer must decide what merchandise to purchase. Most buyers pay careful attention to what customers have purchased in the past.

Buyers use **unit-control records** to keep track of sales and control stock assortments. The information in unit-control records is expressed in units of merchandise. Unit-control records tell buyers at a glance the total history of a particular merchandise item or a particular merchandise style. They show the number of units purchased, sold, ordered, returned, and in stock. Unit-control records help predict buying trends. They help buyers identify what items are "hot" and what items are, in merchandising language, "dogs." Buyers who know how to analyze these records can learn many facts about their customers.

Ms. Martin explains, "There is no standard set of unit-control records. Some stores have an electronic unit-control system that tabulates unit-control data with a computer. And our store is planning to switch over to a computer in the near future. As long as you understand the purposes of unit-control records, which is to help you plan your purchases and control your inventory, you will have no problem using the information.

"Here is the record system the previous buyer of the Dress Down Shop used," Ms. Martin continues. "Let me show you how to interpret these records in a way that will help you plan your merchandise purchases."

USING UNIT-CONTROL RECORDS FOR PLANNING

Ms. Martin begins her explanation of how to use unit-control records. "How a buyer uses unit-control records partially determines that buyer's success," she remarks.

"This unit-control record has two styles of 100 percent cotton corduroy pants, straight leg and flare leg, in three colors," she says. (See Figure 11-2.) "Each straight line on the record represents a merchandise item in stock. Each straight line with a diagonal line through it represents sold merchandise. Each circle shows that the merchandise item was taken out of stock because of a transfer (t) or return to vendor (v). Let's analyze the sales of these two styles of pants. Past sales indicate that the most popular style is the flare leg. The most popular color is navy blue. Sizes 30M, 30L, 32M, and 32L are the big sellers. The retail price on these pants is $13.99. The pants have not taken a markdown.

"To find out which price line is more popular, let's compare these pants to a similar pant group. The unit-control card for the second group shows two styles of polyester/cotton blend brushed denim pants. (See Figure 11-3.) These pants used to retail for $16.99. On October 8, they were marked down to $13.99. Although the colors are not the same as in the first group, the two pant groups can be compared because they are similar in merchandise type, style, and size range. The customers for both pants are the same.

"Even though the polyester/cotton blend pants were $3 more, they have a better sales record. Navy blue is again the most popular color and flare leg is the most popular style. Sizes 30 and 32 medium and long are also the most popular.

"These two unit-control records can help a buyer plan future pant purchases. The records clearly show a customer demand for sizes 30 and 32 medium and long. In fact, the sales figures would make me consider reducing the number of 30 shorts in stock. The records also show customers are willing to pay more for the easy care and comfort of the polyester/cotton blend. The records show a customer preference for navy blue and the flare leg. Due to the poor sales of loden green, I would hestitate to purchase an assortment of this color pant once again, except perhaps in small quantities of samples."

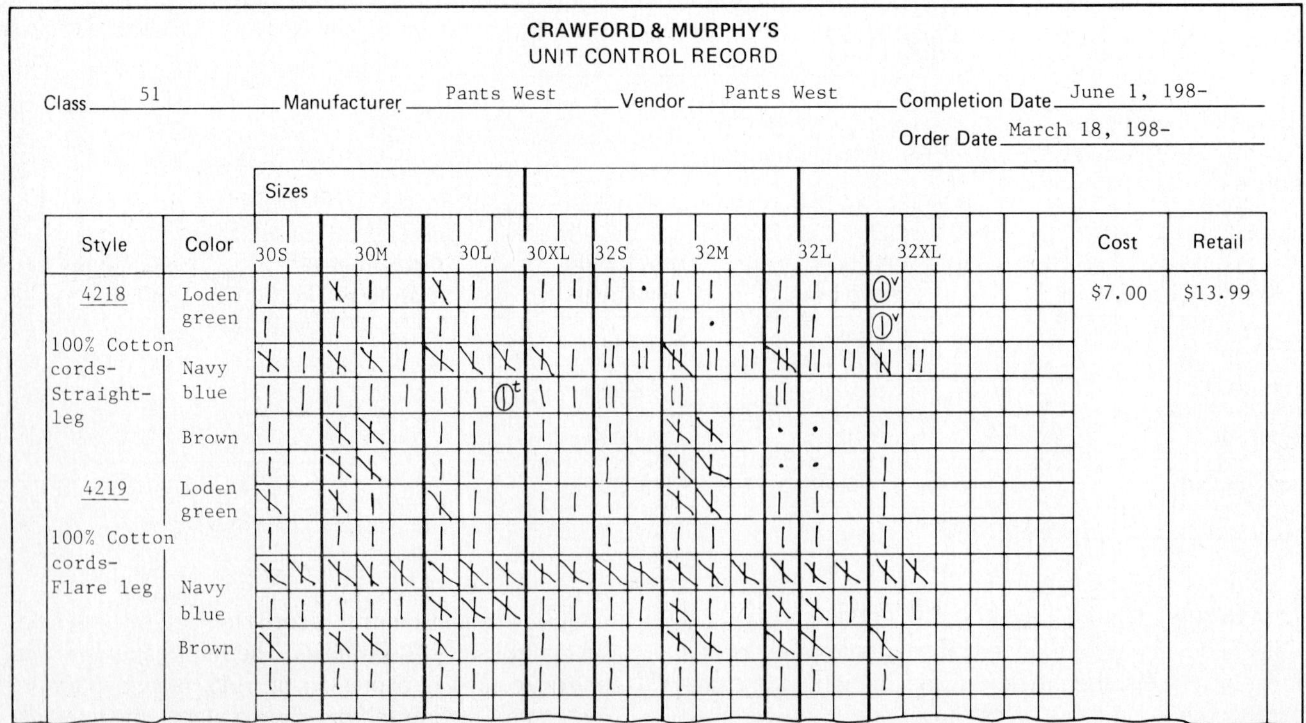

CRAWFORD & MURPHY'S
UNIT CONTROL RECORD

Class 51 Manufacturer Pants West Vendor Pants West Completion Date June 1, 198-

Order Date March 18, 198-

Style	Color	Sizes: 30S	30M	30L	30XL	32S	32M	32L	32XL	Cost	Retail
4218 100% Cotton cords- Straight-leg	Loden green									$7.00	$13.99
	Navy blue										
	Brown										
4219 100% Cotton cords- Flare leg	Loden green										
	Navy blue										
	Brown										

Fig. 11-2 The symbols used on unit-control records are explained in this and the following chapters. Dots, for example, represent goods on order.

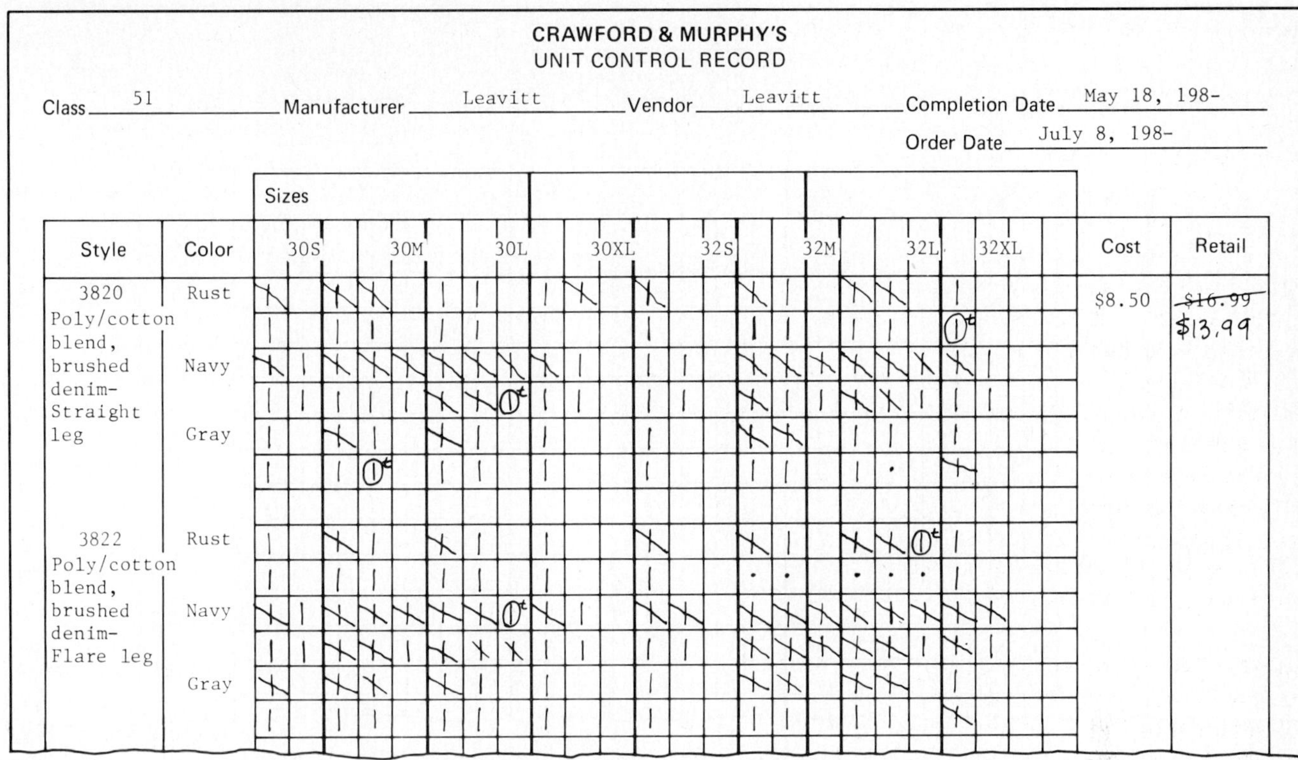

CRAWFORD & MURPHY'S
UNIT CONTROL RECORD

Class 51 Manufacturer Leavitt Vendor Leavitt Completion Date May 18, 198-
Order Date July 8, 198-

Style	Color	Sizes: 30S	30M	30L	30XL	32S	32M	32L	32XL	Cost	Retail
3820 Poly/cotton blend, brushed denim-Straight leg	Rust									$8.50	~~$16.99~~ $13.99
	Navy										
	Gray										
3822 Poly/cotton blend, brushed denim-Flare leg	Rust										
	Navy										
	Gray										

Fig. 11-3 This unit-control record reflects the performance of a fast-selling price line.

Ms. Martin then gave you the following guidelines for analyzing unit-control information:

1. *Identify the best-selling sizes.* These sizes, which change very slowly over time, should be the ones to buy in the largest quantity. Sizes that rarely sell should be dropped or purchased in very limited quantities.
2. *Identify the strongest price lines.* The price lines show the amount of money customers are willing to spend. When buying goods, choose merchandise that fits those lines.
3. *Identify the best-selling merchandise types, styles, and colors.* Some merchandise types, styles, and colors stay popular for long periods of time. Others are out of fashion in a season. Use the unit-control records to identify which items are basic stock items. These items, which have a consistent customer demand, should always be in the store. Apparel and accessory styles and colors change fast so that unit-control records do not show the exact fashion goods customers will purchase. However, the records show if customers are fashion leaders or followers. If last year the "in" look was knickers, and buyers couldn't keep knickers in stock, the customers are then saying that the *customers* are the fashion leaders.
4. *Identify which merchandise had to be marked down.* For example, the pants in Figure 11-3 were marked down on October 8 from $16.99 to $13.99. If past records show that a particular color or style of merchandise must always be marked down, buy a limited merchandise assortment of that color or style.

Experience 11-3

Reading the Records

Ms. Martin has asked you to analyze the unit control record for women's wallets seen on page 154. She wants to know:

1. What color is most popular with customers?

____

2. What style is most popular with customers?

____

3. Have there been any markdowns taken on these wallets?

____

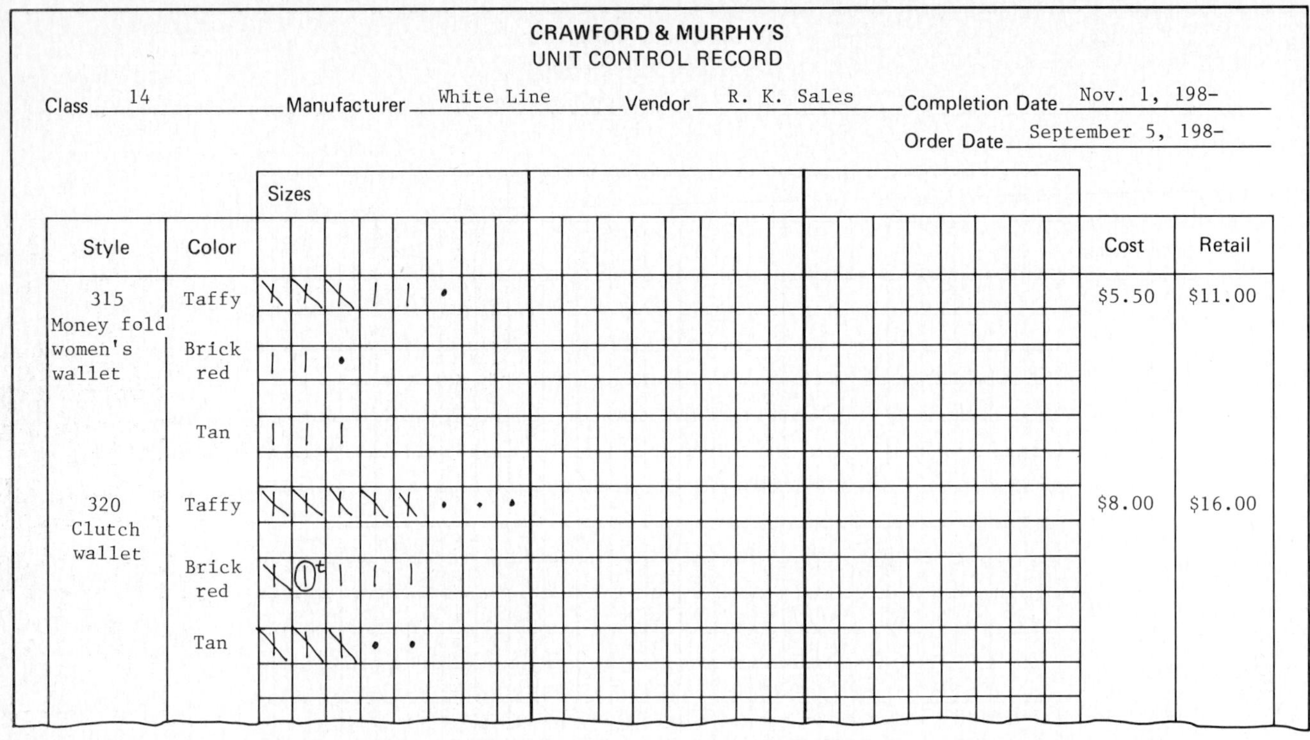

CRAWFORD & MURPHY'S
UNIT CONTROL RECORD

Class 14 Manufacturer White Line Vendor R. K. Sales Completion Date Nov. 1, 198-
Order Date September 5, 198-

Style	Color	Sizes	Cost	Retail
315 Money fold women's wallet	Taffy	X X X | | •	$5.50	$11.00
	Brick red	| | •		
	Tan	| | |		
320 Clutch wallet	Taffy	X X X X X • • •	$8.00	$16.00
	Brick red	X ①t | | |		
	Tan	X X X • •		

4. If you could buy only one style and color wallet, what would you buy? Explain your answer.

EXAMINING CUSTOMER REQUESTS

When customers ask for merchandise that the store does not stock, sales are lost. To minimize lost sales, smart buyers find out what merchandise customers couldn't find in the store. Because buyers don't work regularly with customers, they rely on salespeople to tell them about customer requests for merchandise. Many buyers ask their salespeople to use customer want slips to record information about unavailable styles, colors, and price ranges that customers wanted. (See Figure 11-4.) Buyers should examine customer requests for merchandise when deciding what to purchase before a buying trip.

IDENTIFYING CURRENT FASHION TRENDS

Unit-contol records show what has sold in the past. However, they cannot predict the big fashion news for the future. Buyers must turn to fashion designers, reports, and magazines to find out the latest fashion trends.

CRAWFORD & MURPHY'S

CUSTOMER WANT SLIP

Store 12 Dept. No. 6 Salesperson Nels Laarsen Date 2/13/—

Item Requested by Customer	Style No.	Size	Color	Price	Action Taken (To Be Completed by Buyer)
Rugby Shirt	—	12	blue/green	—	
Tank top	833A	medium	rust	$7.59	
Suede vest	2111	large	beige	$14.99	

Fig. 11-4 A typical example of a customer want slip prepared by salespeople for buyers is shown above.

To keep up with the current trends and fads, buyers read trade journals and magazines. Trade journals, such as *Women's Wear Daily* and *Footwear News,* predict fashion trends and spotlight best sellers. *Vogue, Harper's Bazaar, Glamour, Mademoiselle, Seventeen, Gentlemen's Quarterly,* and *Men's Wear* emphasize fashion news. These periodicals help buyers know the types and styles of apparel and accessories that will be sold by merchandise suppliers. They help buyers form an idea of new items to purchase.

EVALUATING ECONOMIC CONDITIONS

Buyers should realize that economic conditions in their areas influence what sells and what doesn't. For example, the income level and unemployment rate of an area affect apparel and accessory purchases. New industries moving into a town will increase the demand for apparel and accessories. An anticipated strike makes people hesitant about buying unnecessary goods.

Newspapers, television news, and radio reports are good sources about local economic conditions. They help the buyer determine the type and quantity of merchandise to buy and its price ranges.

DETERMINING COMPETITION

Buyers should consider the competitive conditions in their market areas when planning their purchases. They should know their competition—the other stores where their customers make clothing and accessory purchases. They should know which stores carry the same merchandise but at a lower price.

To keep informed of these competitive conditions, buyers need comparison shopping information. Either the buyers or their assistants must visit other stores that serve the same customers. After these visits, buyers sometimes complete a comparison shopping report, which lists facts about the merchandise, price, and promotional atmosphere of the competition.

Experience 11-4

Coming Fashion Attractions

Read two articles in current fashion magazines that predict a future trend in apparel and accessory merchandise. On a separate sheet of paper, prepare a summary of the major points.

Experience 11-5

Do They Have the Money to Buy?

Read one newspaper article that describes an economic situation in your area, such as the unemployment condition or income level. On a separate sheet of paper, summarize the article. Then explain how that economic situation would affect you as an apparel and accessory buyer.

Experience 11-6

What's the Competition?

Choose two stores where you buy your clothes. Also choose two clothing items, of the same brand and style, that both stores sell. Write the names of the stores, clothing items, brands and styles on a separate sheet of paper. Visit the stores and find out the prices of the items. Write the prices on your paper.

If the prices are the same or very close, write an explanation why you think the merchandise is priced that way. If one store sells the items for a lower price than the other, write an explanation of what you think will eventually happen in the pricing of merchandise in these stores.

PREPARING STOCK PLANS

After buyers have determined the money available to spend and have examined past customer purchases, customer requests, current fashion trends, local economic conditions, and local competition, they are ready to prepare stock plans. Stock plans describe the merchandise items the buyers should purchase. Ms. Martin discusses two types of stock plans.

"Apparel and accessory buyers must purchase two kinds of merchandise, basic stock and fashion goods," Ms. Martin explains. "Basic stock items have a consistent customer demand in a complete range of sizes. These items are stocked in the best-selling price lines, sometimes in an entire color assortment. Some basic stock items are seasonal and some are popular all year long. For example, in the summer, there is a consistent

CRAWFORD & MURPHY'S
BASIC STOCK LIST

Store 30 Dept. 7 Effective Date 4/15 Page 2

Vendor / Address	Item Description	Style	Size	Color	Pkg.	Retail	Min Qty	Max Qty	A
Vendor: Westco Apparel Address: 924 Belmont									
Chicago, Illinois	Men's lined	.63	small	black		14.98	4	8	1
	work jacket			gray		14.98	4	8	2
Representative: Sandra Baker				brown		14.98	4	8	3
Address: 416 Harris Boulevard				navy		14.98	4	8	4
Oakland, California			medium	black		14.98	6	10	5
Phone: 286-5188				gray		14.98	6	10	6
Coverage Period 7 Weeks				brown		14.98	6	10	7
Delivery Period 2 Weeks				navy		14.98	6	10	8
Method of Count [XX] Group Mgr. [ ] Vendor			large	black		14.98	5	9	9
Week of Count				gray		14.98	5	9	10
___ 1. First Week				brown		14.98	5	9	11
X 2. Second Week				navy		14.98	5	9	12
___ 3. Third Week									13
___ 4. Forth Week									14
___ See Additional Information Below									15
Additional Information									16
									17
									18
									19
									20
									21
Emergency Orders: [XX] Call Vendor									22
[ ] No Emergency Orders									23
Requisition must be mailed from store by Wednes. of count week									24
Minimum Model Allowed									25

Fig. 11-5 Here's a typical example of a basic stock list.

demand for tank tops. Every winter, pullover sweaters in a variety of colors and sizes are basic stock items. Standard-rise blue denim pants have high sales all year long.

"Fashion goods have a shorter selling cycle than basic stock. They are in high demand for short periods of time and then lose their customer appeal. Most of the pants, shirts, jackets, and sweaters in the Dress Down Shop are fashion goods."

Basic Stock Lists Buyers prepare basic stock lists that show the strong sellers in the store or department. They use these lists to determine the type and quantity of basic stock they need to purchase. Basic stock lists include a description of the merchandise, merchandise vendor, style, size, color, and price. They also include the minimum and maximum quantity of merchandise that should always be on hand in the store. (See Figure 11-5.)

MODEL STOCK PLAN

Item	Style	Price	Color	Sizes 6	8	10	12	14	16
Blouses	Long-sleeved ruffled collar	$15.00	solid	1	2	4	4	2	1
			patterned	1	1	2	2	1	1
		$16.00	solid	2	3	4	4	3	2
			patterned	2	2	3	3	2	2
		$17.00	solid	1	2	4	4	2	1
			patterned	1	1	2	2	1	1
	Roll-up sleeve, pointed collar	$18.00	solid	1	2	4	4	2	1
			patterned	1	2	2	2	2	1
		$19.00	solid	1	2	4	4	2	1
			patterned	1	2	3	3	2	1
		$20.00	solid	1	2	4	4	2	1
			patterned	1	1	1	1	1	1

Fig. 11-6 Model stock plans are not as detailed as basic stock lists as this example shows. Compare it with the basic stock list on the opposite page.

When determining what to purchase, buyers should examine the sales record of their basic stock. Items that are not selling well should be dropped. Items that have become consistent sellers and that are not included on the basic stock list should be added. Basic stock lists show buyers exactly what type merchandise customers are purchasing. They help simplify the buying decision. By examining the sales of basic stock items, buyers can buy the merchandise customers have purchased in the past and will purchase in the future.

Model Stock Plans Buyers prepare model stock plans to determine the kinds of fashion merchandise they should purchase. Ms. Martin explains more about model stock plans: "A model stock plan is not as specific as a basic stock list. Instead of identifying a particular merchandise item by brand or style, the model stock list may describe merchandise by type (such as blouses), size (such as two size 8, four size 10, four size 12, and so on), and price line (such as $15 to $17 and $18 to $20)." (See Figure 11-6.)

Buyers develop their model stock plans from information in the unit-control records, which show price, color, and size preferences of past customers. They also estimate where their customers fit in the fashion cycle, either as fashion leaders or followers.

Fashion goods change so quickly that each season apparel and accessory buyers are faced with different merchandise selections. By preparing model stock plans, buyers take some guesswork out of buying merchandise.

Experience 11-7

Finding Out about the Basics

1. On a separate sheet of paper, set up a basic stock list similar to that shown in Figure 11-5. Write vendor, merchandise description, style, size, color, and retail price on your paper. You will use this basic stock list again in question 2 that follows.
2. Visit a local apparel and accessory store that sells fashion goods and basic stock merchandise. Locate five basic stock items in the store or in a particular department and write the information about these items on your basic stock list. If necessary, ask a salesperson to help you identify five merchandise items that are always in demand.

BUYING MERCHANDISE

Most buyers make several trips to different market areas each year. They visit apparel and accessory fashion centers such as New York, Los Angeles, and Dallas. When arriving "at market," many buyers visit their **resident buying offices** before going to any merchandise supplier or vendor showrooms. These buying offices, which are located in major fashion centers, are paid a fee by apparel and accessory stores to keep buyers informed on current marketing information and fashion trends. The offices provide member stores with facts about merchandise suppliers, hot items, and vendor's deliveries.

There are so many merchandise vendors to buy from that buyers must carefully choose the ones they want to visit. At this busy time, the vendors you choose to visit should depend on the merchandise assortment you want to purchase. Vendors who you have done business with in the past, who produce goods that appeal to your customers, and who deliver on time should be at the top of your list.

Most successful buyers suggest that you see all your scheduled merchandise lines before you write out an order. This will enable you to evaluate all merchandise that interests you and determine the best buy at the best price.

CLASSIFYING GOODS

Let's suppose you're in the vendor's showroom to see a women's shirt line. The shirts may be attractively displayed on hangers or grouped on stock racks. Some vendors use live models and others display the goods on mannequins. Some vendors give buyers an order form that shows a picture and description of the merchandise available.

When examining merchandise in vendor showrooms, try to classify all the merchandise seen. If the vendor gives you a pictured order form, you may assign numbers to the merchandise that you would consider buying next to the pictures on the form. For example, you may assign a 1 to merchandise that you think would be an excellent buy. You assign a 2 to merchandise that you think would be a good buy. Goods that you would never consider buying would be given no rating at all.

If the vendor does not provide you with a pictured order form, you will need to write down the style number and some styling characteristic of the goods you like. To take notes about the merchandise, you will need an excellent knowledge of various styles and fabrics.

EVALUATING THE MERCHANDISE SALABILITY

When deciding what merchandise to buy, try to determine if customers will pay the price your store must charge. Suppose, for example, you are considering the purchase of famous designer blouses that cost $20 each. If your store marks up all its merchandise by 50 percent, the retail price of these blouses will be $40. If you know your customers will not pay more than $25 for a blouse, buying these designer blouses would be a mistake.

Another way to evaluate the salability of merchandise is by comparing the new merchandise with similar items that have retailed for the same price at your store. For example, if you are considering the purchase of blouses that are supposed to sell for $28 each, compare these blouses with other $28 blouses that you have sold. Ask yourself if your customers purchased the blouses in that price range or if the price was too high or low. Determine the quality of the blouses: examine how they are made and check the fabric.

If you think the blouses are overpriced, ask yourself one more question. Is there something unique about the blouse, some style characteristic, that makes you feel customers would pay the price asked? If so, and if the blouse fits into your store's image and price lines, then you may want to include it in your selection.

Another factor buyers must keep in mind is the competition in the local market. If another store is going to sell the item at a lower price or can promote the goods better, it may have an advantage over yours. Buyers often ask vendor salespeople about the purchases of other stores in their areas to find out about competition.

Experience 11-8

"Checking Out" the Merchandise

1. Choose five stores that sell lightweight jackets for men or women.
2. Visit each store. On a separate sheet of paper, list the styles and colors of the jackets in stock.
3. While at each store, write a detailed description of the jackets you particularly like. Comment on the fabric, construction, appeal, and so on.
4. Without looking at the price tags, decide what retail price you think is fair to charge for the jacket. Then look at the price tags and record the real prices of the jackets.
5. When you have finished your shopping trip, assign numbers to the jackets you described in detail. Assign a 1 to all the jackets you liked best. Assign a 2 to all the jackets you liked less than 1 jackets. Assign a 3 to all the jackets you liked least.

DETERMINING THE ORDERING TERMS

When you find merchandise that fits into your buying plan, you should ask the vendor about the ordering terms. Ask questions such as:

When will the goods be delivered? If goods cannot be on your selling floor when you need them, they are useless.

What shipping terms can I get? Because freight costs are increasing, they represent a sizable portion of the total cost of the merchandise. If a vendor quotes you free on board **(FOB) shipping point** or **FOB selling point**, your store is responsible for paying all transportation charges from the shipping or selling point to your store. Title to the goods passes to your store at the time of shipping, so your store assumes all risks of loss or damage to the merchandise. **FOB destination** means the vendor pays the entire transportation charges to the buyer's location. Title to the goods passes to the store when the merchandise reaches its destination.

What discounts can I get? Discounts are deductions off the regular price of the merchandise. Buyers may negotiate quantity discounts when they buy in large quantities or promotional discounts or allowances to help pay for advertising the merchandise. Stores receive cash discounts for paying the bill within a specified time before the bill is actually due. As a general rule, women's apparel vendors offer 8/10,EOM payment terms. That means if the bill is paid within 10 days of the invoice date, an 8 percent deduction off the total price will be allowed. The total amount is due at the end of the month. If, for example, an invoice for $700 is dated March 15, if it has payment terms of 8/10,EOM, and if it is paid by March 25; the total amount due is $644 (.08 × $700 = $56; $700 − $56 = $644). Men's and children's wear vendors usually offer 2/10,EOM payment terms.

Can I reorder? If the goods turn out to be fast-selling items, you will want to be able to reorder. Clothing vendors have a limited amount of fabric. When all the fabric is used, they cannot fill reorders.

Are there any special promotions? Some vendors offer promotional help. Promotions, such as fashion shows or special displays, increase sales.

Experience 11-9

Getting the Best Deal

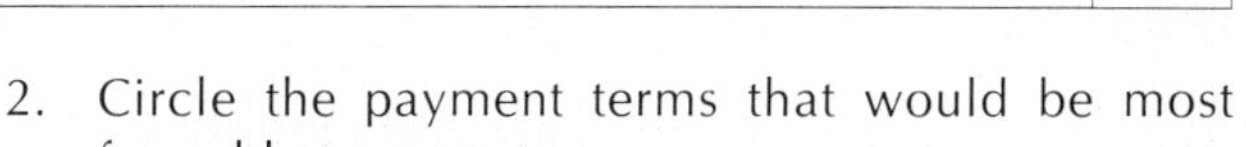

Assume you are a buyer at Crawford & Murphy's in Albuquerque, New Mexico. You are buying macrame belts from a vendor in Los Angeles.

1. Circle the shipping terms that would be most favorable to your store.

   FOB, Albuquerque   FOB, Los Angeles

   FOB, Crawford & Murphy's

2. Circle the payment terms that would be most favorable to your store.

   2/10,EOM   8/10,EOM   8/30,EOM

3. Suppose you purchased 100 belts costing $3 each. The payment terms on the invoice are 2/10,EOM. The date of the invoice is February 3. If your store pays the invoice on February 12, how much did your store pay?

   ____

BALANCING THE STOCK

When buyers have seen the vendors' merchandise selections and are deciding which merchandise they will buy, they may find that the items they like are all very similar. Before writing any orders, buyers should examine their model stock plan so as to buy the clothing their customers like. By balancing the stock, buyers provide a complete assortment of merchandise, in a variety of styles, colors, and sizes, to satisfy all their customers.

When buying new merchandise, buyers must pay special attention to size assortment because rarely can a customer substitute one size for another. On the average, most customers wear the medium-sized ranges. As a buyer of men's sport shirts, sized S, M, L, XL, you would probably buy more medium and large than small or extra large. Following this same principle, some manufacturers package goods in sized assortments, such as one small, five mediums, four large, and two extra large.

Unit-control records provide buyers with an accurate idea of the size ranges of customers. After examining the records, buyers may find that their customers are larger than average and must, therefore, purchase larger sizes.

DETERMINING THE ORDER QUANTITY

There are so many fashion goods to choose from that it is impossible for buyers to predict accurately which items will be the best sellers. Therefore, they purchase new merchandise items, styles, and colors in small quantities. By carefully watching which items are selling, they determine which items to reorder.

In the beginning of a season, the merchandise assortment is usually broad and shallow. That means there are a variety of styles, colors, and price lines (broad) with a small number of items for each size (shallow). As some styles and colors stand out as the strong sellers, buyers reorder the same item or another item in a similar style and color. At the peak of the selling season, the merchandise selection should include only the most popular items and the depth of the stock (in sizes and colors) should be increased. Once the peak of the selling season has passed, buyers try to sell out the remaining stock to make room for the next season.

Sometimes buyers find an item that they are sure will be a big seller. If there are no reorders on the item—this is a usual occurrence in women's apparel, buyers may be daring and order a large enough supply for the expected customer demand. This is a risky situation for buyers. They receive praise if the item becomes a best seller and receive criticism when they have overestimated customer demand.

The total quantity of merchandise that buyers can purchase depends on the open-to-buy amount and demand

CANCEL ANY PART OF ORDER NOT SHIPPED BY: 10/30 19 8- (B)

PURCHASE ORDER
CRAWFORD & MURPHY'S
202 State Street
Albuquerque, NM 87103
(SHIP AND MAIL INVOICE TO ABOVE)

(A) TO Levitt's Pant Company
ADDRESS 482 Harrison Boulevard
CITY New York STATE New York 10001

CRAWFORD & MURPHY'S

(B) DATE OF ORDER August 15, 198-
SHIPPING DATE September 30, 198-
SHIP VIA Air
(C) TERMS AND DATING 8/10, EOM/FOB factory

ORDER NO. 27016
DEPT

IMPORTANT
MARK ALL INVOICES AND PACKAGES WITH OUR ORDER NO. AND DEPARTMENT NO. MAKE SEPARATE INVOICES FOR EACH DEPARTMENT.

PLEASE
SHOW OUR ORDER AND DEP'T NO. ON ANY CORRESPONDENCE ON THIS ORDER. AIRMAIL INVOICES FOR EXPRESS OR PARCEL POST SHIPMENTS.

√REC'D.	QUANTITY	LOT NO.	CLASS	MODEL	COLOR	ARTICLES	DIM	5	7	9	11	13	COST UNIT	COST TOTAL	RETAIL UNIT	RETAIL TOTAL
	18	3842	51		blue	polyester twill weave		2	4	6	4	2	11 50	207 00	23 00	414 00
	18	3846	51		black	polyester twill weave		2	4	6	4	2	11 50	207 00	23 00	414 00
	9	3852	58		blue	match jacket		1	2	3	2	1	22 00	198 00	44 00	396 00
	9	3856	58		black	match jacket		1	2	3	2	1	22 00	198 00	44 00	396 00
																1620.00

(D) (E) (F)

(G) BY Karl Sanford (F) TOTAL ORDER AMT. $ 810.00 M.U. %

Fig. 11-7 Here's an example of a purchase order buyers use. Each of the lettered items is explained in the text below.

within a season. Many buyers do not like to spend all their open-to-buy at one time. They want some in reserve so that they can reorder hot items or buy special promotion goods.

WRITING THE ORDER

Stores usually require buyers to use the store purchase order form when buying goods. (See Figure 11-7.) Buyers complete the order form by:

1. Writing in the name and address of the vendor. (See Figure 11-7, letter A.)
2. Writing the date the order is written, the date the goods are to be shipped, how the goods are to be shipped, and the date the order is canceled because of late shipment. (See Figure 11-7, letter B.)
3. Writing in the terms and dating agreed upon by the vendor and buyer. (See Figure 11-7, letter C.)
4. Writing in the quantity and description of the goods ordered. (See Figure 11-7, letter D.)
5. Writing in the size breakdown of the goods. (See Figure 11-7, letter E.)
6. Writing in the unit cost and total and the unit retail and total. (See Figure 11-7, letter F.)
7. Signing the order. (See Figure 11-7, letter G.)

Experience 11-10

Write that Order!

You're in New York to make your first big buy. You have visited many vendors and have evaluated the merchandise selection. After hours of serious thinking, you decide to place some orders. Complete the purchase order shown on the opposite page for the following women's sweaters:

CANCEL
ANY PART OF ORDER NOT SHIPPED BY:
______ 19____

PURCHASE ORDER
CRAWFORD & MURPHY'S
202 State Street
Albuquerque, NM 87103
(SHIP AND MAIL INVOICE TO ABOVE)

TO ______

ADDRESS ______

CITY ______ STATE ______

CRAWFORD & MURPHY'S

DATE OF ORDER

SHIPPING DATE

SHIP VIA

TERMS AND DATING

ORDER NO. 27016

DEPT ______

IMPORTANT
MARK ALL INVOICES AND PACKAGES WITH OUR ORDER NO. AND DEPARTMENT NO. MAKE SEPARATE INVOICES FOR EACH DEPARTMENT.

PLEASE
SHOW OUR ORDER AND DEP'T NO. ON ANY CORRESPONDENCE ON THIS ORDER. AIRMAIL INVOICES FOR EXPRESS OR PARCEL POST SHIPMENTS.

✓REC'D.	DESCRIPTION							SIZES	COST		RETAIL	
	QUANTITY	LOT NO.	CLASS	MODEL	COLOR	ARTICLES	DIM		UNIT	TOTAL	UNIT	TOTAL

BY ______ TOTAL ORDER AMT. $ ______ M. U. %

1. Vendor: Wooly Knits, 388 Kelly Avenue, Dallas, Texas 75209
2. Stretch nylon knit turtlenecks
   a. Sizes: two small, four medium, two large
   b. Colors: copper, gold, and red
      Lot 615, Class 70, cost: $3.50; retail: $7.50
3. Acrylic knit hooded sweater
   a. Sizes: four small, eight medium, four large
   b. Colors: sage green, dark brown, midnight blue
      Lot 203, Class 40, cost: $5.50; retail: $11.00

Assume the date is July 18, 19——. The shipping date is September 30. The shipping terms are FOB factory. The dating terms are 8/10,EOM.

FOLLOWING UP THE ORDER

When buyers return from market, it is their responsibility to make sure the orders are delivered at the right time, in the correct quantity, and in good condition. Buyers may have to telephone or write merchandise suppliers to find out why delays in deliveries occurred. Often, buyers indicate a delivery date on their purchase orders. If the merchandise does not arrive at the store by that date, the store does not have to accept the merchandise.

Buyers also contact vendors when shipments arrive with more or less merchandise than was ordered. They work with vendors who back order certain items. When vendors **back order** merchandise, it means that they cannot fill the entire order at the time and are sending only a partial shipment. The vendor will send the rest of the order as soon as the ordered merchandise becomes available.

Sometimes the merchandise samples in vendor showrooms are not of the same quality as the goods shipped to the store. When shipments of faulty fabric or poorly sewn garments are received, the buyers must contact the vendors and arrange for merchandise returns and refunds to the store. These refunds are chargebacks.

Of course, merchandise that is returned to vendors is subtracted from the store's inventory records and unit control records. If this subtraction is not made, then the records won't agree with later inventory counts. Improper recording of merchandise will make the managers believe that there was a merchandise shortage caused by shoplifting or employee theft.

Purchase orders usually cannot be canceled without the consent of both the vendor and the store. Therefore, if the store buyer wants to cancel an order, the buyer must ask the vendor for approval. If the vendor cannot meet all the requirements of the order, such as a certain delivery time, then either the buyer or vendor may cancel the order.

PRICING MERCHANDISE

There are no standard rules for setting the retail price of apparel and accessory merchandise. Buyers, who compute the selling prices, must be certain each item can be sold at a price that covers the cost of the merchandise and store expenses and provides a profit. To cover their costs and earn a profit, stores add a **markup**, also called markon, to the wholesale cost of merchandise. The dollar markup equals the difference between the retail price and the cost of the merchandise sold:

$$\text{Dollar markup} = \text{Retail price} - \text{Cost}$$

Two variations of this formula are:

$$\text{Retail price} = \text{Cost} + \text{Dollar markup}$$
$$\text{Cost} = \text{Retail price} - \text{Dollar markup}$$

All buyers should be able to compute the dollar markup, cost, and retail price of any merchandise item. Buyers can compute these amounts by using the formulas shown above. For example, if a merchandise item costs the store $10 and the store sells it for $17, the dollar markup equals $7.

Buyers should also be able to compute the retail markup percentage and retail price when only the cost and the retail mark-up percentage are known. Buyers use the following formulas for these computations:

$$\text{Retail markup percentage} = \frac{\text{Dollar markup}}{\text{Retail price}}$$

$$\text{Retail price} = \frac{\text{Cost}}{100 \text{ percent} - \text{Retail markup percentage}}$$

For example, the merchandise that cost the store $10 and sold for $17, has a retail markup percentage of 41 percent.

$$\text{Retail markup percentage} = \frac{\$7}{\$17} = 41 \text{ percent}$$

If the store purchases an item for $5 and wants to maintain a 50 percent markup, the retail price is $10.

$$\text{Retail price} = \frac{\$5}{100 \text{ percent minus } 50 \text{ percent}} = \frac{\$5}{50 \text{ percent}} = \$10$$

The actual merchandise prices set by buyers are determined by such factors as customer demand, store expenses, needed profit, competitors' prices, and the type of product. Some of the many pricing policies followed by apparel and accessory buyers are:

Predetermined Markup. Some stores determine the amount of markup needed to pay for operating costs and provide a profit, such as 40 percent or 45 percent. These stores initially mark up all their merchandise by this predetermined mark-up percentage. Many apparel stores add a **keystone markup**, which is a 50 percent markup, to all their merchandise items. The keystone markup means that the retail price is double the cost price. If a scarf that costs the store $3 has a keystone markup, it will retail for $6.

Leader Pricing. Some stores follow a leader pricing policy. Prices of some merchandise items are set lower than usual to attract customers to the store. The reasoning behind this pricing policy is that once customers are in the store, they will also purchase other, more profitable merchandise.

Odd-ending Pricing. Stores that set prices that end in odd numbers, such as $5.99 or $4.37, are following an odd-ending pricing policy. This policy usually suggests lower prices and bargains.

Even-ending Pricing. Stores that set prices that end in even numbers, such as $5 or $4.50, are following an even-ending pricing policy. Even-ending pricing suggests high-quality merchandise.

Price Lining. Many apparel stores follow a pricing lining approach to pricing merchandise. They set up distinct price points or ranges of prices and then price all merchandise to fit into the predetermined price points or price ranges. For example, a store may sell gloves at three specific price points: $5, $7.50, and $10. Or it may sell purses in three price lines: $5 to $7, $10 to $12, and $15 to $17. All gloves or purses would fit into one of the store's price points or lines.

Experience 11-11

What's the Price?

On a separate sheet of paper, complete the following:

1. Dollar markup on the following merchandise:
   a. Ties: wholesale cost = $3.25; retail price = $7.50
   b. Cufflinks: wholesale cost = $2.70; retail price = $4.99
2. Percentage of retail markup on the following merchandise items:

a. Earrings: wholesale cost = \$1.85; retail price = \$3.00
b. Socks: wholesale cost = \$1.45; retail price = \$2.50

3. Retail prices of the following merchandise items:

a. Slippers: wholesale cost = \$2.75 pair; desired mark-up percentage = 45 percent

b. Nightgowns: wholesale cost = \$4.40 each; desired mark-up percentage = 42 percent

PRICE MARKING MERCHANDISE

Buyers are responsible for setting retail prices. Seldom, however, do they mark the prices on the price tickets themselves. Usually, employees who work as price markers prepare the price tickets. At smaller stores, merchandise may be price marked by the salespeople. Jack Johnson, store manager at Crawford & Murphy's, explains its price marking procedure to you.

"After merchandise is received and the order is checked," Jack begins, "all the merchandise is taken out of the boxes and stacked in like groups. For example, all the blouses from a particular vendor are grouped together. All the dresses are together. These items are then ready for their price tickets. Crawford & Murphy's has a staff of price markers who marks the price on all our merchandise. They use a price marking machine that prints the information on the ticket."

Jack shows you a price ticket for a dress. (See Figure 11-8.) "We print the style, vendor, size, class, color, season, and selling price on the ticket," Jack says. "This information is taken from the purchase order the buyer has written. Notice that our purchase orders have a column for the retail price of the merchandise being bought. (See Figure 11-7.) At the time the order is placed or at least before the actual merchandise is received, the buyer writes the retail amounts on the purchase orders. This is called **preretailing**. It allows price tickets to be made and attached without delay.

"The numbers that appear on our price tickets, such as vendor, class, season, and color numbers," Jack says, "are assigned by the store. Every store has its own set of numbers, similar to these, that help employees identify the merchandise."

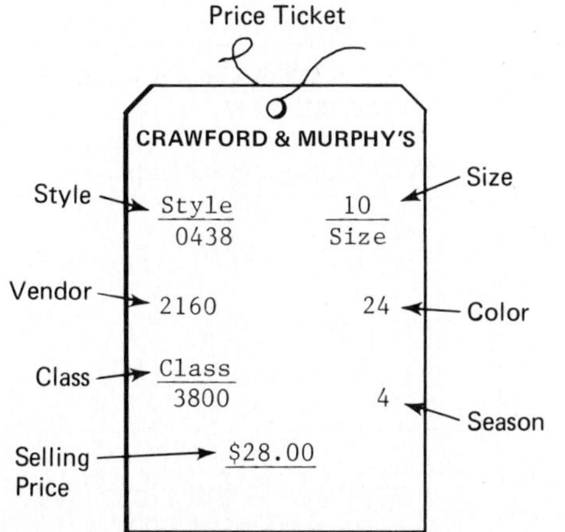

Fig. 11-8 All the numbers used on price tickets help salespeople identify merchandise.

Selecting Price Tickets At Crawford & Murphy's, the price markers use plastic connector tickets, pin tickets, string tickets, gummed tickets, and wedge tickets. The kind of merchandise determines the type of ticket used. For example, a gummed ticket would be a poor choice on a hanging blouse, but it is the best choice for boxed wallets. (See Figure 11-9.)

At this time, the store does not use the special price tickets or shoplifting detection wafers that set off a security alarm when customers pass through a certain area. These wafers identify shoplifters. When customers purchase a merchandise item, the salesperson either detaches or deactivates this special price ticket. When customers pass through an electronic field set up at a doorway or escalator with a price ticket that has not been deactivated, an alarm goes off. Security people approach these customers to determine if shoplifting has occurred.

Attaching Price Tickets "New employees quickly learn which price ticket goes on which item," Jack explains further. "It takes a little longer to learn how to attach the price tickets without damaging merchandise.

"Let's start with the plastic connector. This ticket makes it almost impossible for dishonest people to switch price tickets. A special machine shoots the plastic connector, which is attached to the price ticket, into the garment. We use it on everything we can. On blouses, the ticket is attached to the left sleeve on the inside seam above the cuff. On slacks, it is attached to the left side of the waistband, on the inside seam. On short-sleeve or sleeveless dresses, it is attached where the seams meet under the left arm.

"Because this ticket makes a small hole in the garment, price markers don't use plastic connectors on delicate garments. The hole made by the pricing ticket may run or grow. On delicate garments the price ticket is attached to the garment's label. Also, the plastic connector ticket is not used on leather or vinyl because the hole will also be noticeable and may run.

"We attach all plastic connector tickets to the *left side* of the merchandise. This way, when merchandise is hung on racks and other merchandise fixtures, all the price tickets are hanging on the outside, in easy reach of the customers.

"Not all stores use plastic connector tickets as much as Crawford & Murphy's. Some stores use string tickets or wedge tickets and attach them to a shirt or blouse button. Some stores attach the string ticket by sewing it to the waistband of skirts or slacks at the seams. For

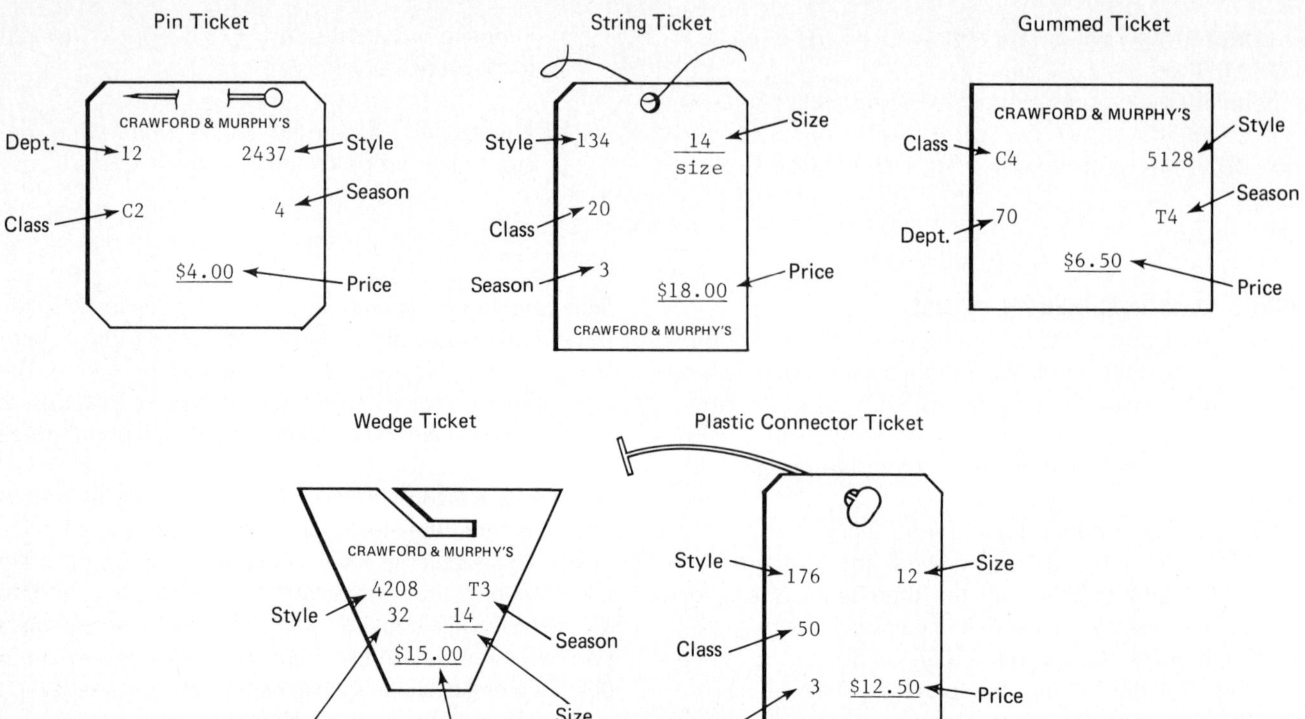

Fig. 11-9 Some common price tickets are illustrated above.

lingerie, many stores use pin tickets so as not to snag the garment.

"Crawford & Murphy's also uses pin, string, gummed, and wedge price tickets. The pin tickets are used on knit caps and scarves. String tickets are attached to handbags at the handle and to jewelry at the clasp. Gummed tickets are attached to earrings, boxed merchandise, and perfume. The wedge tickets are used for leather and vinyl coats. Usually they are attached to the second button."

Experience 11-12

Price Tickets: What Kind Do Stores Use?

Visit an apparel and accessory store or department and examine the price tickets. Examine at least seven different merchandise items. Find as many types of price tickets as possible. (You may need to ask a salesperson to help you. Explain to the salesperson that you are studying for an apparel and accessory career.) Complete the table below. If you need more space, use a separate sheet. Write the merchandise item and the type of ticket. On a separate sheet, sketch the price ticket and determine what the information on the ticket represents. Label the information. Also write where the price ticket is attached to the merchandise item as shown in the example below.

Item	Type of Ticket	Information on Ticket	Where Ticket Is Attached
EXAMPLE: Knitted ski hat	Pin	Dept. 18 Class 5 Price $4.95 Season K3	Attached to knitted fabric, near headband

MARKING AND RECORDING RETAIL PRICE CHANGES

The original retail price is not always the price at which merchandise is actually sold. Because customer demand for merchandise items fluctuates, the retail price of apparel and accessory goods goes up and down. Salespeople are responsible for marking the retail price changes on price tickets. They record the price changes on the appropriate store retail price change forms.

Recording Markdowns Suppose it is early July. The buyer wants to move out the swimsuits and beachwear to make room for the back-to-school merchandise. Your store carries swimsuits in three price lines: $15, $18, and $21. The buyer tells you to take one third off the selling price. (A markdown of one-third is a typical initial markdown for apparel and accessory merchandise.) To make the price changes, you slash the $15 price and write $10. The $18 suits are reduced to $12 and the $21 suits are priced at $14. (See Figure 11-10.)

It is important that all price changes are recorded on a retail price change form, similar to the one in Figure 11-11. Follow the letters on this form to see how to keep track of total inventory dollars in a department. When price changes are not properly recorded, the store does not have the necessary information to determine the accurate amount of profit earned.

To complete the retail price change form, you do as follows:

1. Write the symbol of the type of price change (markdown; MD). (See Figure 11-11, letter A, page 166.)
2. Enter the date the price change is made. (See letter B.)
3. Enter the department number as shown on the price ticket. (See letter C.)
4. Enter the style of the item from the price ticket. (See letter D.)
5. Write the description of the merchandise. (See letter E.)
6. Enter the class of the item from the price ticket. (See letter F.)
7. Write the retail price shown on the ticket before the price change. (See letter G.)
8. Write the new retail price after the markdown. (See letter H.)
9. Write the difference in the present and revised price. (See letter I.)
10. Count the number of items with price changes. (See letter J.)
11. Multiply the quantity by the difference and record the total in the extension column. (See letter K.)
12. Total the extension column. (See letter L.)
13. Write the reason for the price change. (See letter M.)
14. Sign the retail price change form. (See letter N.)
15. The buyer must approve the changes. (See letter O.)

Recording Markups One of the basic stock items has been camel-colored vinyl shoulder bags that retail at $14. When the buyer went to market in April, the purse vendor issued price increases on all the vinyl models. The new cost to the store is $8.75. Your store doubles the cost of every item and follows even price lines, such as $15 and not $14.95. You compute the new selling price of the purse to be $18 ($8.75 × 2 = $17.50, rounded up to $18). The price tickets of the purses in stock must be marked up $4.

Apparel and accessory stores do not record price increases on price tickets by slashing out the old price and showing the new price. This causes too much customer resistance, so stores issue new price tickets. This price change is also recorded on the retail price change form.

Recording Mark-Down Cancellations A mark-down cancellation restores the original price after a special sale markdown. For example, on Saturday your store participated in the town's annual Sidewalk Sale. The buyer marked down tennis shirts from $13 to $8. Your store, like many other apparel shops that run limited time sales, attached a sale ticket to the shirts and did not remove the original price ticket. Now that the sale is over, you must remove the sale price tag and record the mark-down cancellation on the retail price change form. The present price of $8 is revised to $13.

Recording Mark-Up Cancellations The buyer purchased 35 orlon pullover sweaters. Instead of paying the usual cost of $7 each, the buyer paid $175, only $5

CRAWFORD
&
MURPHY'S
Dept. 8 Style 827
Class 41 Size 10
Price
~~$15.00~~
$10.00

CRAWFORD
&
MURPHY'S
Dept. 8 Style 827
Class 41 Size 14
Price
~~$18.00~~
$12.00

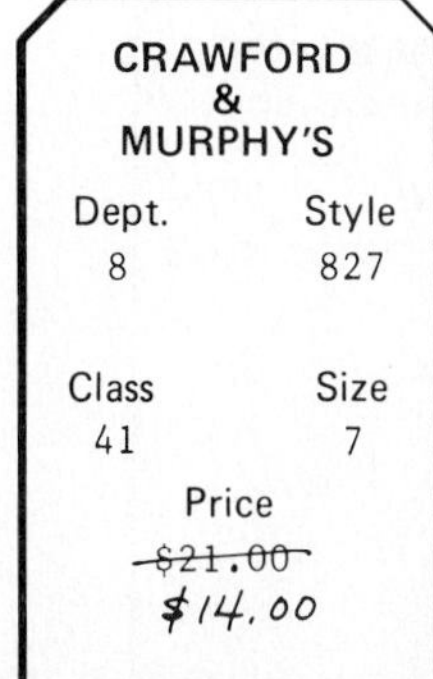
CRAWFORD
&
MURPHY'S
Dept. 8 Style 827
Class 41 Size 7
Price
~~$21.00~~
$14.00

Fig. 11-10 These three price tickets reflect some typical midsummer markdowns.

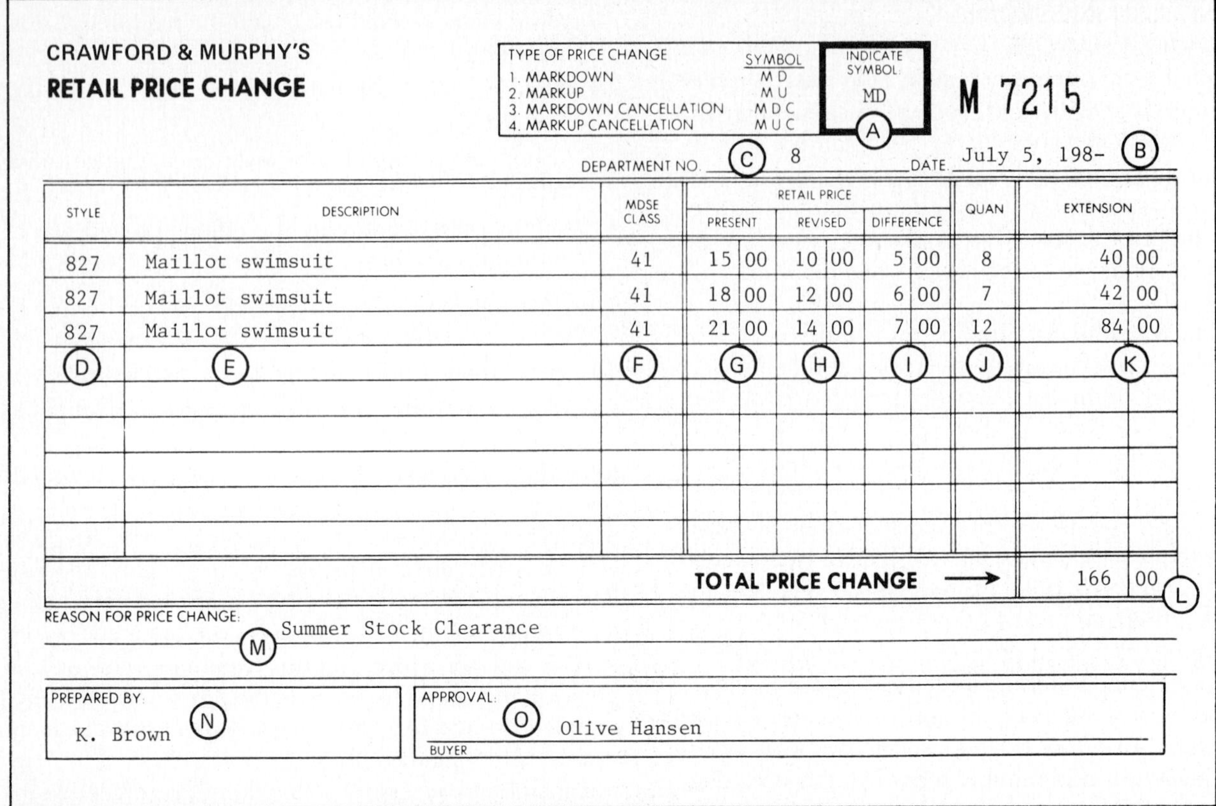

CRAWFORD & MURPHY'S
RETAIL PRICE CHANGE

TYPE OF PRICE CHANGE	SYMBOL
1. MARKDOWN	M D
2. MARKUP	M U
3. MARKDOWN CANCELLATION	M D C
4. MARKUP CANCELLATION	M U C

INDICATE SYMBOL: MD (A)

M 7215

DEPARTMENT NO. (C) 8 DATE July 5, 198- (B)

STYLE	DESCRIPTION	MDSE CLASS	RETAIL PRICE PRESENT	RETAIL PRICE REVISED	RETAIL PRICE DIFFERENCE	QUAN	EXTENSION
827	Maillot swimsuit	41	15 00	10 00	5 00	8	40 00
827	Maillot swimsuit	41	18 00	12 00	6 00	7	42 00
827	Maillot swimsuit	41	21 00	14 00	7 00	12	84 00
(D)	(E)	(F)	(G)	(H)	(I)	(J)	(K)
						TOTAL PRICE CHANGE →	166 00 (L)

REASON FOR PRICE CHANGE: (M) Summer Stock Clearance

PREPARED BY: K. Brown (N)

APPROVAL: (O) Olive Hansen
BUYER

Fig. 11-11 This is an example of a retail price change form. Each of the lettered items is explained in the text on page 165.

each. Even though your store purchased the sweaters "off cost," it still takes the 50 percent markup on the usual cost of $7, making the retail price $14.

After a few weeks of poor sweater sales, the buyer instructs you to take a mark-up cancellation and mark the price to $10. You record the new price by slashing through the original price and writing $10 on the price ticket. The mark-up cancellation, which shows the revised price of $10, is also recorded on the retail price change form.

Experience 11-13

Marking the Changes

Demonstrate how you would mark and record the following retail price changes:

1. Your store has had a difficult time moving sequin evening dresses. The buyers have already taken two markdowns, but there are still five of these dresses on the sale rack. You are instructed to take another markdown of 25 percent. Use the price ticket in the left column below and the retail price change form at the top of page 167.

Dinwoody's
FINE FASHIONS
Dept. 20 Style A43
Class 12 Size 6
Price
~~$75.00~~
~~$50.00~~
$33.00

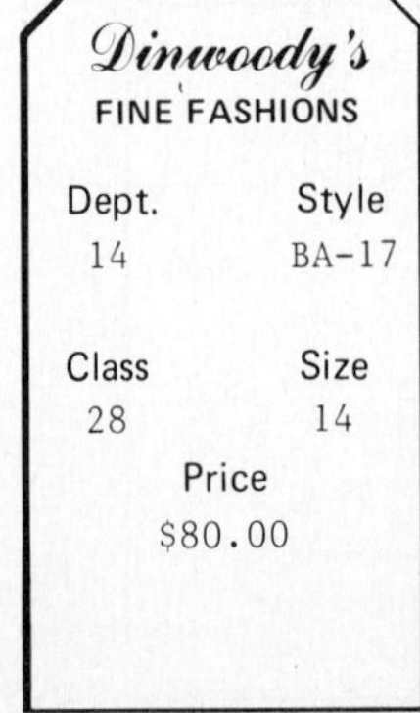

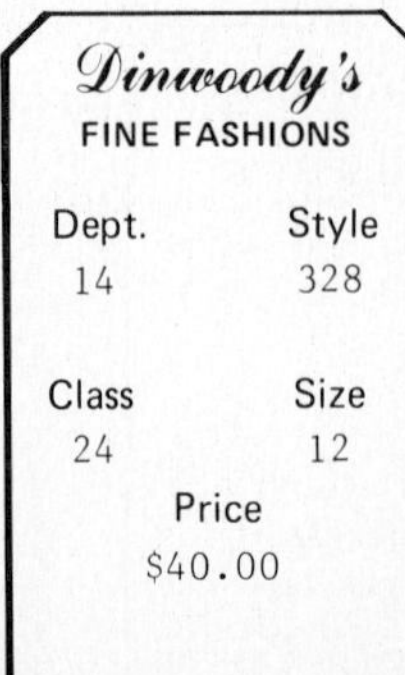

Dinwoody's
FINE FASHIONS
Dept. 14 Style 204
Class 16 Size 16
Price
$72.00

Dinwoody's FINE FASHIONS

RETAIL PRICE CHANGE

TYPE OF PRICE CHANGE	SYMBOL	INDICATE SYMBOL
1. MARKDOWN	M D	
2. MARKUP	M U	
3. MARKDOWN CANCELLATION	M D C	
4. MARKUP CANCELLATION	M U C	

M 7215

DEPARTMENT NO ______________ DATE ______________

STYLE	DESCRIPTION	MDSE CLASS	RETAIL PRICE			QUAN	EXTENSION
			PRESENT	REVISED	DIFFERENCE		
					TOTAL PRICE CHANGE →		

REASON FOR PRICE CHANGE: ______________________

PREPARED BY ______________ APPROVAL ______________ BUYER

Dinwoody's FINE FASHIONS

RETAIL PRICE CHANGE

TYPE OF PRICE CHANGE	SYMBOL	INDICATE SYMBOL
1. MARKDOWN	M D	
2. MARKUP	M U	
3. MARKDOWN CANCELLATION	M D C	
4. MARKUP CANCELLATION	M U C	

M 7215

DEPARTMENT NO ______________ DATE ______________

STYLE	DESCRIPTION	MDSE CLASS	RETAIL PRICE			QUAN	EXTENSION
			PRESENT	REVISED	DIFFERENCE		
					TOTAL PRICE CHANGE →		

REASON FOR PRICE CHANGE: ______________________

PREPARED BY ______________ APPROVAL ______________ BUYER

2. Your store's preseason coat sale has just ended. Customers can no longer purchase coats at 20 percent off the regular selling price. You have 15 fur-trimmed coats (sale priced $80), 45 vinyl coats (sale priced $40), and 32 nylon-wool blend coats (sale priced $72). On a separate sheet of paper, prepare new price tickets for the coats. Information applying to the department, style, class, and size is the same. Use the three tickets in the right column, page 166, and the retail price change form above.

WATCHING SALES

A buyer's work isn't finished once merchandise is on the sales floor. The buyer must also carefully watch sales. Merchandise that shows strong sales needs to be reordered as soon as the need for more stock is discovered, and slow-selling merchandise needs special attention. Buyers must carefully monitor inventory levels so that there is an adequate supply of merchandise to meet customer needs.

REORDERING BASIC STOCK

Many times basic stock lists include the minimum amount of merchandise and maximum amount of merchandise that should be on hand at all times, called **model stock.** These amounts are determined from past sales. As soon as the store's actual supply of merchandise reaches or falls below the minimum quantity, an order for more merchandise should be made.

The amount of merchandise to be reordered is computed by subtracting the quantity on hand and the quantity on order from the model stock. Suppose that there are three packages of men's T-shirts, size 40, on the sales floor. There is no merchandise in reserve stock in the stockroom. Five packages are on order but have not yet been received. The model stock for this item is 12. The buyer should reorder four more T-shirts in size 40. Notice the following:

Model stock (12) − Quantity on hand (3) − Quantity on order (5) = Quantity to be reordered (4)

REORDERING STRONG SELLERS

Sometimes an item hasn't been included on the basic stock list but has shown strong, consistent sales. When the stock supply of this item gets low, the buyer must determine how much to reorder. To do this, the buyer uses these formulas:

1. Minimum stock = Reserve + (Delivery period × Weekly sales)
2. Maximum stock = Minimum stock + (Reorder period × Weekly sales)
3. Quantity to order = Maximum stock − (Stock on hand + Stock on order)

For example, suppose you sell an average of eight medium-sized rugby shirts during a week. Your reorder period is every 4 weeks. Your delivery period for the shirts is 2 weeks. You think you need four extra shirts in stock just to take care of an unexpected increase in sales. At this time, you have a total of six shirts in stock and 10 on order. In this situation, you would reorder 36 shirts.

$$\begin{aligned} \text{Minimum stock} &= 4 + (2 \times 8) \\ &= 20 \\ \text{Maximum stock} &= 20 + (4 \times 8) \\ &= 52 \\ \text{Quantity to order} &= 52 - (6 + 10) \\ &= 36 \end{aligned}$$

Let's suppose these shirts are prepacked in a certain color assortment, such as six to a package in red, blue, and green. You have to order 6 packages to meet your merchandise requirements. This amount is computed by dividing the quantity needed, 36, by the number of shirts to a package, 6.

By following the reorder formula, which is based on weekly sales figures, you will be able to keep your stock in balance with your sales.

Experience 11-14

Ordering, Ordering, and Reordering

1. Using the following information, determine the quantity of basic stock you should reorder.

Merchandise	Quantity on Hand	Quantity on Order	Model Stock	Reorder Quantity
a. Knee socks—navy	3 pair	0	7 pair	
b. Gold button earrings	1 pair	1 pair	4 pair	
c. Men's white shirt, 15½/33	0	2	5	
d. Clear plastic umbrellas	3	2	5	
e. White cardigan sweater, size medium	2	0	5	
f. Tennis shorts, size small	4	2	10	

2. Using the following information, determine the quantity of merchandise you should reorder.

Merchandise	Weekly Sales	Reserve Quantity	Reorder Period (Weeks)	Delivery Period (Weeks)	Stock on Hand	Stock on Order	Reorder Quantity
a. Men's socks	10	20	2	2	3	0	
b. House slippers	5	8	4	3	4	2	
c. Men's black belts	7	9	3	6	6	4	
d. Women's knit shells	12	14	1½	2	8	10	

PROMOTING SLOW SELLERS

Just as a buyer cannot know which items will be the best sellers, a buyer cannot predict unpopular items. To overcome poor turnover and low profits, buyers must stimulate consumer demand for poor-selling items. To stimulate sales, a buyer does those things that cost the store the least amount of money first. For example, the buyer can feature interior displays of the slow-selling items or give salespeople more information about the slow sellers. If sales still do not pick up, the buyer may want to advertise the slow sellers or reduce the price of the merchandise.

Moving Slow Sellers Around An item may not be selling well because of its location on the sales floor. Customers cannot see merchandise that is hidden or blocked from view, and, therefore, will not buy it. The first way many buyers try to stimulate sales is by moving the goods to different sections of the department.

Sales Training Some items may not be selling because the sales force has not received training in the features and benefits of the goods. It is the buyer's responsibility to be certain that salespeople know the features of their merchandise and how to translate these features into benefits for the customer.

Merchandise Transfers Buyers for stores that have more than one branch use merchandise transfers to stimulate sales. The slow sellers are moved to different branch stores. Because the goods are given exposure to new customers, sales often increase.

Merchandise transferred out of the store reduces the stock on hand. Merchandise transfers must be reordered on the merchandise transfer form. (See Figure 11-12.) Follow the letters on this form to see how to keep the unit-control records up to date. The form is completed by recording:

1. Date (See Figure 11-12, letter A, page 170.)
2. Where the merchandise is transferred from (store and department) (See letter B.)
3. Where the merchandise is being transferred to (store and department) (See letter C.)
4. Merchandise class number (See letter D.)
5. Merchandise style number (See letter E.)
6. Description (See letter F.)
7. Merchandise class in the receiving store and department (See letter G.)
8. Retail price of the transferred item (See letter H.)
9. Number of items being transferred (See letter I.)
10. Total dollar amount of items being transferred (See letter J.)
11. Total dollar amount of the transfer (See letter K.)
12. Reason for transfer (See letter L.)
13. Signature of person preparing the transfer (See letter M.)
14. Signature of the person approving the transfer (See letter N.)

Advertising Some items are poor sellers because customers are not aware that the store or department carries the goods. A buyer may increase the advertising of slow sellers to remedy this problem. Of course, every buyer is required to stay within the advertising budget. Because advertising is expensive, a buyer should try to stimulate sales by doing the things that don't cost as much money as advertising before turning to its use as a remedy.

Lower Prices Some items are poor sellers because they are priced too high. Customers who consider the price too high will often purchase goods if the price is lowered. Most buyers use a keystone (or 50 percent) markup at retail. If the goods fail to sell at the original retail selling price, the buyers mark one-third off the price. If the goods still do not sell the buyers mark the goods down again, usually to one-half of the original retail price. After two markdowns, many buyers have special sales. The goods are placed on a clearance table and sold at a very low price.

CRAWFORD & MURPHY'S
MERCHANDISE TRANSFER

DATE September 13, 198- (A) T 86270

TRANSFER FROM		TRANSFER TO	
(B) LOCATION: ☑ 1 Albuquerque ☐ 2 Santa Fe ☐ 3 Phoenix	DEPT 4	(C) LOCATION: ☐ 1 Albuquerque ☐ 2 Santa Fe ☑ 3 Phoenix	DEPT 4

MDSE CLASS (Send Dept)	STYLE	DESCRIPTION	MDSE CLASS (Rec Dept)	UNIT RETAIL		QUAN	EXTENSION	
7	825	Fur-trimmed leather jacket	7	150	00	2	300	00
14	347	Imitation leather Eisenhower jacket	14	45	00	4	180	00
(D)	(E)	(F)	(G)	(H)		(I)	(J)	
		TOTAL TRANSFER →					480	00 (K)

REASON FOR TRANSFER:
Customer requests at Phoenix store (L)

PREPARED BY:	APPROVAL:	MDSE. RECEIVED BY:
Allen Smithstone (M)	Denise Martin (N) BUYER	

FORM A 402 (REV. 8/74) MOORE BUSINESS FORMS INC. M MERCHANDISE CONTROL COPY

Fig. 11-12 Merchandise transfers, which sometimes stimulate sales of goods in other branches of a store, are recorded on a form such as this.

Experience 11-15

Move out the Slow Sellers!

As a buyer for the Dress Down Shop, you recently purchased an assortment of corduroy and velvet jackets. The corduroy jackets retail for $48; the velvet jackets retail for $75. Even though you have three branch stores where you could send the jackets, most of the jackets are located in your downtown store. You have not featured any special promotions for the jackets, even though you have a large advertising budget.

Over the past 2 weeks, you have carefully watched the jacket sales and noticed that the sales are very slow. In the space provided, explain four ways you can stimulate jacket sales. Be sure you put the least costly way of stimulating sales first and the most expensive way of stimulating sales last.

12 Physical Distribution

Every day merchandise enters and leaves an apparel and accessory store at an astonishing rate. Merchandise that buyers purchase at market arrives at the store's receiving dock the same time that customers are leaving the store with their new purchases. To keep track of how much merchandise is in the store at a particular time, apparel and accessory managers use inventory control.

Most inventory control systems include dollar control records and unit-control records. **Dollar control records** show how much merchandise, in dollar amounts, is in the store or department. **Unit-control records** show the actual merchandise items in the store. Both types of information records are needed to keep management and buyers aware of stock levels.

PERPETUAL INVENTORY VERSUS PERIODIC INVENTORY

Dollar control and unit-control records can be based on perpetual or periodic inventory systems. If dollar control records are based on the **perpetual inventory system**, the records will perpetually, or continually, show the retail value of merchandise on hand. If the dollar control records are based on the **periodic inventory system**, the records will be updated only when an inventory is taken.

Unit-control records based on the perpetual inventory system will always show the merchandise items in stock. Under a periodic inventory system, the only way to determine the quantity of merchandise units on hand is by making an actual stock count. Under this system, there is no attempt to keep the inventory up to date.

RETAIL INVENTORY METHOD VERSUS COST INVENTORY METHOD

Most apparel and accessory stores use the retail inventory method. It is easier than the cost inventory method, and it provides more up-to-date information. With the **retail inventory method**, all figures are recorded at their retail price. Stores that use the cost method record all merchandise at its cost price, which is the price the store paid.

ESTABLISHING AN INVENTORY CONTROL SYSTEM

How do apparel stores set up and maintain an inventory control system? There are many variations, especially with computers to keep track of inventory levels. Let's examine how one store, called Rebecca's, handles its inventory control system. Suppose this medium-sized apparel store is just starting in business. To set up its inventory records, the store is taking an initial inventory count of all its merchandise. Suppose you are a salesperson at Rebecca's, and you are helping in the stock count.

TAKING A STOCK COUNT

Your manager, Grace Kinney, explains the stock count procedures to you and the other salespeople. "We are going to use the team method to take the stock count," Grace says. "A team is made up of two persons—a caller and a writer. Each team will be assigned to a particular area and section of the store and will be responsible for counting all the merchandise in that section. Accuracy is most important in taking this stock count. If you overlook any merchandise or call out or write down the wrong information, your errors will show up in the store inventory records."

You have been assigned the job of writer. Your area is the second floor; your section is the selling floor of Department 18. This department sells school clothing for boys, sizes 8 through 18. "As writer," Grace explains, "you are responsible for recording information

Rebecca's

CONTROL NO.
№ 33714

INVENTORY SHEET

Date Jan. 21 Dept. 18 Called By Will Harvey Written By Your name

CONTROL NO.	AREA NO.	SECTION NO.
№ 33714	2	5

	Class	No. of Items	Price		Class	No. of Items	Price
1 (A)	7	13	5 99	24			
2	4	72	2 99	25			
3	2	6	3 99	26			
4		4	4 99	27			
5		8	5 99	28			
6		12	7 99	29			
7		3	9 99	30			
8		5	11 99	31			
9				32			

Fig. 12-1 When salespeople take inventory, they complete a form similar to the one shown above.

on an inventory sheet. (See Figure 12-1.) You are to write the date, department numbers, and the names of the caller and writer on the form. Our store's inventory management team fills in the control number, area number, and section."

Suppose this inventory count is to determine the total dollar value of merchandise in the store. To take this count, you are interested in only three items of information: the class, price, and number of merchandise items in your section. The merchandise class is a number that represents a certain kind of merchandise, such as cotton shirts or pants. The class number is printed on the price ticket. (See Figure 12-2.) The price of each item is also printed on the price ticket. The number of items is the total quantity of merchandise with the same class number and the same price. (*NOTE*: If you were taking a unit-control stock count, you would be concerned with the following information: merchandise brand, size, style, color, price, and quantity.)

The first item you inventory is boys' denim pants. The pants are sized on a tiered counter. Will Harvey, your caller, starts in the top left-hand section of the counter and calls off the class and price. After checking each price ticket to be sure all class numbers and prices are

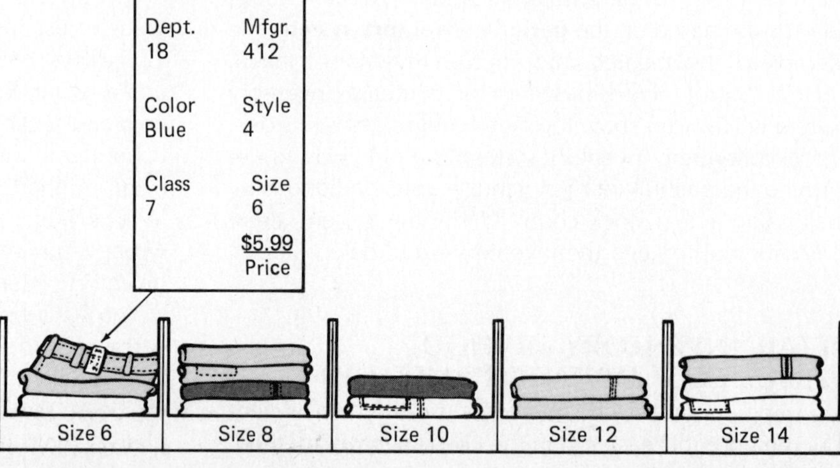

Fig. 12-2 The top portion of the tiered counter you and Will are to inventory is shown at the right. For the merchandise class pictured, what's the total inventory?

the same, Will counts the pants. You notice that he follows a certain pattern when counting the merchandise: from top to bottom and from left to right. After Will has finished counting, he calls out: "Class 7, a total of 13, retailing at $5.99." You record this information on your inventory sheet. (See Figure 12-1, letter A.)

The next item for your count are boys' socks, which are packaged three pairs for $2.99. Your store considers any packaged merchandise, no matter how many items are included in the package, as one set. Will says, "Class 4, a total of 72, retailing at $2.99." You record 72 in the "number of items" column on line 2 of the inventory sheet.

Your next six counts are for shirts, all class 2, but of different price lines. It is not necessary for you to write the class for each shirt, as they are all the same. You write the class once and indicate the class of the shirts of the different price lines by drawing a line through the appropriate class column. (See Figure 12-1.)

You are very careful that all merchandise items are counted and correctly recorded on your inventory sheet. You know accuracy is important in stock counts.

Experience 12-1

Counting the Goods

You're helping take a stock count to update dollar control records. You are to count the men's hanging and packaged T-shirts. Following the proper inventory procedures, count the merchandise shown and complete the inventory sheet below. The hanging T-shirts are $6.98 each and the packaged are $4.98 each.

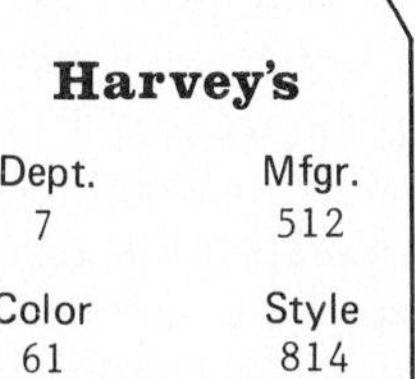

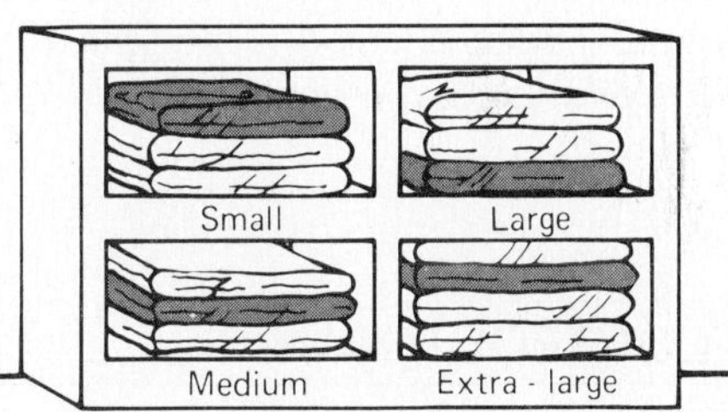

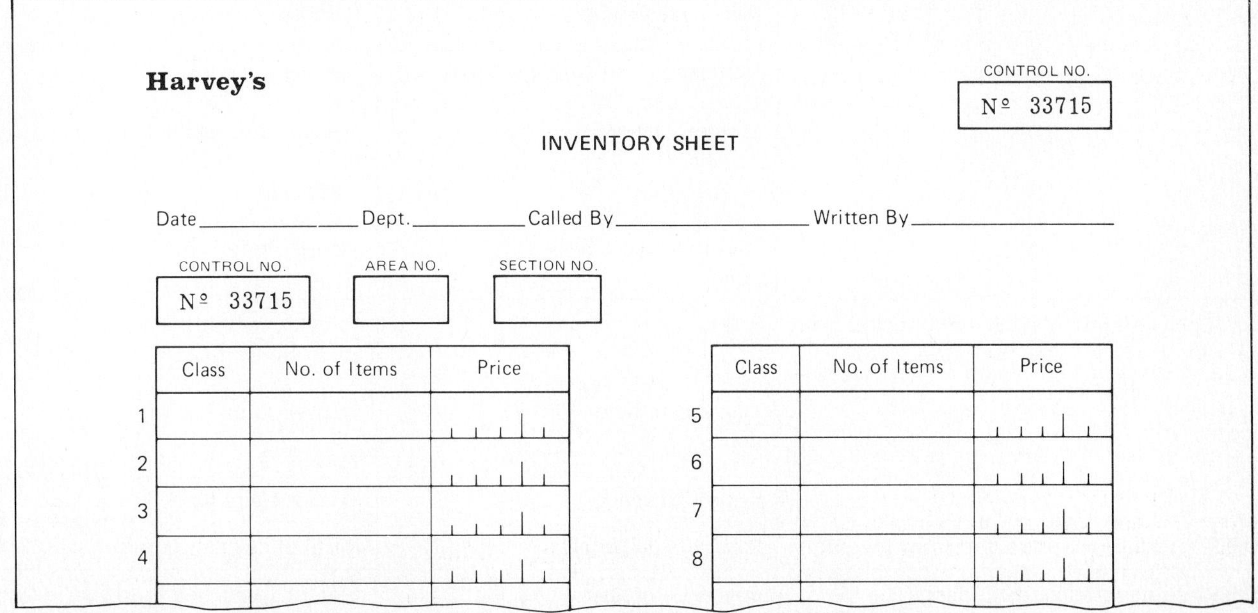

Harvey's

CONTROL NO. № 33715

INVENTORY SHEET

Date __________ Dept. __________ Called By __________ Written By __________

CONTROL NO. № 33715 | AREA NO. | SECTION NO.

	Class	No. of Items	Price
1			
2			
3			
4			

	Class	No. of Items	Price
5			
6			
7			
8			

Experience 12-2

Counting the Units

On a separate sheet of paper, prepare an inventory sheet. Rule six columns and label the columns brand, style, color, size, price, and quantity. At the top of the paper, write the merchandise item that you will be counting. Choose any apparel or accessory item.

Visit an apparel and accessory store that sells the merchandise you chose. Explain to the manager that you are studying inventory control systems in school and would like to make a unit stock count of a certain merchandise item. After receiving permission from the manager to make the count, record the various brands, styles, colors, sizes, prices, and quantities of merchandise. Be sure your information is recorded accurately and that you have not missed any items.

SETTING UP AND MAINTAINING INVENTORY CONTROL RECORDS

Both dollar control and unit-control records require similar types of information. For example, both need an initial stock count to determine the dollar value and type of merchandise on hand. To keep the records accurate and up to date, both types of inventory control records also need information about all merchandise that has entered the store and left the store. They also need information about any changes in the merchandise price or any other cancellations.

Most stores have prepared many kinds of forms that keep track of the value and amount of store inventory. See Table 1.

Dollar Control Records To prepare dollar control records, which are concerned only with dollar values, the total quantity of merchandise counted is multiplied by its price. Notice the example given opposite.

Class	Quantity	Price	Total
7	72	$3.89	$ 280.08
4	15	$5.99	$ 89.85
30	104	$7.59	$ 789.36
		Dollar Value of Stock	$1,159.29

To keep the dollar control records current and up to date, the value of all incoming merchandise is added to the dollar value of stock. All outgoing merchandise is subtracted from the dollar value of stock. The value of markdowns and mark-up cancellations is subtracted from stock; the value of markups and mark-down cancellations is added to stock.

Suppose, for example, that the total dollar value of inventory in the boys' department is $17,895.47. During

Table 1

INVENTORY CONTROL FORMS

	Information Recorded	Form Used
INCOMING MERCHANDISE—Added to Inventory	Merchandise orders	Purchase order
	Merchandise arrivals	Receiving record
	Customer returns	Merchandise return or Credit slip
	Transfers from other stores	Transfer form
OUTGOING MERCHANDISE—Subtracted from Inventory	Sales	Sales slip or Stub of price ticket
	Transfers to other stores	Transfer form
	Returns to vendors	Vendor claim form
OTHER—Added or Subtracted from Inventory	Retail price changes	Retail price change form
OTHER—Subtracted from Orders	Cancelled orders	Order cancellation form

1 month of business, $2,709.84 of merchandise was added to the store inventory. In the same month, $5,309.83 of merchandise was subtracted from the store inventory. The current dollar value of stock is $15,295.48.

Initial stock count		$17,895.47
Merchandise added to stock:		
Merchandise received	$2,380.70	
Customer returns	304.59	
Transfers from other stores	24.55	+ 2,709.84
Merchandise subtracted from stock:		
Sales	$4,835.24	
Returns to vendors	104.39	
Markdowns	295.70	
Transfers to other stores	74.50	− 5,309.83
Dollar value of inventory		$15,295.48

Inventory control records must reflect accurately the merchandise in stock. Employees are extra careful when making entries because counting, recording, and math errors can affect merchandise decisions.

Experience 12-3

How Much Is in Stock?

Using the following information, determine the dollar value of merchandise at the end of August in the shoe department at Rebecca's.

Sales: $5,489.35
Stock count on August 1: $8,342.75
Merchandise transferred to other stores: $105.79
Merchandise transferred to your store: $74.35
Merchandise received from vendors: $2,409.59
Merchandise returned to vendors: $341.20
Markdowns: $850.47
Merchandise returned by customers: $140.35

Dollar Value of Merchandise $______

Unit-Control Records As mentioned in Chapter 11, "Buying and Pricing," there are many different types of unit-control records. Some records are prepared by computer; others are prepared by hand. The information recorded on all unit control records, which tells about orders, sales, returns, purchases, and merchandise transfers, is basically the same.

Suppose you are responsible for the unit-control records. You must record the information as follows:

Use the buyer's purchase orders to record information about merchandise orders. Record the merchandise class, manufacturer, vendor, delivery date (completion date), and the date the order was written on the form. (See Figure 12-3, letter A.) Also record the style, color, and sizes of the merchandise ordered. (See Figure 12-3, letter B.) Record this information by marking a small dot in each square to show a certain size, color, and style is on order. For example, Figure 12-3, letter C, shows that five medium black turtlenecks are on order.

Use the receiving record to record information about what merchandise is actually received. Information listed on the receiving record may differ from the purchase order because vendors do not always send all the

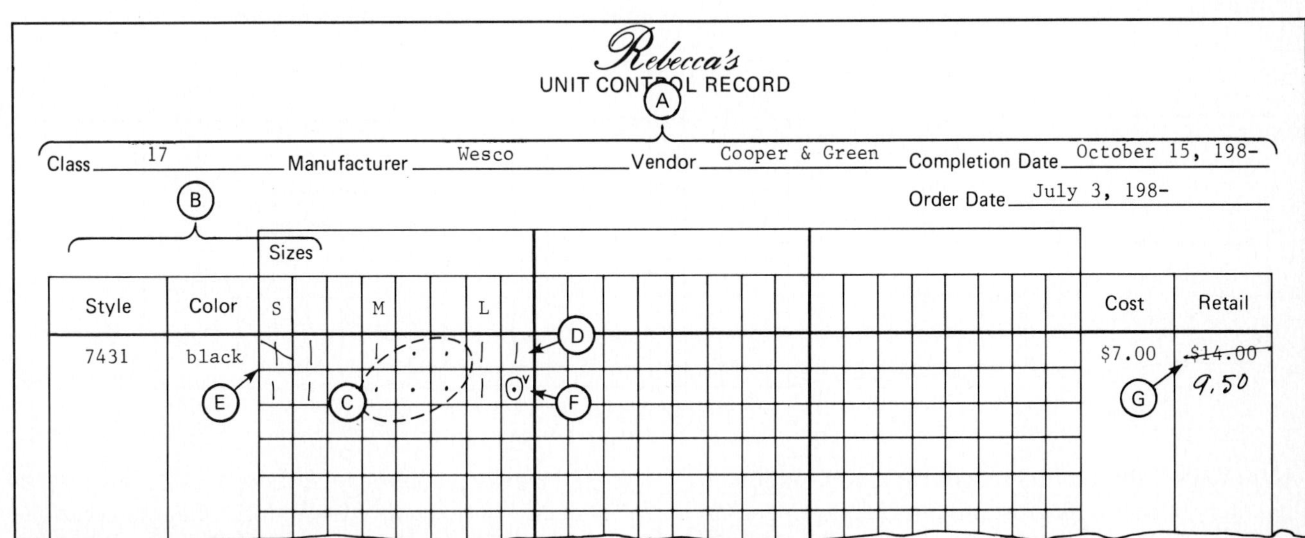
Rebecca's
UNIT CONTROL RECORD

Class 17 Manufacturer Wesco Vendor Cooper & Green Completion Date October 15, 198-
Order Date July 3, 198-

Style	Color	Sizes: S			M			L		Cost	Retail
7431	black									$7.00	~~$14.00~~ 9.50

Fig. 12-3 What other completed forms were used to fill out this unit-control record? (See pages 175 and 176 for the answer.)

merchandise that was ordered at one time. Sometimes, they have to back order merchandise, which means the other items will be sent as soon as they are available. Record information about items that are received by making a straight line in the appropriate squares. (See Figure 12-3, letter D.)

Use the price tickets from sold items to record information about what merchandise is actually sold. Suppose that whenever a sale is made in your department, one section of the price ticket is torn off the item and placed in a box next to the cash register. Use these tickets to record sold merchandise. Make a diagonal line to represent each sold item. (See Figure 12-3, letter E.)

Use merchandise transfers, merchandise returns to vendors, and purchase order cancellation forms to record transactions that reduce inventory. Circle the items that are leaving your inventory and indicate why these items are being removed from stock. Remember *t* means transfer and *v* stands for merchandise returned to vendors; a circled dot with a *v* stands for a canceled purchase order. (See Figure 12-3, letter F.)

Use customer return slips to record customer returns. Customer returns increase inventory. When a customer returns an item that can be sent to the selling floor, erase the sold mark. By doing this, the unit control records show the item is again available for sale.

Use retail price change forms to record price changes of merchandise. Cross out the old price and write in the new retail price on the unit control record. (See Figure 12-3, letter G.)

Experience 12-4

Completing the Records

Using the following information, complete the unit-control record shown below.

1. On February 4, you purchased an assortment of short-sleeve broadcloth shirts in brown, blue, and red. The shirts, which are sized S, M, L, and XL, are to be delivered on April 15. You purchased two small, four medium, four large, and two extra-large shirts in each color. The manufacturer and vendor are Aristocrat Shirt Company. The style number is 8241; the department number is 8; the class number is 72. The cost of the shirts is $6.50. The retail price of the shirts is $13.50.
2. The shirts arrive on April 8. Two medium blue-checked shirts are missing.
3. During the week of April 12–18, you sell all the medium and extra-large red-checked shirts, one small and two large red-checked shirts, three large blue-checked shirts, and two medium and one large brown-checked shirts.
4. One customer returns a medium red-checked shirt for a large red-checked shirt. You return the medium shirt to the selling floor.
5. Your branch store calls and asks for a transfer of one extra-large brown-checked shirt.

UNIT CONTROL RECORD

Class________ Manufacturer________ Vendor________ Completion Date________

Order Date________

Style	Color	Sizes			Cost	Retail

ANALYZING INVENTORY CONTROL RECORDS

Inventory control records provide management and buyers with important information about sales, shoplifting and employee theft, and merchandise reorders. As an apparel and accessory employee, the information from inventory control records can help you prepare financial reports and determine what merchandise should be reordered or closed out. They can also help you pinpoint some problems with your store's security procedures.

Determining Sales from Stock Counts Some stores do not keep track of daily merchandise sales. They do not subtract the sales from the dollar control or unit-control records. By using stock count information, however, these stores can determine past sales. To determine what has sold in the past by the stock count, or periodic inventory system, a store must do the following.

- Physically count and record all stock on hand at the beginning of a time period.
- Add to this amount all the merchandise that has arrived during a particular time period. (This includes all merchandise from vendors, transfers from other stores or departments, and customer returns.)
- Subtract all merchandise that has left the store, such as returns to vendors and transfers to other stores.
- Subtract all markdowns, which reduce the value of the inventory.
- Physically count and record all stock on hand at the end of a time period.

For example, suppose you want to know the sales of men's slacks during February. On the first of the month, the store would take an actual count of all the men's slacks in the store and determine the total dollar value of these slacks. It would add to that amount the merchandise received and subtract the merchandise that left the store, was reduced in value, and was still on hand at the end of the month. The following procedure would be used to calculate February sales.

Value of slacks on hand, February 1		$1,240
Amount of merchandise arriving during the period:		
From vendors	$749	
From transfers	108	
From customer returns	73	+ 930
Amount of merchandise leaving during the period:		
By returns to vendors	$ 82	
By transfers	111	− 193
Amount of markdowns		− 214
Value of slacks on hand, February 29		−1,138
Sales during February		$ 625

This same procedure can be used to determine past sales in units, rather than dollars.

Experience 12-5

How Much Did We Sell?

Using the following information, compute the sales during May for the men's wear department at Rebecca's.

Stock count, May 1: $12,345.72
Stock count, June 1: $13,409.54
Merchandise received from vendors: $3,087.59
Merchandise returned to vendors: $540.79
Merchandise received from transfers: $87.30
Merchandise transferred out of store: $249.39
Merchandise returned by customers: $109.48
Markdowns: $240.55

Sales during May $______

Using Inventory Records to Determine Shoplifting and Employee Theft Inventory records can help store employees spot shoplifting and employee theft. When a store takes a physical count of its stock, it compares the actual value or quantity of merchandise to the value or quantity listed in the inventory records. This is called the "book" value or quantity. If the actual quantity is less than the quantity indicated in the books, merchandise that should be in the store is missing. This merchandise may have been stolen by customers or by employees. For example, suppose today's stock count shows that 82 coats are in stock. Using inventory records, you determine that there should be 84 coats in stock. The difference between the actual number in stock and the "book" value is 2. These 2 coats may have been stolen by customers or store employees.

Sometimes accounting errors are the reason the actual quantity of merchandise from a stock count does not agree with the inventory records. For example, if a store employee records 25 coat sales instead of 27, which is the correct number, the inventory records would be inaccurate. No shoplifting or employee theft problem has occurred, even though the records make it look so.

Other accounting errors that can cause the inventory records to tell an inaccurate story are: customer returns, merchandise received, returns to vendors, transfers to or from the store, sales, or markdowns that were incorrectly recorded or not recorded at all.

Experience 12-6

Why the Difference?

Suppose you are the department manager of the Accessory Department at Rebecca's. You have just completed a total stock count of your handbags and have determined that there is a total of 72 handbags on the sales floor and in the stockroom. Last month, the stock count was 84 handbags. During the month, you have received 24 new bags from merchandise suppliers, 2 bags as transfers from another store, and 3 customer returns. Your sales records show 34 bags were sold and 2 were transferred out of the store. When you compare actual stock count with unit-control records, you find that the total stock figure does not agree.

1. How many handbags should be in stock?

2. On a separate sheet of paper, explain three reasons that could account for the difference between the actual stock on hand and the inventory records.

3. On a separate sheet of paper, explain why inventory control records must be accurate.

Using Inventory Records to Reorder Merchandise One of the most important functions of inventory control records is to help buyers determine what merchandise should be reordered. Unit-control records, which specifically show merchandise sales, markdowns, and customer returns for certain items, can help buyers identify what the customer demand is for merchandise. Fast-selling merchandise or merchandise that has a strong sales record should be in sufficient supply to meet customer requests. Reorders should be placed before all merchandise is gone or future sales will be lost. Slow-selling merchandise or merchandise that must be marked down before customers will buy it often indicates low customer demand. Buyers probably will not want to purchase more merchandise that, in the past, has been significantly marked down. Buyers may also hesitate to purchase a certain item if customer returns have been high.

Often, buyers are not the ones who record the information about sales, markdowns, and customer returns on the inventory control records. If you are responsible for keeping the inventory control records up to date, you are also responsible for keeping your buyer informed of merchandise needs. Be sure to tell your buyer about merchandise that is selling quickly or merchandise that is almost out of stock so that merchandise reorders can be made.

Taking Basic Stock Counts. To be sure that the store never is totally out of basic stock items, some stores have salespeople take basic stock counts once a week, every 2 weeks, or once a month. The salespeople count the items listed on the basic list and record the on-hand stock.

The basic stock inventory figure is usually given to the assistant buyer or buyer, who computes the amount of merchandise to reorder. Sometimes an experienced salesperson computes the reorder. Computing basic stock reorders is discussed in Chapter 11, "Buying and Pricing."

RECEIVING, CHECKING, AND STORING MERCHANDISE

How merchandise is received, checked, and stored at an apparel and accessory store is another part of inventory control. If merchandise is not properly received and checked in, the inventory control records will show inaccurate information. Poor stockroom and storing procedures can cause merchandise to be misplaced or lost.

RECEIVING MERCHANDISE

To make sure that all incoming merchandise is entered into the inventory control system, many stores require all new merchandise to follow certain receiving procedures. These stores realize that inventory control must begin as soon as merchandise arrives at their receiving docks.

Jeff Bateman supervises the receiving, checking, and shipping of merchandise at Rebecca's. He is just beginning to explain the receiving procedure to Sally, a new employee: "We receive many shipments of new merchandise each week. These shipments are delivered to our store as soon as they arrive in town. Some of the merchandise is delivered by motor carriers, such as P.I.E. or Consolidated Freightways. Sometimes, shipments are sent by air, with companies such as Emery Air Freight, and then delivered to our store by truck. We also receive deliveries of packages that weigh between 1 and 50 pounds from companies such as United Parcel Service. All these trucks bring the shipments to our receiving dock, which is located right at the back of the store."

Receiving and Delivery Schedules Apparel and accessory stores receive many merchandise deliveries from vendors. At stores that have more than one branch, there is usually much merchandise being transferred from store to store. At stores with a central storage area, merchandise is sent to the sales floor of different stores every day. Many apparel stores also provide delivery service of merchandise to their customers.

To coordinate the flow of merchandise in and out of stores and their storerooms, apparel and accessory stores follow a receiving and delivery schedule. This schedule, which shows when merchandise will be picked up and delivered, allows for the efficient movement of merchandise. By setting up and following a schedule, salespeople and buyers know when to expect new merchandise shipments and transfers. These schedules can help salespeople plan their stockroom work.

Every morning at Rebecca's, a Rebecca delivery truck visits each of the five local Rebecca stores. This truck picks up merchandise that is to be transferred to other stores and drops off the transfers and merchandise shipments every morning. Every afternoon the truck makes customer deliveries. It delivers merchandise to the North and East sections of the city on Monday, Wednesday, and Friday afternoons. It delivers merchandise to the South and West sections of the city on Tuesday, Thursday, and Saturday afternoons.

Receiving the Freight Bill After a driver pulls a truck up to the receiving dock, the driver hands the store receiver a freight bill. Jeff tells Sally, "As a receiver, you should check to be sure the merchandise to be delivered really belongs to our store. Our store name should be written where it says consignee."

Unloading the Shipment Many receivers help the driver unload a merchandise shipment, especially when the shipment is large. Safety procedures should be followed at all times. "Before you try to lift anything by yourself," Jeff explains, "be sure you can carry it. If you think a package or box is too heavy, ask for help or use special lifting equipment, such as a two-wheel handcart or a forklift. If you can lift a package by yourself, use the following procedure.

1. Spread your feet about 8 inches apart.
2. Stand close to the box.
3. Crouch down and get a good hold on the box.
4. Push up with your legs, not your back.
5. Stand up straight when carrying the box.
6. Put down the package by reversing this procedure.

"When carrying packages," Jeff continues, "you should always be able to see where you are going. Don't carry boxes that you can't see around or over. It's better to make more trips than it is to hurt yourself by running into or tripping on other merchandise or fixtures."

"When stacking boxes," Jeff says, "make the stacks straight so that they will not tumble over. Accidents happen when employees aren't careful."

Experience 12-7

Can You Lift It?

Fill a box with 10 to 15 hardback books. Demonstrate how you would properly lift the box, carry it, and put it down. Have another classmate watch you and check if you are using the proper lifting procedures.

Checking the Freight Bill The freight bill shows the transportation charges due. Usually, apparel and accessory stores must pay the freight cost for shipping merchandise. Jeff continues his explanation of receiving procedures for Sally. "After the boxes are unloaded, you must count the number of boxes that are actually received. Then compare the counted quantity to the quantity listed on the freight bill. If the numbers agree, sign the bill and date it. If the numbers disagree, write the actual number received and sign your name and date. If all the boxes are not received, a copy of the freight bill is sent to the transportation company as evidence of the shortage. You are to keep one copy of the freight bill; the driver keeps the others." (See Figure 12-4.)

"Sometimes," Jeff says, "I open a box or two and examine the merchandise before signing the freight bill.

Fast Transit Inc.
3248 Soda Drive
Los Angeles, CA 90053
Phone 213-492-1083

FREIGHT BILL 138114
PRO NUMBER S 6295S
DATE 2/17/8-

Rebecca's — CONSIGNEE
1211 Main Street Miami, FL 33148 — DESTINATION

Martin's of California — SHIPPER
78 Los Angeles Blvd., Los Angeles, CA 90015 — POINT OF ORIGIN
720 — SHIPPER'S NO.

NUMBER OF PACKAGES, ARTICLES, AND MARKS	WEIGHT	RATE	FREIGHT CHARGES
5 Boxes, sweaters NMFC 49880 RECEIVED 4 BOXES, 1 BOX CRUSHED Jeff Bateman 2-27-8-	65	$74.35	$74.35 Collect
TOTAL PIECES 5 — ICC REGULATIONS REQUIRE PAYMENT OF THIS BILL WITHIN 7 DAYS	TOTAL WEIGHT 65	$74.35	← PAY THIS AMOUNT

Fig. 12-4 When checking freight bills, such as the one at the left, it is important to compare the actual quantity of the shipment with what appears on the freight bill.

If any of the boxes have been opened or if the tape or sealing of any box is broken, I always open the box and check the condition of the goods. Opened boxes are a clue that pilferage or theft may have taken place.

"If any of the boxes are crushed or damaged, be sure to write that information on the freight bill. (See Figure 12-4.) Make it a habit to inspect the merchandise inside the damaged boxes. If the merchandise is still in good condition, accept it. If the merchandise itself is damaged, it should not be accepted. The accounting office will file a claim against the transportation company when it is responsible for damaging the merchandise."

Experience 12-8

Checking the Bill

Suppose you are the receiver at Rebecca's. You have just helped a truck driver from Fast Freight Company unload the merchandise boxes opposite.

1. Write the appropriate information on the freight bill shown below.
2. What is the purpose of the freight bill?

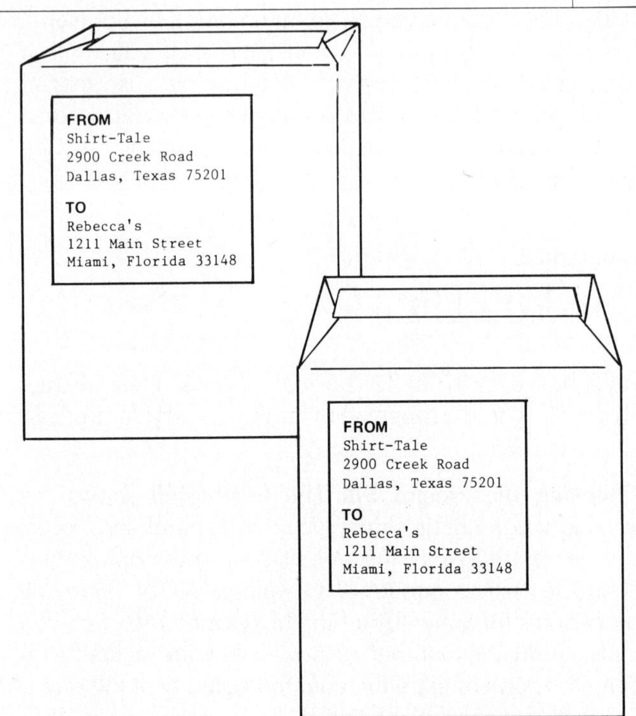

M & M Trucklines
2348 Glenellen Blvd.
San Antonio, Texas 78207

FREIGHT BILL 1847

PRO NUMBER S 6295S

DATE 8/15/8-

Rebecca's — 1211 Main Street — Miami, FL 33148
CONSIGNEE — DESTINATION

Shirt-Tale — 2900 Creek Road — Dallas, TX 75201 — 213
SHIPPER — POINT OF ORIGIN — SHIPPER'S NO.

NUMBER OF PACKAGES, ARTICLES, AND MARKS	WEIGHT	RATE	FREIGHT CHARGES
2 Boxes, shirts NMFC 49880	24 lbs.	$36.40	$36.40 Collect
TOTAL PIECES 2 — *ICC REGULATIONS REQUIRE PAYMENT OF THIS BILL WITHIN 7 DAYS*	24 TOTAL WEIGHT lb.	$36.40	← PAY THIS AMOUNT

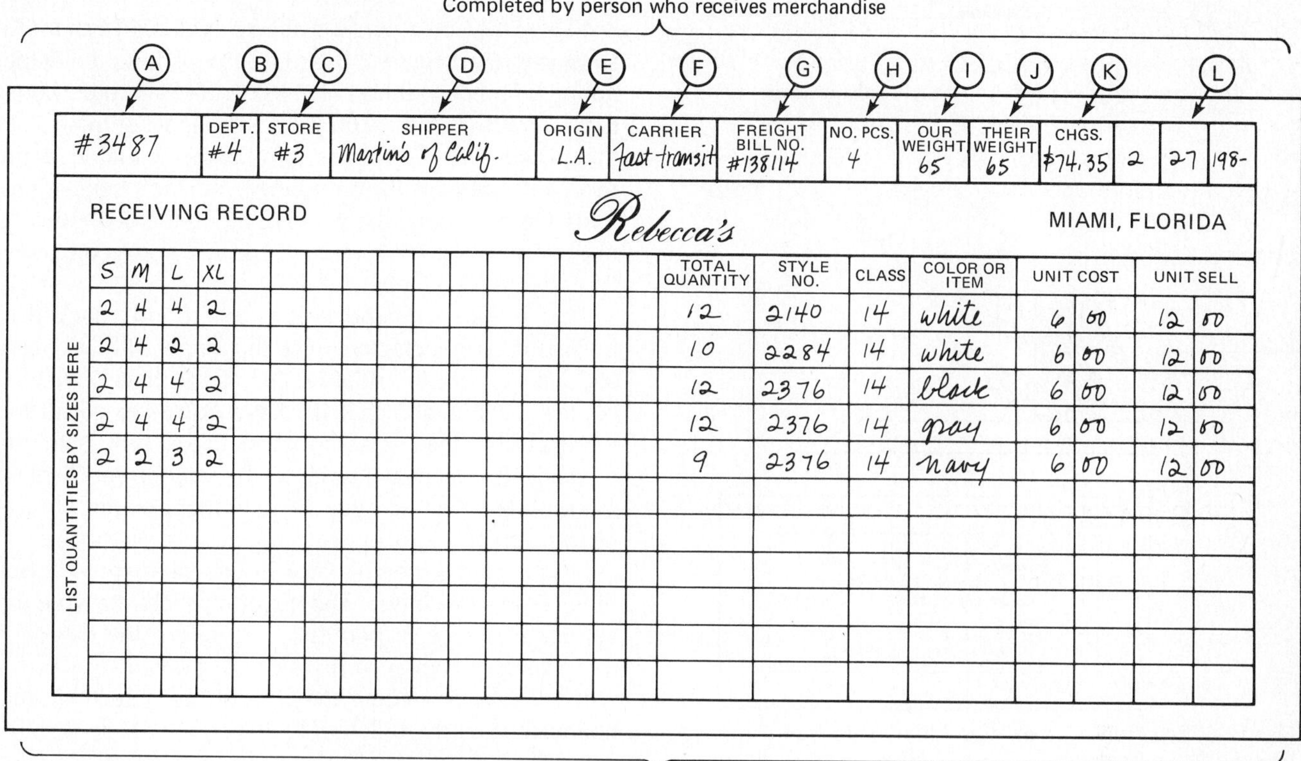

#3487	DEPT. #4	STORE #3	SHIPPER Martin's of Calif.	ORIGIN L.A.	CARRIER Fast transit	FREIGHT BILL NO. #138114	NO. PCS. 4	OUR WEIGHT 65	THEIR WEIGHT 65	CHGS. $74.35	2	27	198-

RECEIVING RECORD — Rebecca's — MIAMI, FLORIDA

LIST QUANTITIES BY SIZES HERE

S	M	L	XL	TOTAL QUANTITY	STYLE NO.	CLASS	COLOR OR ITEM	UNIT COST	UNIT SELL
2	4	4	2	12	2140	14	white	6.00	12.00
2	4	2	2	10	2284	14	white	6.00	12.00
2	4	4	2	12	2376	14	black	6.00	12.00
2	4	4	2	12	2376	14	gray	6.00	12.00
2	2	3	2	9	2376	14	navy	6.00	12.00

Fig. 12-5 From where does the information on the top line of a receiving record come?

Completing the Receiving Record Rebecca's, like most apparel and accessory stores, keeps a record of all incoming shipments on a form called a receiving record. "When a shipment is received," Jeff says, "the top line of the receiving record is completed. This information is taken from the freight bill." (See Figure 12-5.)

"To complete the top line write:

1. Receiving record number (see Fig. 12-5, letter A)
2. Department number (see letter B)
3. Store number (see letter C)
4. Name of the shipper or the company that sent the merchandise (see letter D)
5. Place that the merchandise was shipped from (see letter E)
6. Name of the company that transported the merchandise (see letter F)
7. Freight bill number (see letter G)
8. Number of boxes of merchandise received (see letter H)
9. Weight of the shipment according to the store, Rebecca's (see letter I)
10. Weight of shipment according to the transportation company or carrier (see letter J)
11. Cost of transporting the merchandise (see letter K)
12. Date the merchandise was received (see letter L)

See where this information is found on the freight bill (Figure 12-4)."

Experience 12-9

Preparing the Receiving Record

Using the information from Experience 12-8, complete the top line of the receiving record shown below. Assume the shipment is for Department 12, Store 2. Your weight of the shipment is 24 pounds. Use the current date. The receiving record number is 8043 for this particular shipment.

#	DEPT.	STORE	SHIPPER	ORIGIN	CARRIER	FREIGHT BILL NO.	NO. PCS.	OUR WEIGHT	THEIR WEIGHT	CHGS.			

RECEIVING RECORD — Rebecca's — MIAMI, FLORIDA

				TOTAL QUANTITY	STYLE NO.	CLASS	COLOR OR ITEM	UNIT COST	UNIT SELL

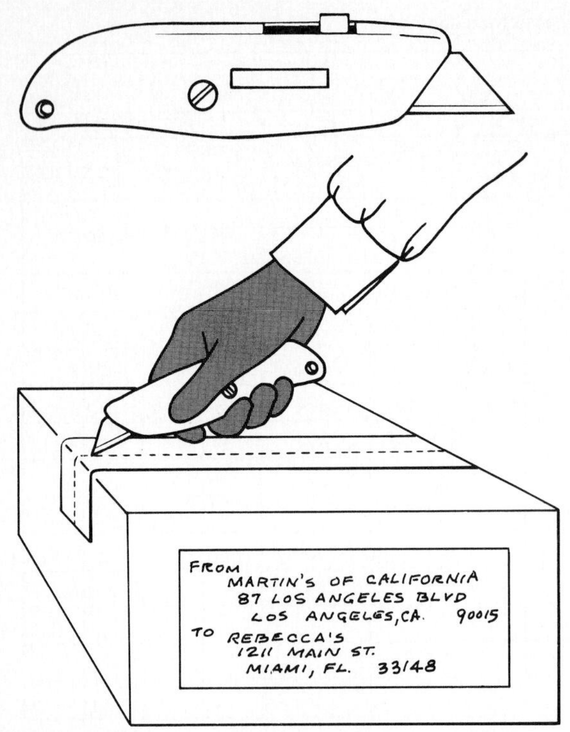

Fig. 12-6 Read Jeff's safety tips (below) on how to use a box cutter (above).

CHECKING NEW MERCHANDISE

"After the new shipment has been recorded on the receiving record," Jeff continues, "open the boxes with a box cutter. Be careful to cut only the edge of the cartons so that the merchandise is not damaged. For safety, always cut away from your body. (See Figure 12-6.)

"There will be a packing slip with each merchandise shipment. (See Figure 12-7.) This form shows the actual quantity and description of merchandise shipped. Count the merchandise in each shipment and compare it to that listed on the packing slip. If the actual quantity received agrees with the quantity on the packing slip, write OK and initial the packing slip. If the quantities do not agree, write the quantity received and your name. (See Figure 12-7, letter A.)

"Once the merchandise is counted and checked to be sure it is not defective, give the freight bill and packing slip to Jean, the bookkeeper. If you have indicated on the packing slip that we have not received all the merchandise that was supposed to be sent with the packing slip, Jean will write to the vendor and explain the problem. She will pay for only that amount of merchandise that we received.

"If any of the merchandise in the shipment is defective, contact the buyer. The buyer must call or write the vendor and receive permission to return the defective merchandise. When permission is granted, the buyer will tell Jean to deduct the cost of the defective merchandise from the bill.

"Before Jean makes payment to the vendor, she also compares the packing slip and invoice, which is the vendor's bill, to the purchase order. Often the packing slip shows that less merchandise was shipped than was ordered. The remaining ordered merchandise is back ordered, which means the vendor will send it as soon as it is available. Jean does not pay for back-ordered merchandise. She only pays for that merchandise listed on the slip received in good condition."

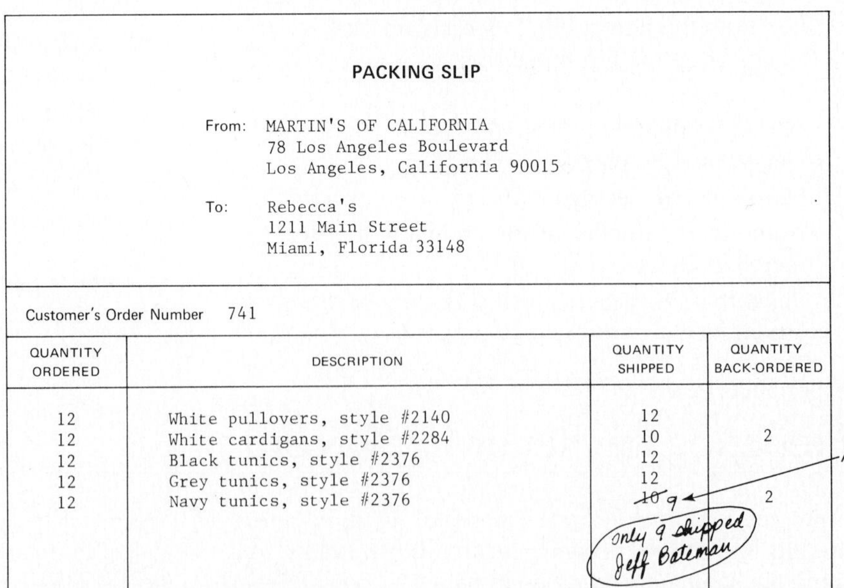

PACKING SLIP

From: MARTIN'S OF CALIFORNIA
78 Los Angeles Boulevard
Los Angeles, California 90015

To: Rebecca's
1211 Main Street
Miami, Florida 33148

Customer's Order Number 741

QUANTITY ORDERED	DESCRIPTION	QUANTITY SHIPPED	QUANTITY BACK-ORDERED
12	White pullovers, style #2140	12	
12	White cardigans, style #2284	10	2
12	Black tunics, style #2376	12	
12	Grey tunics, style #2376	12	
12	Navy tunics, style #2376	~~10~~ 9	2

Fig. 12-7 If the quantities received in a shipment do not agree with those shown on the packing slip, write the amount received and your name on the form as Jeff did here (A).

Experience 12-10

Comparing the Merchandise with the Packing Slip

1. A shipment of blouses you received is shown on page 183. Compare the actual shipment with the packing slip below it. Record any problems on the packing slip and initial it.

PACKING SLIP

From: Shirt-Tale
2900 Creek Road
Dallas, Texas 75201

To: Rebecca's
1211 Main Street
Miami, Florida 33148

Customer's Order Number 328

QUANTITY ORDERED	DESCRIPTION	QUANTITY SHIPPED	QUANTITY BACK-ORDERED
2	Size small, Plain blouses	2	
3	Size medium, Plain blouses	2	1
3	Size large, Plain blouses	3	
2	Size extra-large, Plain blouses	2	
2	Size small, Checked & striped blouses	2	
3	Size medium, Checked & striped blouses	3	
3	Size large, Checked & striped blouses	2	1
2	Size extra-large, Checked & striped bl.	2	

2. Suppose you are to pay the vendor for the shipment. You check the buyer's purchase order and find that ten solid blouses (two small, three medium, three large, and two extra large) and ten checked and striped blouses (two small, three medium, three large, and two extra large) were ordered. Each costs $6. What would you pay the vendor? (Assume your store doesn't pay for back-ordered merchandise.)

____

PRICE MARKING MERCHANDISE

After merchandise is received and checked in, it is price marked. The type of price ticket used and the information written on the price ticket are explained in Chapter 11, "Buying and Pricing."

STORING MERCHANDISE

Buyers often purchase large quantities of basic stock merchandise. Because of lack of room, only some of this merchandise may be placed on the sales floor. The extra merchandise is kept in a stockroom. When the stock on the sales floor begins to sell, merchandise from the stockroom is used to replenish the missing items.

Sometimes merchandise arrives too early or too late for its buying season. For example, a buyer may purchase a large quantity of close-out swimsuits in July. The swimsuits won't arrive at the store until late August, just when the buyer is featuring new fall merchandise. These swimsuits are kept in the stockroom until the next February when the store starts its swimsuit promotion.

Occasionally, buyers instruct salespeople to keep merchandise in the stockroom until the day before an ad appears. This practice ensures that a sufficient supply of merchandise will be available for the ad.

You may work at an apparel and accessory store that has a large warehouse where all merchandise shipments are received, checked in, price marked, and stored. Or you may work for a very small store where the only storeroom is a small area off the selling floor. No matter what size store or type of merchandise you work with, you will need to understand basic storeroom and stocking procedures.

STOCK CARD											Location: AISLE 18, SHELF 3	
Terms: NET 30		Discount: 2% 10 DAYS		Reorder Period: 30 DAYS							Vendor: WESTCO ACCESSORIES MONTGOMERY, ALABAMA	
Stock Number	Description	Cost	Current Inventory								Stock Max.	Stock Min.
284	MEN'S WHITE HANDKERCHIEFS	$3/pkg	Date	7/12	7/18						60	25
			Stock on hand	46	41							
			On order									

Fig. 12-8 Stores with large stockrooms operate on a stock card system. Here's a typical stock card used in such a system.

Arranging the Stockroom So that merchandise can be easily located, stockrooms should be arranged in a logical, orderly way. If the store uses a central warehouse to keep the extra stock for many departments, each department should be assigned a particular location in the warehouse.

Stores with large stockrooms usually divide the storage area into sections. They number the aisles and shelves so that merchandise is easy to find. They also set up a stock card system. Each stock card lists the description, location, and quantity of the merchandise on hand. Some stock cards also list the order quantities and terms of the merchandise. (See Figure 12-8.)

In all stockrooms, like merchandise should be stored with like merchandise. If appropriate, merchandise in the stockroom should be sorted into styles, sizes, and colors. For example, girls' pajamas should be stocked together in one section of the children's wear department stock area. All size 3 pajamas should be together, followed by sizes 4, 5, 6, and 6x. Within each size, each style should be grouped. For example, in size 3 the pullover pajamas could be grouped before the button-down styles. Within each style, the colors should be grouped. For example, all the yellow pullovers size 3 pajamas would be before the green pullovers size 3 pajamas. Within each color, the oldest merchandise should be stocked before the newest.

Rotating Stock Most apparel and accessory stores follow a stock rotation system called *f*irst *i*n and *f*irst *o*ut (FIFO). Under this system, merchandise that comes into the store first should leave the store first. The FIFO system guarantees fresh merchandise moving through the store at all times. It keeps merchandise from getting dirty, turning yellow, and losing its appeal to customers.

To use the FIFO system, you will need to know when merchandise comes into the store. Many stores print a season code on price tickets that dates the arrival of the merchandise. For example, a store may use the letters A–L to represent the months of the year and numbers to represent the days of the month that merchandise is received. Merchandise coded B-10, or February 10, would be older than merchandise dated F-5, or June 5.

Following the FIFO system, all merchandise should be stored so that the oldest items are to the front and the newest items are to the back of the shelf or rack. It makes no difference what kind of merchandise it is, where the merchandise is stored, or how it is stored; all merchandise should follow this procedure. For example, robes hanging on racks in the stockroom should be arranged so that the oldest robes are to the front and the newest robes are in the back. When additional robes are needed on the sales floor, the oldest robes are taken from the front of the rack to the selling area.

Merchandise on the sales floor should also follow this stock rotation system. For example, when adding boxes of diapers to a merchandise shelf, the oldest boxes should be placed to the front. The newest boxes should be placed to the back.

Keeping Stored Merchandise Clean Dust, dirt, and yellowing from sun or age can make stored merchandise lose its fresh look and appeal to customers. To guard against old, soiled-looking merchandise, apparel and accessory stores often store merchandise in plastic bags or boxes. They also dust the stock area frequently to eliminate a buildup of dirt and dust. By preventing stored merchandise from getting dirty, stores are avoiding the additional work and expense of cleaning stored items.

Experience 12-11

FIFO

Answer the following on a separate sheet of paper.

1. Suppose your store follows the FIFO stock rotation system.
   a. What does FIFO mean to you as a stockperson?
   b. What are the advantages of following a FIFO stock system?
2. Your buyer recently purchased a large quantity of white tennis shorts, a basic stock item at your store. In the past month, you received four shipments of the same shorts, one shipment every Tuesday. You checked and price marked the merchandise in all the shipments, but at this time there's no room for any of the merchandise on the sales floor.
   a. How should you stock the merchandise, which is on hangers, in the stockroom?
   b. When the sales floor needs white shorts, which shipment should you send?

Controlling Merchandise in the Stockroom Stores that have large stock areas or warehouses where many kinds of merchandise is stored usually have established a procedure for releasing merchandise from stock. These stores require buyers, department managers, or other authorized employees to prepare a stock requisition that lists all needed merchandise. This requisition is sent to the stockroom personnel, who locate the merchandise and assemble the order.

The stockroom employees use the stock cards to locate the ordered merchandise. They record all merchandise that leaves the storage area on its appropriate stock card. For example, the stock card in Figure 12-8 shows that on July 18, 5 packages of men's white handkerchiefs were removed from stock and 41 packages are remaining. At inventory time, the actual merchandise is compared to the quantity listed on the stock cards. The quantities should be identical. If they are different, it is evidence of an accounting error or theft. So when filling an order, it is very important for stockroom employees to list exactly what merchandise is being sent to a store or department.

Stockroom employees usually send the ordered merchandise plus a copy of the requisition back to the department or store requesting the merchandise. If any merchandise is not available because of out-of-stock conditions, this information is written on the form.

GETTING THE MERCHANDISE READY FOR SALE

As soon as merchandise arrives on the sales floor, an employee must check the actual merchandise received against the form that shows what merchandise was sent. Any errors in quantity, size, color, or style must be reported to the supervisor immediately. Shortages may be the result of stockroom errors or theft.

Safety in the Stockroom After the merchandise is checked in, it is usually placed in the stockroom off the sales floor until sales personnel have a chance to prepare the merchandise for the selling area. As in all stockkeeping situations, it is necessary for salespeople to follow safety procedures when storing this merchandise in the stockroom.

When stacking boxes, the boxes should be put in straight stacks so that their weight is evenly distributed. If they aren't straight, boxes may easily tumble off shelves and injure someone. Broken boxes, that is boxes that are opened and have had some merchandise removed, should be on the top of the stack. If a box that isn't full is put on the bottom of the stack, the weight of the other boxes may collapse the bottom box and cause the stack to fall.

Round objects should be stacked in a pyramid. A boundary should be used on each side of the pyramid to keep the stack from slipping. Sometimes, boxes are stacked in tall rows. When getting one of these boxes, you will need to use a stepladder. Before climbing the ladder, be sure it is sitting firmly on the floor. Test the ladder by putting some of your weight on it first.

Changing Clothes Hangers, Buttoning, Belting, and Dusting Salespeople should make merchandise look as attractive as possible so that customers will want to purchase it. Sometimes, this involves changing the hangers from the flimsy plastic hangers sent by the vendor to the store's own hangers. Sometimes, salespeople add a foam padding insert to the hanger so that merchandise does not slip off its hanger or lose its shape. Dresses or blouses should be buttoned and belted before going on the sales floor; plastic, leather, or boxed merchandise should be dusted.

Experience 12-12

Getting the Overall Picture

Visit an apparel and/or accessory store. Explain to the manager that you are studying how merchandise shipments are received, checked in, stored, and made ready for the sales floor. Ask the manager if you can watch how that store handles these operations. If there are no new shipments of merchandise at the time of your visit, make an appointment to return to the store at another time.

13 Sales Promotion: Advertising

Apparel stores use many methods, called promotion, to influence customers to purchase merchandise. There are two types of promotion, personal and nonpersonal. In **personal promotion,** there is one-to-one communication between the store and the customer. An example of personal promotion is retail selling in which a salesperson and a customer communicate on a one-to-one basis. In **nonpersonal promotion**, there is one-way communication from the store to the customer. One example of nonpersonal promotion is advertising.

A store may use all phases of promotion to attract customers. Newspaper, radio, television, and mail advertisements may be used to arouse interest and bring customers into the store. The store may create attractive displays that encourage customers to examine its merchandise. A staff of trained salespeople may be hired.

ADVERTISING RESPONSIBILITIES OF SALESPEOPLE

The goal of advertising is to create interest and desire in customers to bring them into the store to make purchases. Yet advertising alone cannot make a sale. An efficient sales force must work with a store's advertising to help customers make buying decisions.

Salespeople must know what's being advertised and answer customer questions about the advertised goods. They must fill mail and telephone orders that result from the ads. They must make sure there is sufficient quantity of advertised merchandise and prepare sale signs. Also, salespeople must keep customers informed of the store's special promotions.

KNOW WHAT'S BEING ADVERTISED

Advertising draws customers into a store to look at merchandise. Salespeople must be prepared for the questions customers ask about advertised items.

Examine the salesperson's reaction in the following situation:

A customer hurriedly enters a store, clutching a newspaper ad.

CUSTOMER: Where's this robe? I've been looking for a robe just like this for months.

SALESPERSON: I'm not sure. I just started working here. Just look around, I'm sure you'll see it.

In this situation, a salesperson showed a lack of knowledge about the advertised merchandise. The salesperson was not prepared to handle customer questions about merchandise location, price, and features. How could you, as an apparel and accessory salesperson, handle this and similar situations?

Know the Merchandise Being Featured Apparel and accessory stores may use newspaper, radio, television, and special mailing inserts to advertise their merchandise. Medium- and large-sized stores circulate store bulletins that tell their salespeople what merchandise will be featured in ads. In smaller stores, buyers, managers, or owners usually tell salespeople about the upcoming ads. As an apparel or accessory salesperson, some stores will ask you to tear out the newspaper ads for your department and place them by the cash register. This will help you remember if an ad that ran 2 days ago is still in effect.

Apparel and accessory stores do most of their advertising in newspapers. Make it a habit to look through newspapers for ads from your store. A customer who has just purchased women's shoes may want to know where the men's wallets that are on sale are located. By making it a daily routine to read your store's ads, you will be able to answer your customer's questions more thoroughly.

Know the Location of Advertised Merchandise You may be aware of what is being advertised, but do you know where that merchandise is stocked in your department? Generally, buyers supplement their advertisements with special displays. This coordination between advertisements and displays increases sales. Be sure to walk through your department when you come to work each day. Make a mental picture of where merchandise is. Note where advertised merchandise is stocked.

Know the Availability of the Advertised Merchandise Apparel and accessory stores often run fashion ads. **Fashion ads**, which often appear in the Sunday paper, feature new merchandise at full price.

Because buyers are never sure which fashion merchandise will be a big seller, they purchase limited quantities of new styles or colors and then reorder the popular items. This practice prompts customers to ask questions about the availability of the advertised merchandise. For example, you may be faced with questions such as: "The size 12 is a bit snug and there isn't a size 14 on the rack. Does your branch store in Ridgewood have a size 14?" You will have to know about merchandise reorders and transfers.

Merchandise advertised at reduced prices in a "sale ad" may be available in limited sizes, colors, and styles if the buyer is not reordering. You will be able to answer customer questions quickly about sale merchandise by keeping orderly displays in which merchandise is grouped by style, color, and size. Make it a practice to talk to your buyer or department manager about the availability of advertised merchandise. Ask questions about what is on order, what can be reordered, and what is at the branch stores.

Know the Features and Benefits An ad that runs on Tuesday may bring 15 customers into the store to see the advertised merchandise. During the day, a salesperson may be asked to explain the features and benefits of the advertised goods to each customer. For example, customers may want to know the price; available sizes, colors, and styles; durability and care of the merchandise; and manufacturer reputation. To promote the sale of the goods better, salespeople should be able to discuss the features and benefits of advertised merchandise. You can prepare for customer questions about advertised merchandise by completing a product analysis sheet. This form is discussed in Chapters 9 and 15.

Experience 13-1

Salesperson + Advertising Awareness = Sale?

Look through a newspaper and identify two fashion ads and one sale ad for apparel or accessories. Try to find ads from three different stores. Visit the stores and make the following observations. Record your findings on the rating form provided.

1. When you enter the store, ask a salesperson where you will find the advertised item. (Mention the item by name.) If the salesperson knows, give the store one point on the rating form.
2. When you enter the department, ask the salesperson where the merchandise featured in the newspaper is located. Give the store one point if the salesperson knows what merchandise is advertised. Give the store another point if the salesperson knows where the merchandise is located.
3. Examine the advertised merchandise for color, style, and size. Ask the salesperson if you can purchase the merchandise in a color, style, or size that is not available among the merchandise you have examined. Give the store one point if the salesperson knows if the merchandise can be reordered or transferred into the store.
4. Ask the salesperson questions about the merchandise. (Examples: How does the merchandise wear? How should the merchandise be cared for?) Give the store one point if the salesperson knows the features and benefits of the advertised goods.
5. Total the points on the rating form. Describe how you feel about the store that has the most points. Describe how you feel about the store that has the least. At which store do you prefer to shop?

Description of Salesperson	Store 1	Store 2	Store 3
a. Salesperson knew location of advertised merchandise in another department.			
b. Salesperson in department of advertised merchandise knew what merchandise was being advertised.			
c. Salesperson knew the location of the advertised merchandise.			
d. Salesperson was aware of reorders and merchandise transfers.			
e. Salesperson knew features and benefits of advertised goods.			
f. Total			

FILL MAIL AND TELEPHONE ORDERS

Many stores include mail and telephone order blanks for the products featured in their newspaper ads. Small mail-order businesses use order blanks in their newspaper and magazine ads. See Figure 1-7, Chapter 1, for an example. They also include order blanks in the ads they mail to customers. These ads are called direct-mail inserts, or **stuffers**. See Figure 3-5, Chapter 3, for example. Large stores have an order department that receives the merchandise orders returned by customers and sends the orders to the appropriate departments.

The salespeople read the orders and get the requested merchandise, checking that the merchandise is the requested size, style, and color. If the customer has included cash or a check, the salesperson rings the order on the cash register. If the customer wishes to pay at a later date, the salesperson writes a charge slip. Then the salesperson puts the goods in a box and sends the merchandise to the shipping department.

In small apparel and accessory stores, salespeople may answer the phone and write and fill orders. They may also wrap the merchandise, determine the postage, and mail the merchandise to the customer.

COUNT THE MERCHANDISE

In apparel and accessory stores, salespeople are often asked to count the quantity of advertised merchandise on hand before an ad appears. This quantity count is recorded on an ad response sheet. Salespeople also count the merchandise 3 days after the ad appears. The number of units sold during the 3 days, which is the difference between the two counts, also is recorded on the ad form response sheet. (See Figure 13-1.) Buyers and store management use this information to determine the effectiveness of an ad.

Merchandise counts help salespeople become more aware of what merchandise is being advertised. Salespeople can see the range of styles, colors, and sizes that is available for customer selection. When making merchandise counts, the salespeople must be careful to include merchandise in the **understock** (that is, merchandise in the drawers under the counters) and in the storeroom.

PREPARE THE ADVERTISED MERCHANDISE

Salespeople are often asked to "set the ad" or prepare the merchandise for the upcoming advertisement. For a fashion ad, this may involve arranging a display in a prominent location. For a sale ad, this involves marking and recording the price changes. Salespeople become aware of the quantity of advertised merchandise needed to satisfy customer demand.

Chain stores use ad merchandise inventory reports, sometimes called store ad information sheets, to tell their department managers when to set a sale ad. (See the store ad information sheet in Figure 13-2.) These sheets show when reduced price merchandise will be featured in the newspaper. The department manager is responsible for making sure there is sufficient merchandise on hand to handle customer demand and that the items are priced for the ad.

INFORM CUSTOMERS OF SPECIAL PROMOTIONS

Medium- and large-sized department stores have a sales

AD RESPONSE SHEET

DATE OF AD *Dec. 3, 198-* ADVERTISED ITEMS

Item	Dept.	On Hand	Selling Price	3-Day Unit Results	Comments
Men's PVC vinyl jackets	35	40	$19.99	29	*Good ad. The price was reduced $10 to encourage customers to purchase.*
Men's down-filled vests	35	23	$14.99	6	*Ad didn't produce the results expected. Gunther's Sporting Goods ran an ad that featured these vests for $12.99.*
Men's wool-blend shirts	35	28	$12.99/ 2 for $25	18	*Many customers requested sizes medium and large, but we ran out. We could have sold many more.*

Fig. 13-1 An ad response sheet, such as this, contains information which can help buyers and store managers determine the effectiveness of an ad.

Courtesy K-Mart Apparel Corp.

STORE AD INFORMATION SHEET

STORE STAMP

AD DATE July 15, 198-

EVENT Wednesday Newspaper Insert

(Merch. Areas 6, 7, 8)

MERCHANDISE AREA	AD SPACE	DEPT	ITEM	REGULAR PRICE	AD PRICE	EST. QTY. FOR AD	QTY. SHIPPED HOLD-FOR-AD	ACT. QTY. ON HAND	QTY. IN TRANSIT (WHSE. CHARGES)
All	Full	36	Lds. Dusters	4.00	2.88	20-42dz	6-12dz	22dz	
All	page	49	Lds. Short sleeve shirts	4.57-4.97	3.22	13-29dz	2-4dz	15dz	
All		78	Lds. Short sleeve T-shirts	3.97-4.57	3.22	40-60dz	3dz	43dz	
All		77	Lds. Shirts	3.97	2.88	18-18dz	4dz	20dz	
All		25	Lds. Coats	16.96-18.88	14.44	36-80pc	24pc	15pc	

NOTE: IF THERE IS AN AREA NUMBER OTHER THAN "ALL", BE SURE TO REFER TO YOUR MERCHANDISE AREA LISTING ON YOUR AD BOOK.

INSTRUCTIONS FOR COMPLETION OF THIS FORM

THREE WEEKS PRIOR TO THE AD, A COUNT MUST BE TAKEN OF THE "ACTUAL QUANTITY ON HAND". IN ADDITION, CHECK YOUR WAREHOUSE CHARGES TO DETERMINE THE "QUANTITY IN TRANSIT". REFER TO THE MARKDOWN AUTHORIZATION SHEET FOR SPECIFIC MFG., STYLE, AND ITEM. BE SURE TO CHECK YOUR MERCHANDISE SIZE AND COLOR ASSORTMENT, AND IF LACKING, NOTIFY YOUR DISTRICT MANAGER IMMEDIATELY AND RETAIN THIS COPY FOR YOUR FILE.

Fig. 13-2 Store ad information sheets keep department managers informed so that they can have merchandise ready for upcoming sale ads.

promotion department that coordinates the store's advertising, display, and publicity.

This department watches the details of major promotions and makes sure a special promotional theme is followed. For example, in Salt Lake City, Auerbach's Department Store, Kennington Shirts, Disneyland, and Western Airlines combined forces for a Mickey Mouse special promotion. The store held a "Welcome Mickey" Parade and sponsored a family vacation to Disneyland. The Auerbach's Sales Promotion Department coordinated the special event. It continued the Mickey Mouse theme in the store's advertising. (See Figure 13-3.) Buyers purchased Mickey Mouse clothing and the salespeople reminded their customers of the special upcoming parade.

© 1975 Walt Disney Productions

Courtesy Auerbach's, Inc.

Fig. 13-3 Mickey Mouse provided the theme for a special promotion sponsored by Auerbach's Department Store in Salt Lake City, Utah. Kennington Shirts, Disneyland, and Western Airlines joined the store in this promotional event.

The success of special events or promotions often depends on salespeople informing customers of the happenings. To keep the sales force aware of future events, stores may hold special meetings or issue bulletins. Salespeople can easily inform customers of special events by casually mentioning the event at the end of the sale. For example, after ringing up a customer's purchase, a salesperson may add, "Mrs. Jones, I want to remind you of our Sidewalk Sale on July 16 and 17. The store will be offering some exceptional bargains. I hope you will be able to come." This practice builds customer goodwill and helps ensure the success of promotions.

Experience 13-2

Special Events

1. Discuss special events that unite the community and local merchants in your area. List these events and the approximate times they occur.
2. Role play the possible ways you, as a salesperson, could inform customers about these special events using the following steps.
   a. Choose a particular apparel or accessory item. Assume the customer has entered the store to examine that item.
   b. Explain the product, overcome any customer objections, and close the sale of the item.
   c. Before the customer leaves, mention one of your community's upcoming future events. Be enthusiastic and try to make the customer want to attend the event.
   d. At the end of your role playing, ask the customer if you made him or her want to attend.
   e. Change places with the customer and repeat steps a–d.
3. After you both have role played the salesperson, discuss ways apparel and accessory stores could encourage salespeople to inform customers of special events. List each possibility and what the stores would have to do to make it work. Rate your possibilities. Give the possibility that you think is most workable a 1 and so on.

AD RESPONSIBILITIES OF BUYERS

Apparel and accessory buyers have the major responsibility of determining what to advertise. They must prepare an advertising budget, choose the advertising media, prepare monthly advertising plans, and check the "ready to print" advertisements. They must also evaluate the effectiveness of the advertisements.

No matter how the advertising dollars are spent, buyers want all their ads to accomplish a goal. For example, the goal of one buyer may be to create interest and desire for a particular item. Another buyer may want to increase sales in the department. Buyers may use ads to introduce new products or display a new use for a product. Managers may want to keep the store's name current in the public's mind. Because advertising is one way a store builds an image, advertisers may use ads to establish and maintain a reputation for quality, fashion, low prices, or any combination of these.

Experience 13-3

The Purpose of Advertising

Leaf through a newspaper and tear out five apparel and/or accessory ads. Examine each ad. Complete the following rating chart. (Place a check mark in the appropriate column.)

Description	Ad 1	Ad 2	Ad 3	Ad 4	Ad 5
1. The main goal of the ad is: a. To introduce a new fashion item					
b. To increase sales of a basic item					
c. To increase sales of an established fashion item					
d. To promote the image of the store					

Description	Ad 1	Ad 2	Ad 3	Ad 4	Ad 5
2. The image that the store projects is: a. Fashion					
b. Quality					
c. Low prices					
d. Combination of above (Specify)					
3. Does the ad create interest and desire for the goods? (Answer yes or no.)					

PREPARE ADVERTISING BUDGET

The actual decision of how much money a buyer can spend for advertising is made by store management. Management may use a number of methods to determine the total advertising figure, but one of the commonest is percentage of sales. When determining the specific percentage, management considers such factors as store competition, store location, and future goals. A common figure for apparel and accessory stores is to budget between 2 and 5 percent of net sales for advertising expenses.

Once the total store advertising budget has been determined, each buyer prepares an advertising budget for his or her department. The buyer reviews past sales figures and upcoming calendar events that have an impact on future sales. Past ads and their effectiveness, as well as competitors' advertisements, are also examined. For example, suppose Valentine's and Company, an apparel and accessory store, earned $500,000 in net sales last year. The store may project future net sales to be $575,000, which is a 15 percent increase. Using next year's projected figures, management may budget 3.5 percent of $575,000, or $20,125, for advertising.

Let's see how Jeannie Harris, buyer for the children's coat department at Valentine's and Company, prepares her advertising budget. Last year, the children's coat department sold approximately $50,000 worth of goods, or one tenth of the total sales volume of the store. Based on these sales figures, management has given Jeannie one tenth of the advertising budget, or $2,010.00, to spend this year. To determine how she will spend the advertising money, Jeannie first examines past sales figures. She identifies the best selling periods in her department. (See Table 1.) Jeannie realizes there are three busy times of the year that produce the majority of sales in children's clothing: Easter, back to school, and Christmas. These peak periods are reflected in higher sales.

The next step in preparing the advertising budget is anticipating what the coming sales figures will be. Jeannie anticipates a 15 percent increase in sales over last year. She prepared a chart of next year's sales figures. (See Table 2.) Notice that Jeannie increases all the dollar amounts by 15 percent. The peak sales periods of back to school and Christmas come at the same time every year. Jeannie adjusts the Easter sales figures because Easter will be in late April in the coming year.

Table 1

CHILDREN'S COAT DEPARTMENT PAST SALES FIGURES
Total: $50,000

Month		Dollars	Percentage of Total Sales
January		$2,000	4
February	Easter	3,500	7
March	Easter	4,000	8
April		2,000	4
May		2,000	4
June		2,500	5
July		2,000	4
August	Back to School	9,000	18
September	Back to School	6,000	12
October		2,000	4
November	Christmas	6,000	12
December	Christmas	9,000	18

Table 2

CHILDREN'S COAT DEPARTMENT PROJECTED SALES FIGURES
Total: $57,500

Month		Dollars	Percentage of Total Sales
January		$ 2,300	4
February		2,300	4
March	Easter	4,025	7
April	Easter	4,600	8
May		2,300	4
June		2,875	5
July		2,300	4
August	Back to School	10,350	18
September	Back to School	6,900	12
October		2,300	4
November	Christmas	6,900	12
December	Christmas	10,350	18

Jeannie determines how much money she can spend for advertising each month by multiplying the percentage of total sales by her total advertising budget. Table 3 shows Jeannie's monthly advertising budget for this year. For example, because she anticipates that 8 percent of her total sales will occur in April, Jeannie distributes 8 percent of her total advertising budget to April.

Jeannie has based her advertising budget on factual information of past peak selling periods and projected sales. Periodically, she will review the advertising plan to see if it is producing the expected amount of sales. If not, she may rearrange her plans and distribute more dollars to different months. How Jeannie spends her advertising dollars is her decision. Although not all buyers use percentage of sales and calendar events to prepare their budgets, many do. No matter what system is used, buyers are responsible to stay within their total budgeted amount.

NOTE: This example is based on high sales periods in the children's wear departments. The important selling times will be different for the women's, men's, junior women's, and young men's departments. The calendar in Table 4 shows the peak sales periods for all departments. (In Table 4, important sales periods are in bold print and less important periods are in italics.)

Table 3

CHILDREN'S COAT DEPARTMENT MONTHLY ADVERTISING BUDGET Total Budget: $2,010

Month	Dollars	Percentage of Total Sales
January	$ 80.00	4
February	80.00	4
March	141.00	7
April	161.00	8
May	80.00	4
June	101.00	5
July	80.00	4
August	362.00	18
September	241.00	12
October	80.00	4
November	242.00	12
December	362.00	18

Table 4

IMPORTANT SALES PERIODS

<table>
<tr><th></th><th>Children's Department</th><th>Young Men's Department</th><th>Junior Women's Department</th><th>Men's Department</th><th>Women's Department</th></tr>
<tr><td>JANUARY</td><td colspan="5">← Clearance of Winter Goods →</td></tr>
<tr><td>FEBRUARY</td><td colspan="5">← Valentine's Day →</td></tr>
<tr><td></td><td colspan="5">← Washington's Birthday Sale →</td></tr>
<tr><td>MARCH</td><td colspan="5">← *Easter →</td></tr>
<tr><td>APRIL</td><td></td><td></td><td></td><td></td><td></td></tr>
<tr><td>MAY</td><td></td><td></td><td></td><td></td><td>Mother's Day</td></tr>
<tr><td>JUNE</td><td></td><td>Graduation</td><td>Graduation</td><td>Father's Day
Graduation</td><td>Graduation</td></tr>
<tr><td>JULY</td><td colspan="5">← Clearance of Summer Goods →</td></tr>
<tr><td>AUGUST</td><td colspan="3">← Back to School →</td><td></td><td></td></tr>
<tr><td>SEPTEMBER</td><td colspan="3">← Back to School →</td><td></td><td></td></tr>
<tr><td>OCTOBER</td><td colspan="5">← Halloween →</td></tr>
<tr><td></td><td colspan="5">← Columbus Day Sale →</td></tr>
<tr><td>NOVEMBER</td><td colspan="5">← Thanksgiving →</td></tr>
<tr><td></td><td colspan="5">← Christmas →</td></tr>
<tr><td>DECEMBER</td><td colspan="5">← Christmas →</td></tr>
</table>

**Changes from year to year.*

Experience 13-4

Prepare the Ad Budget

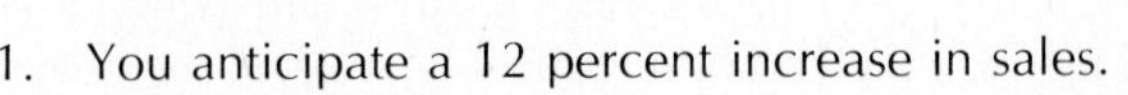

You are the buyer for the young men's department. Every 6 months you prepare an advertising budget for this department. Study the past sales figures for this department, page 193, top left column.

First prepare a chart of the projected sales figures in the space provided on page 193. Then prepare a monthly advertising budget. When preparing the monthly advertising budget, consider the following:

1. You anticipate a 12 percent increase in sales.
2. Your merchandise manager has given you a total advertising budget of $1,820.
3. You want to advertise every month to keep the merchandise and your store in the public's mind.
4. Last year Easter was in March. This year Easter is in late April.

YOUNG MEN'S DEPARTMENT—SHIRTS

PAST SALES FIGURES Total Sales: $28,560

Month	Dollars	% of Total Sales
February	$4,284	15
March	8,568	30
April	2,856	10
May	4,284	15
June	7,140	25
July	1,428	5

PROJECTED SALES FIGURES Total sales:__________

Month	Dollars	% of Total Sales
February		
March		
April		
May		
June		
July		

YOUNG MEN'S DEPARTMENT—SHIRTS MONTHLY ADVERTISING BUDGET

Total Budget:________

Month	Dollars	% of Total Sales
February		
March		
April		
May		
June		
July		

This space is for your calculations.

Courtesy Castleton's

Fig. 13-4 Handouts can be distributed near a store entrance to call customers' attention to a special promotion. Handouts are an inexpensive advertising medium.

CHOOSE ADVERTISING MEDIA

Apparel and accessory buyers can distribute their advertising budget among various media. For example, most buyers use newspapers, radio, and television stations, and direct-mail advertising to get their advertising messages to customers. Each of these media costs different amounts and reaches different customers.

Most buyers use newspapers to advertise because newspapers reach the most customers for the least cost. Also, newspapers usually allow retailers to make last-minute changes, such as canceling an ad when the merchandise has not arrived. This flexibility is very important in the constantly changing world of fashion.

Some apparel and accessory shops use radio advertisements, called radio spots, to reach teen-age customers who don't read the paper. Radio spots are particularly effective for young men and junior women's clothing and accessory stores or departments. Few apparel and accessory stores use television advertisements because they are expensive.

Stores that send out monthly statements often insert small direct-mail advertisements in the statements. Manufacturers provide stores with these printed inserts free of charge. See Figure 3-5, Chapter 3, for an example of a direct-mail insert. Apparel and accessory departments in large department stores often print customer handouts. These handouts are placed near the store entrances and call customer attention to special promotions. They are a very inexpensive means of advertising. (See Figure 13-4.)

Another advertising medium is the use of public address (PA) systems for in-store advertising spots. These spots alert customers who are already in the store to particular merchandise. An example of this in-store advertising is: "Shoppers! For the next 15 minutes, our boys T-shirts will be reduced 25 percent. These shirts are made of 100 percent combed cotton and come in a variety of colors. Be sure to visit the Boys' Department on the second floor near the up escalator for this tremendous bargain."

Experience 13-5

In-Store Promotions

Buyers or department managers may be responsible for preparing in-store advertising messages. Try your skill at preparing a message for one of the following apparel items:

Girls' Summer Tops in Three Styles. Self-tie midriff, tank top, or Western-look short sleeve; price $1.88; variety of colors; sizes 6 to 14.

Boys' Dress Jeans. Polyester/cotton fabric; price $6.98; plaids and checks; regular and slim sizes 8-18.

Write the advertising message. Time it to be sure it is no more than 10 to 20 seconds. (Customers will not listen to long messages.) Read the advertising message into a tape recorder. Evaluate your message using the following chart. Circle the appropriate response.

Description	No				Yes
1. Ad effectively captured attention?	1	2	3	4	5
2. Ad explained the merchandise in detail, yet was short enough to keep the customer's attention?	1	2	3	4	5
3. Ad flowed smoothly?	1	2	3	4	5
4. When read aloud, ad was clear and easily understood?	1	2	3	4	5

PREPARE MONTHLY NEWSPAPER ADVERTISING PLANS

Every month the buyer chooses the sizes of the upcoming month's newspaper advertisements and the dates when the ads will appear in the newspaper. These are important decisions. The larger the ad, the more it costs the store. And when the advertisement appears in the paper often determines how many customers see the advertisement. Buyers also choose the brands and styles of merchandise to be advertised.

Choosing the Size of the Advertisement The size of the advertisement depends on the merchandise items to be featured in the ad and the amount of money in the advertising budget. Most apparel and accessory newspaper ads include:

Illustration or picture of the merchandise items
Headline, which attracts the reader's attention to the advertisement
Body copy, which is the information or selling message under the headline; usually includes information about available sizes and colors, fabric and style, and price
Logotype, often called logo, is a kind of trademark or distinctive design that represents the store; some well-known apparel and accessory store logotypes are shown in Figure 13-5.
Location of store and store hours

The layout of the advertisement also influences the size the buyer chooses. The **layout** shows the arrangement of the various parts of the advertisement. Layouts for stores that have a fashion or quality image usually include only one or two items and much white space. The items are relatively large in size. Layouts for stores that have a discount image usually include small-sized illustrations or pictures of many merchandise items.

Some of the factors that buyers consider when choosing the size of an advertisement are:

- Advertisements that illustrate clothing on people are more realistic and more effective than pictures of the clothing items alone. Advertisements for apparel are usually larger than advertisements for accessories. Accessory advertisements often show only the accessory items.
- Advertisements that feature more than one item need more space than advertisements that feature only one item. Additional clothing items must be pictured and explained in the body copy.
- Large advertisements, such as quarter-page, half-page, or full-page, draw more customer attention to the merchandise than do smaller advertisements. However, these large advertisements are very expensive. Many apparel stores have found small, more frequent advertisements to be just as effective.

Fig. 13-5 Do these store logos look familiar to you? It's important that a store's logo be distinctive.

Although buyers are not responsible for the prepera-tion of advertising layouts, they are responsible for the technical information in their store's ads. They're responsible for the selling power of their ads also. Many buyers work closely with the ad specialists at their stores, at the advertising agency, or at the newspaper to develop attractive advertisements that will produce the highest sales volume possible.

Computing the Cost of a Newspaper Advertisement The size of a newspaper advertisement is determined by the number of agate lines it contains. To determine the number of **agate lines** in any newspaper ad, multiply the height of the ad, in inches, by the width of the ad, in columns, by 14.

Agate Lines = Height of ad (measured in inches) × Width of ad (measured in columns) × 14

The width of a newspaper column varies from newspaper to newspaper. You can determine the column

Fig. 13-6 Point out the headline, body copy, and logotype in this ad. It ran in the newspaper on a 2-column width and was 6 inches deep. This is a reduced version of the ad.

width of any paper by locating the narrowest typed column in the paper. This is the width of one column of advertising space. For example, the advertisement in Figure 13-6 was 6 inches high and 2 columns wide. Using the formula above, the advertisement contained 168 agate lines.

Agate lines = Height × Width × 14
168 = 6 inches × 2 × 14

Once a buyer knows the number of agate lines for a particular newspaper advertisement, the buyer refers to a newspaper rate card supplied by the newspaper to determine the cost of the ad. (See Figure 13-7.) Notice that the cost of a 168-agate-line advertisement that appears in the Sunday newspaper is $222.60.

Cost of the advertisement = Number of agate lines × Price per line
$222.60 = 168 × $1.325

RETAIL ADVERTISING RATES

	Weekday Per Line	Sunday Per Line	N.W. Magazine Per Line**
Less than 350 lines	$.955	$1.325	$1.456

CONTRACT RATES

Space in 12 Months Agate Lines			
350	.738	1.041	1.135
700	.716	1.005	1.098
1,400	.701	.969	1.057
3,500	.673	.932	1.019
7,000	.665	.896	.975
14,000	.658	.882	.963
20,000	.652	.875	.954
30,000	.643	.860	.942
50,000	.636	.854	.932
90,000	.628	.832	.905
130,000	.622	.818	.896
170,000	.600	.809	.882
210,000	.579	.803	.868
260,000	.572	.788	.860
400,000	.563	.766	.845
550,000	.558	.751	.818
700,000	.550	.744	.809
Theatres	.694	.963	1.048
Churches	.622	.796	.868
*Amusements	.954	1.431	1.570

*Commission allowed to recognized agencies
**Less than full page units

Source: *The Oregonian*, Portland, OR

Fig. 13-7 Rate cards supplied by newspapers enable an advertiser to determine the cost of running an ad.

Experience 13-6

Determine Newspaper Advertising Costs

Look through your paper and find three apparel or accessory advertisements. Try to find advertisements that are different sizes. Tear out the advertisements. In the same paper, determine the narrowest column of type (the size of one column of advertising space). Measure the three ads and determine the number of agate lines in each. Record the size of each advertisement on the ads. Have one person from your apparel and accessory group obtain a rate card from the advertising department of your paper. Use the rate card to determine the total cost of each ad. Try to estimate the size of other apparel and accessory ads without measuring. Look through the paper and select three more apparel or accessory ads. Estimate the total column inches and total number of agate lines of each. Write your estimates on the ads. Measure the ads. Compare your estimates with the ads.

Experience 13-7

Choose the Ad Size

One of the best ways to learn how to choose ad sizes is by fitting illustrations of the merchandise, body copy, and logos in ads. In this experience, you will prepare an attractive apparel or accessory ad. Choose one of the following merchandise items.

Boy's Shirt and Sweater Vest (illustrated on page 197):
Shirt—In two styles: polyester/cotton plaids and nylon/acetate jersey prints; sizes 8-20; price $7.50.
Sweater Vest—solids and patterns, acrylic knit; navy, green, or brown; sizes 12-20; price $5.00.

Woman's Blouse (illustrated on page 197):
Blouse—Cotton and polyester blend; rust and black plaid; sizes 5-13; $11.

1. Determine the total column inches you need to advertise the merchandise attractively. Be sure your ad is a particular number of columns wide, such as three or four.
2. Sketch the ad space on a separate sheet of paper.
3. Sketch the merchandise in the ad space. You may scale down or increase the size of the illustration given.
4. Prepare body copy for the ad using the merchandise facts given. Write copy that will create interest and arouse attention.
5. Include the store logotype on page 197.
6. Evaluate the ad. Is your ad attractive? Could you have used less space? Does your ad look cluttered?

Choosing the Time to Advertise Many buyers keep files of their past advertisements, as well as of their competitors' advertisements. This record of past ads helps them remember what happened in the past so that they can make better decisions about current advertising.

Fashion buyers often run their ads on Friday and Saturday, the two busiest shopping days of the week. Ads that run on these days produce better customer response than weekday, Monday through Thursday, ads. Sunday papers usually feature fashion ads that show the current fashion trends. Weekday and week-end ads are often used for apparel and accessory sale items.

Experience 13-8

When Do Local Apparel and Accessory Stores Advertise?

Choose a particular apparel department, such as men's clothing. Check the newspaper every day for 1 week and locate all the ads for that department.

Record the ads on the following chart and indicate whether they were fashion or sale ads. If you were the buyer for a department such as the one whose ads you have been watching, when would you advertise? Why?

Department:___________

Day of Week	Name of Store	Fashion Ad	Sale Ad
EXAMPLE: Sunday	Wilson's Clothing	X	
Sunday			
Monday			
Tuesday			
Wednesday			
Thursday			
Friday			
Saturday			

CHOOSING THE MERCHANDISE TO ADVERTISE

A buyer must choose appropriate merchandise for ads and the merchandise chosen must be seasonal and timely. Even though a department's best seller may be winter parkas, it is not logical to advertise the parkas in May. Fashion novelty items, such as the puka shell necklaces or mood rings of a few years ago, may be big sellers one year and out of fashion the next. Before placing an ad, buyers make sure the merchandise fits in with the season and current trends. Buyers also must determine what merchandise to advertise at regular prices and at sale prices.

Regular Price Ads When choosing merchandise for regular price ads, buyers consider best-selling items, name brands, name brands that offer cooperative advertising money, and fashion trends. Buyers who advertise their best sellers often get the best results from their ads. Customers will not buy merchandise they don't want, no matter how much advertising the slow sellers receive. Buyers refer to their unit control records to find out which items have the best sales.

A department's best-selling items may be name-brand merchandise. Customers often have more confidence in name brands or purchase name brands because of status appeal. Manufacturers who produce name-brand merchandise may provide stores with cooperative advertising dollars. In **cooperative advertising**, the manufacturer shares the cost of the ad with the store. For example, suppose a store purchases a supply of name-brand slacks. Under cooperative advertising, the manufacturer gives the store an advertising allowance. The allowance is based on a percentage of the store's purchases during a certain period. The manufacturer may offer to pay 65 percent of the net newspaper space cost. There are certain requirements the store must meet before the manufacturer will pay a share of the costs. See Figure 13-8 for an example of some requirements in a cooperative advertising plan.

Fig. 13-8 Campus Casuals Cooperative Sales Plan

Campus Casuals is pleased to announce our newly created cooperative sales plan. Our plan has been established to aid our customers in diverting a portion of our National Advertising Funds to local newspaper advertising, available to all dealers alike on a proportionately equal basis.

To qualify under this plan an advertisement must:

1. Feature Campus Casuals exclusively.
2. Prominently display the Campus Casuals name in a type size not smaller than 36-point type (½ inch).
3. A maximum of two quarter-page black-and-white advertisements or one half-page advertisement may be run during any one quarter of the calendar year.
4. Not advertise: closeouts, discountinued merchandise, seconds, or irregulars.
5. Appear in a A. B. C. daily or Sunday newspaper.
6. Not misrepresent merchandise advertised.

The rate of cooperation will be based entirely on the circulation of newspapers in which the advertisement is run and is not in any way subject to quantity of purchases of Campus Casuals products. An average rate of payment per thousand in circulation has been established for all newspapers in the United States, divided into four circulation groups.

The group classifications and rate of payments are as follows:

Group	Circulation	Quarter-Page (Half-Page Tabloid)	Half-Page (Full-Page Tabloid)
1	200,000 and over	$ .37½ per thousand	$ .75 per thousand
2	100,0000 to 199,999	.50 per thousand	1.00 per thousand
3	25,000 to 99,999	.75 per thousand	1.50 per thousand
4	Under 25,000	1.00 per thousand	2.00 per thousand

Example:

275,000 (circulation) × \$.75 per thousand (half-page) = \$206.25 allowance

50,000 (circulation) × \$.75 per thousand (quarter-page) = \$37.50 allowance.

To collect for newspaper advertising, you need only send a full-page tear sheet of the ad within 60 days after publication to:

Campus Casuals of California Co-op.
The Advertising Checking Bureau, Inc.
P.O. Box 3419
Rincon Annex
San Francisco, California 94105

If the advertisement meets the six listed requirements, a check for the exact amount, determined by the circulation rate table, will be sent by return mail by the Advertising Checking Bureau. It is not necessary to send invoices.

Claims for advertising allowance cannot be deducted from Campus Casuals accounts payable. **Do not send invoice or claim to Campus Casuals.**

If a dealer is unable in a practical way to utilize this cooperative newspaper plan, every consideration will be given to the use of other media, such as radio, television and catalogs. Campus Casuals of California will pay 50 percent of the actual cost not to exceed 2 percent of the accounts purchases for the season. Prior approval must be given by submitting your plans to: Advertising Department, Campus Casuals of California, 1200 South Hope Street, Los Angeles, California 90015.

This offer is subject to change or cancellation upon 15 days' written notification.

We reserve the right to submit any requests for an exception to this program to the Federal Trade Commission for its approval.

November 19___

Courtesy Campus Casuals of California

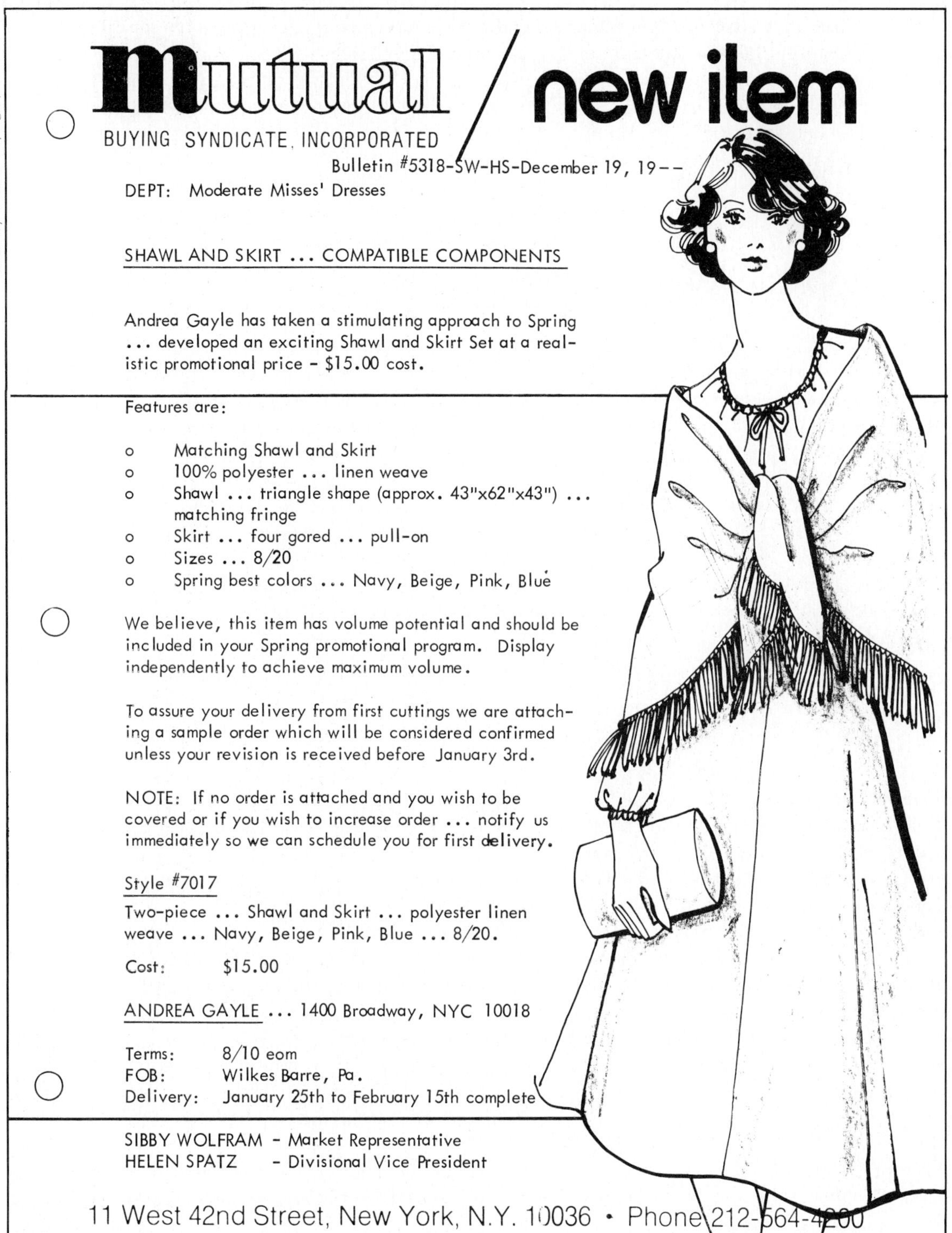

Mutual / new item

BUYING SYNDICATE, INCORPORATED

Bulletin #5318-SW-HS-December 19, 19--

DEPT: Moderate Misses' Dresses

SHAWL AND SKIRT ... COMPATIBLE COMPONENTS

Andrea Gayle has taken a stimulating approach to Spring ... developed an exciting Shawl and Skirt Set at a realistic promotional price - $15.00 cost.

Features are:

- Matching Shawl and Skirt
- 100% polyester ... linen weave
- Shawl ... triangle shape (approx. 43"x62"x43") ... matching fringe
- Skirt ... four gored ... pull-on
- Sizes ... 8/20
- Spring best colors ... Navy, Beige, Pink, Blue

We believe, this item has volume potential and should be included in your Spring promotional program. Display independently to achieve maximum volume.

To assure your delivery from first cuttings we are attaching a sample order which will be considered confirmed unless your revision is received before January 3rd.

NOTE: If no order is attached and you wish to be covered or if you wish to increase order ... notify us immediately so we can schedule you for first delivery.

Style #7017

Two-piece ... Shawl and Skirt ... polyester linen weave ... Navy, Beige, Pink, Blue ... 8/20.

Cost: $15.00

ANDREA GAYLE ... 1400 Broadway, NYC 10018

Terms: 8/10 eom
FOB: Wilkes Barre, Pa.
Delivery: January 25th to February 15th complete

SIBBY WOLFRAM - Market Representative
HELEN SPATZ - Divisional Vice President

11 West 42nd Street, New York, N.Y. 10036 • Phone 212-564-4200

Fig. 13-9 Fashion reports help buyers to determine which items may be their best sellers.

Many apparel and accessory buyers take advantage of cooperative advertising money. The main advantage of the "co-op money" is that the store is able to afford more advertising. One problem of cooperative advertising is that some buyers may buy advertising rather than merchandise. When at market, some buyers may base their decisions on advertising arrangements rather than the merchandise. These buyers should remember that advertising cannot sell unwanted merchandise.

Besides choosing their best sellers, which are often name brands with cooperative advertising plans, buyers of fashion goods also advertise fashion trends. Buyers look to fashion reports from their resident buying offices and fashion magazines to find out about upcoming best sellers. (See Figure 13-9.) Then buyers estimate the potential of each fashion item in their local area. If the potential seems strong, a fashion ad may be requested. However, a fashion report that lists the best-selling items for a season based on sales in New York cannot be used to predict accurately the best-selling items in Tennessee.

Usually, discount apparel and accessory stores do not stress fashion. Their ads feature big sellers at low prices.

Sale Price Ads Buyers are responsible for choosing appropriate merchandise for sale ads. Sale ads promote merchandise that is marked down. End of season merchandise that is reduced in price and available in broken assortments often appears in apparel and accessory sale advertisements.

Experience 13-9

Choosing Appropriate Merchandise for Ads

The decision of which merchandise items to feature in advertisements is not easy. In this experience, you will help a buyer decide what merchandise to feature in a May advertisement.

Elizabeth's store has a fashion quality image that it wants to project in all its ads. Elizabeth's best seller is a 100 percent worsted wool pantsuit. It is a very heavy material and looks soft and fuzzy. Sales of this pantsuit peak in October–November.

Elizabeth features two name-brand lines of sportswear. Both lines are good sellers. One of the manufacturers offers cooperative advertising dollars equal to 4 percent of the total purchase. (This amounts to approximately $7,200 in extra ad dollars per year.)

Elizabeth is considering featuring the new fashion look of scoop-neck shells and matching overblouses. Also in the department are some Easter promotion leftovers. The goods are poor sellers and have been marked to one half of the original retail price. With so many items to choose from, Elizabeth doesn't know what to advertise. What advice could you give her? Give reasons to support your decisions. Write your advice and reasons on a separate sheet of paper.

PREPARE ADVERTISING REQUESTS

Two or 3 weeks before an ad is scheduled for the paper (longer for radio and television ads), the buyer completes an advertising request. (See Figure 13-10.) The request identifies the item, its brand name, and the central theme of the ad. The form asks for information about the merchandise, such as sizes, colors, fabric, and price. The store's advertising agency, advertising department, or the newspaper's advertising department uses the information on the advertising request to prepare the ad.

Before a buyer can complete this form, he or she has to verify the price, available sizes, colors, and styles of the goods. If the goods have not yet been received, the buyer is responsible for checking on the delivery date. If the supply of goods on hand is not sufficient to handle the customer demand, the buyer must reorder the goods. Although a buyer is never sure of the exact quantity of merchandise needed for an ad, it is a waste of advertising dollars to run an ad when there is not enough merchandise to handle customer demand. Apparel and accessory stores also advertise by radio spot, TV commercial, or direct mail. Buyers work with the store's advertising department or advertising agency to create the ad desired. Usually, buyers complete a form similar to the one shown in Figure 13-10. Copywriters, who are not as familiar with the merchandise, use this information to create interesting, persuasive ads.

Advertising request forms are planning tools. They help buyers decide what merchandise will be advertised, when it will be advertised, and the advertising media that will best meet the store's ad goals.

CHECK ADVERTISING PROOFS

Advertising **proofs** are copies of ads before they run in the newspaper or magazine. Proofs must be checked carefully so that inaccuracies are found and changed before the ads run. In large chain stores, in which one buyer purchases merchandise for all the stores, department managers check advertising proofs. In smaller stores, the buyers or their assistants check the proofs. Check proofs for the following elements:

Quantity. The quantity of merchandise on hand must be sufficient. If merchandise reorders have been written, buyers must check the receiving and marking department to be sure the goods are ready for sale. If the ad is for sale merchandise and only limited quantities are available, the ad should say so. (See Figure 13-6.)

Price. Is the price correct? Smart buyers check the price ticket rather than rely on their memory.

Headline and body copy. Has the ad copywriter omitted any important facts? Does the copy have a message that can be believed by the customer?

Size and color assortment. Do the sizes and colors listed reflect the stock on hand? Should another style or color, which was not in the store when the advertising request was made, be included in the ad?

Courtesy ZCMI, Salt Lake City, UT

ZCMI NEWSPAPER ADVERTISING INFORMATION

DEPT. Women's Sportswear DEPT. NO. 15 BUYER Margaret Clawson

	Day of Week	Date	Space
DESERET NEWS			
TRIBUNE	Sunday	Nov. 21	half page
STANDARD EXAMINER	Sunday	Nov. 21	half page
PROVO HERALD	Sunday	Nov. 21	half page
LOGAN HERALD JOURNAL			

IMPORTANT This form must be in the advertising office 18 days before running date (add one extra day for holidays) Color ads and double trucks 21 days before running date

IF REPEAT ATTACH TEARSHEET

INCLUDED WITH AD COPY (check): MDSE. XX GLOSSIES ☐ SLIX OR MATS ☐

IF OLD ART TO BE USED GIVE DATE OLD AD RAN —

MAIL ORDER COUPON YES ☐ NO ☒

CO-OP ☒Yes ☐No ☐Yes, BUYER YOU MUST: (1) INCLUDE ALL CO-OP REQUIREMENTS (2) ATTACH CO-OP FORM #280

ITEM: What is the item(s)? (1) bolero, shirt, pants; (2) tunic, pants

BRAND NAME(S): Lively Look

IS THIS: (Check one) Regular Promotion X Sale ______

WHAT'S THE BIG IDEA? (What is the one thing you want the reader to remember about this product or products.) The fashion look of plaid: red, white & black. The lively look to get you through the winter.

COPY INFORMATION Please include sizes, colors, fabrics (other vital information to meet FTC regs.), patterns. List unique selling points and how these are translated into customer benefits. List how to use the product to best advantage, or how to take care of it.

	SPECIFY "REG." "LIST" "IF PERFECT"	SELLING PRICE
100% polyester - This Makes Them Practical		
Plaid bolero - sizes 8-18; red, white & black plaid		$22.00
Shirt - long sleeve; sizes 8-18; red		$21.00
Pants - pull-on; sizes 8-18; red, white & black		
plaid or red or black		$24.00
Tunic - multi-stripe; V-neck; 100% acrylic		$24.00

For promotional (box type ads) multiple items use additional sheets. Allow one space between items.

Fig. 13-10 This is an example of an advertising request. It should give all the information needed to prepare a desired ad.

Illustration. Is the picture of the merchandise realistic? Does the person pictured in the ad resemble a typical user of the product?

Logotype. Are the store name and logotype (and store location, if needed) included in the ad?

Besides checking ads for accuracy, buyers or some assistants should evaluate their selling power also. As a buyer, ask yourself if your ads persuade customers to visit your store and personally investigate the merchandise featured.

Experience 13-10

Proofing Ads

Assume you are the buyer for the shoe department. You are having a boot sale. Children's boots, sizes 8–3, are $12.99 and sizes 4–6 are $15.99. Women's boots are selling for $49 and men's boots are $52. Proof the ad shown below. Write in the corrections, if any, that should be made.

Courtesy Cooper's Western Wear, Albuquerque, NM

go back-to-school in boots from Cooper's

This is the look that's making news. And Cooper's is the place to get it! Cooper's boots are priced to give you exceptional value. And you can always be sure of a proper fit. Shown, 3 styles in russet driftwood leather. More to see when you come in!

Children's 8-3 **13.99**
3-6 **15.99**

Ladies' **49.00**

Men's **52.00**

The Best of the West

COOPERS

Western & Casual Wear

PROOF

FASHION PLACE — MURRAY — 262-6771

BankAmericard — Master Charge — American Express

Mc Goo's MEMO

DATE: July 6, 198_

TO: Merchandise Managers, Buyers, Assistant Buyers

FROM: John Parkin, Promotion Director

SUBJECT: Window Schedule and Ad Responsibility for Sunday Paper

Window Schedule - Theme	Ad Responsibility
July 29 Children's BTS - "Getting on the Bus"	Fashion Ad, runs Sunday 8/1 Dept. 34 - children's shoes 18 - boys' wear 4 - girls' wear
Aug 5 Children's BTS - "In the Classroom"	Volume Ad, runs Sunday 8/8 Dept. 47 - boys' budget 56 - girls' budget
Aug 12 Young Women's - "Campus Scene"	Fashion Ad, runs Sunday 8/15 Dept. 26 - junior dresses 33 - junior sportswear 22 - handbags 21 - jewelry
Aug 19 Young Women's - "Can You Top This?" (Outerwear)	Fashion Ad, runs Sunday 8/22 Dept. 29 - junior coats 33 - junior sportswear
Aug 26 Young Men's - "Can You Top This?" (Outerwear)	Fashion Ad, runs Sunday 8/29 Dept. 45 - men's coats 11 - prep sportswear

Fig. 13-11 Well-done window displays carry the same theme as store ads to reinforce customer interest. Here's an example of a bulletin sent buyers to alert them to the themes planned for some upcoming window displays. Buyers use such bulletins to coordinate their ads with themes in the window displays.

COORDINATE ADS WITH THE DISPLAY DEPARTMENT AND SALES FORCE

Advertising is a powerful tool that can arouse customer interest and draw people into the store. The effectiveness of the best advertisements, however, is strengthened when the ads are coordinated with merchandise displays and well-trained salespeople.

Coordination with Display Department Well-done window displays that carry the same theme as the newspaper, radio, or television ads reinforce customer interest. Apparel and accessory stores of all sizes try to coordinate their ads with their displays to project a unified image to the public.

In large- and medium-sized stores, usually the buyers, advertising department, display department, sales promotion department, and merchandise managers work out promotion themes. The sales promotion department usually sends buyers a bulletin that lists the window schedule. This bulletin helps buyers choose merchandise for ads that is appropriate for the window displays.

For example, the bulletin in Figure 13-11 shows that children's back-to-school windows are planned for the weeks of July 29 and August 5. There will be a fashion ad in the Sunday paper featuring merchandise from departments 34, 18, and 4. The next Sunday there will be a volume ad that shows a variety of merchandise items from Budget Departments 47 and 56. Buyers, who are responsible for turning in advertising requests 3 weeks before the ad runs, need this coordination to know what merchandise to feature.

Advertising is also strengthened by good interior displays and signs. Customers may be enticed into the store by excellent ads. Their interest for the merchandise may increase when they pass the window displays in the front of the store. If, once they are in the department, they cannot find the advertised and displayed goods, their interest may be lost. They may turn their attention to merchandise that is attractively displayed in the department across the aisle. Therefore, merchandise promoted in ads and window displays should be prominently displayed in the department.

Experience 13-11

Coordinating Advertising and Display

Look through the Sunday section of your paper. Choose two apparel or accessory stores featuring ads in the paper. Visit both stores to evaluate the coordination between advertising and display. Answer the following on a separate sheet. (You may want to complete the comments for Store 1 before going to Store 2.)

1. Write the theme or main message of each ad.

   Store 1

   Store 2

2. Visit each store. Examine the window displays, if any. Write the message the window displays are telling you.

   Store 1

   Store 2

3. Visit the department where the advertised merchandise is located. Find any interior display. Record the theme of the displays.

   Store 1

   Store 2

4. In your opinion, how well were the ads and displays coordinated? What suggestions could you make about their coordination?

   Store 1

   Store 2

Coordination with the Sales Force Many sales are lost because the buyer or department manager failed to tell the salespeople about advertised merchandise. Some buyers hold regular meetings to discuss merchandise that will be featured in ads. They discuss questions that the salespeople may be asked and possible answers to those questions. Often, buyers role play with their salespeople a sales presentation for the advertised goods, covering price, brand name, and available sizes, colors, and styles.

Before giving these training classes, buyers must research the merchandise information themselves. This process makes the buyers or managers more aware of the merchandise featured and better able to help the customers.

EVALUATE ADVERTISING EFFECTIVENESS

Effective ads bring customers into the store and increase sales. Because advertising costs so much money, buyers want to request only those ads that will be effective. They want the ads to cover at least the cost of the ad, which includes the salary of the people who prepare the ad, the materials used to produce the ad, and the media space or time. They also want the ads to bring the store a profit.

Because the effectiveness of an ad cannot be determined until after the ad runs, buyers refer to old ads to see what's worked in the past. To keep track of past advertising results, most stores use an advertising report or advertising evaluation sheet. The person responsible for completing the report records which items were advertised. Also recorded is the merchandise on hand before the ad ran and the quantity of merchandise sold 3 days after the ad. The advertising report also records comments about the ad. A typical comment may be, "The weather was terrible. We had 3 days of constant snow and rain."

Advertising reports, as well as a file of competitor ads, help buyers plan future ads. By skillfully examining the facts, buyers can change advertising appeals and eventually come up with the appeal that works best.

Experience 13-12

Evaluating Advertising Effectiveness

Evaluate the following advertising report. Would you run the ad again? Explain your decision on a separate sheet of paper.

ADVERTISING REPORT

- Fill out a form each week you have advertising and send it in with your audit & recap.
- On sale ads, it isn't necessary to list the items, just indicate general response.
- Under COMMENTS, include any suggestions you have and mention any conditions that might have affected response (weather, competition, etc.).

STORE # 14 FOR WEEK OF August 17

ADVERTISED ITEMS	MDSE. ON HAND	MDSE. SOLD
gym suits ($7.95)	42	12

MEDIA: NEWSPAPER (attach tear sheet) x RADIO ____ TELEVISION ____ OTHER ____

SALES FOR WEEK $1082.75 PLANNED SALES $1325

COMMENTS: Weather conditions: Clear

This ad involved extra art work, cost $70. The ad space cost $125. Past sales record for gym suits has been very poor.

14 Sales Promotion: Display

Think about the clothing stores where you shop. Each has its own special atmosphere. One reason for this is visual merchandising. **Visual merchandising** includes all parts of the store that the customers see: the design and style of the store's architecture, window displays, interior displays, display fixtures, cash registers, floor coverings, and department layouts. An apparel and accessory store combines these visual merchandising elements in a variety of ways to produce a unique store image.

One of the most important factors in visual merchandising is display. Displays play a major part in developing a store's image. For example, if a store sells fashion apparel and accessories, its displays try to create a fashion image. The window and interior displays include only a few items and the displays are uncluttered. Price is not stressed.

On the other hand, displays in discount stores are different. They include a great many items. Discount stores sell as much merchandise as they can for the lowest prices possible. Thus, their displays stress price.

The duties of employees in different size apparel and accessory stores vary. Many chain-operated specialty apparel stoes and large department stores have separate display departments. Employees in the Display Department design and build the window and interior displays. Some examples of stores with their own display departments are J. C. Penney, Bloomingdale's, Sears, and Jordan Marsh. In small, independently owned and operated stores, salespersons often prepare the store displays.

SELF-SELECTION DISPLAYS

Suppose you are employed as a salesperson at Rosco's, an independent fashion apparel and accessory store. The store is planning some new displays. Part of your job is to help with these displays, and Terry Simpson, your department manager, is giving you some display tips.

Terry asks, "Do you know what self-selection displays are?" You tell her that they are the shelves, tables, counters, and racks inside the store that hold merchandise that the customers can physically examine. "That's right," Terry says. She goes on to explain that these displays allow customers to inspect and choose merchandise without the salesperson's help. "In the Boys' Department, where you will be working, all the bins, racks, and shelf fixtures are self-selection displays. In other departments, though, such as the Jewelry Department, there are both self-selection displays and displays that are out of the customers' reach."

Terry explains one of the most important functions of self-selection displays. When self-selection displays are orderly and have clearly written signs, customers who know what they want can easily find the merchandise. In fact, one of the major benefits of self-selection displays is that salespeople can devote their time to customers who need help choosing merchandise.

BUILDING SELF-SELECTION DISPLAYS

"To build a self-selection display," Terry says, "be sure it tells a story. Also, make your displays visually attractive. They should have a good balance and be color coordinated."

You remember hearing that displays should tell a story, but you tell Terry that you never understood what that meant. Terry explains, "When you look at a display, don't you get a feeling about the merchandise? Doesn't the display say something to you? For example, if you walk into a department and everywhere you see black and variations of black—black shirts, black sweaters, and so on—the display is telling you that black is in fashion. To get a better idea of what I mean, let's take a short tour of the store."

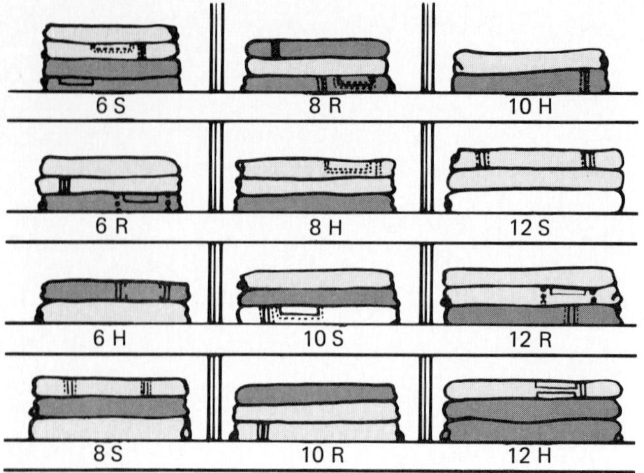

Fig. 14-1 In vertical stock arrangements, the sizes move from top to bottom and from left to right.

Shelf, Bin, and Table Arrangements As you walk through the Boys' Department, Terry explains that most stores use vertical stock arrangements when displaying merchandise in shelves or bins. This means that the merchandise is stocked so that the sizes progress from top to bottom and from left to right. (See Figure 14-1.)

At Rosco's, the boys' casual slacks are stocked in bins. Similar items are grouped by size. In each bin, the slacks are also grouped by color. Most stores have their own color arrangements. At Rosco's, the pants are stocked from top to bottom by black, brown, gray, blue, green, and yellow and then plaid, stripes, and checks. This size and color arrangement lets both customers and salespeople see the total selection of merchandise at a glance.

Walking through the Men's Department, you see that some merchandise is on tables. You ask Terry why they aren't in bins. Terry tells you that sale merchandise is usually arranged on tables. In table arrangements, the merchandise is folded neatly and stacked according to size. But table merchandise gets messy very quickly, so it will have to be refolded and resized many times a day. Shirts and sweaters are folded so that the front is facing up and the sleeves are tucked inside. Pants are folded first by the seams and then just above the knee.

Counter Arrangements Terry points to a wallet display on a counter. "Accessory items, because of their size, are popular counter display items," she says. "Inexpensive costume jewelry, leather goods, handkerchiefs, scarves, and hats are often displayed on small display fixtures on top of counters." She tells you that merchandise boxes are often used to make counter display arrangements. You notice a display of boxed wallets that looks like stairsteps.

Terry mentions **related items**, those merchandise items that naturally go together. You learn that related

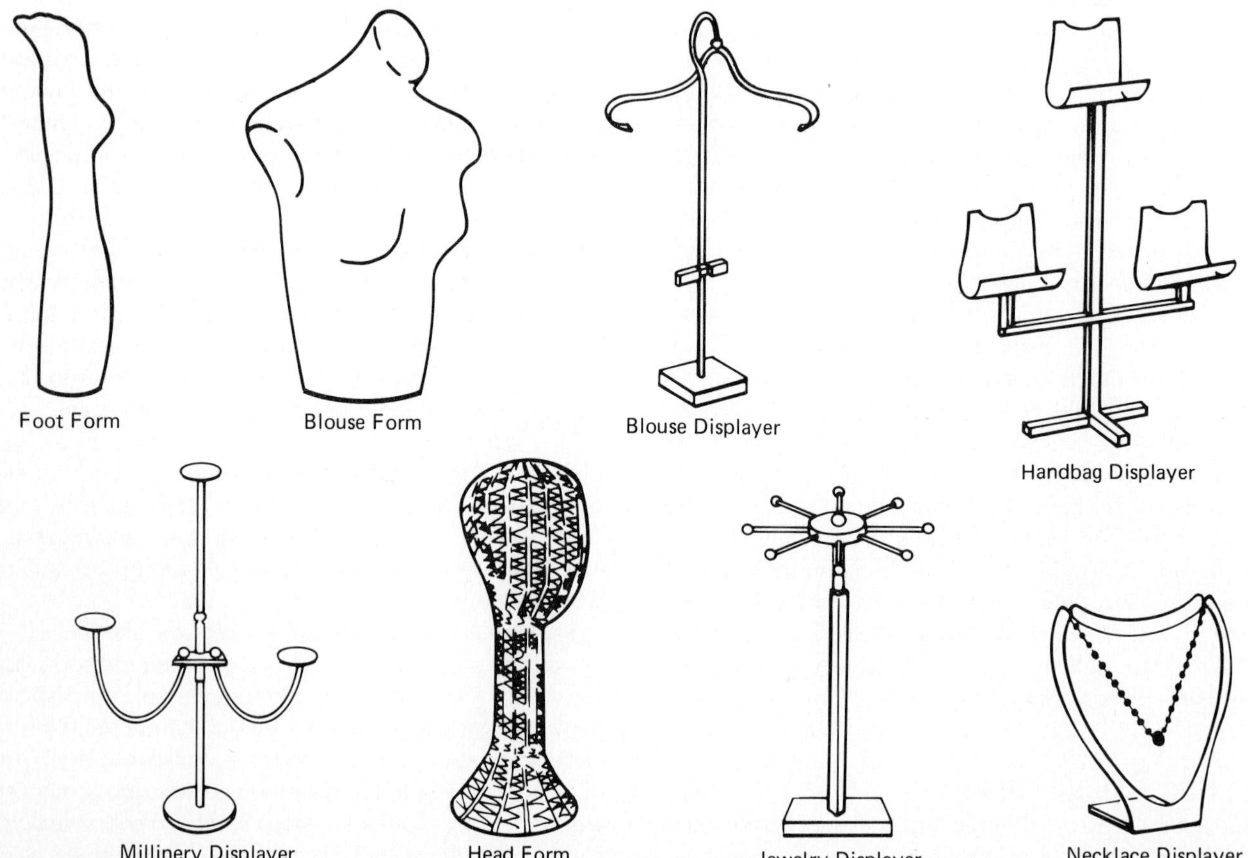

Fig. 14-2 This illustration shows the wide variety of display props available for counter displays.

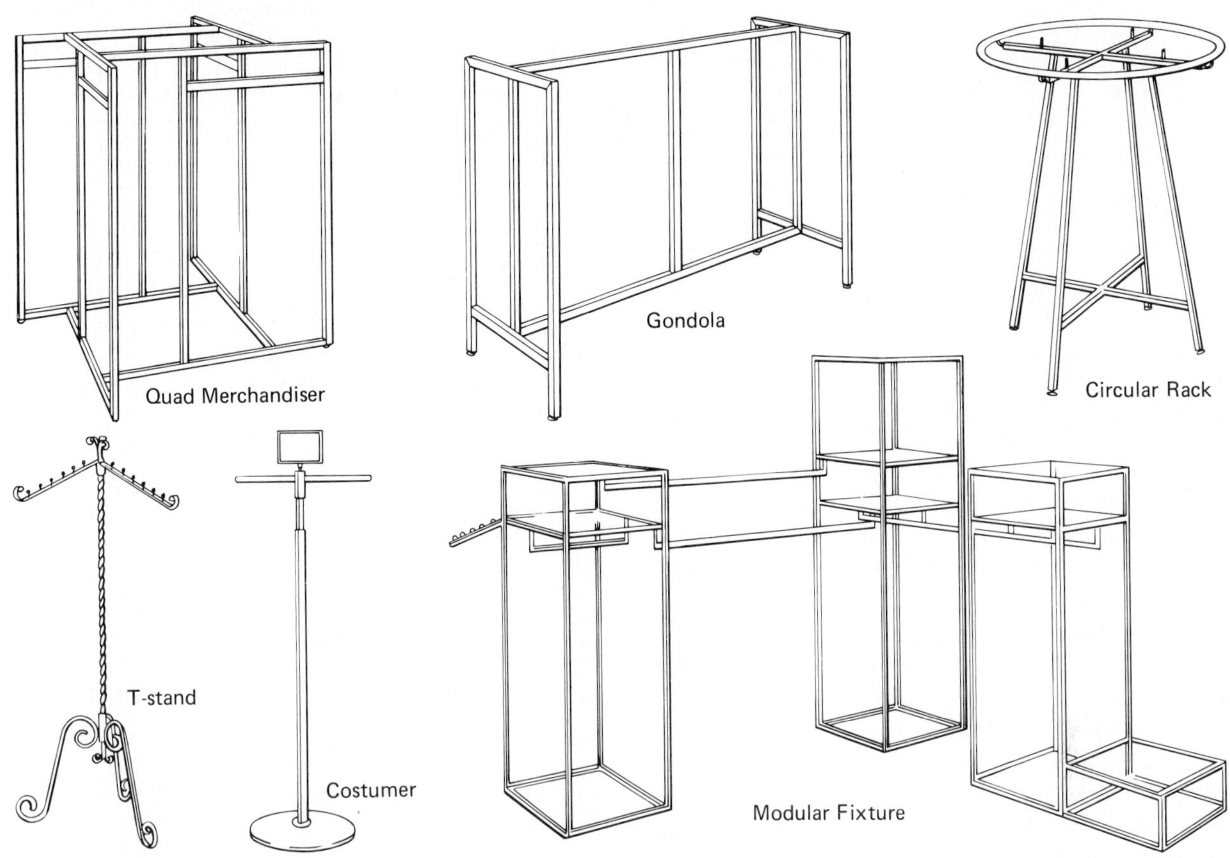

Fig. 14-3 Display fixtures, such as those shown above, can be arranged in a variety of ways to give a new look to stores or departments.

accessory items are often combined into one counter display. For example, in the Women's Accessory Department, you see a display that includes a purse, scarf, sunglasses, and umbrella. Terry points out that the combination adds more selling power to the display. In fact, someone looking only for a purse may be so impressed with the scarf in the display that he or she buys both the purse and the scarf.

Looking at the counter displays, you notice that Rosco's uses props to make attractive displays. Hand forms display gloves, foot forms show socks, and head forms hold hats and scarves. Some scarves are also hanging from scarf racks and jewelry from jewelry posts. (See Figure 14-2.)

Rack Arrangements Walking over to some racks, Terry says, "Our self-selection displays include a variety of merchandise racks. We use wall fixtures, floor circular racks, T-stands, tri-racks, and tubular fixtures to hang pants, blouses, coats, and jackets. Most of these fixtures can be moved to give the departments a new look." (See Figure 14-3.)

Racks are well suited for displaying certain types of items. For example, folded or prepackaged merchandise that is not selling well is often hung on racks to help customers better see what the merchandise looks like. Men's and women's pants look best when displayed on racks. Shirts, blouses, and sweaters with a unique or different design also make attractive rack merchandise.

You ask Terry about the best way to group merchandise on racks. She tells you to think about the most important feature of an item and then try to build a story around that feature. "For example," she says, "look at this tapestry yoke shirt. What do you think would make a customer buy that shirt? Is it the brand, style, color, size, or price?"

You note that the design is different, "I've never seen a tapestry yoke shirt before." Terry agrees and says that this design feature should be emphasized in the display. If it were put on a wall rack with other shirts, it wouldn't get much customer attention. By being put on top of a rack of shirts, the shirt will attract more attention.

Terry adds that the arrangement of a display is also important. At your store, merchandise is grouped by size—S, M, L, and XL (small, medium, large, and extra large) and then by color within each size. "This arrangement lets the salesperson see immediately if a shirt is available in a particular size and color," Terry says. "Some stores arrange items by color and then size."

Some bright ponchos catch your attention in the next department. "T-stands are often used to feature new arrivals or hot fashion items, such as these ponchos," Terry explains.

Walking through the store, you have noticed that racks are used to display many kinds of merchandise. In the Sportswear Department, you comment on this. Terry explains that sportswear can be purchased either separately or in a combination by style or coordinated colors. She points to a rack with a group of coordinates consisting of blue solid and checked pants, vests, jackets, and shirts.

Color Arrangements Coordinated groups are easy to display because the manufacturer has already color coordinated the various items. Terry says that after a few weeks the rack "sells down," and the department may be left with many pairs of pants and no jackets or shirts. Part of your job will be to color coordinate the remaining merchandise with other apparel items in stock and build new rack displays.

I've always had a hard time with color," you tell her. "It seems like such a personal thing. All customers have individual color preferences."

"You're right," Terry says. "Color is personal. And, of course, if the colors clash or are displeasing, the display will have no impact or a negative impact on sales. Don't worry though. People who haven't made many displays are often unsure about matching colors."

Terry goes on to explain that a **monochromatic color scheme**, which is a combination of various shades and tints of only one color, is the easiest color group to coordinate. As an example of a monochromatic color scheme, she points to a group that includes navy pants and vest and a powder blue shirt.

"As people gain more experience in working with color," Terry continues, "they go on to combine colors that are next to each other or opposite each other on the color wheel."

"Color wheel?" you ask.

Terry tells you that a **color wheel** shows the relationships between colors. (See Figure 14-4.) It contains all the colors in the solar spectrum. The **primary colors**—blue, red, and yellow—are the colors from which all other colors are derived. **Secondary colors** are made by mixing two primary colors, for example, red and yellow make orange. **Tertiary colors** are obtained by combining those secondary and primary colors that are next to each other on the color wheel. The tertiary colors are blue-violet, blue-green, yellow-green, yellow-orange, red-orange, and red-violet.

Besides monochromatic color schemes, there are also analogous color schemes and complementary color schemes. An **analogous color scheme** is a combination of colors that are next to each other on the color wheel, such as red, red-orange, and orange. A **complementary color scheme** is a combination of colors that are opposite each other on the color wheel, such as purple and yellow.

SIGNS

"Terry," you ask, "who is responsible for all the signs?" Terry tells you that the department manager or buyer prepares the sign requests for counter or rack display signs. Part of your job will be putting the signs in the sign holders and placing them on or in the displays.

You wonder aloud if signs are really that important. Terry says that signs are a very important part of a display. They help customers locate the merchandise they want and they attract attention. Terry points out the following guidelines for adding signs to displays:

- Check the signs to be sure they are correct. If the printing department misspelled a word, don't alter the sign by writing on it. Have your supervisor requisition a new sign.
- Check the signs to be sure they are neat, clean, clear, and unmarked.
- Put the sign in a holder that fits—not one that is too big or too small. Never use tape or staples to fasten the sign to the merchandise rack or shelf.
- Do not have blank sign holders facing customers. Unless customers cannot see the blank side, there should be a sign on both sides of the holder.
- Remove any blank sign holders from displays. Store them where they will not be damaged.

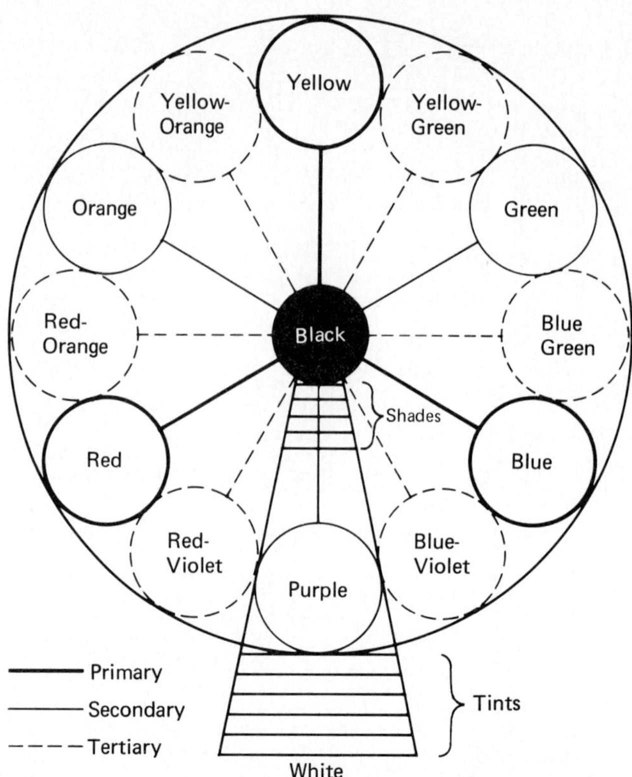

Fig. 14-4 Color relationships are illustrated in this color wheel.

During a coffee break, Terry says she realizes you may feel a little overwhelmed. She talks to you about display principles used in self-selection displays. You will learn to use color to attract customer attention. You will also learn the various display arrangements.

Terry explains that some of the most interesting and attention-getting displays can't be classified by type. Some creative displays cannot be found in books. When you are preparing displays, don't be too concerned with formal or informal balance and so on. Instead, evaluate your display to see if it attracts attention, looks attractive, tells a story, and holds customer interest.

Experience 14-1

Build a Shelf Display

In this experience, you will build a shelf display for pants. Read all the directions before you begin.

1. Collect 10 to 12 fairly large boxes. The boxes will be the shelves of the display where you will stock your merchandise selection.
2. Collect as many pairs of men's, women's, or children's pants as you can. (Try to find 10 to 15 pairs. They don't have to be new.)
3. Check the time and write down when you begin to build the display.
   Time you begin:______
4. Properly fold the pants and sort them into size groups.
5. Arrange the boxes in a vertical stock arrangement. According to the sizes you have sorted the pants into, prepare a size marker for each box and attach the markers to the boxes. Be sure you assign a box and prepare a size marker for those sizes in the size range that are missing. For example, if you have pants in sizes 6, 10, 14, and 18, prepare boxes with size markers for sizes 6, 8, 10, 12, 14, 16, and 18.
6. Choose a color arrangement for the pants within each size. Stack the pants, according to size and color, in the appropriate boxes.
7. When you are satisfied that your self-selection shelf display is neat and properly sorted, record the time. Subtract your beginning time from your ending time to determine how long it took you to build the shelf display.

   Time you finish:______
   Number of minutes to build this display:______

Experience 14-2

Sketch Related Merchandise Counter Displays

1. Visit a men's or women's apparel and accessory store or department. On a separate sheet of paper, list the accessory items that would be appropriate for a counter display. Using the accessory items you found in the store, make four sketches of related merchandise counter displays on a separate sheet of paper. Be sure each sketch includes at least three different items.
2. Using colored pencils or crayons, color your sketches. Give one sketch a monochromatic color theme, another sketch an analogous color theme, and another a complementary color theme. Use your creativity to color coordinate the fourth sketch.

   After coloring the sketches, examine each sketch as though it were a counter display. Decide which display has the most exciting colors and label it. Label the sketch that attracts the most attention.
3. Collect the items needed and build one of the counter displays you sketched. (The items in your display do not have to be new.) Determine the minimum amount of space needed to build the display on a table or counter top.
4. On a separate sheet of paper, answer the following questions:
   a. What story does your display tell?
   b. How does your display attract attention?

Experience 14-3

Check the Sign

As an apparel salesperson, you will be responsible for attaching signs to the displays. Suppose you work in the Girls' Department. You are starting your Christmas promotion and have received a large quantity of new stock. This morning you helped your department manager put the merchandise on racks.

1. You have just received the following signs. Identify any signs that you think should be redone.
   a. Should this sign be redone? If so, why?

A

For the little Girl in Your Life

DENEM JEANS
- **Western cut**
- **permanent press**

$5.98

______

B

> **Perfect for Schol**
>
> **CARDIGAN SWEATERS**
> - **V-neckd**
> - **100% acrylice**
>
> **$5.98**

b. Should this sign be redone? If so, why?

____

____

2. While you were at lunch, another salesperson attached some improper signs to the merchandise. How would you change the sign opposite?

____

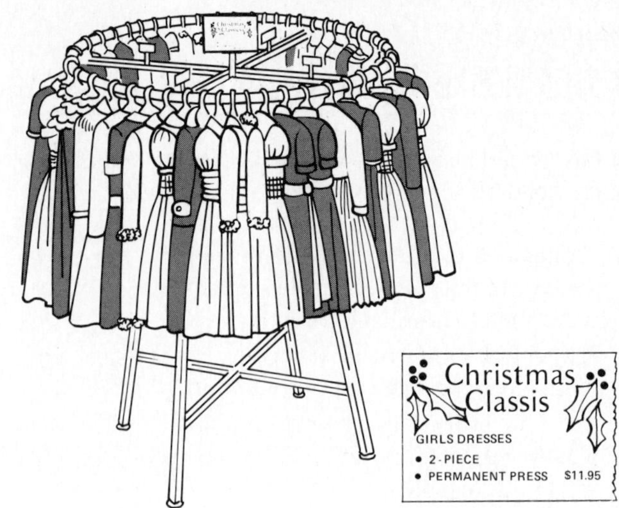

CARING FOR SELF-SELECTION DISPLAYS

Walking back to the Boys' Department, Terry says, "One of your main responsibilities is to keep the self-selection displays neat and orderly. Regroup the stock according to size and color and make sure the merchandise is properly folded or hung on hangers." She also notes that before closing, you will need to go through each rack and adjust the hangers so that all the items hang straight and are an even distance apart. Terry expects you to dust the counter tops, fixtures, and merchandise also.

"It will be your job to replenish the stock when it gets low," she says. Under the counters are drawers that contain merchandise used to refill the self-selection displays. This merchandise is called **understock**. When there is not enough merchandise in understock, more merchandise is gotten from the stockroom. This merchandise is called **reserve stock**.

"When you refill the shelves or counters, be sure to use the oldest merchandise," Terry says, picking up a price ticket. She explains the date code on the ticket (See Figure 14-5.) At Rosco's, August is coded 1, September 2, October 3, and so on. A second digit stands for the year. For example, if an item was received in December 1980, it would have the date code of 50. If it were received in July 1981, its date code would be 121. "It is really important to watch the date code when you restock," Terry says. "If you don't, the store may have 3-year-old stock sitting under the counter gathering dust and losing value."

ROSCO'S	
Dept. 6	Class 8
Date 50	Size 6B
Price $12.95	

Fig. 14-5 Follow Terry's explanation of date coding as you look at the price ticket shown above.

Experience 14-4

First in, First out

As a salesperson at Ric's, you need to restock the men's pajama shelves, sizes M and XL, on the sales floor. In the stockroom you have three shipments of men's pajamas. Examine the price tickets opposite and decide which shipments you should use. Your marking department uses the date code A for January, B for February, C for March, and so on. The second digit of the code represents the year.

Shipment to use first ______________________________

	A	B	C
Store	Ric'S	Ric'S	Ric'S
Dept.	10	10	10
Class	42	42	42
Date	L1	J2	K1
Size	M	M	M
Price	$9.99	$9.99	$9.99

Experience 14-5

Straighten, Straighten, Straighten

An apparel and accessory salesperson must recognize when self-selection displays need to be straightened. Examine the self-selection displays shown below. On a separate sheet of paper, list what you would have to do to make these two displays have a neat and orderly look.

DISPLAY PLANNING

Mrs. Logan is the manager of Junior World, a specialty shop for junior-sized women. This week she has run an advertisement for jumpsuits at 20-percent off the regular price. To prepare for the sale, Mrs. Logan decided to feature various store displays. She also scheduled a staff meeting to inform the salespeople about the jumpsuit promotion.

Mrs. Logan realizes that advertising, display, and personal selling all work together to produce sales. Advertising is the force that gets the customers into the store. Displays catch customers' attention inside the store or department. And the sales force encourages customers to make buying decisions.

Mrs. Logan knows that displays promote and establish a store's image. Some displays also introduce new styles and educate the public. For example, when some customers were unsure how to coordinate shawls with their wardrobe, Mrs. Logan featured a shawl display. This display helped customers see how shawls create a new fashion look.

Whenever Mrs. Logan builds a display, she plans what she is going to do before she starts. She always keeps in mind four important ideas in display planning:

1. A display must reflect the image the store wants to project. Junior World appeals to young people. Therefore, Mrs. Logan's displays are daring, have some movement, and feature merchandise that appeals to young customers.
2. All displays must fit into the display budget. The owner, Mr. Harvey, prepares the display budget for Junior World. It details the amount of money that can be spent on display props, such as backdrops, lighting, and mannequins.
3. Each display must tell a story. Displays that tell stories sell merchandise. After she builds a display, Mrs. Logan always checks to see what it says. She knows that if the message is not clear to her, it won't be clear to customers.
4. Displays should show how merchandise is used and looks when worn. For example, Mrs. Logan rarely lets a scarf hang on a display. She ties it in some interesting way. Mrs. Logan displays some of her merchandise on mannequins to give customers a better idea of how the merchandise drapes. Wall displays help customers see the fullness of each garment.

SELECTING APPROPRIATE MERCHANDISE FOR DISPLAYS

Mrs. Logan gives salespeople a chance to plan and build displays. The salespeople like to prepare displays because it is a change from their regular job of selling and stock work. It also gives them an opportunity to express their creativity.

Suppose you have worked with Mrs. Logan for about 6 months, and she has decided to let you prepare your first major display. "Mrs. Logan," you say. "I appreciate the chance to make a display. I'm a bit scared, though. I'm not quite sure where to begin."

Mrs. Logan smiles. "Everybody has that problem. Let's start at the beginning. First of all, no matter what type of display you're building, you need to choose appropriate display merchandise."

"What's that?" you ask.

Mrs. Logan explains that the store's buyer purchases a variety of seasonal merchandise—timely merchandise that corresponds to the seasons of the year. Because you want people to think of the store as a fashion leader, the staff promotes these new fashions as soon as they are received. For example, in April, the first shipments of swimsuits and summer dresses are received. At that time of year, these new merchandise items are displayed.

"The next step," Mrs. Logan tells you, "is to try to coordinate the displays with ads." Every large department store sends each department a schedule of upcoming ads so there can be close coordination between advertising and display. At a small store, the owner, who may also be the buyer, prepares an ad schedule based on the goods purchased. When building a display, you should always check the ad schedule so that you can build displays that feature the same items that are being advertised.

You ask Mrs. Logan about times when the store doesn't run ads. Mrs. Logan tells you that ads are expensive and the store cannot afford to run them every week. But coordination between displays and other advertising is still possible. For instance, such magazines as *Seventeen, Vogue, Gentlemen's Quarterly,* and *Men's Wear* feature ads of the latest fashions. Customers who read these ads will remember them and the merchandise when they enter stores and see the displays. Adding a sign, such as "As seen in *Seventeen,*" to the merchandise display will help jog the customers' memory.

You start thinking about the display you are going to build. "Yesterday I checked in a shipment of different styles of sweaters—cowl-necked, bulky cardigans, tabards, and pullovers. These sweaters were featured in almost every fashion magazine this month. And Mr. Harvey has a quarter-page newspaper ad running on Sunday that features the sweaters. It seems as though everything points to a sweater display."

Mrs. Logan compliments you on your decision. She then asks what your display theme, or display story, is. You wonder aloud if sweaters are your theme.

Mrs. Logan replies, "Yes and no. Certainly the featured merchandise is the main element in your display theme, or story. But color is also important. What colors will you show?"

"Most of the sweaters," you tell her, "are rust, beige, or gray—the three big colors this season. What I choose depends on the other clothing and accessory items I put with the sweaters. Right?"

"Yes," Mrs. Logan answers. "You want your sweater display to tell a total fashion story. Include the sweaters along with pants and skirts. Your accessory items could include belts, scarves, and jewelry. You will want all your colors to be coordinated."

You say excitedly, "When I was checking in the merchandise, I put together the sharpest outfit. I saw a cowl-necked rust sweater, black tabard trimmed in rust, and rust pants. There is a gold necklace in the jewelry display case that would set off the sweater perfectly!"

"You have just chosen some appropriate related items," Mrs. Logan tells you.

As you are talking about your merchandise colors, Mrs. Logan reminds you to consider the color of the display background. Dark or bright-colored sweaters look best on a light-colored background. Light or neutral colors look best on a dark-colored background. Because you are going to be working with a pale green background, your choice of black and rust items will make an attractive, appropriate display.

Experience 14-6

Display and Advertising: Do They Tell the Same Story?

Suppose you work in a small clothing store that does not advertise often. When you prepare in-store displays, you usually refer to fashion magazines for ideas of what merchandise styles and colors are currently fashionable.

1. Look through current copies of two fashion magazines. On a separate sheet of paper, prepare a list of clothing items that are being featured as "most fashionable." Also, list the colors being promoted.
2. Visit a fashionable clothing shop. (This shop should have the same types of customers, in terms of clothing preference, as the magazines you examined.) Look through the shop's merchandise and locate clothing items that reflect the same fashion looks as seen in the magazines. On a separate sheet of paper, record the merchandise type (dresses, sweaters, pants, and so on), brand name, and color.
3. Examine both lists to be sure the merchandise type and color are the same.
4. Why is it important for an apparel store to coordinate its advertising and display? Write your answer on a separate sheet of paper.

Experience 14-7

Plan a Related Merchandise Display

1. Assume you are dressing two female mannequins that stand together on a platform at the entrance of the store. The big fashion news this season is the feminine look, featuring soft flowing fabrics.
   a. On a separate sheet of paper, list all the apparel and accessory items that you need to dress the mannequins. Try to use as many related merchandise items as possible without making the display cluttered. Use the most popular colors and accessories.
   b. Sketch the mannequins and their clothing and accessories on the same sheet of paper. Color the sketches. (You may want to trace the forms or clothing from fashion magazines.)
2. Assume you are dressing two male mannequins that stand together on a platform at the entrance of a sporting goods store. It's the season to promote golf sportswear. Follow steps a and b for planning this display.

TYPES OF DISPLAYS

Most apparel stores feature several types of displays. For example, window displays are designed to capture the walking or driving customer's attention. These displays often influence customers to enter the store. Window displays may be designed to promote specific merchandise items or an idea. They also help in establishing a store's image.

Usually, apparel and accessory stores have many interior displays, or displays inside the store. Mannequins, wall and ledge displays, and rack-top displays are all examples of interior displays. (See Figure 14-6.) Before choosing merchandise for a display, you need to know what type of display you will be making. For example, merchandise used in a ledge display gets soiled and dirty much faster than merchandise in a glass counter display. Because stores do want to sell displayed merchandise, items that can be easily cleaned are best for a dirt-catching ledge. Vinyl coats, umbrellas, and shoes, merchandise that can be wiped clean, are examples of ledge display items.

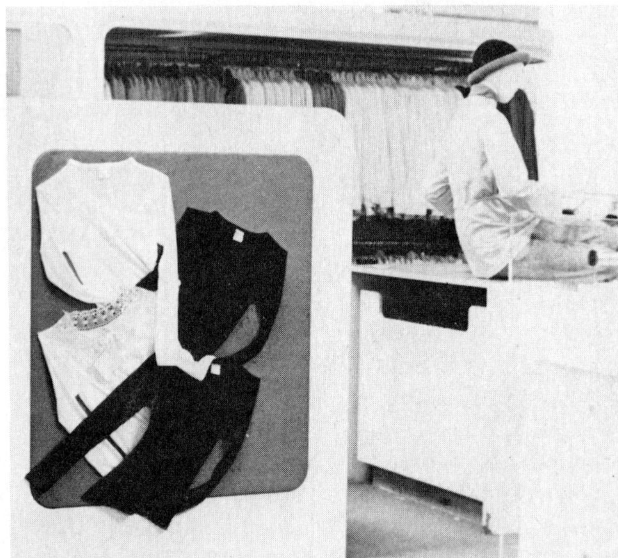

Fig. 14-6 How many types of displays can you find in the above illustration?

The weight of the merchandise also affects the appropriate display. For example, items that rip easily or are exceptionally heavy would be poor choices for a wall display. Another consideration in choosing the type of display used is prevention against shoplifting. Expensive items are often displayed in glass counters or closed, glassed-in window displays. These items are not usually displayed near department or store entrances.

Experience 14-8

Merchandise Arrangement

Visit a women's or men's clothing store or department. On a separate sheet of paper, sketch the arrangement of merchandise. Record the type of each interior display (mannequin, counter, ledge, wall), the type of merchandise being featured in each, and the price of the display merchandise, if possible. Answer the following questions about the merchandise arrangement:

1. Is the merchandise in each of the interior displays appropriate? (Example: fur coats are inappropriate for a wall display.)

____

____

____

2. Is the merchandise displayed in areas where shoplifting is difficult?

____

____

____

3. Would you suggest display merchandise be moved to areas that are more secure? If so, sketch the new arrangement on a separate sheet of paper.

PLANNING A WALL DISPLAY

Mrs. Logan asked you to prepare a wall display for your store, Junior World. The merchandise you have chosen—the slacks, cowl-necked sweater, tabard, and jewelry—are appropriate items for this type of display. You ask, "Mrs. Logan, now that I know what merchandise I'm going to use for my wall display, may I start it?"

Mrs. Logan answers, "Before building any display, window or interior, you should plan your display on paper. Planning will save you time and help you to build a more effective, pleasing display. Why don't you make a scaled-down version of how your display will look?"

You ask, "You mean draw everything in proportion?"

"Right," says Mrs. Logan.

You get pencil and paper and begin to work. The wall area you will use for your display is 7 feet high and 4 feet wide. To make your drawing in exact proportion, you decide to let 1 foot equal ½ square inch. You then make rough sketches of the sweaters and pants in the available space. You make three to four sketches before you decide which merchandise arrangement looks best. You sketch your displays so that they look natural and show the merchandise as it is used. Some displays achieve the natural look by showing the clothing on a slant and with natural bends. In your sketches, you also try to give your wall display movement. Mrs. Logan says that the feeling of movement makes displays more exciting to look at. (See Figure 14-7.)

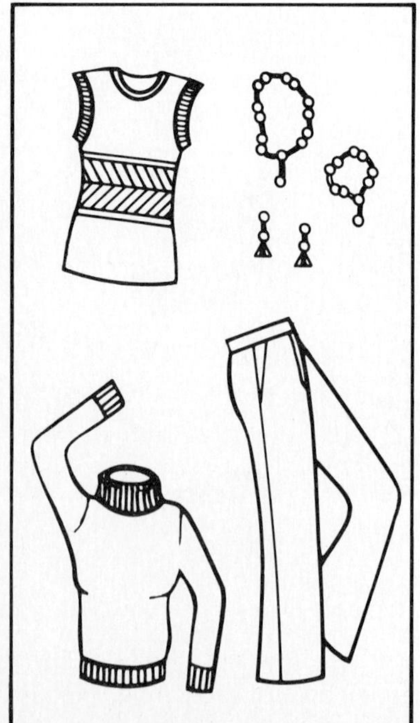

Fig. 14-7 Which one of these sketches of merchandise arrangements would you prefer to use for your wall display?

"After you have chosen a sketch, try to evaluate the balance of the display," Mrs. Logan comments.

"What is balance?" you ask.

"Balance refers to the arrangement of the items in the display," Mrs. Logan tells you. "There are two kinds of balance, formal and informal. **Formal balance** means that one half of the display is identical to the other half. You can determine if a display has formal balance by drawing an imaginary vertical line through the middle of a display. If items on both sides of the display are the same distance from the center and are in similar order and size, the display has formal balance. **Informal balance** is when the size or number of items on both sides of the display are not identical." Mrs. Logan then shows you some pictures of formal and informal balance.

She then looks at your sketch and asks, "What catches your eye when you first look at your sketch?" She explains that the item you first look at is the **dominant item** in the display. Be sure that the dominant item is the one that you want your customers to see first. Also find out where your eye goes after it sees the dominant item. Check to see if there is easy eye movement. Be sure all parts fit together; this is called harmony.

After you have selected your final sketch and have checked that it has all of the elements of good display design, you start working with your merchandise. You don't immediately start pinning up your display, however. First on a flat surface, you experiment with how you will pin the clothing to the wall. You bend the sweaters and pants in natural places, such as the elbow and knee, to see how they will look. You experiment with folding the neck of the cowl-necked sweater to show it off to its best advantage. Mrs. Logan tells you to gather the sweaters and pants in the back to give them a "thin," tapered look. This display tip makes the merchandise appear more desirable to customers.

Experience 14-9

Sketch It Out

As manager of the Menswear Department, you are responsible for the merchandise displays. Assume you are building a men's pant, shirt, and sweater display. The display area is your wall—an area 7 feet by 7 feet. On a separate sheet of paper, make four scaled-down sketches of the clothing display. Include related items. Using colored pencils or crayons, color your sketch. Choose the sketch you like most. Collect the clothing and accessories needed to build the display. On a flat surface, 7 feet by 7 feet, arrange the clothing according to the sketch. Experiment with various ways of folding the clothing.

1. In the space provided, answer the following questions about your sketches:
   a. Do your sketches look natural and show the merchandise as it is used?

      ______

   b. Do all the parts of each display sketch fit together? Explain why.

      ______

      ______

2. When you have completed the display, evaluate it:
   a. Does it attract attention?

      ______

   b. Is it as interesting as you thought it would be in your sketch? If not, how can you improve it?

      ______

      ______

      ______

PINNING A WALL DISPLAY

Excitedly, you call to Mrs. Logan, "I'm ready to pin up the display!"

"Do you have your T-pins, ladder, and masking tape?" she asks.

"I have my pins and ladder," you reply. "But why do I need masking tape?"

Mrs. Logan explains, "You have to clean the background area. Masking tape picks up any lint on the background. If you were doing a window display, you would need to vacuum the display floor. You must also press the clothing used in any display. The display merchandise must be clean and wrinkle free. I made a short checklist to help you build your first display. Here it is. Good luck." (See Figure 14-8.)

DISPLAY CHECKLIST

1. Clean the display area.
2. Press the display clothing.
3. Gather your needed equipment: ladder, pins, fishline, and so on.
4. Pin the merchandise to the wall.
   a. Using T-pins, pin the pants to the wall according to the display sketch. Be sure to give the clothing a thin appearance by folding in the waist. Keep the pins invisible.
   b. Arrange the cowl-necked sweater inside the tabard before climbing onto the ladder. Use T-pins to pin the shoulders and neckline to the wall. Give the sweaters a thin appearance by folding in the sides. Keep the pins invisible.
   c. Pin the accessory items to the display. Keep the pins invisible.
   d. Pick up the display area.

Fig. 14-8 Here is Mrs. Logan's checklist for setting up a merchandise display.

Experience 14-10

Build a Wall Display

Pin up on a bulletin board the display you sketched and arranged in Experience 14-9. You will need T-pins, background paper, and staples to build the display. (Staple the background paper to the bulletin board.) When you have completed your display, answer the following questions in the space provided.

1. Does your display tell a story? What is the story?

____

____

2. Does your display attract attention? What part of the display attracts attention?

____

____

3. Identify the factors that make the display interesting to look at.

____

____

____

____

4. Are the colors in the display coordinated? Does the display have a particular color theme?

____

____

5. Does the display have a "thin" appearance?

____

6. Are the accessories appropriate?

____

7. Is the clothing firmly attached to the wall?

____

8. Are the T-pins out of view?

____

PREPARING DISPLAY SIGNS

"You really did a nice job on the wall display," Mrs. Logan tells you. "How about preparing some signs for the merchandise racks?"

PREPARING MERCHANDISE SIGNS

A display sign should briefly state reasons that customers should buy the merchandise. When preparing signs, remember that just the name of the merchandise is not enough information. Avoid writing too much copy on the signs. Try to limit the words on a sign to two to three per line.

1. On the top line, write the reason the customer should buy the merchandise. This is the most important line of the sign. Write customer benefits. Ask yourself what the merchandise will do for the customer. If the merchandise item is the newest fashion accessory or never needs ironing, line 1 should say so.
2. Line 2 should identify the merchandise by name, brand name, or trade mark.
3. Lines 3 and 4 (or the additional lines on an 11-inch by 14-inch sign) should describe sales features that are not obvious to the customer. The construction, quality, ease of care, selection of colors, and size are ideas for these lines.
4. The last line of the sign may give the price and unit of quantity, such as $3.19 per package.

Fig. 14-9 Here are Mrs. Logan's guidelines for the preparation of signs.

Fig. 14-10 What are the customer benefits of the featured merchandise on these signs?

"Sure," you say. "Do I print them myself?"

"We send the signs to a printer," Mrs. Logan replies. "but we have to tell the printer what information to print on the sign. That's what I want you to do. Here are some guidelines that will help you decide what the signs should say." (See Figure 14-9.)

Mrs. Logan gives you some examples of signs that follow these guidelines. (See Figure 14-10.)

You ask her what size the signs should be. She says that the size depends on the sign holders, the merchandise, and the amount of copy on the sign. Usually 5½-inch by 7-inch signs are used for accessory items, such as small leather goods. A ½-inch heading and no more than four lines of ¼-inch print on a 5½-inch by 7-inch sign are used. These signs are usually displayed on counter tops.

Signs 7 inches by 11 inches are used on top of ready-to-wear racks. They hold about six lines of ¼-inch print with a ½-inch heading. Signs 11 inches by 14 inches are found in fitting rooms and hold nine lines of ½-inch print with a ¾-inch heading. Upper- and lower-case letters are used to make the sign easy to read.

Experience 14-11

Sign It

1. On a separate sheet of paper, write the information you would include on a display sign that will appear on top of a rack of men's mid-thigh-length suede lambskin coats. The coats have a zip-in acrylic pile lining as well as a rayon inner lining. The suede is specially treated to repel water and non-oily stains. Price: $150. Sizes: 36–44 regular and long. Color: brown.
2. Prepare a 7-inch by 11-inch sign for the suede coat display. If you have access to a sign-making machine, use the machine to make your sign. If not, use ¼-inch and ½-inch stencils and a black felt-tipped pen to letter the sign on a sheet of unlined paper or posterboard. Use upper- and lower-case letters. Be careful to make your signs neat, attractive, and accurate.

MERCHANDISE AND FIXTURE DISPLAY

Salespeople, department managers, and buyers make decisions daily about how merchandise and fixtures should be displayed in a department. How can new items receive the best customer exposure? How should the department be arranged so that customers feel comfortable? How much merchandise can a display fixture hold and not topple over? How can shoplifting of the smaller items be reduced? When making these decisions, customer convenience, security, and ease of restocking are considered.

Suppose you are a management trainee at Cordova's. John Bradshaw, the manager of the Men's Furnishings Department, is telling you about some display essentials. He explains that customer exposure and customer convenience must be considered as well as ease of restocking merchandise.

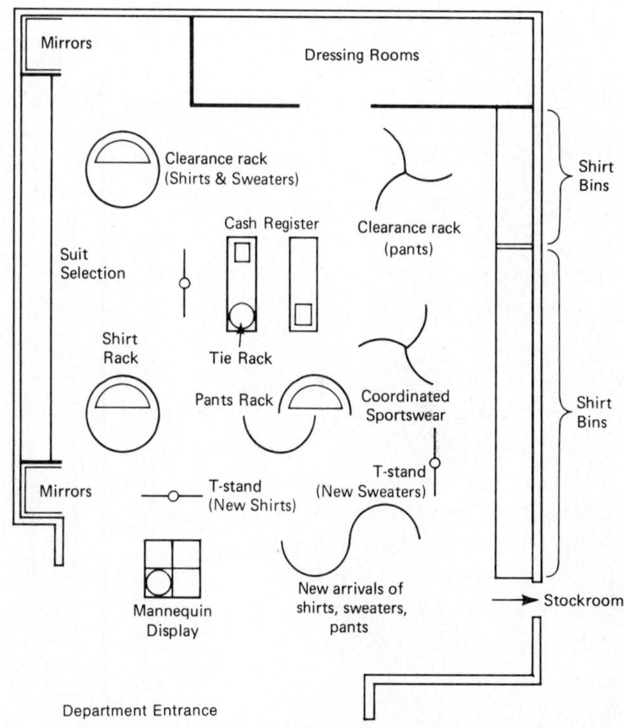

Fig. 14-11 Here's one of John's weekly sketches used in rearranging the department.

CUSTOMER EXPOSURE

"Merchandise items that are visible from the entrance of the department," John says, "have a much better chance of being seen and purchased." He goes on to say that because there is limited space at the front of the department, merchandise must be rotated. Merchandise that is not selling at the back of the department may become its hottest items when moved to the front. Moving merchandise to another rack is a better way to stimulate sales than markdowns.

CUSTOMER CONVENIENCE

You say to John, "It seems that where fixtures are located and the way customers move around them affect the way customers feel about shopping in a store."

"You're right," says John. "When the racks are too close together, customers have a hard time walking down the aisles and they have trouble examining the merchandise. A crowded arrangement makes it difficult for them to get to the cash registers or fitting rooms."

John goes on to explain how he tries to rearrange the merchandise and fixtures every week. "I prepare sketches, like this one, that show where the fixtures and merchandise will be displayed. (See Figure 14-11.) I prefer this arrangement because it has better balance."

You say, "New merchandise seems to be in the front of the department."

"Yes," says John. "This is so that customers can see at a glance what's new. The older merchandise and clearance racks are placed at the back."

John says that he always tries to use round fixtures in displaying merchandise because customers can easily walk around them. By grouping related items together, customers are encouraged to move from one floor rack to another.

"When I was in the Boys' Department," John says, "I used long floor racks to display pants and jackets. I tried to make sure that no rack was longer than 12 feet so that salespeople could easily approach customers and offer assistance."

EASE OF RESTOCKING

You ask John about how he stocks the department. He tells you that additional stock is kept behind the selling department in the forward stock area. When stock is moved from the stockroom to the selling floor, stock bins and racks are used. Therefore, the aisles must be wide enough for the stock equipment to move into the department. "Remember," he says, "when you prepare a merchandise and fixture display layout, leave room for the bins and racks that travel through the sales floor."

Experience 14-12

Build a Department

Using the following department layout and fixtures, prepare a merchandise and fixture display layout. Cut out the fixtures and arrange them so that the department looks balanced, not lopsided. Stock the newest merchandise to the front of the department. Allow sufficient aisle space so that customers may move freely.

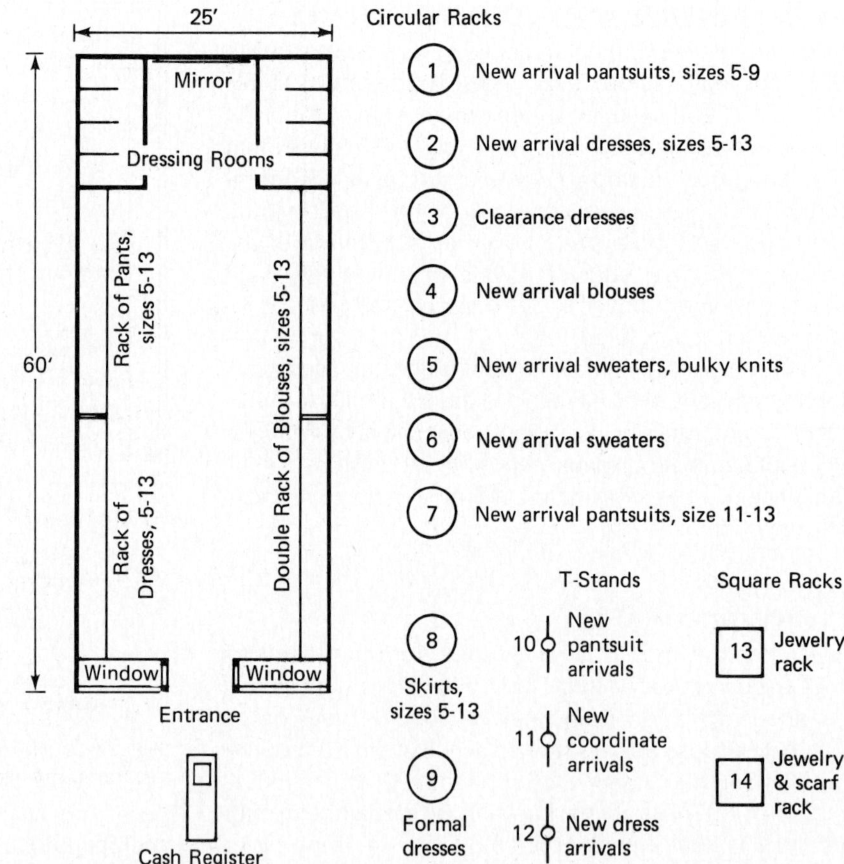

15 Selling

Evans' Department Store is located in a medium-sized Midwestern town. Twenty-five years ago, Mr. Evans opened a small men's apparel shop. As his reputation for high-quality merchandise and service grew, Mr. Evans increased his merchandise assortment. First he added women's apparel, then children's, and then a complete assortment of fashion accessories. His one store expanded to seven.

Mr. Evans says he owes his success to his sales force. Let's listen to him as he opens a sales training seminar for his salespeople. Mr. Evans: "Knowledgeable salespeople are important to a store and its customers. We have people in our store who try to buy the most desirable merchandise, create the best displays, and write the most exciting, effective advertisements. But it is you, the salespeople, who are responsible for keeping the customers happy and coming back. This is probably the most important job in the store. Without satisfied customers, there would soon be no store.

"To be a good salesperson, you have to be proud of what you do. You have to believe in selling. You have to believe that customers need help in purchasing apparel and accessories. To provide that help, you have to know enough about the merchandise to explain to the customer why a particular item is the one he or she should buy. You have to believe the customer needs the merchandise you are trying to sell.

"If you are a professional salesperson, you will be able to find out what people need or want and then convince them that it is a good purchase. Your job will never be boring, for you will come in contact with thousands of people, each different. You will have to be a cordial host or hostess, a psychologist, and a communications specialist."

Mr. Evans continued, "For example, when customers enter our store, you approach and greet them. You try to make them feel welcome and glad they came, just like a host or hostess. Just like the psychologist, you ask questions to find out what customers want or need. Often, customers don't tell you because they don't know themselves. You've heard about hidden needs. You, as a salesperson, have to uncover those hidden needs. As a communications specialist, you talk in terms that mean something to the customers. You talk about product benefits. You overcome an objection in a way that is meaningful to the customer.

"Those of you who have sold before may say that selling isn't so difficult. I've heard that from many people. Just remember that selling is not 'order taking' or 'cashiering.' It is helping the customer obtain maximum personal satisfaction for the money spent.

"Our store believes that salespeople need sales training. We believe selling is a skill that can be learned. That is why we are holding these sales seminars. We are going to talk about different parts of a sale: the approach, determining the customer's needs, sales demonstration, objections, closes, and suggestion selling. And we'll talk about product knowledge. But first, let's discuss the types of customers with whom you will be working."

CUSTOMER TYPES

It takes many customers to make a store a success. Each customer who walks through the door is different, with different needs and feelings. Because all customers do not act or react the same way, some successful salespeople class customers into certain types. This helps them determine the best way to help customers with their, particular needs. Table 1, which is shown on the following page, lists some of these typical types.

Table 1

TYPICAL CUSTOMER TYPES

Customer Type	Method for Handling
Ms. Iwanna Argue will give you all sorts of reasons why your merchandise is bad.	Keep cool, calm, and courteous. Don't try to win an argument, for you might lose a sale. Use Ms. Argue's own arguments to prove your points. "You're right, Ms. Argue, durability is important to consider when buying a pantsuit. This 100 percent polyester suit will give you long wear, wrinkle resistance, and easy care."
Mrs. Hesi Tant is never sure if she should buy. Just when you think she's made a decision, she changes her mind.	Help this customer make a decision. Give her your opinion. Reassure her. "That's a very good choice, Mrs. Tant. I'm sure you'll be pleased with your purchase."
Mr. Izit A. Bargain is always looking for a sale.	Know the quality of merchandise you sell. Sell him on the additional quality and service you can offer him.
Mr. Si Lent is the toughest customer of all. He just doesn't talk, even though he's quietly thinking about what you're saying.	Ask open-ended questions that give Mr. Si Lent a chance to talk. Don't hesitate in trying to close the sale. He only needs to say one word—yes.
Miss Ina Hurry is impatient and easy to irritate if you're slow.	Give her fast service and the important facts. Don't bore her with details or she will leave.

Of course, this table doesn't include all of the types of customers you'll meet. Remember that each customer is an individual and must be treated as such.

SELLING APPAREL AND ACCESSORIES

Successful selling hinges on (1) a salesperson having adequate product information, (2) the customer understanding the salesperson, and (3) the salesperson's personality and desire to help. Mr. Evans, owner and manager of Evans' Department Stores, continues the sales training seminar: "As you know, this store firmly believes in product knowledge. We distribute pamphlets about fabrics, construction, and fashion. Also, we meet with clothing and accessory manufacturer reps. Customers have the right to ask questions about the merchandise they purchase and they deserve the correct answers.

"I've asked two experienced salespeople to role play a sales situation. You will see the value of product knowledge in making a sale." Two women walk to the front of the room. One takes the part of the salesperson; the other is the customer.

SALESPERSON: Good morning. How are you today?

CUSTOMER: Fine, thank you. *(The customer is examining a shelf selection of boys' shirts.)*

SALESPERSON: What size are you looking for?

CUSTOMER: Size 10. My nephew's birthday is coming up. Roger's mother mentioned that he could use a dress shirt.

SALESPERSON: Do you think Roger would prefer short sleeves or long sleeves?

CUSTOMER: Summer is coming, so short sleeves would be cooler.

(The salesperson, without hesitation, leads the customer to another shirt counter.)

SALESPERSON: These 50 percent cotton/50 percent polyester shirts are our most popular sellers. Because cotton is a cool, absorbent fabric, it is especially nice to wear in the summer. Polyester makes the shirt easy to care for. This shirt can be machine-washed in warm water and tumble-dried. The boy's mother will appreciate the no-ironing.

CUSTOMER: This shirt is too plain. I've seen other boys wear brightly colored patterned shirts. Roger's shirts are mostly solid, so I really wanted something in a patterned shirt.

(The salesperson moves to the next counter, where the patterned shirts are stocked. She quickly locates the size 10s.)

SALESPERSON: Here's a blue, green, and yellow floral pattern. It would look nice with solid blue, green, or yellow pants. Your nephew could also wear gray, black, or white pants with this shirt. *(The salesperson carefully hands the shirt to the customer. She handles the merchandise with care and respect to show that the shirt is valuable.)*

SALESPERSON: Notice how nicely the shirt tail and sleeves are hemmed.

CUSTOMER: Do you have any of those "silky" looking shirts that are popular?

SALESPERSON: We have some boys' nylon jersey print shirts. *(Taking the customer to another rack.)* These shirts have a lustrous finish. They can be machine-washed and -dried, and require little ironing.

CUSTOMER: I like the print of those other patterned shirts.

SALESPERSON: That's a good choice. *(Walking the customer back to the patterned shirt counter.)* Your nephew will be able to wear the shirt with many colors. This shirt collar looks equally nice when worn open or with a tie. I'd suggest a white tie as a finishing touch for a dress outfit. *(The salesperson puts the tie next to the shirt.)* Younger boys often prefer these clip-on ties. This tie is made of 100 percent polyester, so spots can be removed easily. The tie gets its interesting design from a special weaving process. Doesn't the weave give the tie an interesting pattern?

CUSTOMER: Yes, it does look nice. In fact, I like it very much. *(Picking up the shirt and tie and walking the customer to the cash register.)*

SALESPERSON: I'll take the price tags off this merchandise for you and put the shirt and tie in a gift box. That should reduce your wait at the gift-wrapping desk. Will this be cash or charge?

"Thank you," says Mr. Evans. "Now let's discuss what we just observed."

APPROACHING THE CUSTOMER

Mr. Evans discusses the importance of making an effective approach. He explains that the first step of a sale is called the **approach**. In the approach, the salesperson gets the attention of the customer and tries to make the customer feel welcome in the store.

Mr. Evans asks, "Did you notice that the salesperson in the sale we just observed promptly approached and greeted the customer? Sometimes this is impossible, though, because you will be helping another customer. Even if you are busy with someone else, be sure to acknowledge all customers who enter your department. Look up from your sale and make eye contact with the new customer. Say, 'I'll be with you in a minute.' Remember to keep looking up and making eye contact so they won't think you've forgotten them.

"I'm sure you've heard of the greeting, service, and merchandise approaches. These are the three best ways to open a sale. The **greeting approach** invloves saying such things as 'Hi,' 'Hello,' 'Good morning,' and 'How are you.' These friendly greetings make the customer feel welcome.

"The **service approach** involves asking the customer a question. You might ask, 'What may I show you today?' A combination greeting and service approach is: 'Good evening. I'm Hal Evans. Perhaps I can save you some time and help you get the best value for your money. What are you looking for?' This approach says that you can help the customer and provide a service. Notice that the service approaches could not be answered with a simple yes or no. These questions, and all questions that begin with words who, what, where, when, why, and how, are called **open-ended questions**. Open-ended questions make the sales presentation a two-way conversation. The customer has a chance to talk, giving the salesperson a chance to find out what the customer wants.

"In the **merchandise approach,** you say something specific about merchandise the customer is examining. A typical merchandise approach is: 'We just received this spring suit selection. Attractive, don't you think?' You can't use the merchandise approach all the time. Often you approach customers who are not looking at particular items, and sometimes customers approach you. In these cases, the service or greeting approach is more appropriate."

Mr. Evans continues, "The approach won't make a sale, but it can lose a sale. It's important to learn how to begin a conversation with a customer. Learn to approach the customer with a friendly, helpful attitude and a suitable remark."

Experience 15-1

Say What's Appropriate

Assume you are a salesperson in a young men's sportswear store. Have classmates be the customers. Your store stocks casual and dress clothes. Use a tape recorder and record how you would approach customers in each of the following situations. Also, record why you believe each approach was appropriate. (If you do not have a tape recorder, write your dialog on a separate sheet of paper. Explain why you think your remarks are appropriate. Also write what you believe is the most important part of the sale. Then explain why you think it is the most important part.)

1. Customer, not particularly interested in any one item, wanders around tables and racks.
2. Customer stops to look at table of sale pants. Customer remains at table.
3. Customer stops to look at table of sale pants. After a minute or two, customer walks to the wall of sport coats and then to the shirt racks.
4. You are showing golf shirts to a customer when another customer enters your store. Another customer enters and walks directly to the cash register.

DETERMINING NEEDS

Before you can successfully sell a particular item, you need to know if the item would be appropriate. Find out what customers want by questioning, observing, and listening. You need to know *who* the item is for; *where* the clothing or accessories will be worn; *what* size is needed; and *what* color, style, and fabric are preferred by customers.

Fig. 15-1 Identify each of the shoppers pictured above. Which one is just browsing? Decided? Undecided?

One of the fastest ways to determine customer needs is by asking open-ended questions. These questions encourage customers to talk because they cannot be answered with a simple yes or no. Some examples of open-ended questions are: "What color did you have in mind?" "How often do you travel?" and "Which style do you like best?"

By asking questions, a salesperson finds out that all customers are not alike. Decided shoppers have a very specific idea of what they want to purchase. The customer who was looking for a dress shirt for her nephew in the role-playing situation was a decided shopper. Undecided shoppers only have a general idea of what they want. For example, an undecided shopper may be looking for a father's birthday present, but will consider buying anything a man can use. Shoppers who are browsers are not looking for anything in particular. They may be just bargain-hunting. Once the salesperson finds out whether or not a customer is a decided shopper, undecided shopper, or browser, he or she can better meet that customer's needs. (See Figure 15-1.)

During the discussion period, Leon Richards asks, "What if, after asking some questions, I find out that the customer wants something we don't stock?"

Mr. Evans answers, "You should try to suggest some substitutes. Suppose the customer wants a powder blue tie blouse. We don't have any tie blouses, but we do have powder blue blouses. Show her that it can be worn open, with scarfs, and with jewelry. The customer may leave with our blouse because it fits her needs better. Be courteous because customers return to stores where they receive friendly, helpful service."

Experience 15-2

Which Size, Style, Color?

1. Before you can successfully sell apparel and accessory items, you have to find out if the items would be appropriate. What does that mean?

____

____

____

____

____

____

2. Situation: Assume you are a salesperson. While helping another customer, a man enters the store. He spends some time looking at casual woven polyester slacks. You have just approached this customer. What five questions could you ask him to determine his needs?

3. Play the part of a salesperson in a men's clothing store. Have someone pose as a customer looking for an overcoat. Demonstrate how you would determine this customer's needs. Record this role-playing situation on a tape recorder or write what you said on a separate sheet of paper.

Courtesy Tiberius Fashions Ltd. Photo: Daile Kaplan

Fig. 15-2 Why does an aware salesperson always watch for the customer's reaction to items of merchandise?

BUYING MOTIVES

Mr. Evans explains buying motives to his sales staff in more detail. "**Buying motives** are reasons why people purchase something," he says. "Very few people purchase clothing just to stay warm. Rather, people have a variety of reasons to justify their clothing purchases. These reasons can be classified as rational or emotional needs. Some of the **rational needs** are to save money (economy), to save time (convenience), for health reasons, for warmth, and for modesty. Some of the **emotional needs** are for pleasure, to attract attention, to be different, to be a follower, for variety, to be a leader, to attract the opposite sex, and to win recognition for social approval.

"We all have rational and emotional needs in different degrees. That's what makes every customer unique and different. Discovering buying motives is not difficult. You can discover buying motives by listening carefully to what a customer says and observing how he or she reacts to what you say.

"Suppose a woman wants a new dress to wear to work. Most working people want to save time. The easy-care features of polyester appeal to such customers. By showing this customer a 100 percent polyester dress, you can appeal to her need to save time. Explain the easy-care features of polyester, so she can see why this dress suits her needs. By matching the merchandise to the customer's needs, you can persuade her to make the purchase."

At this point, Jonas Morris interrupts, "Mr. Evans, you make it sound as though all customers' needs can be determined right after the approach. I don't think that's true. Usually, I learn more about the customer needs during my sales presentation and when the customer makes objections."

"That's a good point, Jonas," says Mr. Evans thoughtfully. "I didn't intend to make it sound as though you don't show merchandise until you've asked all the right questions and pinpointed customer needs. Sometimes the best way to determine customer needs is by showing the customer a particular item and just watching his or her reaction. A scowl means 'forget it.' A twinkle in the eye may mean 'That's what I'm looking for!' " (See Figure 15-2.)

Experience 15-3

Buying Motivators

Salespeople must be able to analyze customer needs. Read each of the following customer statements. Determine which emotional or rational need the customer seems to be expressing.

1. Have you received your first shipment of designer fashions for spring?

   ____

2. A friend of mine bought a crepe de chine dress here about a week ago. Do you still have any in stock?

   ____

3. I already have red, green, and orange turtleneck sweaters. I want something different.

4. I heard you were having a sale on leather wallets. Do you have any of the tri-fold kind?

   ____

5. I'm looking for a pair of riding boots. I have plans to go riding with someone very special whom I want to impress.

   ____

Experience 15-4

Body Language Tells the Story

People react to merchandise with their bodies. For example, if a customer sees something she likes, she may nod her head.

1. What are four ways customers may react nonverbally toward merchandise they like?

2. What are two ways customers may react nonverbally toward merchandise they don't like?

PRESENTING MERCHANDISE

After you approach customers and discover what merchandise they need or want, you follow up with the presentation. During the **presentation**, you show customers how your merchandise will satisfy their needs. To make an effective presentation, you need to know your product and be familiar with special selling skills.

Mr. Evans explains the important points for presenting merchandise, "Did you notice how the salesperson in the role-playing situation had selling confidence? That's the kind of confidence you get when you know your merchandise. Merchandise knowledge will help you choose the product best suited for the customer. It will help you explain product features and benefits and overcome customer objections. Merchandise knowledge will give you more interest in merchandise.

"Customers want to know certain information about the apparel and accessories they buy. They will ask such questions as the following:

About Fabric How will it wear? Will it hold its shape? Will it shrink? Can it be washed? Will it fade? Does it need to be ironed? What kind of material is this?
About Construction Is it true to size? Can it be altered?
About Fashion Is it in fashion?
About Coordination What do you have that goes with this?

Some customers also want to know the history of the product or the many different ways to wear an item.

"To learn about the many different apparel and accessory products you sell, prepare a **product analysis chart**. Look at the example of a product analysis sheet found in your seat at the beginning of this seminar. They are simple to prepare. List all the facts or features about a product on the left side of the chart. Across from each fact, write an advantage or benefit of it. (See Table 2.)

"Product analysis charts help you prepare for a sale. They help you know exactly what you want to say about a product on the spur of the moment. When a customer asks an unexpected question, you won't lose the sale because you couldn't answer. By analyzing the merchandise beforehand, you can coordinate other garments or accessories that complement the merchandise.

"Because you know the merchandise doesn't mean you'll be able to sell it. You need to have special selling skills too. I've made a list of the selling skills that are important when presenting merchandise." Mr. Evans points to a poster containing the following list. After a pause, Mr. Evans asks, "Any questions about any of these nine points?"

1. Limit the amount of merchandise shown.
2. Point out the obvious features first.
3. Talk about benefits.
4. Handle the merchandise with care and respect.
5. Let the customer participate in the sale.
6. Appeal to the customer's senses.
7. Point out the hidden features.
8. Be enthusiastic.
9. Show the medium-priced item first, unless the customer requests otherwise.

Point One: Limit the Amount of Merchandise Shown "Why limit the amount of merchandise shown?" asks Jake Cartega. "We stock a large selection of merchandise. Why not let the customer see it all?"

Mr. Evans replies, "It's harder to make a choice when you have to consider 20 alternatives rather than just two or three. Too many alternatives confuse customers. Some customers will leave the store rather than be forced to choose a particular product. (See Figure 15-3.)

"In our role-playing situation, there may have been 15 shirt styles in the department. Yet the salesperson showed only three. The customer purchased one of those three shirts because the salesperson correctly determined the customer's needs. The salesperson made it easy for the customer to buy."

Point Two: Point out the Obvious Features First "What's an obvious feature about a dress or pair of pants?" asks a new salesperson, Harriett Clark.

Fig. 15-3 Limiting the amount of merchandise shown to a potential customer is an important selling skill for salespeople to remember and practice.

Mr. Evans answers, "An obvious feature is the first thing that catches the customer's eye. It may be a color or a special style detail. For a dress, it may be the cool, summery, mint green color. For a pair of pants, it may be the contrast stitching on the Western-cut pockets. By pointing out the obvious features first, you are drawing the customer's attention to the merchandise. By commenting on a garment's color or style, you are reinforcing what the customer can see and already knows. If you prepare a Product Analysis Chart on a merchandise item, you can determine the features to be emphasized. This will also help you determine benefits, which I will explain shortly. Here is an example of a Product Analysis Chart." (See Table 2.)

Table 2

PRODUCT ANALYSIS CHART

PRODUCT: Three-piece plaid woman's suit—skirt, jacket, and vest

Sales Features: Facts	Selling Points: Benefits
1. FABRIC: Made of 100 percent polyester knit	1. Fabric is easy to care for—it can be machine-washed and -dried; the suit is a good traveling companion because the fabric resists wrinkles.
2. CONSTRUCTION: Matched plaids, preshrunk fully lined jacket, handsewn collar	2. The plaids are matched at the seams—a mark of excellent workmanship; the jacket will not lose its shape when the coat is cleaned because the lining is preshrunk; the lining also adds to the way the jacket drapes the body; the lining adds to the feel and wearing comfort of the jacket; extra care has been taken in making the handsewn collar lay flat.
3. FASHION: Three-piece plaid suit includes an A-line skirt with fitted vest and jacket.	3. This suit is a classic and will continue to be fashionable for years to come.
4. ACCESSORY COORDINATION: Brown and gold plaid suit	4. This brown and gold plaid suit is versatile; it can be worn together with blouses and sweaters or separately with a shirt and skirt or the vest and another pair of pants.

Point Three: Talk about Benefits "I understand why I should limit the merchandise selection and point out obvious features," says Jon Harper. "What do you mean when you say 'talk about benefits'?"

"**Benefit statements** tell customers what they will receive when they buy that dress, or coat, or hat," Mr. Evans replies. "They answer the customer's question, 'What's in it for me?' Customers want to hear what items will do for them. Some customers really don't care about the name of the fabric as long as a garment is easy to care for. By talking about the benefits that are important to the customer, you will be able to create desire and interest in the merchandise so that he or she would want to buy it.

"You should be skillful in relating merchandise benefits to customer needs. As we discussed before, customers give hints about their needs. If a customer has stressed a desire for economy, point out the economical aspects of the item, such as quality workmanship or always in fashion."

"But why is it important to point out the benefits?" Jon asks.

Mr. Evans says, "Features only *imply* benefits. Suppose you are showing a customer a pair of slacks that have an elasticized waistband. You may know the band keeps the shirt from slipping out, but the customer may not. If you assume the customer knows this benefit, you are losing the opportunity to tell the customer the special features of the slacks.

"For most of us, Jon, money is a scarce item. Because we don't have as much money as we'd like, we are selective in our spending. Like us, customers don't buy everything they see. By stating the benefits, you give the customers reasons to make a purchase."

Point Four: Handle the Merchandise with Care and Respect "No one," Mr. Evans explains, "wants to spend money for something that someone else doesn't think is valuable. If a salesperson handles merchandise carefully, as though it is truly valuable, customers will believe the merchandise has real value too. They will be more likely to make the purchase."

Point Five: Let the Customer Participate in the Sale "Isn't it hard to get the customer to participate in the sale?" asks Janice Henzke.

"Not when you're selling apparel and accessories!" laughs Mr. Evans. "When you're selling accessory items such as wallets or purses, get the customer to hold the merchandise and open it. Have customers try on scarves and jewelry and look at themselves in a mirror. When showing coats, help the customer off with his or her coat and on with the merchandise. Then have the customer look in a mirror to see how the coat looks."

Point Six: Appeal to the Customer's Senses "By letting customers participate in the sale," Mr. Evans says, "you will be appealing to their senses of sight, touch, speech, and hearing. The more senses you can appeal to, the better you will be able to hold a customer's attention. Customers will get a feeling of ownership for the item that can be hard to resist."

Point Seven: Point out the Hidden Features Rodney Valenti states: "Point seven, point out hidden features, makes it sound as though everything we sell has a secret compartment."

"In a way, that's true, Rodney," Mr. Evans says. "The suits you sell have some secret compartments. Customers won't know about the handsewn seams or fine quality wool blends unless you tell them. Hidden features are things customers are not interested in at first, but they help customers reach a decision to buy. They help customers justify spending their money."

Point Eight: Be Enthusiastic "This point, be enthusiastic, applies to everything you do as salespeople," Mr. Evans adds. "If you're excited about the merchandise, the excitement will be carried over to the customer. Customers can sense when salespeople are genuinely interested in merchandise they sell. They increase their desire for the merchandise when they see the salesperson thinks the merchandise is valuable."

Point Nine: Show the Medium-priced Item First, unless the Customer Requests Otherwise "So far," Mr. Evans continued, "we haven't said anything about price. Price is an important consideration. Much of our merchandise is available in three price lines: high, medium, and low. If customers don't mention the exact price range, show them the medium-priced range. Be sure to listen carefully to what customers say and how they react to the medium-priced product. Stress the quality benefits the customer will receive from the product. If customers mention, 'This is a bit more than I wanted to spend,' take them to the next lower-priced line. If customers say, 'Is this the best quality item in stock?' show them a higher-priced line. Avoid asking them, 'How much do you want to spend?' That boxes you in and doesn't give you freedom to 'trade up' to a better quality, but more expensive item."

Experience 15-5

Product Analysis

Choose an apparel item from a catalog, magazine, or store.

1. On a separate sheet of paper, prepare a Product Analysis Chart. Write the features and benefits of a particular apparel or accessory item. Be sure you include information about the garment's fabric, construction, and style.
2. List other apparel and accessory items that turn the apparel items you analyzed in 1, above, into a coordinated outfit.
3. Why is merchandise knowledge so important?

Experience 15-6

What's in It for Me?

Examine the following statements. Decide if each statement is a "benefit" statement or a "feature" statement and place a check mark in the appropriate column.

	Benefit	Feature
1. This jacket is versatile; it can be used as a blazer or a suit coat.		
2. This fabric resists wrinkles and will be easy to care for.		
3. The elastic waistband will keep your shirt in.		
4. These natural fabrics are the "in" look this season.		
5. This is a wool and nylon blend.		

Experience 15-7

Appeal to the Needs

Customers give hints about why they are purchasing apparel and accessory items. Examine each of the following sales situations. Under each situation, write a benefit statement that would appeal to the customer's expressed need. Assume you are a salesperson in a children's store.

1. You are helping a mother purchase a coat for her 3-year-old son. The woman has mentioned she wants a long-wearing warm coat. You are showing her a coat that is machine-washable.

   ____

   ____

2. Another customer wants to see your selection of sleepers. This customer is most concerned that the sleepers are warm because his 2-year-old niece refuses to sleep under a blanket. You are showing him a one-piece garment with attached feet.

   ____

   ____

3. Another customer is looking for a special party dress for her 5-year-old daughter. She doesn't want to spend a lot of money on a dress that her daughter will wear only once. You are showing her a sleeveless dress with a plain bodice and colorful skirt. The dress has a matching jacket and a 3-inch hem.

   ____

   ____

Experience 15-8

Present the Merchandise

Role play how you, as a salesperson, would present merchandise to a customer. Ask another student to pose as a customer.

1. Choose an apparel or accessory item your customer may be interested in purchasing. Bring that item to class for your sales presentation.
2. On a separate sheet of paper, prepare a product analysis chart for your product. Be sure to include features and benefits about its fabric, construction, and style. Also identify other apparel and accessory items that would coordinate with the product.
3. Using a tape recorder, record how you would present the merchandise to your customer. Assume you have already greeted the customer and determined the customer wants to see the product you are about to present. Be sure to follow the nine points of a presentation on page 224.
4. After the merchandise presentation, ask your customer to evaluate your performance by completing the following evaluation form.
   a. Did the salesperson talk about the merchandise benefits? Give three examples.

____

____

____

b. Give two examples that show the salesperson handled the merchandise with care and respect.

____

____

c. How did the salesperson let you participate in the sale?

____

____

____

d. How did the salesperson appeal to your senses of sight, touch, smell, and hearing?

____

____

____

e. How would you rate this salesperson's enthusiasm? (Circle one)

Very enthusiastic Somewhat enthusiastic
Not so enthusiastic

f. Any suggestions for improving the presentation?

____

____

The salesperson's job would be very easy if, after every presentation, customers said, "I'll take it." Usually, customers have questions or comments about the merchandise. When these questions or comments indicate reasons why customers may honestly refuse or hesitate to purchase merchandise, they are called **objections.**

As a salesperson, you will hear many objections and you will need to know how to handle them. Remember that objections are a natural part of the sale. They indicate that the customer is sincerely interested in the merchandise. In some situations, customers may raise an objection because they want more information before deciding to buy.

Kinds of Customer Objections. Customer objections to merchandise can be classified in three categories. These are (1) need, (2) price, and (3) objections to particular features. A salesperson must successfully overcome these objections to make the sale.

Need Objections. When customers say, "I don't need that," they cannot see how the merchandise will benefit them. When customers try to put off buying merchandise, they don't think they need it now. Some common objections salespeople hear are, "I don't think I'll get enough wear out of it," or "I'd like to think it over."

Anticipate need objections. Find out why customers are uncertain about making the purchase. Ask, "What do you want to think over?" or "Why do you feel this merchandise won't fit your needs?"

Remember that when a salesperson and customer meet, there is always a sale. Either the salesperson sells the customer the merchandise or the customer sells the salesperson on the idea that he or she doesn't need the merchandise.

Price Objections. Salespeople often meet price objections, such as "It costs too much." If a customer really can't afford the merchandise, there's not much a salesperson can do. If you have not pointed out the value of the merchandise, show customers that the merchandise offers full value for the money spent. People do not buy price; they buy value and benefits. Price is related to style, fit, construction, quality, and store services.

Don't apologize for the price. Explain why the price is justified. Consider the following example:

CUSTOMER: This blazer costs too much.

SALESPERSON: I admit that this is not an inexpensive jacket. Let me tell you why. This is 100 percent worsted wool. You will be warm and comfortable when you wear it. Because this jacket has straight, tailored lines, it will be fashionable for years to come. All the seams are hand-stitched. This quality construction feature adds to the strength and appearance of the jacket. The jacket also has a full lining, which definitely adds to the jacket's appearance and fit.

Objections to Particular Features. Throughout a sale, customers may object to various features of the merchandise shown. Some samples of these objections are; "I don't like the color," or "That style makes me look terrible." Sometimes customer objections about style, color, and fit help you better determine customer needs. When you show an item the customer objects to, you have a better idea of what the customer really does want to purchase. This helps you choose more appropriate merchandise.

Some objections about the fabric or construction may be based on wrong information. The salesperson should try to overcome such objections. Consider the following example:

CUSTOMER: This really is a beautiful coat, and it is so comfortable. But, it's too lightweight to keep me very warm.

SALESPERSON: I felt the same as you did until I bought a coat like this. It's made of lightweight wool. You may not know that wool absorbs dampness from the air in the cold weather. You'll feel warmer when wearing wool than when you wear other fabrics.

General Tips on Handling Objections. Every customer objection must be handled with respect. You are a salesperson; you are not supposed to win an argument with a customer but lose the sale. To overcome customer objections, follow these simple rules:

- Let customers state their objections.
- Be sure you understand the objection. Restate the objection in your own words.
- Agree with customer's objection. By doing this, you will show the customer you think the objection is important. Also, by agreeing, you show the customer that he or she is not wrong in making the statement. Agreement avoids a possible argument.
- Point out other factors that show the customer the objection is not necessarily true.

Some examples of how salespersons can effectively overcome objections by using these rules are:

- **EXAMPLE 1**

CUSTOMER: I don't like the length of these new dresses. They make me look so old.

SALESPERSON: I can understand why you say that. New styles are hard to get used to. However, in a short while you'll be seeing this skirt length all over town. In fact, you'll feel uncomfortable wearing the length you wear now.

- **EXAMPLE 2**

CUSTOMER: This suit is all right, I suppose. But I always wear (brand name) originals.

SALESPERSON: You have good taste, sir. That brand is excellent, but, you may want to consider this brand. As you can see, this suit has an exceptional style and cut. This designer is new to the fashion world, but already has an excellent reputation.

Anticipate Objections If you can anticipate possible customer objections, you will be able to handle them. To help you overcome objections, prepare an **objection analysis sheet**. List the type of objection, why the customer will state the objection, and what you can say to overcome the objection successfully. See Table 3 for an example of an objection analysis sheet.

Table 3

OBJECTION ANALYSIS SHEET

PRODUCT: Man's Two-piece Gray Woven Wool Suit

Type of Objection	Customer's Possible Objection	Salesperson's Suggested Answer
NEED	"I like the suit. I just don't think I'll get enough wear out of it."	"You mentioned, sir, that you will soon be graduating from college and will be interviewing with employers for a job. This suit will serve your interviewing needs well. It is also versatile enough to wear to work, church, or an evening out. This jacket, which is a blazer style, can also be worn with other pants."
PRICE	"This suit costs a bit more than I wanted to pay."	"I agree that this suit is not inexpensive. However, it has many quality features that add to its value. For example, this is a quality wool that will retain its crisp, neat look. The manufacturer is also a leading designer of men's clothing. Much time and care have been taken to size this suit to give you a good fit."
PARTICULAR FEATURE: FABRIC	"Won't this suit be too hot during the summer? It's wool, isn't it?"	"Wool is an absorbent fabric. It can absorb body moisture produced in hot weather up to 30 percent of its weight."
PARTICULAR FEATURE: COLOR	"The color is so drab."	"Gray is a very versatile color in a man's wardrobe. You can wear it with so many colors to get many different looks."

Objections Versus Excuses Salespeople must be able to distinguish between customer objections and customer excuses. Objections are honest, real reasons why the customer hesitates to purchase the apparel or accessories you are presenting. Excuses are reasons customer's have made up for not purchasing the product. The best way to find out if the customer has a real objection is to ask questions.

For example, suppose the customer says, "These shoes aren't really the style I had in mind." The salesperson could say, "Can you describe the style you wanted?" If the customer answers with a definite answer, the customer has a real objection. If the customer says, "I want a more casual looking shoe—perhaps a loafer," the customer has a real objection. The reply, "I'm not sure what I want" is an excuse.

Experience 15-9

Why Won't They Buy?

1. Choose a specific apparel or accessory item. On a separate sheet of paper, write a description of this item.
2. On the same paper, prepare an objection analysis sheet. On the sheet, list every reason why you would not purchase the item. Next to each objection, write what the salesperson could say to overcome your objection.

Experience 15-10

Make Them See It Your Way

Using a tape recorder, record how you, as an apparel salesperson, would overcome the following customer objections. Assume you are showing the customer a $35 silk blouse.

1. "It is a nice blouse. I'm just not sure I need it right now. I want to think about this. Perhaps I'll be back to get it later."
2. "Thirty-five dollars is a lot of money. In fact, I think this blouse costs a lot more than it's worth."
3. "Silk is so hard to care for, and dry cleaning is awfully expensive."

CLOSING A SALE

If a salesperson has successfully determined the customer's needs, presented the merchandise, and overcome any objections, the customer should be ready to buy. Most customers, however, don't say, "I'll take it." They need a salesperson's help to decide to buy.

Usually, a salesperson who is paying close attention to customers can tell when they are ready to buy. Customers make positive statements about the merchandise or their actions indicate they want to buy. For example, handling the merchandise again, after it's been set aside, is a buying clue. When the buying signals indicate that customers are ready to buy, the salesperson should try to close the sale.

There are many ways to close a sale. If the customer has been examining two different items, a salesperson may say, "Which do you like better, the striped or the plaid?" If the customer is sending buying signals, a salesperson could ask, "Should I charge this to your account?"

Be ready to close the sale as soon as the customer seems ready to buy. Some customers are ready to buy much sooner than others, so don't drag out the sale longer than needed. Salespersons who don't know when to stop talking and start closing talk customers out of buying. (See Figure 15-4.)

Fig. 15-4 What valuable advice could you give to the salesperson who waited on this customer?

Experience 15-11

Be Alert, Watch for Buying Signals

1. List five verbal buying signals that indicate it's time to close the sale.

2. List five nonverbal buying signals that indicate it's time to close the sale.

3. You are a salesperson in the men's shoe department. You have successfully approached a customer and found out the customer wants a white patent leather slip-on. You have sized the customer's foot, located the shoe in the stockroom, and explained the shoe's comfort and wear features. The customer keeps nodding his head in approval, agreeing with everything you say. List three ways you could close this sale.

SUGGESTION SELLING

The sale should not end when the customer agrees to purchase a merchandise item. Suggestion selling, another important part of the sales process, should follow the close. In suggestion selling, the salesperson suggests other merchandise for the customer to purchase. The salesperson may suggest related items that accessorize the customer's first purchase or an additional number of the item the customer is purchasing. The suggestion should be made *after* the customer has made a decision about the first item, but *before* the package is wrapped.

For example, suppose a customer has decided to buy a pair of mint green gabardine pants. The salesperson can suggestion sell by saying, "We have some polyester hooded jackets that match the color of those pants perfectly. Let me show you how they look together."

Suggestion selling is beneficial to the store and to the salesperson because it increases the amount of the sale. Higher sales mean more profit for the store and more commission to the sales personnel. Suggestion selling is also beneficial to the customer. By mentioning other items that a customer may need, the salesperson is saving the customer from the inconvenience of another trip to the store.

You will get the best results from your suggestions if you remember these points:

- Make your suggestion specific, don't say, "Is there anything else?" Say, "Let me show you."
- Make your suggestion customer-oriented. Tell customers how they will benefit if additional merchandise is purchased.
- Suggest with enthusiasm. If you're not excited about the additional merchandise, why should the customer want to see it?

Experience 15-12

Suggestion Selling: It Helps the Customer and You

On a separate sheet of paper, list three merchandise items you could suggestion sell to the following customers described.

1. The customer has purchased a pair of school shoes for his daughter. (You work in the Children's Shoe Department.)
2. The customer has purchased a scarf. (You work in the Women's Accessory Department.)
3. The customer has purchased a man's blue corduroy bathrobe. (You work in the Men's Furnishings Department.)

BUILDING GOODWILL

Every store wants its customers to leave the store with a good feeling about the salespeople and merchandise. As a salesperson, you can build this good feeling by treating all customers courteously. Tell customers you appreciate their business. Say, "Thank you, and please come in again."

As you work in a store, you will notice some regular customers. Regular customers are very important to the success of a store; they should get "special" treatment.

Of course, a store always wants its sales staff to increase the number of loyal customers. That's where you, as a salesperson, can be a real asset to the store. By knowing the merchandise and having a sincere desire to help people find the merchandise they want and need, you will become a productive, satisfied employee.

MERCHANDISE RETURNS

Customers return merchandise to an apparel store for many reasons. Sometimes, the merchandise is defective. For example, a garment may be constructed poorly or may be made from a poor-quality fabric that fell apart when it was laundered. Sometimes customers make a mistake when choosing merchandise. When they arrive home with their purchase, they become dissatisifed with the color, size, or style of the item.

Most stores establish their own return policy that guides employees in deciding which returned merchandise items to accept from customers. Usually, all stores accept the return of defective merchandise, except items that are sold at final closeout, "all-sales-final" sales. Often stores allow merchandise to be returned if the return is made within a reasonable time period, such as 1 or 2 weeks after it was purchased. Most stores require the sales slip to accompany the returned merchandise as a proof of purchase. Most stores also require the merchandise not to have been worn.

Today, merchandise returns are a problem at many apparel stores. Because returns are a drain on profits, management tries to reduce the number of returns as much as possible. One way of doing this is by training salespeople to help customers purchase merchandise that best fits their needs and wants.

During their sales training, salespeople should be warned against misrepresenting merchandise, that is, making false claims about a merchandise item. Salespeople should also realize that every customer return is another potential sale. Because the item the customer is returning is not exactly right, the customer is still in the market for another merchandise item—one that better fits his or her needs.

Whenever you deal with a customer who is returning merchandise, be as cheerful and pleasant as you were when the customer originally made the purchase. Listen to why the customer wants to return the merchandise. If the merchandise meets your store's return policy, process the return by completing your store's return forms. Look upon each customer return as an opportunity to increase your sales. At the time of the return, always suggest other merchandise that will better meet your customer's needs.

Experience 15-13

Put It All Together

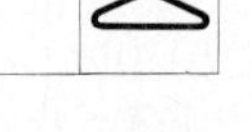

Choose a particular apparel or accessory item. Bring that item to class for your sales presentation. On a separate sheet of paper, prepare a product analysis chart for the item. On another sheet of paper, prepare an objection analysis sheet.

Bring to class five related items that you could suggestion sell with the item. Ask a classmate to pose as your customer. Set the stage for the customer. Explain the type of store, price range of your merchandise, and type of merchandise the customer is going to buy. Ask the classmate to act like a customer who seriously wants to buy the merchandise. Ask the customer to come up with some real objections about the merchandise.

Role play a sales presentation. Use a tape recorder to record your sales presentation. Do as follows:

1. Use an appropriate approach.
2. Determine the customer's needs.
3. Point out the benefits of owning the merchandise.
4. Demonstrate the merchandise.
5. Overcome objections.
6. Close the sale.
7. Suggestion sell.
8. Build goodwill.

16 Management and Administration

Cindy Palmer and Nick Stead went to school together. After graduation, both got good jobs. Cindy went to work as a unit control clerk at Stockman's Southside branch. This store was 1 of 30 in the Stockman apparel chain and had over 200 employees. Nick started as a salesperson at Cassidy's, a small specialty store in the center of town. Mr. Cassidy and Joe Sinclair are the only other employees besides Nick.

"You know, Cindy, I think my job at Cassidy's is really preparing me to advance into management," Nick mentioned one day at lunch.

"Sure it is," Cindy remarked. "As soon as Cassidy decides to retire, which may be never, you can be the manager. You should have applied for a job at Stockman's if you wanted to go into management. We have so many managers I can hardly keep track of them all. There are eight department managers, two assistant store managers, and a store manager."

"You missed my point," Nick replied. "I know there are lots of management jobs at your store. There are more managers because there are more employees to supervise. What I meant was that my job at Cassidy's is really showing me the different phases of management. Because it's a small store, I get to do some of the things a department manager or assistant buyer does at your store. Last week, Mr. Cassidy hired a high school student to help us receive, price mark, and stock merchandise, and I get to train him. That's a management job. And last month, Mr. Cassidy asked me to work out the advertising budget for the next 6 months. That's also a management job. I suppose it doesn't make any difference what title you have," Nick continued. "If you're responsible for people and for planning and organizing certain store operations, you're a manager."

WHAT IS A MANAGER?

There are many different tasks involved in keeping an apparel and accessory store operating smoothly and efficiently. Some of these tasks are buying, receiving, stocking, and selling merchandise. Others are providing store security and store credit and controlling store finances. In a small store, all these tasks are done by the owner and probably two or three helpers. In large stores, however, there may be hundreds of people doing these tasks. In all stores, someone must coordinate the work of the other employees in order to achieve the store's goals. This "someone" is the manager. (See Figures 16-1A and 16-1B.)

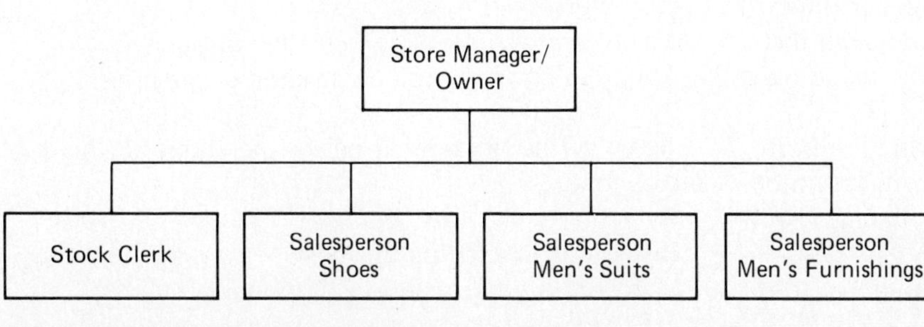

Fig. 16-1A Here's a typical example of an organization chart of a manager-owned store.

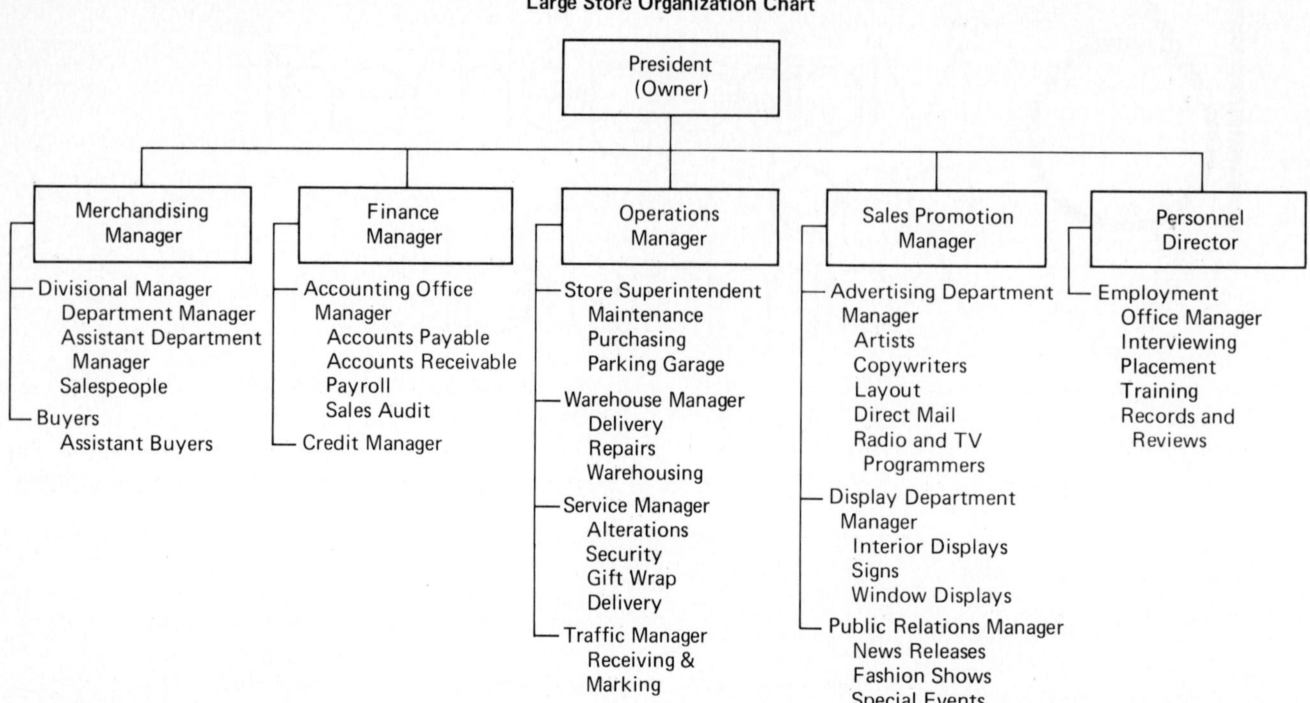

Fig. 16-1B Here's a typical example of the organization chart for a large department store.

Nick has a good idea of the tasks performed by a manager. He realizes that although there are many different types of managers, with many different titles, they all basically perform the same management tasks. They are all involved in planning, organizing, directing, and controlling other store employees and store operations.

Some of the management tasks to be discussed in this chapter are:

- Recruiting and hiring for various jobs
- Training employees in their job responsibilities
- Supervising and evaluating employees
- Planning and controlling store expenses
- Planning and controlling store finances

The examples in this chapter will deal with managing a department in an apparel store. The basic management principles presented will help you to be a more effective manager.

RECRUITING AND HIRING

In small stores, the owner or store manager is usually responsible for recruiting and hiring new employees. In larger stores, this task is often handled by the personnel manager. The personnel manager often works with the store manager and department manager in deciding which applicant is best suited for the job.

The basic procedures for finding and hiring the best person for the available job are the same, no matter how large or small the apparel store is. The manager in charge of hiring is looking for a person who is physically, mentally, and emotionally able to perform the duties of the job. By choosing the right person to fill a job, the store is reducing employee turnover and training costs. The store is also gaining an employee who is satisfied with his or her job and who has a good effect on the other employees' morale.

Although each apparel store has different recruiting and employment guidelines, most stores use employment application forms, job interviews, and sometimes tests when deciding which applicants to hire. Before starting the recruiting process, many stores prepare job descriptions.

PREPARING JOB DESCRIPTIONS

A job description lists in detail the skills and attitudes needed by the worker to do a particular job. For example, some of the skills listed on the job description for a salesperson in the accessory department may include the following:

- Ability to communicate with customers
- Ability to operate the cash register
- Ability to add, subtract, multiply, and divide accurately and quickly
- Ability to make change
- Ability to use courtesy and tact when working with customers
- Ability to make pleasing, effective displays
- Ability to color-coordinate fashion accessories

Some of the attitudes a person needs to fill this job are as follows:

- Fashion is an exciting business
- Merchandise information is important

- Responsibility to get along with customers, coworkers, and supervisors
- Honesty and integrity are important personality traits for all employees

Experience 16-1

What Kind of Job Did You Say This Was?

1. If you are employed by an apparel and accessory store, prepare a job description for your job. If you are not employed, visit a local apparel and accessory store and prepare a job description for one of the apparel sales jobs. It will be necessary for you to talk to the salespeople to find out what types of work they are expected to do. Be sure the job description you prepare includes all of the needed skills and attitudes.
2. After you have prepared the job description, show it to your boss. If you don't work, ask the manager of the apparel store you visited to read the job description. Find out if you were able to explain the basic responsibilities of the job. Add any omitted.

IDENTIFYING RECRUITING SOURCES

Employees at an apparel store can be classified into three groups: management, sales, and sales-supporting. (This last group includes stock workers, secretaries, display assistants, tailors, and so on.) When there is a job opening in any of these groups, the person in charge of recruiting and hiring looks for qualified people inside and outside the store.

Often, managers may fill an opening by promoting a person who already works for the store. The promotion usually requires the employee to accept greater responsibility and do more difficult work. When there are no store employees who are qualified, the manager looks to other recruiting sources to find qualified applicants. Some stores prefer to hire top management people from outside the store.

Some stores always accept applications for jobs at the store. When there is an opening, the manager reviews these applications for qualified candidates. Many stores list employment opportunities in the classified advertising section of local newspapers. Sometimes stores recruit new employees through personnel recruiters who visit schools or colleges. Other stores recruit new employees from Distributive Education, fashion merchandising, and vocational school programs. Some stores find qualified applicants through employment agencies.

READING EMPLOYMENT APPLICATIONS

Most stores ask all job applicants to complete an employment application (called an "ap" for short) before interviewing the applicant. The "ap" gives the manager information about the job applicant's personal life, education, and work history. (See Figure 16-2.) Managers read the application carefully before meeting the job applicant. They take special notice of the applicant's handwriting and the neatness with which the form was completed. They believe that a messy or hard-to-read application is an indication that they will have a hard time reading the forms the applicant must complete when working at the store.

The completed application form helps managers decide what questions they should ask job applicants during the job interview. For example, when applicants write "worked as salesperson at Bank's Clothing Store," it is natural for the manager to ask the applicants about their duties at the store.

Experience 16-2

What Does the Ap Say?

1. Read the completed employment application on page 236. On a separate sheet of paper, list five questions that you, as manager, could ask this job applicant during a job interview.
2. Based on the information in the application on page 236, decide if this person is qualified to fill the job you described in Experience 16-1. On a separate sheet of paper, give reasons to support your answer.

CONDUCTING JOB INTERVIEWS

As a manager, you will interview job applicants. Your interviews will be more meaningful and easier to conduct if you can make the applicant feel comfortable. Smile, shake hands with the applicant, and ask him or her to sit down.

APPLICATION FOR EMPLOYMENT JCP-6300-1 (REV. 5/73) FRONT — **JCPenney** — PRINT IN INK

DATE OF APPLICATION: 7 / 1 / --

NAME: FIRST MARK M.I. E. LAST ROMAN — SOCIAL SECURITY NO. 127 – 42 – 8248 — TELEPHONE NO. (AREA CODE) (301) 123-4567

STREET ADDRESS 22 MAIN STREET — CITY SHAWSVILLE — STATE MARYLAND — ZIP 21738

DATE OF BIRTH* 5/7/-- — HAVE YOU EVER BEEN EMPLOYED BY J.C. PENNEY CO? ☐ YES ☒ NO — IF "YES," WHERE? — WHEN? / / — WHY DID YOU LEAVE?

NAME OF RELATIVE WITH PENNEY'S: NOT APPLICABLE — LOCATION — POSITION — RELATIONSHIP

DESCRIBE YOUR GENERAL HEALTH: EXCELLENT — HAVE YOU EVER HAD A SERIOUS ILLNESS OR INJURY? ☐ YES ☒ NO — HAVE YOU EVER RECEIVED COMPENSATION FOR INJURIES? ☐ YES ☒ NO — HAVE YOU EVER HAD TUBERCULOSIS? ☐ YES ☒ NO

HAVE YOU EVER HAD A RUPTURE OR A HERNIA? ☐ YES ☒ NO — IF "YES," WHEN / / — WAS IT CORRECTED BY AN OPERATION? ☐ YES ☒ NO — DESCRIBE ANY PHYSICAL LIMITATIONS YOU FEEL SHOULD BE CONSIDERED IN JOB PLACEMENT

WHAT TYPE OF WORK ARE YOU APPLYING FOR? RETAIL SALESPERSON — WHAT EXPERIENCE HAVE YOU HAD IN THIS TYPE OF WORK? PART-TIME RETAIL SALES PERSON IN THE BRADY'S DEPARTMENT STORE LAST 2 YEARS OF HIGH SCHOOL — ARE YOU APPLYING FOR ☒ FULL TIME ☐ PART TIME — DATE YOU CAN START 8/1/--

IF YOU ARE EMPLOYED AT PRESENT, WHY DO YOU WISH TO CHANGE? — HAVE YOU EVER BEEN CONVICTED OF A FELONY? ☐ YES ☒ NO — IF "YES," WHERE? — WHEN? / /

DESCRIBE ANY BACKGROUND EXPERIENCE EDUCATION OR TRAINING WHICH YOU CONSIDER APPLICABLE TO THE POSITION FOR WHICH YOU ARE APPLYING.
DISTRIBUTIVE EDUCATION MAJOR AT HIGH SCHOOL; STUDENT IN DE COOPERATIVE PART-TIME PROGRAM (WORKED 2 YEARS AS PART-TIME RETAIL SALESPERSON); STUDIED GENERAL BUSINESS, RETAILING, BOOKKEEPING, AND SALESMANSHIP; MANAGER OF MIDDLETON HIGH BASKETBALL TEAM DURING SENIOR YEAR; WORKED AS STOCK CLERK FOR DALE'S VARIETY STORE DURING SUMMER OF 19--

NAMES AND LOCATIONS OF SCHOOLS ATTENDED	DATES ATTENDED FROM	TO
HIGH SCHOOL: MIDDLETOWN HIGH SCHOOL, SHAWSVILLE, MARYLAND 21738	9/--	6/--
COLLEGE	/	/
OTHER (NAME OR TYPE)	/	/

*Federal law and a majority of state laws prohibit discrimination in employment because of age, sex, race, color, religion and national origin. The Age Discrimination in Employment Act of 1967 prohibit discrimination on the bais of age with respect to individuals who are at least 40 but less than 65 years of age.

APPLICATION FOR EMPLOYMENT JCP-6300-1 (REV. 5/73) BACK

WORK HISTORY

EMPLOYED FROM MO./YR.	EMPLOYED TO MO./YR.	EMPLOYER (START WITH LAST OR PRESENT EMPLOYER)	NATURE OF WORK DURING EACH EMPLOYMENT	EARNINGS STARTING	EARNINGS LEAVING	REASON FOR LEAVING
9/--	6/--	BRADY'S DEPARTMENT STORE, CENTER STREET, SHAWSVILLE, MARYLAND, 21738	RETAIL SALESPERSON (DE COOPERATIVE PART-TIME PROGRAM); WORKED IN SEVERAL DIFFERENT DEPARTMENTS	$2.10 PER HOUR	$2.50 PER HOUR	PART-TIME POSITION ONLY
6/--	9/--	DALE'S VARIETY STORE, 10th STREET, SHAWSVILLE, MARYLAND 21738	STOCK CLERK	$2.00 PER HOUR	$2.00 PER HOUR	SUMMER POSITION ONLY
/	/					

MAY WE CONTACT THE EMPLOYERS LISTED ABOVE? IF NOT, PLEASE NOTE THOSE YOU DON'T WISH US TO CONTACT.

I understand that; If employed, any misrepresentation of facts on this application is sufficient cause for dismissal. Classification as a regular associate depends upon successfully performing work assigned me during a trial period of up to 30 days and upon the further need of my continued employment by the company. The company in considering my application for employment may verify the information set forth on this application and obtain additional information relating to my background. I authorize all persons, schools, companies, corporations, credit bureaus and law enforcement agencies to supply any information concerning my background.

SIGNATURE AS SHOWN ON SOCIAL SECURITY CARD: Mark E. Roman

DO NOT WRITE BELOW THIS LINE

Fig. 16-2 Careful handwriting and neatness are two things managers notice when they read an employment application.

Begin the interview meeting with general conversation. For example, you may want to start off by talking about the applicant's extracurricular school activities. Or, you may offer the applicant a soft drink or cup of coffee. Any subject that does not refer to the applicant's eligibility for the job will ease his or her tensions.

As the interviewer, you should guide the job interview. It is your responsibility to tell the applicant about the job as well as find out if the applicant has the ability to do the job.

Finding Out about the Applicant After you have put the applicant at ease, find out about the applicant's qualifications. Even though much information about the applicant is written on the employment application form, you will want more details about the applicant. Some of the questions you may ask will relate to the applicant's past jobs, courses in school, school schedule if the person is a student, skills, personal qualities, and desire and availability for work. Some usual questions are as follows:

- What kind of work did you do at your last job?
- Why did you quit that job?
- What kind of work would you like to be doing in 5 years?
- In school or in any of your past jobs, were you ever in charge of planning and organizing a program or project? Tell me about it. How did it turn out?
- Have you ever supervised people? When?
- Is your school schedule flexible so that you can work nights and weekends?
- How soon can you start work?

When asking questions, try to use words the applicant will understand. Ask the questions one at a time so that the applicant will not be confused.

Explaining the Job Some of the information you should provide the applicant are:

Duties the applicant will be expected to complete, such as know product information, answer customer questions, make sales presentations, operate cash registers, handle money, and make change.
Working conditions, such as the surroundings the applicant will work in, the hours the applicant is expected to work, and the types of people with whom the applicant will work.
Fringe benefits, such as vacation time, insurance programs, and employee discounts.
Wages, such as how much and how often the applicant will be paid and when paydays are.
Opportunities for advancement, such as how fast the company is growing.

The interviewer should describe the job to the applicant as realistically as possible. The interviewer should not oversell the job by painting a rosy picture that just isn't true. After explaining the job, the interviewer should find out if there are any questions the applicant has about the job. Those questions should be answered at this time.

Closing the Interview Close the interview in a polite, cordial way. If, during the interview, you are convinced that the applicant is the best person for the job, you may want to end the interview by offering the job to the applicant. And you may arrange the time when the applicant should report to work.

Sometimes an interviewer wants more time to decide whether or not to hire the job applicant. In this case, you may end the interview by saying, "I appreciate the time you spent with me this afternoon discussing the job opening in our shoe department. We have had several applications for the job. I want to review everyone's qualifications before making my final decision. By the end of the week, I'll let you know my decision."

It's important to tell the applicant when the decision will be made. It is not fair or ethical to keep an applicant waiting any longer than necessary to find out your decision. While the applicant is waiting to hear from you, he or she may pass up other job opportunities.

Sometimes you will interview a job applicant who is obviously not qualified for the job. At the end of the interview, it will be your job to tell the applicant that she or he is not acceptable. This need not be an unpleasant task. Be tactful and honest. The applicant probably realizes that there are several people applying for an opening and not everyone can be hired. In situations like this, you may say, "I appreciate your coming in to talk with me about this opening. From our conversation, I can tell that you possess some special personal and work characteristics. I do not believe, however, that you would be happy as a unit control clerk. The job involves reading forms and working with numbers most of the day, tasks that you said you do not enjoy. I will keep your application in our files and call you in the future if there are any other job openings that match your skills and interests. Again, thanks for coming in."

CHOOSING THE BEST APPLICANT

There are no definite guidelines to help a manager choose the best applicant for a job. Sometimes one applicant is obviously the best qualified for the job and the decision to hire him or her is easy. Other times one applicant may not have as much experience as another, but will be more enthusiastic and eager to do a good job. The person in charge of hiring should carefully consider the needs of the job and hire the applicant who best fits those needs.

For example, suppose a manager has interviewed two people for a selling job in the shoe department. One of the applicants has had a DE class and past sales experience in a small shoe store. The other has not had this special training. If both applicants are similar in their desire to work and in their attitudes, the manager would probably hire the person with the additional training. This person would best meet the needs of the job.

Managers should verify or check the information the job applicant wrote on the application form and said during the interview. A previous employer is the best source to verify the applicant's past work history. The references listed on the employment application give managers added insight into the job applicant's character and personality.

Form **W-4**
(Rev. Aug. 19--)
Department of the Treasury
Internal Revenue Service

Employee's Withholding Allowance Certificate

(This certificate is for income tax withholding purposes only; it will remain in effect until you change it.)

Type or print your full name	Your social security number
Susanna B. Anastasio	410-56-1776
Home address (Number and street or rural route)	Marital status
205 Carson Dr.	☒ Single ☐ Married
City or town, State and ZIP code	(If married but legally separated, or wife (husband) is a nonresident alien, check the single block.)
Teton Village, Wyoming 83025	

1 Total number of allowances you are claiming 1

2 Additional amount, if any, you want deducted from each pay (if your employer agrees) . . . . $

I certify that to the best of my knowledge and belief, the number of withholding allowances claimed on this certificate does not exceed the number to which I am entitled.

Signature ▶ Susanna B. Anastasio Date ▶ June 10, 19--

For Company Payroll information, please supply the additional information: Date of birth 5/16/62 Sex: ( ) Male (X) Female

Fig. 16-3 The first day on a job, new employees usually fill out an Employee Withholding Allowance Certificate, or W-4 form.

Following the Employment Laws There are various federal and state laws that apply to recruiting and hiring new employees. All stores must abide by these laws. All managers must follow the Equal Employment Opportunity Act. This law prohibits discrimination in hiring or promotion because of race, color, sex, religion, or national origin. Stores that discriminate against any applicant because of one of these reasons can be prosecuted.

Under the Federal Labor Standards Act, the government has established a minimum hourly wage for employees of retail businesses. Employees in nonsupervisory jobs, such as salespeople, who work more than 40 hours per week must receive one and one-half times their regular pay rate for hours worked beyond 40.

Today the law requires employers to give equal pay for equal work to both men and women. Retailers may employ minors who are at least 16 years old in any job, except in those jobs declared hazardous. Employees must be 18 before they can work at hazardous jobs. There are many other labor laws that managers should know about. Contact your State Employment Commission for more information.

Tax Information and Fringe Benefits Usually, the first day on the job the manager conducts an indoctrination meeting with the new employee. At this time, the manager has the employee complete a form called a W-4, Employee's Withholding Allowance Certificate. (See Figure 16-3.) This form, which asks for the employee's social security number, is used to determine how much to deduct from the employee's paycheck for taxes. If there is health insurance, life insurance, or other fringe benefit programs offered by the store, the manager explains these benefits to the employee. The employee signs up for these benefits during this meeting.

Experience 16-3

You're the Interviewer!

Ask a classmate to play the part of a job applicant. Tell the classmate to assume that he or she filled out the application form on page 236. Be sure the applicant reviews the completed application form before role playing the job interview.

Role play how you, the manager, would interview the job applicant for a sales position in your clothing store. This position has similar duties to the ones you described in Experience 16-1. Assume you have already reviewed the employment application. You will pay the new employee $3.00 per hour and offer an employee discount, health and life insurance, and two weeks vacation time.

During the interview, decide if the applicant's qualifications meet the requirements of the job. End the interview by either offering the applicant the job, postponing your decision, or telling the applicant that you are not going to hire her or him. Ask another classmate or your instructor to observe the interview and complete the rating sheet that will be provided by your teacher.

TRAINING EMPLOYEES

As a manager, it is your responsibility to train persons who work for you. This involves explaining the store's policies and procedures as well as teaching the skills and information workers need to do their jobs well. To train employees, you need to know how to do all the

Courtesy Hess's

DEPARTMENT SPONSOR MUST COMPLETE CHECKLIST AND RETURN TO THE STORE MANAGER WITHIN 3 DAYS FROM DATE OF ISSUE.

- ☐ Show where to put personal belongings.
- ☐ Show where nearest restrooms and water fountains are.
- ☐ Introduce to department personnel and Floor Supervisor.
- ☐ Show Department Manager's office location.
- ☐ Explain lunch time and location of weekly schedule.
- ☐ Give a tour of your department(s) to show stock by type, brands, sizes, reserve stock location.
- ☐ Ask Buyer or Sales Manager to assign specific stock responsibility.
- ☐ Explain PRICE tickets in detail and, if you STUB, go over this thoroughly.
- ☐ Show where supplies are kept and how they may be ordered.
- ☐ Show location of department bulletin board.
- ☐ Get selling supplies needed.
- ☐ Explain delivery procedure.
- ☐ Show how to handle gift wraps.
- ☐ Tell how to answer department phones, take messages and transfer calls.
- ☐ Review how to call Security.
- ☐ Explain alteration procedures if applicable.
- ☐ Show location of fitting rooms.
- ☐ Explain telephone and mail order procedures.
- ☐ Show how to handle co-worker package.
- ☐ Take person to location for depositing register media, keys, etc.
- ☐ Go over dress standards, grooming, selling, floor conduct, etc.
- ☐ Review co-worker's part in accepting bank checks.
- ☐ Show location of numbers to call for charge authorization.
- ☐ Show list of wanted charge plates and list of checks which are not to be accepted.

Fig. 16-4 This example of a manager's checklist for training new employees lists the many activities involved.

tasks you expect your employees to do. For example, if you are training your salespeople to operate the cash register, you have to know how to operate the register yourself. Some stores have training checklists for their managers. These checklists show the information that must be explained to a new employee before beginning the job. An example of such a checklist is shown in Figure 16-4.

Training employees is time consuming and costly, but the results are worthwhile. Effective employee training produces efficient workers and a store that operates smoothly.

EXPLAINING STORE RULES, POLICIES, AND PROCEDURES

Each store establishes basic rules, policies, and procedures so as to present a unified image of the store to customers and the general public. For example, the policy of a store may be to make promotions from within. Stores also establish procedures that are guidelines for how a certain activity is to be accomplished. For example, how to ring up a charge sale is a store procedure.

New employees must be familiar with policies and procedures in the store where they work. As their manager, you must inform them of the importance of working within the policies and procedures. A store's policies and procedures help employees determine how they should act to fit into the store's image and operations.

TRAINING METHODS

The purpose of training is to increase an individual's knowledge and skill in a particular area so that the individual can do a better job. To train a person to do a particular task, you must communicate your directions and information in a clear, logical way. There are many different ways to train apparel workers. Some of these methods are lecture, demonstration, and role playing.

Lecture Some managers use lectures, in which they tell new employees about new ideas or new processes. Lectures are often used to explain store rules and regulations or to introduce a special store promotion. At the end of a lecture, managers often have question and answer sessions, which allow two-way communication between the employees and the managers. Many times, managers use visual aids to make their lectures more interesting and keep the attention of the employees. Visual aids, such as filmstrips, videotapes, charts, or graphs, help employees learn and retain information.

Demonstration Managers often use demonstrations to teach employees. Usually, they *tell* the new employees about the task they are going to do. Then they *demonstrate* how to do the task. Finally, they give the new employees an opportunity to perform the task themselves. This "learning by doing" gives employees an opportunity to understand the task they are to do and how they are to do it. By becoming actively involved in learning the procedure, new employees have a better grasp on the information.

Role Playing Many managers use role playing to teach new employees to handle certain situations at work, especially those that involve working with people. When using the role-playing training method, the manager describes a situation and assigns employees to play the different roles. Employees are instructed to "ad lib" or spontaneously act out their parts.

After the role play is over, the manager asks the employees to analyze what happened. For example, suppose you are training employees how to handle customer complaints. As manager, you may assign one employee to play the role of the salesperson and another to play the part of the angry customer. By role playing the situation, the employees are able to determine how they should respond in a similar real-life situation. Because they are actively involved, employees often more clearly understand training concepts that they have role played. Role playing also helps employees see a problem from both sides.

MOTIVATING EMPLOYEES DURING TRAINING

A manager can make training fun and satisfying in many ways. Compliment employees for trying to learn and praise them when they do a good job. This way, you can motivate your employees to learn and become more productive.

Experience 16-4

Good Managers = Effective Trainers

Salespeople must be kept informed of new merchandise, new styles, and new merchandising trends. As a department manager, you may be asked to provide training for your employees.

1. Choose a particular merchandise item, style, or trend in apparel merchandising for a training topic, such as preparing merchandise displays, discussing new fabrics with customers, or color coordinating clothing.
2. Plan and conduct a training session in which you train two or three classmates in the topic you chose. Try to use as many different training methods as possible. Prepare charts or use pictures to help you communicate your concepts.
3. Devise some type of activity to test your "trainees" to see if they understand the concepts you presented. If possible, make the test an "active" test, such as making an actual display based on the information you presented.

SUPERVISING EMPLOYEES

As a manager, one of your major responsibilities is to supervise people. Your employees will look to you for guidance, direction, and encouragement. You are also expected to plan and organize your own work as well as that of your employees. And you schedule your employees' working hours, give orders, and evaluate job performance.

PLANNING WORK

Planning means deciding in advance what needs to be done, who will do it, and when it will be done. To be successful, you must be a good planner. You must learn how to set your goals and those of your employees. And you must identify how to achieve those goals.

Principles of Planning You will be involved in planning what you and your employees should accomplish every day as well as what should be accomplished in the future. The principles of short-range (today) and long-range (in the future) planning are basically the same. They are as follows:

Identify exactly what you want to accomplish. Make your goals as specific as possible. For example, instead of setting the goal "increase sales in the Women's Sportswear Department," set the specific goal "increase the sale of blouses in the Women's Sportswear Department by 10 percent."

If you want to accomplish more than one goal, prioritize your work. That is, decide what goal you want to achieve first, second, third, and so on. Write a 1 by the goal that is most important. Write a 2 by the next most important goal, and so on. (See Figure 16-5.)

Identify what you must do to accomplish each goal. It's easier to reach a goal that is divided into smaller tasks. *Set realistic deadlines for completing each subgoal.* By setting a time limit for accomplishing each subgoal, you will be able to achieve your major goal.

When planning, realize that even the best plans sometimes do not work out. You may have overlooked an important fact that affects your plans or you may have set an unrealistic deadline. Remember to remain flexible. Evaluate your plans occasionally to see if they are being met or need to be revised.

Daily Planning Guide

1—Prepare next week's work schedule.
4—Record yesterday's sales on unit control records.
3—Prepare last week's sales report for buyer.
5—Make appointment with store manager to discuss advertising program.
2—Make new counter top display for accessories.

Fig. 16-5 On this planning guide, what is the most important goal of the day?

Experience 16-5

How's Your Planning?

Planning involves identifying a goal and what you must do to achieve that goal. If you work, refer to your work situation when answering the following questions. If you don't work, think about your career goal when answering the questions. Answer these questions as thoughtfully as possible.

1. What specific new goal do you want to achieve for the coming year?

2. Divide your major goal into subgoals. In the space provided, write all those things you must do to achieve your major goal.

3. Set realistic deadlines for completing each of your subgoals. Write those deadlines next to the corresponding subgoals above.

4. Are other people involved in helping you achieve your goal? If so, explain how you will communicate to them what they have to do to help you reach your goal.

ORGANIZING WORK

A manager must organize his or her work and the work of others to get each job done efficiently. When you are organizing work, you should:

- Have a clear idea of what work has to be done to meet your goal.
- Prepare a logical, systematic plan of how the work will be completed.
- Decide how many people will be needed to do the work.
- Decide who will do the work.
- Explain the work to the people involved.
- Follow up on the workers' progress.
- Be available to help the workers with any problems or questions.

SCHEDULING EMPLOYEES

As a department manager, you prepare your employees work schedule. This is a written schedule showing the days and hours each employee is scheduled to work. You want to have enough employees to handle customer sales and store security. You don't want so many employees that some have nothing to do. Apparel and accessory retail stores follow several different methods of scheduling employees. Many stores use projected or expected sales figures and a salary/sales ratio when preparing employee work schedules.

Computing Projected Sales Suppose, for example, you are the department manager of the junior sportswear department. Last year, on the third Monday of June, your department sold $900 of merchandise. This year, on the third Monday of June, your store is projecting a 20 percent increase in sales. Thus, your expected sales figure for the day is $1,080.

$$\$900 \times .20 = \$180$$
$$\$900 + \$180 = \$1{,}080$$

Computing Salary/Sales Ratios Let's also suppose that your store operates on a salary/sales ratio of 10 percent. That means that the total salaries of your salespeople should equal 10 percent of your day's sales. Using a 10 percent salary/sales ratio, your total salaries should not exceed $108.

$$\$1{,}080 \times .10 = \$108$$

If all employees in your department earn $3 per hour, you have enough money to pay for 36 hours of sales work for this particular third Monday in June.

$$\$108 \div \$3 = 36$$

Of course, you do not have to use all the time available.

Computing the Hours to Be Worked Once you know how much time you can schedule for employees (36 hours in this situation), you need to determine when the employees will work. Suppose that your store is open from 10 a.m. until 9 p.m. on the third Monday of June. You need at least one employee in the department at 9:30 a.m. to open the cash register and put out new stock. You also need one employee to stay from 9 p.m. to 9:30 p.m. to close out the cash register and clean the dressing rooms. Therefore, let's assume you need at least one person in the department from 9:30 a.m. to 9:30 p.m., a total of 12 hours.

During the day, you will need more than one salesperson in the department. Usually between 11 a.m. and 2 p.m. and 5 p.m. and 8 p.m., the busy hours of the day, more salespeople are needed to handle all the customers. There must also be enough salespeople working so that all workers can take lunch and rest breaks.

Completing the Staffing Sheet Most stores have some type of staffing sheet on which the manager writes each employee's name and the hours when that employee will work. This sheet is prepared in advance and should be posted where all employees can read it.

One possible schedule for the junior sportswear department for the third Monday of June is listed on the staffing sheet in Figure 16-6. Notice that the time each employee comes to work, goes home, and eats lunch is different. Like the store in Figure 16-6, most apparel

WEEKLY STAFFING SHEET

DEPT. Jr. Sportswear WEEK OF June 20–25

Day of Week	Employee	9	10	11	12	1	2	3	4	5	6	7	8	9	Total Hours
Monday	Kay				X	X	X	X	L.	X	X	X	X		8
	Dennis					off									0
	Ron	X	X	X	L.	X	X	X	X	X					8
	Herb										X	X	X	X	4
	Corina				X	X	X	L.	X	X	X	X	X		8
	Jessica			X	X	X	L.	X	X	X	X	X			8

X = Times Worked   L. = Lunch

Fig. 16-6 How many of the above staff members work 8-hour shifts? 4-hour shifts? Who is on vacation?

stores schedule their employees to work 4- or 8-hour shifts. Stores schedule their employees so as to have maximum coverage of the sales floor during the busiest times of the day.

Scheduling Lunch and Rest Breaks Most apparel stores allow their employees either a 30-, 45-, or 60-minute lunch break and one 15-minute rest break for every 4 hours worked. The rest breaks are not usually written on the schedule sheet; they are taken during slack times.

Before your employees take their break, be sure there are enough salespeople remaining on the sales floor to handle sales and store security. If there are not enough salespeople to handle the work load, call in other salespeople from slow departments to help. Or reschedule the employee's break to a later, slower time.

ANOTHER SCHEDULING METHOD

Stores that do not use projected sales or salary/sales ratios usually rely on the common sense of their managers when they prepare work schedules. The managers realize that there must be at least one person in the department at all times, no matter what the sales are, for security reasons. When this person goes to lunch or on a rest break, a store floater may be assigned to enter the department and take over. A **floater** goes from department to department when needed to fill in for the regular salespeople. A group of floaters are sometimes called the "flying squad."

A FINAL WORD ABOUT SCHEDULING

Scheduling employees is a tricky business. Even though there are elaborate formulas to help managers determine how many people should work and when they should work, these formulas are not foolproof. Sometimes a department will have more workers than needed, even when the manager has followed the formula. This problem shows that it's very hard to guess how many people will be shopping in your store at any particular time of the day.

Experience 16-6

How Many Workers?

As a department manager of children's wear, you must prepare a written schedule for your six salespeople. Your store uses past sales information and salary/sales ratio to determine how many salespeople can work on any particular day. The store allows you to determine when these workers will come to work, leave, and eat lunch.

1. Compute the projected sales for the fourth week in July for the children's wear department. The needed information appears in the opposite column.
2. Your store management asks you to follow a salary/sales ratio of 10 percent. Using the projected sales

Last Year's Sales	Projected Increase	This Year's Projected Sales
Monday—$940	10%	
Tuesday—$820	5	
Wednesday—$900	10	
Thursday—$1,050	7	
Friday—$1,120	10	
Saturday—$1,180	20	

figures from 1 above, compute the number of employee hours you will be allowed each day. Assume each of your employees earns $3 per hour.

a. Monday ________ d. Thursday ________
b. Tuesday ________ e. Friday ________
c. Wednesday ________ f. Saturday ________

3. Using the following information, as well as the number of employee hours you determined were allowed from 2 above, complete the work schedule for the week. On a separate sheet of paper, make a weekly Staffing Sheet using Figure 16-6 as a guide.

Assume your store allows each employee who works 5 hours a day a 1-hour lunch break. There are five employees in your department. Two of the employees, Raphael and Smitty, are full-time employees who have been averaging 38 hours per week. The other employees, Glenn, Margo, and Allyn, are part-time employees and work an average of 20 hours per week, 4 hours per day. Wednesday is Raphael's day off; Smitty prefers Tuesday off. Your store is open from 10 a.m. to 9 p.m. on Monday through Friday and from 10 a.m. to 6 p.m. on Saturday. The store is closed on Sunday. One employee must be in the department at 9:30 a.m. and one usually stays until 9:30 p.m. to close out the department. The busiest times of each day are 11 a.m. to 2 p.m. and 4 p.m. to 8 p.m.

ASSIGNING WORK AND GIVING ORDERS

As manager, you have the authority to make decisions and give orders to the people who work under you. The way you give orders and directions affects your employees' work attitude. You will want to be the kind of manager whom employees want to work for rather than feel they have to do what you say just because you're the supervisor.

Think about the many times someone has asked you to do something. How do you feel when someone *orders* you to do something? Clean up your room! Do your homework! Get a haircut! How do you feel when someone *asks* you to do something? Will you clean up your room this afternoon? How about spending tonight working on your homework?

There's a big difference between being ordered to do something and being asked to do it. When someone is asked to do something, he or she will do it and feel good about doing it. But when someone is ordered to do something, the person often becomes uncooperative. As manager, try to use the request method of giving orders as often as possible. The results may surprise you.

Experience 16-7

Ask Me, Don't Order Me

1. On a separate sheet of paper, rewrite each of the following. Make them requests, not demands.
   a. Make a rack top display for sweaters in the front of the department.
   b. Transfer this merchandise to your Eastwood store.
   c. Go to lunch.
2. Sometimes it is necessary to demand rather than ask an employee to do a certain task. Give two examples of when a demand would work better than a request.

EVALUATING EMPLOYEE PERFORMANCE

Most employees want to know what their manager thinks about the work they are doing. They want to know whether or not they are doing a good job. They want their managers to give them feedback so that they know where they stand.

Today, many stores have established a formal procedure for evaluating employees. At least once each year, the manager discusses with each individual employee his or her progress. This meeting is called a performance appraisal. It is designed to provide a report of how well individuals are meeting company standards.

CRITERIA FOR EVALUATING EMPLOYEES

Many companies prepare a specific set of standards on which employees are evaluated. These standards are written on an employee performance rating form. (See Figure 16-7.) Before each performance appraisal meeting, the manager completes the employee's rating form. The manager should use objective data when completing the employee performance rating form. For example, the manager can use the employee's sales records to evaluate the quantity of the employee's work. The manager can refer to time cards to evaluate the employee's promptness.

Many employee performance rating forms ask the manager to evaluate certain traits of the employee. When making this type of evaluation, a manager should back up his or her comments with specific examples. For example, the rating in Figure 16-7 asks about the employee's cooperative attitude. The manager must make a fair judgment of this trait.

When you complete an employee performance rating form, try to be fair and objective. Look at all the facts

EMPLOYEE PERFORMANCE RATING REASON FOR THIS REPORT		Berry's
Periodic Review (check one) ☐ Annual ☒ Semi Annual ☐ End of Trial Period	☐ Commendation or ☐ Corrective Interview	O-Outstanding, G-Good, NI-Needs improvement, U-Unsatisfactory.

NAME	STORE NO.	REGION	DATE OF HIRE	DATE:
Gwen Matshusita	3	4	2/5/8-	8/17/8-

POSITION	HOW LONG IN PRESENT POSITION
salesperson	six months

O G NI U	
☒ ☐ ☐ ☐	KNOWLEDGE OF JOB —A clear understanding of the facts or factors pertinent to the job. COMMENTS extremely good knowledge of fibers and fabrics
☐ ☒ ☐ ☐	QUALITY OF WORK —Thoroughness on assignments and routine matters. Neatness and accuracy of work. COMMENTS usually has good follow through
☒ ☐ ☐ ☐	QUANTITY OF WORK —Volume of acceptable work under normal conditions. COMMENTS consistently leads other salespeople in amount of merchandise sold
☐ ☐ ☒ ☐	DEPENDABILITY —Conscientious, thorough, accurate, reliable with, respect to attendance and punctuality (starting time, lunch periods, reliefs, etc.) COMMENTS needs work on returning from lunch on time
☐ ☒ ☐ ☐	JUDGMENT —Ability to arrive at sound conclusions and make intelligent decisions. COMMENTS sometimes makes snap judgements
☐ ☐ ☒ ☐	INITIATIVE —Ernestness in seeking increased responsibilities. Self starting. Unafraid to proceed alone. COMMENTS would like employee to take more initiative on stock work
☐ ☐ ☒ ☐	ATTITUDE —Ability and willingness to work with associates, supervisors and subordinates, toward commen goals. COMMENTS needs to work more closely with other salespeople in completing sales supporting jobs
☐ ☒ ☐ ☐	PERSONAL QUALITIES —Personality, Appearance, Sociability, Leadership, Integrity. COMMENTS always well groomed and very friendly with customers

Fig. 16-7 Which traits does this employee need to work on and improve? Name her outstanding traits.

and don't let your emotions sway your judgment. Use specific examples and facts to back up your comments. Because someone's future may depend on the rating you give, take your job of completing employee performance rating forms seriously.

THE PERFORMANCE APPRAISAL MEETING

During a performance appraisal meeting, a manager should give the employee a firsthand report of the employee's progress. Areas in which improvement is needed should be discussed. The performance appraisal meeting should also create a deeper, better understanding and communication between the employee and manager.

Many managers begin the meeting by discussing the good work the employee has done since the last performance appraisal. They then talk about areas in which they think the employee needs to improve. Some employees act defensively and try to justify their past mistakes during the meeting. They get upset and say the manager is unfair to rate them in a certain way. For this reason, the manager should stress the fact that employees are rated according to objective standards that apply to all employees. The manager should also practice tact and consideration during the meeting. He or she should try to see the situation from the employee's viewpoint.

A manager should encourage employees to participate in their performance appraisal meetings. To encourage participation, the manager may ask an employee how the company can make the employee's job more satisfying. Or the manager may ask about any on-the-job problems the employee has.

Both the manager and the employee should leave the appraisal meeting with a good feeling about what has happened. The meeting should build employee morale and give the employee a sense of direction and participation in the development of his or her career. It should make the employee realize that the quality and quantity of work done and his or her work attitudes really do matter and are appreciated.

NAME ______________________ DATE ______________________

Experience 16-8

Employee Appraisals—They're Not Easy

Using the following facts and the completed employee performance rating form in Figure 16-7, demonstrate how you would conduct an employee performance evaluation. Assume you are the manager of the menswear department. Ask another classmate to play the part of the employee.

Background Information: This employee is your best salesperson and continually leads the other salesworkers in sales. However, this salesperson refuses to help with any of the stock work or displays that are also part of the job. This has caused friction with the other salesworkers. They feel they are doing part of this employee's job and not earning as much commission as they could. This salesperson is always well groomed and friendly. Seldom does this salesperson incorrectly ring up sales. The salesperson is also very dependable except when it comes to stock or display work.

CONTROLLING EXPENSES

Besides hiring, training, and supervising employees, most managers are also responsible for controlling expenses in their department and store. They are supposed to make sure that employees and customers carefully handle merchandise, fixtures, and equipment. They instruct their employees to use only those supplies that are needed. They also have their employees follow strict check acceptance and credit procedures as well as shoplifting precautions so that customer theft is kept to a minimum.

PROFIT = SALES − EXPENSES

An apparel and accessory store receives income by selling merchandise. From this income, the store pays for merchandise and the salaries of all store personnel. The store also pays for fixtures, supplies, utility bills, taxes, and insurance. Other items a store must pay for are shown in Table 1.

If there is money left over after a store has paid its salaries and bills, the store has earned a profit. If no money is left over, the store has suffered a loss. Most stores hope to make a profit of 2 percent to 5 percent of the total amount of sales. Remember, sales minus expenses equal profit (or loss).

Expenses are very important in determining how much profit or loss a store earns. In the following examples, you can see what happens when sales remain the same but expenses increase.

Sales		Expenses		Profit or Loss
$100,000	−	$ 95,000	=	Profit of $5,000
$100,000	−	$ 99,500	=	Profit of $500
$100,000	−	$104,000	=	Loss of $4,000

As expenses go up, profit goes down. To obtain a profit, all personnel must try to control expenses.

Table 1

TYPICAL EXPENSES IN AN APPAREL AND ACCESSORY STORE

Cost of Merchandise

Menswear	Children's Wear
Women's Wear	Accessories

Building Fixtures and Equipment

Insurance—Fixtures	Insurance—Building
Depreciation—Fixtures	Store improvements
Rent—Fixtures and equipment	Store maintenance
Personal property taxes	Store security

Utilities

Telephone	Heat
Lights	Water

Personnel

Payroll	Worker's compensation
Payroll taxes	Group insurance

Customer Services

Credit promotion	Deliveries
Fashion shows	Special events
Gift wrap	

Store Supplies

Postage	Wrapping and packing
Display supplies	General office supplies
Selling supplies	Freight expenses and parcel post
Mannequin maintenance	Checkers' and markers' supplies

Other Expenses

Donations
Bad checks
Sales overs and shorts

HANDLING MERCHANDISE, FIXTURES, AND EQUIPMENT

Apparel and accessory employees can decrease store profits by carelessly handling merchandise, fixtures, and equipment. For example, it's not unusual for an employee to rip a garment when putting it on a hanger, especially when in a hurry. It's very easy to damage a mannequin when changing displays. Even cash registers require repairs when they are abused.

The money lost on damaged merchandise and broken fixtures or equipment can easily increase the store's expenses and thus dip into profits. The worst part about these expenses is that they all can be avoided if store employees are careful. As manager, show your employees the proper way to handle merchandise, fixtures, and equipment. Be sure employees know that it is better to take their time to do a good job rather than a fast job.

CONTROLLING SUPPLIES

Apparel and accessory stores use a wide variety of supplies. When added together, the cost of these supplies is expensive and can quickly drain profits. A careful use of supplies is necessary to control expenses.

For example, every time a salesperson gives a customer a large bag when a small bag will do, the salesperson increases the store's expenses by 1½ cents. If this happens twice a day, 5 days a week, 52 times a year, the store loses $7.80 a year. If 10 salespeople in the store do this, the tore loses $78 a year. If 100 salespeople do this, the store loses $780 a year—a substantial drain on profits.

ACCEPTING CHECKS

Many customers use checks to pay for their purchases. Most customers' checks are good; some, however, are bad. A customer's check is bad when the amount of money the customer has in the bank is less than the amount written on the check. It is hard to collect bad checks. Usually, stores have to write off the merchandise purchased by a bad check as a total loss. Apparel and accessory employees who carefully examine every check they accept can help protect their store from bad checks, reduce the store's expenses, and protect the store's profit.

In most apparel stoes, management has a definite set of policies for accepting checks. These policies, although they vary from store to store, must be followed carefully.

Examining the Check As manager, you must instruct your salespeople in how to accept a customer's check. Tell each salesperson to examine the front of the check for the following parts. (Look at Figure 16-8 as you read this checklist.)

- Bank transit number (letter A).
- Customer's full name, address, and telephone number (letter B). If a phone number is not printed on the check, the salesperson must ask the customer for the number and write it on the check.
- Correct date (letter C).
- Payee (letter D). The check must be written to your store.
- Amount in words and numbers (letter E). These amounts must agree.
- Customer's signature (letter F). The signature on the check must agree with the customer's identification.

Checks that are written in pencil, payable to a second party or another store, postdated or payroll checks are not acceptable at most apparel stores. Checks that have been changed in any way or checks without the printed customer's name and address are also not acceptable.

Getting Proper Identification Most stores require the customer to present two forms of proper identification, or ID, before a check can be accepted. These proper forms of ID show either the customer's signature or picture. Some examples of acceptable forms of ID are a permanent driver's license; a national bank credit card, such as Visa or Master Charge; charge cards from other stores; military or student ID; or a check guarantee card. A check guarantee card from a bank shows that the check will be paid even though there not be sufficient funds in the customer's account. Unacceptable forms of ID include a social security card, temporary driver's license, library card, birth certificate, lease, and marriage license.

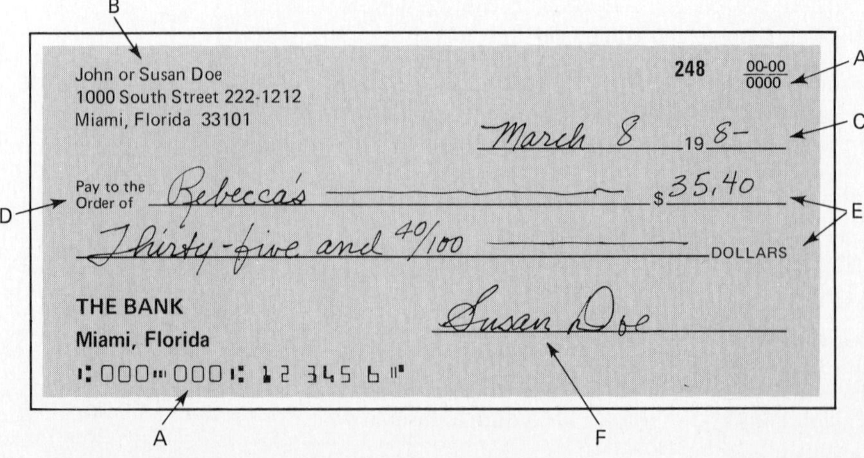

Fig. 16-8 Salespeople must examine these parts of a customer's check: (A) bank transit number; (B) customer's name, address, and phone number; (C) date; (D) payee; (E) amount of payment in words and numbers; and (F) the signature.

The purpose of the ID is to be sure the person writing the check is who he or she says. The ID is also a means of locating the person if the check is returned to the store by the bank.

Recording the ID Both forms of ID are usually recorded on the back of the check. Many stores stamp the check with an ID chart and use this chart to record the information. It's important that the type of ID presented and its number are both written on the check. (See Figure 16-9.) In this example, Fl. Lic. stands for a Florida driver's license and M.C. stands for a Master Charge card.

Getting Additional Approval At many apparel stores, checks over $50 and out-of-state checks need to be approved by the department manager. By having two people examine these checks, the store is taking extra precautions to make sure the check is correctly written. Often, a department manager or supervisor catches errors that a busy salesperson overlooks.

Endorsing the Check After all the store's check-acceptance procedures have been followed and the check is accepted as payment, it should be stamped with the store's endorsement stamp. This makes the check the property of the store.

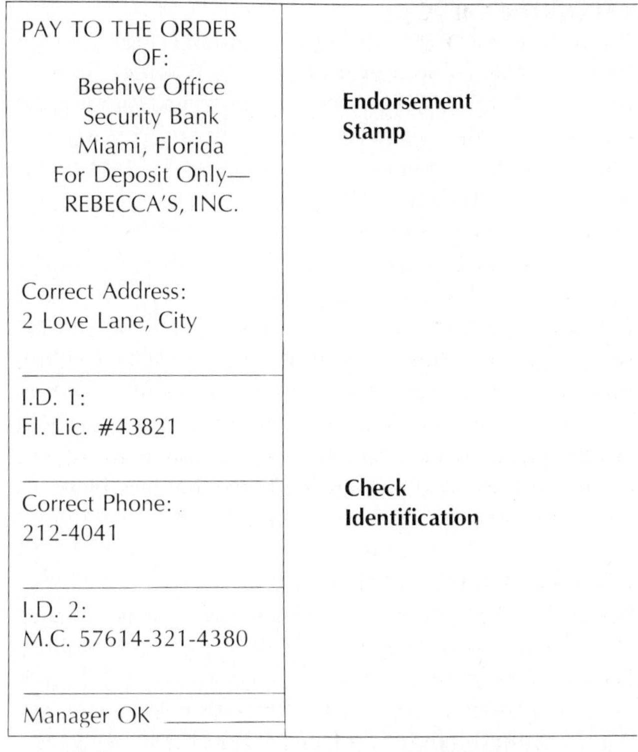
PAY TO THE ORDER OF:
Beehive Office
Security Bank
Miami, Florida
For Deposit Only—
REBECCA'S, INC.

Endorsement Stamp

Correct Address:
2 Love Lane, City

I.D. 1:
Fl. Lic. #43821

Correct Phone:
212-4041

Check Identification

I.D. 2:
M.C. 57614-321-4380

Manager OK ______

Fig. 16-9 After a check is accepted for payment, the customer's ID is recorded and the store's endorsement is stamped on the back.

Experience 16-9

Can You Spot the Rubber Checks before They Bounce?

Suppose you are a department manager at Robertson's, a local accessory store. A customer wants to purchase a $19 scarf and $24 necklace. The total sale, including tax, is $45.15. The customer gives you the check below. Answer the following on a separate sheet.

1. What are the six parts of the check you must examine before accepting the check as payment?
2. Assume that the date is correct and this is an in-state check. Is this check acceptable? If not, what is wrong with the check?
3. Name four other acceptable forms of identification.
4. Name four unacceptable forms of identification.
5. What are two purposes of examining and recording identification before accepting customer checks?

Allen or Robyn White
849 Grand Avenue
San Diego, California 92138

24 00-00/0000

June 2 19 8–

Pay to the Order of Robertson's $ 45.15

Forty-five and 51/100 DOLLARS

THE BANK
San Diego, California

Robyn White

⑆000⑈000⑆ 11 398 7⑈

CREDIT CONTROL

Today, over half the sales in many apparel stores involve credit. Credit services provide many advantages to customers. Credit makes it easier for customers to purchase merchandise they want and need when they want and need it. It eliminates the customers' worry about carrying large amounts of cash.

Credit also provides the apparel and accessory store with many advantages. It produces sales that might never have been made because customers can make purchases even though they may not be able to pay for the purchase at that moment. Credit also makes a store customer more loyal. The "charge," or credit, customer will continue to return to the store to make additional purchases.

Credit is an expense to the store. It costs the store money to set up a credit department and have employees administer the credit policies of the store. The cost of providing credit is further increased when some customers refuse to pay for their credit or charge purchases. That's why stores set up credit policies for their managers and salespeople to follow when accepting customers' charges. It is the apparel and accessory manager's responsibility to see that salespeople know the credit policies and handle the credit transactions according to these policies.

Store Credit Procedures Some apparel and accessory stores issue their own credit cards to customers. These stores have a credit department that approves credit applications, authorizes store charges, and handles customer collection and billing. Once a customer's application is approved, the store issues the approved customer a plastic or metal charge card that can be used to buy merchandise at any of the store's outlets.

The credit department at these stores establishes certain credit guidelines to keep the number of "bad" charges under control. All managers and salespeople must follow these guidelines when accepting a store credit card as payment for merchandise. The following guidelines are examples of common credit rules at apparel and accessory stores.

Guideline 1. The customer wishing to charge merchandise must present his or her charge card to the salesperson. Customers who have left their charge cards at home must present some other form of valid identification. Salespeople must call the credit office for approval when a customer without a charge card wants to charge merchandise.

Guideline 2. Each salesperson and manager has the authority to accept customer charges up to a certain limit. The largest amount for which you are permitted to accept charges without authorization is called the **floor limit**. Salespeople in chain stores usually have a floor limit of $50. Department managers usually have a floor limit of $100. In many small stores, the floor limit is less. When charges are more than the floor limit, the salesperson or manager must call the store's credit office for charge approval. After being told the customer's name, account number, and the amount of the purchase, the employee in the credit office checks on the status of the account to be sure it is in good standing. If the account is in order, the credit department gives an authorization number, which is to be written on the charge slip.

Guideline 3. The customer's charge card or name and account number must be imprinted or written on the store's charge slip. The charge slip is then inserted into the cash register where the other information about the sale is recorded.

Guideline 4. Every charge slip must be signed by the customer. According to the law, if the customer does not sign the slip, the customer is not responsible for paying for the merchandise.

Guideline 5. The customer's signature on the back of the charge card must be compared with that on the charge slip. This is one way of recovering lost or stolen cards. If the signatures do not agree, the salesperson or manager should not accept the charge card as payment for the merchandise. The store employee should call the store manager and try to detain the customer until the store manager arrives and determines why the customer has another person's charge card.

Bank Credit Card Procedures Many apparel and accessory stores also accept bank credit cards, such as Visa and Master Charge. The bank credit card companies also establish guidelines to control the number of "bad" charges. These guidelines, which are similar to retail store credit guidelines are:

Guideline 1. The customer must present his or her bank credit card.

Guideline 2. Every salesperson or manager has authority to accept the card as payment for any purchase less than $50. On purchases over $50, the bank credit card company requires a store employee to telephone its office and get an authorization number before ringing up the sale.

Guideline 3. The salesperson or manager must check the expiration date on the card to be sure it has not expired. The bank credit card companies will not pay for purchases made with an expired card.

Guideline 4. The employee ringing up the sale should consult a booklet issued by the bank credit card companies that lists all stolen and lost cards. If the account number of the card is listed in the booklet, the card is probably lost or stolen. Without letting the customer know what's happening, the employee should call the bank credit card office and store manager and explain the situation. Under no circumstances should the employee give the card back to the customer.

Bank credit card companies pay a reward for any recovered lost or stolen cards.

Guideline 5. The bank credit card purchase must be recorded on a bank credit card slip. The date, department, salesperson number, merchandise, price, tax, and total should be listed on this slip. (See Figure 4-6 on page 42.)

Guideline 6. The customer must sign the sales slip. (See Figure 4-6.)
Guideline 7. The salesperson must check the signature on the sales slip with the customer's signature on the back of the card to be sure they match.

Some stores also accept American Express, Diners Club, and Carte Blanche credit cards. The procedure is basically the same as accepting bank credit cards.

Experience 16-10

Check the Charge

Suppose you are the manager at Hershey's, a specialty shop for women. Your store offers customers a Hershey's store charge. You have a floor limit of $100. Your store also accepts Visa and Master Charge. Answer the following on a separate sheet of paper.

1. Mrs. Gilroy, a well-known customer, wants to purchase a $125 trench coat on her Visa bank credit card.
   a. Do you need credit authorization on this sale? Why or why not?
   b. Her Visa card has expired, but she says her new one is in the mail. Can you accept this? Why?
   c. If you did not know this customer, what way may you be able to tell if this was a lost or stolen card?
2. Mr. Halston is using his Hershey's charge card to purchase a $35 pair of pearl earrings.
   a. Do you need credit authorization before ringing up the sale? Why or why not?
   b. Suppose this sale required credit authorization. Which credit office would you call?
   c. What information would you need to give the credit office?

SHOPLIFTING

When customers take merchandise from a store without paying for it, they are shoplifting. This criminal act decreases the amount of profit a store earns. In some stores, the value of merchandise that is stolen is as high as 5 percent of sales. As a manager, you will train salespeople to watch for shoplifters and in ways to prevent shoplifting.

Spotting Possible Shoplifters Most customers who enter a store are honest. They are more interested in examining the merchandise than in looking around to see if someone is watching them. Shoplifters are different, often more nervous, than the honest customers. They keep looking around to see who is watching them. They may look behind themselves as they leave the department. They either don't want the salespeople to see them at all or they do something to distract the salespeople's attention.

Anybody may be a shoplifter—the best-dressed one in the store, the wealthy person, or a regular customer. Managers should instruct salespeople to watch for any suspicious behavior.

Store Conditions that Make Shoplifting Easy There are certain conditions that make it easier for customers to shoplift. Shoplifters like working in a crowded department where people can't keep too close a watch on them. They also like stores with inattentive salespeople who pay little attention to customers. Store employees should make a special effort to acknowledge all customers who enter their department. Salespeople who are busy helping another customer should tell new customers, "I'll be with you in a moment." They should then keep glancing toward the customers so that the customers know they haven't been forgotten.

Ways to Prevent Shoplifting Most stores try hard to prevent shoplifting. They try to display the merchandise so that it is difficult to shoplift. For example, some stores use locking hangers to display expensive coats. When customers want to try on one of these coats, they must ask a salesperson to unlock the hanger. Most stores also keep expensive jewelry in locked display cases, out of the customers' reach.

It is difficult for salespeople to keep track of all the merchandise, especially the merchandise customers take to the dressing rooms. On busy days, many stores station a security person at the entrance to the dressing room. This person counts each of the garments and gives the customers a numbered tag corresponding to the number of items being tried on. When the customers come out of the dressing room, they must give the person the printed tag and the merchandise items. When there is no security person stationed at the dressing rooms, salespeople must be especially on the lookout for shoplifters.

Some ways you as a manager can help control shoplifting in your department are:

- Tell your salespeople to remove any garments left in the dressing rooms.
- Encourage your salespeople to inspect the clothing their customers take into the dressing rooms. Ask them to make a mental note of the style and quantity.
- Instruct your salespeople to check with dressing room customers often. Neglected customers may leave the store with merchandise for which they haven't paid.

How to Apprehend Shoplifters Almost every store has established policies and procedures that explain what employees should do if they see a shoplifter in action. Some of these rules are:

- Never accuse the person of stealing. If the employee is mistaken, the store may become involved in a lawsuit for false arrest.
- Call the security department or store manager immediately. Many stores employ people who are trained in handling shoplifters.
- Write down a description of the shoplifter. Include the height, general build, color of hair and eyes, and color and type of clothing. This information will help the security department, store manager, or police to locate the shoplifter.

Experience 16-11

Shoplifting: It's a Real Problem

Make an appointment to visit a police station. Ask a member of the police department about the shoplifting laws in your town. Also ask how apparel and accessory managers can reduce the shoplifting in retail stores. Write the essentials of the law on a separate sheet of paper.

EMPLOYEE THEFT

Another cause of higher expenses and lower profits is employee theft. As manager, you know that stores must trust their employees to work honestly with the store's money and merchandise. You will find some dishonest employees who betray their employer's trust by stealing from the store. Employee theft is a very real problem. As manager, you should be aware of some methods and preventions of employee theft. Table 2 outlines some of these methods and preventions.

Table 2

EMPLOYEE THEFT METHODS AND PREVENTIONS

Methods	Preventions
1. Outright theft of merchandise from the sales floor.	Provide employees with a locker so that no purses or packages are allowed on the sales floor.
2. Outright theft of money from cash drawer.	Carefully check the cash register tape to determine the flow of money.
3. Giving employee discounts to unauthorized persons.	Require management approval on all employee discount sales.
4. Stealing merchandise from receiving and marking area.	Keep receiving room area locked when receiving and marking employees are off duty; do not allow unauthorized persons in this area.

Clever, dishonest employees can think of many ways to steal from their employers. Prevention programs cannot stop all employee theft. Most stores realize that they must rely on honest employees and managers to report internal theft. Store management encourages all store employees to help fight rising expenses and theft.

PREPARING BUDGETS AND REPORTS

Another important manager's job is keeping track of the store's money. Most stores require their managers to plan and follow budgets, which show how money should be spent. For example, in Chapter 13, "Advertising," you prepared an advertising budget. Examples of other reports that you will prepare or analyze are (1) sales reports, which show the quantity and type of merchandise sold; (2) payroll reports, which show the amount of earnings paid to employees; and (3) tax reports, which show the amount of taxes paid to the city, state, and federal governments.

ARE YOU READY TO BE A MANAGER?

By now, you should realize that a good manager, one who is successful, has many special talents. The successful manager is a team builder. She or he is a person who can get other people to work together and accomplish common goals. The manager is a planner and organizer. This person can really make things happen.

Besides exceptionally good "people skills," the successful manager also understands how a business operates and what has to be done to make money. In fact, the successful manager knows something about almost everything in the store. Are you ready for the job?